The History of the Origin, Progress, and Termination of the American War

HISTORY

OF THE

AMERICAN WAR.

VOLUME THE FIRST.

THE

HISTORY

OF THE

ORIGIN, PROGRESS, AND TERMINATION

OF THE

AMERICAN WAR.

By C. STEDMAN,

WHO SERVED UNDER SIR W. HOWE, SIR H. CLINTON, AND
THE MARQUIS CORNWALLIS.

IN TWO VOLUMES.

VOL. I.

LONDON:

PRINTED FOR THE AUTHOR;

AND SOLD BY J. MURRAY, FLEET-STREET; J. DEBRETT, PICCADILLY; AND
J. KERBY, CORNER OF WIGMORE-STREET, CAVENDISH-SQUARE.

1794.

TO

THE RIGHT HONOURABLE

THE EARL OF MOIRA.

MY LORD,

THE pain of recording that spirit of faction, that weakness, indecision, indolence, luxury, and corruption, which disgraced our public conduct during the course of the American war, is relieved by the contemplation of those talents and virtues that were eminently displayed on the side of Great Britain, in various important, though subordinate, stations.

Although the issue of that war was unfortunate, our national character was not impaired, nor the contest, while

it

it was maintained, on the whole inglorious. Neither martial ardour was wanting among our countrymen, nor military enterprife, nor patriotic zeal. In that rank, and those circumstances of life which are at once a temptation and an apology for dissipation and a love of pleasure, the military spirit of Britain shone forth with undiminished lustre; and the noblest families exhibited bright examples of true courage, exalted genius, and consummate wisdom.

Whilst I indulge with exultation this general reflection, permit me to acknowledge that my attention is irresistibly drawn towards the Earl of Moira. Accept, then, my Lord, this humble effort to transmit to posterity the glorious actions of our countrymen, as a mark of personal refpect for your Lordfhip ; for that happy union of enthusiasm in the cause of virtue, of invention, intrepidity, and decision of character, with cool reflection and patient perseverance, which directs the public eye to your Lordship, as the hope and the pride of your country.

That your Lordfhip may long live still to sustain in a frivolous age, the dignity of true nobility, the virtue of

I   chivalry

chivalry without its spirit of romance, is the ardent wish and hope of,

MY LORD,

Your Lordship's most obedient,

And most humble Servant,

Denham, Bucks,
Jan. 1, 1794.

C. STEDMAN.

CONTENTS.

VOL. I.   A   CHAP.

CHAP.

A 2

CHAP.

C H A P. XII.

C H A P. XIII.

C H A P. XIV.

CHAP.

CONTENTS.

CHAP. XVII.

CHAP. XVIII.

CHAP. XIX.

CHAP.

CONTENTS.

CHAP. XX.

Sir William Howe resigns the Command of the Army—Festival
called Mischianza, in honour of Sir William Howe—He is suc-
ceeded in the Command of the Army by Sir Henry Clinton—
Returns to England—Complains of Defamation, and solicits and
obtains a Parliamentary Inquiry into his Conduct.—1778.   380

HISTORY

OF THE

AMERICAN WAR.

INTRODUCTION.

SO natural is the love of liberty, and such the averfion of mankind to reftraint, that it feems to be in the very nature of colonies, and all fubordinate governments, to feize every favourable opportunity of afferting their independence; and the external afpect of nature, varie-gated and broken by mountains, favannahs, rivers, lakes, and feas, confpires with that noble paffion to check the progrefs of empire, and to maintain an interefting diverfity among tribes and nations.

But when the Britifh colonies, now the Thirteen United States of North America, took up arms, and declared themfelves free and independent, they were not encouraged by any conjuncture that could juftify that meafure in point of policy, or by any cir-cumftances that could yield any reafonable hope of fuccefs in the arduous ftruggle that was to enfue.   On the contrary, if we take a

VOL. I.   B   view

Introduction. view of the ſtrength and reſources of Great Britain at the commencement of hoſtilities, and contraſt theſe with the weakneſs and almoſt total inability of the revolting colonies, we ſhall have reaſon to conclude that the termination of the war in favour of the latter, with their final ſeparation from the Britiſh empire, was one of thoſe extraordinary and unexpected events, which in the courſe of human affairs rarely occur, and which bid defiance to all human foreſight and calculation. A people, not exceeding two millions of ſouls, widely ſcattered over half the weſtern hemiſphere, in the peaceable occupations of fiſhing, agriculture, and commerce; divided into many diſtinct governments; differing from each other in manners, religion, and intereſts, nor entirely united in political ſentiments; this people, with very little money, proverbially called the ſinews of war, was yet enabled to effect a final-ſeparation from Great Britain, proud from ſuccefsful and glorious war, flouriſhing in arts and arms beyond the example of any former period; capable of raiſing an annual revenue of ſixteen millions of pounds; and, on the whole, the moſt formidable nation in the world: And all this, although the continent of North America, deeply indented and penetrated by navigable rivers and lakes, preſented a fit theatre for the diſplay of naval power, in which chiefly the ſtrength of Great Britain conſiſted. It is the object of the preſent Work to deſcribe with fidelity the war that involved this great event—a wonder to the preſent, and an example to all future ages. But I ſhall firſt run over the train of circumſtances by which that war was produced.

The colonies of New Hampſhire, Maſſachuſet's Bay, Rhode Iſland, Connecticut, New York, Penſylvania, the three lower counties on the Delaware, Maryland, Virginia, North Carolina, South Carolina, and Georgia, the hiſtory of whoſe revolt it is propoſed to relate, are ſituated on the eaſtern coaſt of North America,

rica, where they are washed by the Atlantic Ocean, ranging from north to south, in the order in which they have been enumerated. On the west they are separated from the immense regions, not fully explored, of Canada and Louisiana, by the Apalachian or Allegany mountains. The countries situated to the west of that magnificent barrier, and at a vast though unknown distance from the Pacific Ocean, are watered by mediterranean seas, called the Lakes of Canada, which not only communicate with each other, but send forth several great rivers, among which the Mississippi, and the St. Laurence, by the weight of their waters and the length of their course, are particularly distinguished.

The Mississippi, running in a winding course near five thousand miles from north to south, and receiving in its progress the Illinois, the Miasures, the Ohio, and other tributary rivers, scarcely inferior to the Rhine or the Danube, discharges itself in the Gulf of Mexico. The St. Laurence, on the contrary, stretching in a north-easterly direction from the Lakes of Canada, falls into the ocean near New-foundland. All these, with the Hudson, Delaware, Susquehannah, Chesapeak, Potowmack, and other noble rivers on the eastern side of North America, being navigable, for the most part, to their very heads, encourage and stimulate commerce in times of peace; but, in those of war, expose the colonies to the attacks of a superior naval force, as already mentioned.

The North American provinces lie between the thirtieth and fiftieth degrees of northern latitude, having about twelve hundred miles of sea-coast. As such a situation would denote a great degree of temperature, it is necessary to observe, that within those bounds they experience much vicissitude of weather, and higher degrees of heat and cold than are to be found in European climates similarly situated.

The northern, commonly called the New England provinces, comprehending New Hampshire, Massachuset's Bay, Rhode Island,

Introduction. and Connecticut, are the least fertile in point of soil; but their land produces excellent timber, and their seas abound with fish. The inhabitants here, as elsewhere, led by the hand of nature, employ themselves in those occupations which are suitable to the productions of their climate. Fishing is the business of some, ship-building of others; and the bulk of the people are more or less engaged in trade or navigation.

The soil of the New England province of Connecticut being richer than that of the others, its inhabitants are occupied in agriculture and raising of cattle; of which, and also of grain, considerable quantities are annually exported.

The productions of the colonies of New York, New Jersey, Pensylvania, and the three lower counties on the Delaware, usually called the Middle Colonies, resemble those of Connecticut; and their inhabitants are engaged in similar occupations. Their most common articles of exportation are wheat and flour, with furs from New York.

As you proceed from Pensylvania to the southward, the heat of summer becomes excessive; and the African alone can endure the labour of working in the fields. Hence it is, that in the southern colonies the number of white inhabitants bears only a small proportion to that of the negroes; whereas in the middle colonies very few, and in the northern scarcely any, Africans are to be found.

The provinces to the southward of Pensylvania have been usually called the Southern Colonies. In those, almost all the white inhabitants are proprietors of lands, which they keep in their own possession, and cultivate by means of slaves. These landowners, or planters, as they have been called, lead easy and luxurious lives, are fond of amusements of all sorts, and to labour and fatigue utter strangers. The business of their plantations, and the management of the African cultivators, are committed to the care

of

of perfons called Overfeers; a fort of middle men between proprietors of lands and the flaves who cultivate them. In the fouthern provinces are raifed the moft valuable articles of commerce exported from North America: Tobacco in Virginia, Maryland, and a great part of North Carolina; and rice and indigo in South Carolina and Georgia.

The philofopher, in travelling through thofe regions, which were all originally peopled from Great Britain, the middle colonies excepted, will find amufement in contemplating the effect which is produced upon the human frame and conftitution, by the influence of climate, of foil, and of the courfe of employment in which the inhabitants are engaged.

In the provinces of New England, where nature has been lefs bountiful in the productions of the earth, he will find a race of men, healthy, ftrong, and vigorous; keen, penetrating, active, and enterprifing, with a degree of dexterity and management in all the common affairs of life, which approaches to cunning and artifice, and fuch as the habits and purfuits, not of a liberal and enlarged, but of a detailed and minute trade, are accuftomed to form.

In the middle colonies, he will fee farmers robuft, frugal, perfevering, and induftrious; plain and honeft in their dealings, but of rude and unpliant manners; with little penetration and lefs knowledge.

And, in moft of the fouthern colonies, he will meet with a people of pallid complexion and fwarthy hue, of form rather tall and flender, unfit and unaccuftomed to labour, with an averfion to bufinefs, and a fondnefs for pleafure and diffipation; luxurious, fhewy, and expenfive; yet fenfible, fhrewd, and intelligent; of open and friendly difpofitions, and in their houfes hofpitable even to extremity. But this muft be underftood only of the fea-coaft and interior parts of the fouthern colonies. For the frontiers of thefe, reaching far to
the

the weftward, extending over various ridges of high mountains, and bordering upon the Indian country, are inhabited by a people unacquainted with luxury and refinement, active and vigorous, with minds fierce and intractable, and, in habits, bearing some refemblance to their favage neighbours.

The inhabitants of Maryland, Virginia, and South Carolina, more than any others of the colonifts, imitated, in drefs, equipage, furniture, and modes and habits of life, the manners and cuftoms of the people of England; and thefe circumftances will account for the vaft fums due from thence to Britain.

The bulk of the natives of North Carolina are hardy and robuft. Their chief employment confifts in hunting and rearing cattle; and their principal amufement in fhooting, for wagers, with rifles at a mark.

The natives of Georgia, from the influence of climate, were a poor, emaciated, debilitated, indolent, and death-like people; and like the inhabitants of South Carolina, ignorant, idle, and inactive.

But thefe are not the only differences that merit attention. There are others which are to be afcribed, not to climate, foil, or employment, but to the principles and tenets, whether civil or religious, of the primary fettlers, which, being handed down from father to fon, may maintain their influence for many ages.

The colony of Virginia, which is the moft ancient, was eftablifhed in the early part of the peaceable reign of James the Firft, about the beginning of the feventeenth century. And, as the colonifts by whom it was fettled removed from their native country, not from any caufe of uneafinefs or diffatisfaction with government, but urged merely by the fpirit of adventure, propagated at that period from Portugal and Spain into other parts of Europe, it may reafonably be fuppofed that they carried with them the prevailing notions and

opinions

opinions of the times, which were peculiarly favourable to monarchy and high church government. So inveterate were thofe principles amongft this people, that Virginia was the laft of all the Britifh dominions that yielded to the fuccefsful arms of Cromwell, and the firft, too, that renounced obedience to his ufurped authority by proclaiming the reftoration of King Charles the Second. And fo uniform were the inhabitants in religious matters, that, until the middle of the prefent century, not a fingle place of worfhip either for Roman Catholics or Proteftant Diffenters was any-where to be found within the colony.

The northern colonies were planted about the end of the fame reign, but not till England began to be torn with internal feuds and diffenfions. Thofe who planned and carried into execution the fettlement of Maffachufet's Bay, which was the firft of the New England colonies, were men who had either fuffered, or expected to fuffer, perfecution during the intolerant adminiftration of archbifhop Laud; puritans in religion, republicans in their notions of government, and of the fame party and principles with thofe who afterwards overturned the government of England in both church and ftate, and brought their fovereign to the block. To thefe fettlers a charter was granted, empowering them to chufe whatever form of government fhould be moft agreeable to themfelves, with only one refervation, that their laws fhould not be repugnant to thofe of Great Britain. What motive could induce the king to grant a charter with powers fo extraordinary and extenfive to a people fo little favoured in that reign as the Puritans, it is not now eafy to difcover; unlefs it was meant as an enticement to encourage the emigration of thofe reftlefs fpirits whofe refractory conduct, machinations, and plots, had begun to give fo much difturbance to government. But, whatever was the motive, the meafure produced a greater effect than had been forefeen. Such numbers in a fhort time withdrew to New England, that government,

in

in the following reign, was obliged to interpose, by forbidding all persons to emigrate, except such as were specially licensed.

The settlements at Massachuset's Bay, reinforced by such numbers from England, soon began to flourish. But scarcely had the new inhabitants taken entire possession of the country which they were to occupy, when they fell into internal dissensions. The majority of the colony being Puritans, the presbyterian mode of worship was declared to be the established religion, to which all were required to conform. Having just escaped from persecution themselves, they, in their turn, became intolerant. A strict compliance with religious ordinances was rigorously exacted; and the persecution that followed, at length became so intolerable as to produce fresh emigrations from this infantine settlement. One class withdrew to New Hampshire, another to Rhode Island, and a third to Connecticut, where they formed establishments, and laid the foundations of their respective governments.

The tract of country which contains the provinces of New York, New Jersey, with the three lower counties on the Delaware, was anciently called the New Netherlands; for the original settlers were Dutch and Swedes, in whose possession it remained until it was conquered by the English in the reign of king Charles the Second, to whom the sovereignty of it was finally ceded, and confirmed by the treaty of Breda in 1667. A grant of a great part of this tract of country, with full powers of sovereignty, was made by Charles to his brother James duke of York, who afterwards sold that district since called New Jersey, to lord Berkely and sir George Carteret, reserving to himself only the province of New York; which province, on the accession of that prince, reverted of course to the crown.

The remaining part of this ceded territory was granted by Charles the Second, towards the end of his reign, to William Penn, the celebrated Quaker, who gave it the name of Pensylvania. By Penn it

was

was originally planted with a colony, consisting of persons of his own religion, who fled from England to avoid the persecutions to which they, though a quiet and inoffensive people, in common with other sectaries, were subjected. For his new settlement he composed a code of laws, of so equitable and liberal a spirit, and in all respects so well adapted to the situation of the colonists, that his name has deservedly been transmitted to posterity with those of the most eminent legislators; and, under the influence of his wise institutions, the colony prospered greatly, and soon became one of the most flourishing of the British settlements.

The counties of Newcastle, Kent, and Suffex, usually called the three lower counties on the Delaware, forming a separate establishment, and electing an assembly for themselves, are attached to the government of Pensylvania, by having the same governor.

Adjoining to Pensylvania, on the south, is the province of Maryland; which, like its neighbouring state, though at a different period, took its rise from religious persecution.

In the reign of Charles the First, when, in consequence of repeated addresses from both houses of parliament, the king was obliged to enforce against the Roman Catholics the execution of those penal and sanguinary laws, which a more enlightened and liberal age has thought fit to repeal, Charles lord Baltimore, a Roman Catholic, and a favourite at court, obtained a grant of that part of Virginia which has since been called Maryland, as a place of refuge for himself, and his persecuted brethren of the Roman religion. And, to the everlasting disgrace of that narrow-minded and intolerant age, it is recorded, that when he embarked for his new settlement, he was accompanied by no fewer than two hundred popish families, and many of these of distinction, who chose to encounter the dangers of the sea, the fury of savages, and all the multiplied inconveniences, evils, and hardships of a new, unexplored, and unsheltered country,

Vol. I.   C   rather

rather than longer remain expofed to the cruel oppreffion of their unrelenting perfecutors. And in this manner was Maryland fettled about the year 1635.

The firft fettlements in the provinces of North and South Carolina, originally comprifed in the fame grant, under the general name of Carolina, were begun a few years after the reftoration of king Charles the Second. A grant of them was made to feveral noblemen and perfons of rank, who employed the celebrated Mr. Locke to form a fyftem of government and code of laws for their new colony. But, however wife in theory thofe inftitutions might have been, it is neverthelefs certain, that the fettlement did not thrive under them, although fupported by the wealth and influence of its rich and powerful proprietors : Nor did it even begin to profper until government, many years afterwards, refumed the grants, took the colony under its own immediate protection, laid afide the inftitutions of Mr. Locke, and gave the inhabitants a conftitution fimilar to that of Viriginia ; and from that period its advances in improvement were as rapid as they had been before flow and unpromifing. So complicated are human affairs, and fo intricate the chain that unites the caufe with the effect, that it is very unfafe, in the formation of political fyftems, to go far beyond the line of experience. The more exalted and refined our ideas of liberty and government, the wider they are apt to lead us aftray ; if, in oppofition to facts and circumftances, we obftinately perfevere in endeavouring to reduce them to practice.

At the end of the war with France, which concluded in 1763, there was, and there had been for near a century paft, a fmall revenue collected in the American colonies, which was fubject to the difpofition of parliament. This revenue arofe from duties impofed by two acts of parliament, one in the 25th year of the reign of king Charles the Second, and the other in the fixth year of the reign

reign of king George the Second ; in the firft inftance on goods exported from, and in the fecond, on goods imported into, the colonies.

By the act of navigation, certain enumerated goods, *viz.* fugar, tobacco, cotton wool, indigo, ginger, fuftic, and other dying wood, the produce of the plantations, were reftrained from being carried from thence to any other place than to fome of the other Britifh plantations, or to Great Britain ; and by the 25 Car. II. duties were impofed upon thefe articles when carried to any other place than Great Britain, and confequently upon fuch of them as were exported to any of the other colonies ; and thefe duties were to be paid before the goods were laden on board any fhip for exportation.

At the time when this act paffed, only one of thefe articles was produced on the continent of North America, which was tobacco ; and upon the exportation of it to any of the other colonies, this duty was regularly paid and collected from that period down to the time of the feparation of the colonies from the mother-country; as was alfo the duty upon indigo, after it was introduced as an article of produce and exportation in the fouthern colonies. The other enumerated articles upon which the duties were laid, were all of the produce of the Weft India iflands ; and upon fuch of them as the inhabitants of the North American colonies imported into their own country, the duties were regularly paid in the Weft Indies, before they were laden on board the veffels.

The duties impofed by the 6 Geo. II. are thofe which have been already mentioned payable on the importation of foreign rum, fugar, and molaffes, into the colonies. To thofe the colonies alfo fubmitted, except fo far as they were eluded by clandeftine importation.

But

But this illicit importation, either from the remiffnefs of the cuf-tom-houfe officers in the colonies, or their inability to prevent it, was carried on, in the courfe of time, to fuch an extent as not only to alarm the Weft India planters, by its tendency to leffen the de-mand for their produce, and to lower its price, but alfo to attract the attention of the Britifh miniftry, who, notwithftanding the ex-tent to which this trade was carried on, found the revenue arifing from it very unproductive ; and who were alfo given to underftand, that through the fame channel fome of the manufactures of Europe, and many of the productions and manufactures of the Eaft Indies, were introduced into the colonies, in breach of the act of naviga-tion, and to the manifeft injury of the trade of the mother-country.

Smuggling was carried on, not only upon the American, but upon the Britifh and Irifh coafts alfo, to fuch an extent, that the parliament, in this year, thought fit to pafs a new act for more ef-fectually fuppreffing it ; and the Britifh miniftry, feconding the views and intentions of the parliament, adopted a new plan for carrying the act into execution, and for checking the evil which it was intended to remedy, by calling in the aid of the officers of the navy. For this purpofe a number of the fmaller fhips of war, with cutters and tenders, were put into commiffion, and ftationed in dif-ferent quarters of the coafts of Great Britain and Ireland ; and to the officers who commanded them fimilar powers were delegated with thofe ufually granted to revenue officers, and they were alfo required to take an oath for the due performance of this part of their duty.

This regulation having taken place in Great Britain, it was alfo thought expedient to extend it to North America and the Weft India iflands ; for, as the minifter had it in contemplation to impofe further taxes in the colonies, it was undoubtedly a primary duty to

I   endeavour

endeavour to make thofe taxes which had been already impofed more productive. And if this regulation was found ufeful on the Britifh fhores, it was thought it would be ftill more ufeful on the American coaft, where opportunities for fmuggling were more abundant, by the numerous inlets with which that coaft abounds, fome of them unfettled, and many others but thinly inhabited; and in confequence of the great extent of their ports, and of the very limited number of cuftom-houfe officers who were appointed to do duty in thofe ports.

The new plan for enforcing the laws of trade produced no murmuring or difquiet amongft the people of Great Britain. It was directed only againft the illicit trader, a character as diftinct from the Britifh merchant as darknefs is from light.

But in the northern colonies of America, many of their principal merchants were engaged in clandeftine trade, and in thofe colonies it was no difparagement to be fo: On the contrary, whenever a feizure was made, the difpleafure and refentment of the people were directed againft the officer who had done his duty, and not againft the party who had offended againft the law. And hence, the cuftom-houfe officers, finding it impoffible to live happily with their neighbours, if they exerted themfelves vigoroufly in the difcharge of their duty, became remifs, and feldom made feizures, except in cafes of fuch palpable breaches of the law as came fo openly under their own obfervation that it was impoffible to overlook them.

The reception which this regulation met with in America was fuch as might have been expected, from a people habituated to thofe illicit practices in trade which it was intended to reprefs. In the northern colonies it produced univerfal alarm, difcontent, and diffatisfaction. As the navy officers were not ftationary, nor their refidence on fhore, it was forefeen that they would not be influenced by motives of friendfhip, fellowfhip, or neighbourhood; neither could they be

over-

overawed or intimidated from doing their duty. The merchants in thofe colonies could, therefore, no longer depend, or, to fpeak in mercantile language, they could no longer value themfelves, as formerly, upon the profits of their illicit traffic. But thefe caufes of difcontent, however aggravating and mortifying to themfelves, were not to be urged to the miniftry and parliament; they were by no means calculated to procure that redrefs which they wifhed, becaufe, inftead of fhewing the impropriety, they juftified the expediency, of the meafure. Their oftenfible complaints were founded on different grounds; they complained, that the fair and the clandeftine trader were equally expofed to the operation of this indifcriminating regulation, inafmuch as the fhips and veffels of both were equally liable to be fearched, and confequently to detention upon their voyages: They alfo objected, that the officers of the navy were, of all others, the moft improper to be appointed to fuch a fervice, fince, by the former courfe and habits of their life, they could not be fuppofed to be acquainted with the revenue laws, and were of themfelves prone enough to fall into irregularities, without being put into fuch a ftation of executive authority as to render thofe irregularities almoft unavoidable.

It has been already obferved that this new regulation to prevent fmuggling extended not only to the colonies upon the continent of America, but to the Weft India iflands alfo; and there it produced an effect which probably was not forefeen, otherwife fome means would have been devifed to prevent it. Between the Britifh iflands and the Spanifh fettlements in America a confiderable clandeftine trade had been carried on for many years, which was beneficial, not only to thofe iflands, but to Great Britain alfo; becaufe, through this channel, Britifh manufactures were introduced into the Spanifh fettlements, and the returns were principally, though not entirely, in gold and filver; and if any inconveniences arofe from this commerce,

merce, they were greatly overbalanced by the profits which were derived from it. But this trade, beneficial as it was, for want of proper inftructions to the officers of the navy, fell a facrifice, for a time, to the new regulation.

The enterprifing fpirit of the inhabitants of the northern colonies had, notwithftanding the remotenefs of their fituation, induced them to take a fhare in this lucrative trade; and when they found themfelves cut off from it by the new regulation, their chagrin, vexation, and difappointment rofe to a pitch fcarcely to be defcribed. Neverthelefs this incidental effect of the new regulation raifed up advocates for them in quarters where their complaints, heretofore, had been very little attended to.

The inhabitants of the middle colonies were not themfelves engaged in the Spanifh trade to any great extent; but had an intereft in the continuance of it *. The ftock of grain and other provifions, raifed in the northern colonies, was not fufficient for the confumption of their inhabitants, and the deficiency was fupplied from fome of the fouthern and fome of the middle colonies. The rum and falted fifh of New England were received in exchange for thofe provifions, but fome part of the price was always paid in fpecie; and by means of this coafting trade carried on by the people of New England, the gold and filver which they received in their traffic with the Spaniards, or at leaft part of it, was in time circulated through the other colonies. A very confiderable trade was carried on from New York, Philadelphia, and Baltimore, to Lifbon, and the ports up the Straits, in flour, wheat, &c. The returns were moftly made in fpecie, halfjohannes's, the remainder in port wine; and it was not until after the late peace that the court of Lifbon forbad the Americans to carry away more than a certain fum in fpecie on board each veffel, the remainder of the barter to be in the produce of the country. But

* Vide Chalmers's late publication.

another

another very important branch of their illicit trade was carried on
through the Weſt India iſlands, who ſmuggled from the French and
Spaniſh iſlands ; and then the Weſt Indians bartered their ſmuggled
commodities with the Americans for proviſions; for South Carolina
in particular ſent great quantities of maize, or Indian corn, and live
ſtock, to the Britiſh Weſt Indies. The inhabitants, therefore, of the
ſouthern as well as the middle colonies, ſaw with extreme concern one of the channels through which they had been ſupplied
with gold and ſilver in danger of being ſhut up, eſpecially at a time
when the ſcarcity of ſpecie was felt as a general evil throughout the
Britiſh part of the American continent; and they were the more
ready to join in cenſuring the meaſure by which this trade was likely
to be ſuppreſſed, as they thought it apparent that the continuance
of the trade would not only be beneficial to the colonies, but alſo
to the mother-country.

And thus it happened, that this new regulation was the cauſe of
more or leſs uneaſineſs throughout the Britiſh colonies, whether on
the continent of America, or in the Weſt Indies ; and certain it is,
that it excited much more ill-humour amongſt the people of the
northern colonies than any other meaſure of the Britiſh miniſtry or
legiſlature ever had produced. When their trade with the foreign
iſlands had been burthened by the impoſition of duties, it is true, a
ferment aroſe ; but, after the firſt ebullition of reſentment had ſub-
ſided, they conſidered the operation of the act of parliament as unavoidable, and quietly ſubmitted ; hoping, perhaps, to elude its effect
by clandeſtine importation. But theſe hopes were now either cut
off, or rendered precarious, by the new regulation; and as it operated
by intervals, every ſeizure was a freſh cauſe of diſcontent, and not
only kept alive, but added to the general maſs of ill-humour. Their
newſpapers were, for ſeveral ſucceſſive years, filled with complaints
of the detention and ſeizure of their veſſels, and with abuſive, con-
temptuous,

temptuous, and provoking paragraphs againſt the officers of the
navy: And theſe vehicles of clamour being circulated through the
continent, excited not only a ſpirit of hatred and reſentment againſt
thoſe officers, but of oppoſition to the ordinances of the mother-
country amongſt the people of the colonies in general, which made
a ſtrong impreſſion upon their minds, and prepared them for adopting
more eaſily thoſe violent meaſures which a few years afterwards
ended in open revolt.

The miniſter, in purſuance of the plan which he had laid down
for obliging the inhabitants of the colonies to bear a ſhare in the
expence which might be neceſſary for their future protection, introduced a bill into the houſe of commons for impoſing duties on
certain kinds of merchandize, when imported into the colonies, requiring the payment of thoſe duties to be made in gold and ſilver,
and containing the uſual clauſe in the revenue bills for ordering
them, when collected, to be paid into the exchequer, where they
were to be ſet apart as a ſeparate fund, together with the future
produce of all the former parliamentary duties and taxes which had
been heretofore collected in America; and this fund was to be applied, under the diſpoſition of parliament, for defraying the future
charges of protecting, defending, and ſecuring the colonies. The
bill having paſſed through both houſes, received the royal aſſent on
the 5th of April in this year.

The miniſter, by procuring the act to be paſſed, had a two-fold
object in view; the firſt, to regulate the commerce of the colonies;
and the ſecond, to raiſe a revenue. So far as duties were impoſed by
it on the importation of foreign ſugars, indigo and coffee, Eaſt India
wrought ſilks and calicoes, foreign cambricks and French lawns, the
intention ſeems to have been to diſcourage the uſe and conſumption
of thoſe articles, and thereby to encourage and promote the uſe and

Vol. I.   D   conſump-

confumption of Britifh manufactures, and of Britifh Weft India produce of the like kinds; but if, notwithftanding the impofition of the
duties, thofe articles of foreign manufacture and produce fhould ftill
continue to be imported into America, then the act produced its fecondary effect of raifing a revenue. The other duties impofed by this
act; thofe, namely, on Madeira wine, on port and Spanifh wines, and
on coffee and pimento of the growth of the Britifh Weft India iflands,
were for the fole purpofe of raifing a revenue; and in fixing the rates
and proportions of thefe, the minifter feems to have been abundantly
cautious of avoiding any juft imputation of dealing hardly by the
colonies. On the contrary, it would appear that he wifhed to
imprefs them moft ftrongly with the idea, that although they were
now to be called upon to bear fome part of the burthens of the
ftate, ftill their proportion fhould be far, very far, below what was
borne by the inhabitants of the mother-country. Thus the duty
impofed by this act on Britifh coffee imported into the colonies
was only feven fhillings per cwt. or three farthings per pound;
whereas the people of Great Britain paid an inland excife duty of one
fhilling and fix-pence upon every pound of coffee which they con-
fumed, befides a farther duty payable at the cuftom-houfe on importation.

In the fame feffion of parliament an act was paffed refpecting the
paper currency of the colonies, the grounds and motives for the enacting of which it is neceffary here to explain. During the late war,
the colonial affemblies had been in the practice of iffuing bills of
credit to anfwer their prefent exigencies; and that thefe bills might
more effectually fupply the place of money, they were made a
legal tender in the payment of all debts, as if they had been gold or
filver, and were made redeemable after a certain time, either by the
collection of taxes impofed by the affemblies for their redemption,

or

or by the money allotted to the refpective colonies, by the votes of
parliament, as a compenfation for their fervices. The emiffion of
fo much paper money, iffued perhaps in fome of the colonies with
more profufion than was abfolutely neceffary, produced one effect
very injurious to the colonies, by raifing the courfe of exchange
between them and the mother-country; fo that in fome of them bills
of exchange on Great Britain could not be procured but at a lofs to
the purchafer of between thirty and forty per cent.; and as Britifh
money, and indeed every kind of coin which was current in the
colonies, paffed only at certain rates fixed by law, whatever the
courfe of exchange might be; it happened, that when the courfe
of exchange rofe above thofe rates, not only the Britifh money,
but all the other current coin in the colonies, was either withheld by
individuals from circulation, or remitted to the mother-country in
lieu of bills of exchange; and thus in the courfe of a few years the
fcarcity of fpecie was felt as a general evil in all the colonies. This
fcarcity of fpecie was alfo very injurious to the Britifh merchants;
becaufe it happened not unfrequently that the paper bills of credit,
which their agents in the colonies were obliged to receive in payment of their debts, for want of another medium of commerce, were
depreciated in value by the rife of exchange, even whilft they remained
in their poffeffion, and before they could lay them out in the purchafe of bills of exchange, or any other commodity which would
ferve as a remittance to Great Britain. This evil was more or lefs
felt in all the colonies, but more efpecially in Virginia, where, from
the mifconduct of the treafurer, the bills of credit received by him
from the collectors of the taxes were lent out by him to individuals
for his own benefit, and thrown back into circulation, inftead of
being locked up and fecured until they were burnt by order of the
affembly. A reprefentation on this fubject had been made to the

Britifh

Britifh minifter by the merchants trading to Virginia, in which
the evils arifing from a fuperabundance of paper money had been
more feverely felt than in any of the other colonies. But as the
evil was more or lefs felt in all the colonies, it was neceffary that
the remedy to be provided fhould be as extenfive; and thus the act
of parliament above mentioned was paffed, whereby the colonial
affemblies were reftrained from making their bills of credit a lawful
tender in payment of money.

The act for impofing duties on merchandize was only a part of
the plan which the minifter had in contemplation. At the time when
the refolutions upon which this act was founded were moved in the
houfe of commons, he alfo moved another, of the following import:
" That towards further defraying the expences of protecting and
" fecuring the colonies, it may be proper to charge certain ftamp
" duties in the colonies." But he did not think fit during this feffion
to introduce any bill for carrying this laft refolution into effect; leaving it thus open, that if the inhabitants of the colonies fhould diflike
fuch a mode of levying money upon them, they might have an
opportunity of fuggefting fome other which would be more agreeable; and undoubtedly this manner of proceeding was not only a
proof of the minifter's candour, but of his inclination to accommo-
date himfelf to the wifhes and defires of the colonies, as far as the
neceffities of the ftate would permit. The refolution which was
moved, was a notice to the colonial affemblies that the Britifh
treafury ftood in need of a fupply; and it alfo pointed out to them
the manner in which this fupply was propofed to be raifed; but
as the minifter declined bringing in a bill to carry the refolution
into effect until the next feffion of parliament, it was an evidence
that he did not chufe to take the colonies by furprife, or to levy
money upon them in a mode to which they had not yet
                                                          been

been accuftomed, without giving them previous and timely notice.

But however tenderly the minifter had dealt with the colonies in the duties already impofed, and whatever appearance of accommodation he affumed in the impofition of thofe which he difplayed in paffing the previous refolution concerning ftamp duties, without following it up the fame feffion of parliament with a bill he meditated; his general policy with refpect to America, which in confequence of the regulation of laft year had produced fevere ftrictures in fome and given umbrage in all the colonies, was neverthelefs become the theme of general clamour.

The inhabitants of New England, rendered uneafy by the regulation of the laft year, and ftill fmarting under its effects, were not in a fit temper of mind to fubmit quietly to any further impofitions on their commerce; and the lefs fo, becaufe they faw that in confequence of the vigilance and activity of the officers of the navy in the exercife of their new authority, fuch impofitions would in future be more productive, and lefs eafily evaded, than in times paft. They thought too, that they faw in the minifter's proceedings the appearance of a fettled plan gradually unfolding itfelf, but not yet fully difclofed, which in detail and in extent might even go beyond their prefent apprehenfions: And, inftead of waiting to combat particular parts of this plan, as they fhould appear, they boldly refolved to controvert at once the general principle upon which the whole was founded, by queftioning the right and authority of parliament to levy duties or taxes upon the colonies in any form or fhape whatever; and by maintaining that the exercife of fuch an authority by parliament was an infraction, not only of the privileges of the colonifts as Britifh fubjects, but of their rights as men. Such was the import of a refolution entered upon the journals of the lower

house

houfe of affembly of Maffachufets Bay, in the fall of the year 1764, and of a letter to Mr. Mauduit, their agent in England*; from which it appears that they founded their pretenfions of being free from taxation by the Britifh parliament upon the broadeft bafis that they could affume—their rights as men ; a bafis which, if admitted as a ground of argument againft parliamentary authority, placed them at once not in the condition of colonies, or of fubordinate dominions, but of independent ftates, unconnected with the mother-country by political compacts, and owing her no other obligations than thofe which nature impofed. Hence alfo it is manifeft, that the republican principles which diftinguifhed the earlieft fettlers of Maffachufets Bay were not forgotten, but were ftill recognized and ftill acted upon by their pofterity, after the lapfe of near a century and a half.

By another refolution of the fame affembly, a new complaint was added to the lift of their other grievances, " The late extenfion of " the powers of the court of admiralty," on pretence that the right of trial by jury was violated. It is not certainly known upon what late proceeding of the mother-country this complaint was grounded. If it was upon the regulation of the preceding year, it was altogether unfounded, for that regulation did not enlarge the powers of the admiralty courts, it only extended the power of feizing veffels for breaches of the laws of trade to a greater number of perfons than thofe who poffeffed it before. It is true, that in confequence of this regulation, a veffel feized upon the coaft of New England might be carried into one of the other colonies, and might there be tried; but this effect refulted not from the regulation, but from the general powers incident to courts of admiralty, and fo ancient as to be coëval with their original inftitution. Whatever is

* Report of the Committee of the Houfe of Lords, in 1774.

1   done

done upon the fea is fubject to their jurifdiction, and they are not confined in their cognizance to things which happen within any particular diftrict or portion of the fea, but their jurifdiction is as unlimited as the fea itfelf.

But if the complaint was founded on the claufes in the act of the laft feffion of parliament, directing the penalties thereby inflicted on breaches of the laws of trade, to be recoverable in the courts of vice-admiralty in America, this was no new fubject of complaint; for fimilar claufes had been inferted in former acts of parliament refpecting the trade of the colonies, fome of them made fo long ago as the reign of William the Third *.

It appears, too, to have been the determination of the members who compofed this affembly, that the other colonies fhould be invited to unite with that of Maffachufets Bay, in a joint oppofition to the exercife of the parliamentary authority condemned by their abovementioned refolution †; but for the prefent they prudently delayed fuch an invitation, until, by diffeminating their republican notions of government, and difperfing through the continent their political pamphlets on the rights of the colonies and the encroachments of the mother-country, they fhould in fome meafure prepare the minds of the inhabitants of the other colonies for acceding to fuch a propofal; and, in the mean time, in behalf of themfelves and their own conftituents, they refolved to fet forth their complaints in a petition to the king and parliament.

It has been already noticed, that, in the laft feffion of parliament, an act was paffed for reftraining the paper currency of the colonies. This act, too, had the misfortune to give offence; and it was more offenfive in the fouthern than in the northern colonies: Neverthelefs its beneficial confequences were very foon experienced; for within

* 7 and 8 W. 3. c. 22.   3 Geo. 2. c. 28.   6 Geo. 2. c. 13.
† See the Report of the Committee of the Houfe of Lords, in 1774.

two

two years after it had paffed, the courfe of exchange between Great Britain and the colonies, which had been fo injurious to the latter, was reduced to its proper level.

What proportion of paper currency fhould be admitted in the general circulation of a country, to fupply the place of gold and filver, is a fubject of fo complicated a nature, that the moft enlightened men have differed in their opinions about it, even in countries where experience could be brought in aid of their inveftigations. It cannot therefore be a matter of great furprife, that the American politicians of the fouthern colonies * fhould have been miftaken in their opinions about the effect of this act. The want of a fufficient quantity of fpecie to fulfil the purpofes of circulation was obvious to all; and they thought that an act which had a tendency to hurt the credit of the medium which fupplied the place of gold and filver, muft neceffarily be injurious. They looked upon themfelves as the moft competent judges of their own neceffities, and confidered the interference of the Britifh parliament, in paffing this act, as an unneceffary and wanton exertion of power, the ultimate utility of which they more than doubted, whilft they deprecated its prefent effects as ruinous and deftructive.

The fouthern provinces, being but very little engaged in trade, would not, perhaps, have thought themfelves fo much affected by the act of the laft feffion of parliament for impofing duties, had it not been for the claufe which required the payment of thofe duties to be made in fpecie, and this money to be paid into the exchequer in England, before it was to be applied towards the expence of protecting and defending the colonies; and even with this claufe, had not the act been alfo accompanied with the other, refpecting the paper currency, it is poffible that the northern and middle colonies

* In New England they had fome experience on this fubject, having before felt the benefit of a fimilar act.

might

might have been fuffered to murmur by themfelves, as on former occafions. But the act for reftraining their paper currency affected all the colonies in fome degree; and, in confequence of a greater fcarcity of fpecie, it affected the fouthern colonies more than any one of the reft: And when different communities, however difunited in other refpects, confider themfelves as fuffering under the fame common grievance, mutual fympathy arifes, which, by a natural movement, gradually extends itfelf beyond the caufe by which it was originally excited, and, in time, involves as well their feparate as their common caufes of complaint. At this juncture, too, it fo happened, that thofe meafures of the Britifh adminiftration which had given the greateft offence to the northern and middle colonies had fome relation to that by which the fouthern colonies thought themfelves principally aggrieved. The regulation againft fmuggling had put an end to the trade carried on with the Spanifh fettlements, and in confequence deprived the inhabitants of the colonies of the means of obtaining further fupplies of fpecie; whilft the act of the laft feffion of parliament for impofing duties in America, which required thefe duties to be paid in fpecie, and to be remitted to England, would, it was thought, in a fhort time, drain the colonies of the little of the precious metals which they now poffeffed; and, as the climax of their misfortunes, the act which related to their paper currency, had a tendency to deftroy the only medium of commerce which remained.

By this ftrange accidental connection between thefe three different regulations, the complaints of the New England provinces, which were principally directed againft the two firft of them, were heard with more attention, were better received, and made a deeper impreffion in the fouthern colonies than had been ufual. The people of New England were not wanting, on their part, to improve the favourable moment, for the purpofe of laying the foundation of

a general oppofition. The prefs was reforted to. The grievances
of the colonies were painted in the moft impreffive language; and
the Britifh miniftry were boldly charged with harbouring defigns
againft the liberty, property, and future profperity of the colonies:
And thus a general murmur of difcontent began to run through the
whole extent of the Britifh fettlements on the continent of America,
which was not a little increafed by the refolution of the houfe of
commons, which manifefted an intention in that houfe, at fome
future period, to impofe ftamp duties in the colonies.

There were, in all the colonial affemblies, as indeed there are in
all public affemblies, certain popular characters to whom the great
body of the people looked up for advice and information in matters
of difficulty. Thefe leading men, even in the colonies which were
the moft fincerely attached to the mother-country, entertained,
about this time, ftrong fufpicions and apprehenfions of the arbitrary
defigns of the Britifh court. Such fufpicions originating perhaps,
at firft, in the violence and animofity of party, with which the beginning of the prefent reign was fo much diftracted, had, a little
before this time, been very generally diffufed through Great Britain
itfelf, and were from thence probably tranfplanted into America.
And unfortunately for the fuccefs of Mr. Grenville's American
meafures, perhaps unhappily for the general intereft of the Britifh
empire, and, without doubt, unfortunately for the internal peace
and tranquillity both of Great Britain and America, fuch fufpicions were countenanced by one of the greateft men * of that, or
perhaps any other period, whofe recent fervices, and the unparalleled fuccefs of whofe meafures, whilft he conducted the affairs
of the nation, ftamped an irrefiftible authority upon whatever
opinion he thought fit to efpoufe. If thofe fufpicions, however

* Mr. Pitt.

originating,

originating, were countenanced * · by this great man, the American patriots, placed at such a diftance, and deftitute of equal means of information, may be eafily excufed for adopting them : But certain it is, that they prevailed very much about this time amongft the leading men in all the colonies, and were, through them, inftilled into the minds of the people at large. And from thence it happened, that every act of the Britifh government refpecting America was viewed with more than common jealoufy.

Such was the ftate of public opinion and fentiment in the North American colonies towards the end of the year 1764, and the beginning of the year 1765. But, notwithftanding the threatening fymptoms of difcontent, uneafinefs, and jealoufy, which had begun to appear, the minifter was not deterred from profecuting the defign which he had fo long meditated, of raifing a revenue in the colonies by means of ftamp duties. Having previoufly inquired of the agents for the colonies, whether they had any inftructions from their conftituents to propofe any other method of raifing money in the colonies than that of which he had given intimation the preceding year; or whether they had authority to offer a compenfation for the revenue which was propofed to be raifed ; and receiving for anfwer, that they had no authority for either of thefe purpofes ; he now refolved to lay his plan before the houfe of commons, and, on the 29th of January, in a committee of that houfe, moved fifty-five refolutions for impofing ftamp duties on certain papers and documents ufed in the colonies. Thefe refolutions having been agreed to, a bill grounded upon them was foon afterwards introduced, which, although it met with vehement oppofition, particularly from that party which has fince diftinguifhed itfelf by the name of the Whig party, and at the head of which was the marquis of Rock-

---

* Mr. Pitt's fpeech on the repeal of the ftamp act.

ingham,

ingham, was nevertheless carried through both houses of parliament by a considerable majority, and received the royal assent on the 22d of March.

By this act, which was to take effect in America on the 1st of November following, stamp duties were imposed on such papers and documents as are used as evidence in the common dealings and transactions of life between man and man; or on such as are used in legal proceedings, in appointments to offices, in admissions to professions, and in the entry and clearance of vessels at the custom-house; and had the authority of parliament to pass it been free from all objection, it must be confessed that the scheme of taxation proposed by this act, was perhaps one of the best which could have been devised for raising a revenue from a people spread over such an extent of the continent, and parcelled out into so many different governments, inasmuch as it was not only simple and practicable, but equitable in its operation, equally well adapted to all the colonies, and, in its nature, efficacious. It excluded all jealousy and envy, because it extended to all the colonies, and was to be raised on papers and documents which were common to them all. It must be efficacious, because these papers and documents were declared to be invalid, unless they were stamped; and the stamps could not be obtained without the payment of the duty. And it was also equitable, as the weight of it would fall chiefly upon those classes of people who were best able to bear it; and as it would be most productive in those colonies which were the most flourishing, and in which the transactions between man and man were the most frequent.

The resolutions on which the bill was founded, together with the debates which it had produced in its passage through the house of commons, were, without loss of time, transmitted to America by the agents for the colonies; so that the leading men in that quarter

of

of the world had full time to deliberate on the confequences of the act, with all its attendant circumftances, before it took effect, and to prepare the minds of the great body of the people for yielding to thofe impreffions which they wifhed them to receive. Prepof-feffed as they were with fufpicions of the arbitrary defigns of the Britifh court, they now thought that thofe fufpicions were converted into certainties; and that America, thus taxed without her confent, was deftined to be the firft victim to arbitrary power; and they refolved not to fubmit to fuch a melancholy fate without the moft ftrenuous refiftance. A gleam of hope arofe from feeing the powerful oppofition which had been made to the act in its paffage through the houfe of commons. They were thereby encouraged to purfue the line of conduct marked out by their prefent feelings; and they determined to exert themfelves with vigour in ftirring up fuch a ferment as might diftrefs, if not overturn, the adminiftration, who were the authors of this meafure, and as would certainly defeat the effect of the act for a time, and perhaps eventually produce its repeal: And this refolution feems to have been adopted by the leading men in all the colonies, without any apparent concert except what arofe from a general knowledge of one another's fentiments, in confequence of the tranfactions of the preceding year.

With this view the arguments which had been ufed by the members of oppofition in the Britifh parliament were retraced, enforced, and enlarged; and in this form publifhed in pamphlets or circulated in newfpapers. Thefe publications were adapted to all capacities. It was contended with great ftrength and force of reafoning, that as the inhabitants of the colonies were Britifh fubjects as much as the inhabitants of Great Britain, fo were they entitled to the fame conftitutional rights and privileges: That it was the birthright of every Britifh fubject to give and grant his own money for the

support

fupport of government, and not to be taxed but by his own confent or that of his reprefentative: And as the people of the colonies were not reprefented in the Britifh parliament, fo the Britifh parliament could not conftitutionally impofe taxes upon them. And to fuch arguments other topics were added, not perhaps more convincing, but better calculated to draw the attention, and imprefs the feelings of the American colonift. The act was reprefented to be oppreffive in its operation, by converting the plainnefs and fimplicity of their former proceedings, whether legal or commercial, into labyrinths of doubt, difficulty, and perplexity. It was faid that the act was peculiarly inapplicable to a country fo extenfively fettled, and fo thinly inhabited, as America; for it might, and frequently would happen (to give one example inftead of many), that the planter or farmer, upon fo common a tranfaction as the purchafe of a horfe, might be obliged to ride many miles to procure a piece of ftamped paper, on which he could write a bill of fale, and even when he had performed his journey, he might be in doubt what kind of ftamp was proper for his purpofe. In this manner the fuppofed evils and inconveniences attending its operation were magnified and heightened in language fuited to the apprehenfions of the mafs of the people; a defign in the Britifh miniftry to enflave America was fuppofed to be difcovered; and the ftamp act, it was pretended, was only to be regarded as the forerunner of innumerable other oppreffions which were to follow. And thus the people were taught to confider the period when the act was to take effect as the commencement of their flavery, unlefs they manfully refifted its execution.

Independent of all the previous means which were ufed to bring about an oppofition, it was rather to be expected, that an act which impofed new burdens, and at the fame time rendered the tranfactions between man and man in the common affairs of life fomewhat lefs

plain

plain and eafy, 'and, above all, which was fo open and liable to objection on conftitutional grounds, would not be well received amongft
fome of the colonies at leaft, nor acquiefced in without reluctance;
but it excited no fmall fhare of furprife when it was known that the
firft legiflative oppofition which it met with, took place in the ancient
colony of Virginia, famed beyond all the reft for loyalty to the fovereign, and attachment to the mother-country.

Thofe to whom this event was the caufe of furprife, did not reflect, that during the preceding war the importance of the colonies
in the general fcale of the Britifh empire had been blazoned forth
and magnified in various debates in both houfes of parliament, as if
the exiftence of Great Britain as a commercial nation had depended
upon her trade with the colonies; that it had been made a favourite
theme of declamation with minifters whenever they preffed for fupplies to fupport the war; and that the colonies would at leaft eftimate their confequence equal to what it had been reprefented. Neither did they reflect, that heretofore the colonies had been kept in
fear by the vicinity of the French and Spaniards, whilft the former
were in poffeffion of Canada, and the latter of the two Floridas;
but that now, fince the ceffion of thefe provinces to Great Britain,
they were relieved from all future apprehenfions on account of fuch
formidable neighbours, and faw themfelves placed in a ftate of fecurity which they had never before experienced. Neither did they
reflect, that in proportion as the protection of Great Britain had become lefs neceffary, fo it would be lefs valued; and that the treaty
of Paris, which gave fecurity to the colonies, did, at the fame time,
weaken their dependence on the mother-country.

And this proceeding in the legiflature of Virginia will ftill lefs be
the caufe of furprife, if to thefe confiderations we add, that foon
after the commencement of the prefent reign, a bold and daring

I   fpirit

spirit of oppofition to government had broken forth and fpred itfelf
amongft the people of England; and that it muft neceffarily happen
that fome portion of this predominant fpirit would be imparted to
the inhabitants of the colonies in the profecution of that clofe and
conftant intercourfe which fubfifted between them and the mother-
country. Indeed fuch had been the violence of faction in England,
and fo bold and daring its partifans, that even the fplendour of the
crown could not fhield the head which it adorned againft the in-
venomed fhafts of flander: And fuch was the perverfenefs of the
people, that punifhments inflicted by the courts of juftice for the
moft heinous offences againft government were in fome inftances
converted into public rewards *.

That the colony of Virginia fet the example in this oppofition
to the ftamp act, was perhaps, after all, chiefly owing to accident.
It happened that the general affembly of that province was fitting at
the time when a copy of the act arrived in that country, together
with certain intelligence that it had paffed through both houfes of
parliament and received the royal affent. The act, it is true, was
not to have any effect till the month of November, but they knew
not whether they would have another opportunity of deliberating
upon it as an affembly, until after that event had taken place. The
leading men too were anxious to fhew to their conftituents, that in
their legiflative capacity they were not backward in avowing thofe
fentiments which, as individuals, they had taken fome trouble to
promulgate. The people had been already prepared by reiterated
publications in the newfpapers, and it remained only for the affembly,

---

* The author of the North Briton, and of the Effay on Woman, is a living example of the
truth of this remark. In a valuable appointment beftowed upon him by the corporation of
London, he quietly enjoys the fruits of thofe flanders which filled his fovereign's breaft with
anguifh, whilft every good man muft execrate fo nefarious a publication, and fo diabolical an
author.

2   - by

by some expreffion of their will, to give a fanction to the intended oppofition. Indeed, without this · fanction, the refiftance which they meditated would have been incomplete. The confent of the governor and council was not to be expected; whatever therefore could be done muft be the act of the lower houfe of affembly only ; and the fubject was there introduced without lofs of time, and gave occafion to one of the moft violent and intemperate debates which had ever been known in that country. Some idea may be formed of the manner in which this debate was conducted, by the following paffage, extracted from a fpeech of one* of the members, who afterwards made a confpicuous figure in the beginning of the rebellion. After declaiming with bitternefs againft the fuppofed arbitrary meafures of the prefent reign, he added, " Cæfar had his " Brutus, Charles the Firft an Oliver Cromwell, and George the " Third—" But before he·could proceed farther, a cry of, Treafon ! was heard from one quarter of the houfe, and the fpeaker foon afterwards rifing up, called him to order, and declared that he would quit the chair, unlefs he was fupported by the houfe in reftraining fuch intemperate fpeeches.

This debate was concluded by propofing four refolutions of the following effect, which were agreed to by the houfe, and entered upon their journals on the 29th day of May. The firft declared, that their anceftors brought with them from England, and tranfmitted to their pofterity, all the rights, privileges, and immunities, enjoyed by Britifh fubjects: The fecond, that thefe were confirmed and declared by two royal charters, granted by king James the Firft : The third, that they have ever fince enjoyed the right of being governed by their own affembly in the articles of

---

* Mr. Patrick Henry.

taxes

taxes * and internal police; which right has not been forfeited or yielded up, but has been recognized by the king and people of Great Britain: And the fourth, that the general affembly of Virginia, with his majefty or his fubftitute, have, in their reprefentative capacity, the only exclufive right and power to lay taxes and impofitions upon the inhabitants of that colony: And that every attempt to inveft fuch a power in any perfon or perfons whatfoever, other than the general affembly aforefaid, is illegal, unconftitutional, and unjuft, and has a manifeft tendency to deftroy Britifh as well as American freedom.

Two other refolutions were offered by the committee to whom this matter was referred, which were rejected by the houfe: But as they ferve to characterize the kind of fpirit which had begun to gain ground, and which poffeffed fome of the members of that affembly, the fubftance of them is here inferted. The firft amounted to a declaration that the inhabitants of Virginia are not bound to yield obedience to any law impofing taxes upon them, other than the laws of the general affembly; and the fecond denounced thofe to be enemies to the colony who fhould maintain, by fpeaking or writing, that any perfon or perfons, other than the general affembly, had a right to impofe taxes upon them.

But however intemperate the debate had been, which preceded thefe refolutions, and whatever heat and violence were difcoverable in individual members of this affembly, there was neverthelefs a manifeft and ftriking difference between the refolutions of the Maffachufets affembly of the preceding year, and thofe which were

---

* That thefe refolutions may be fully underftood, it is neceffary to obferve, that in Virginia, and indeed in all the *colonies* of North America, a diftinction was made between taxes, and duties on the importation or exportation of merchandize; fo that the former of thefe terms was not fuppofed to comprehend the latter.

now paffed by the lower houfe of affembly in Virginia; a difference

defcriptive both of the particular views and of the general political character which diftinguifhed the inhabitants of thefe refpective colonies. The former, as if they had been already independent, refort at once to their rights as men—as a ground to exempt them from taxation by the Britifh parliament: The latter, venerating the Britifh conftitution, fenfible of its benefits, and happy in their connexion with the mother-country, found their claims wholly upon their rights as Britifh fubjects, which had been declared and confirmed by their charters. The former claim an unlimited exemption from duties as well as taxes, thereby undermining the whole fabric of the colonial fyftem: The latter, avowing the relation in which they ftand to the mother-country, confine their claim of legiflative jurifdiction to taxes and internal police, thereby tacitly conceding to the Britifh parliament the impofition of duties on merchandize, and the ordering and regulation of their commerce.

The affembly of Virginia having entered into thefe refolutions, was diffolved as foon as the governor was made acquainted with them. But it was now too late to ftop the progrefs of the flame which had burft forth: Indeed the mifchief was already done, becaufe the refolves of the affembly were fuppofed to fanction whatever irregularities might enfue, in oppofing the execution of an act which, by thefe refolves, was pronounced to be illegal, unconftitutional, and unjuft; and the conflagration, which had been kindled was now deftined to fpread through the colony at large, by the return of the members to their refpective counties.

The affemblies of the other colonies, in the courfe of the year, entered into refolutions, fimilar to thofe of the affembly of Virginia; and whatever differences there might be between them in other refpects, there was but one opinion on the fubject of the ftamp act.

F 2 . They

They all concurred in voting it to be an act that was unconstitutional, and an infringement of their rights.

We have seen that the assemby of Massachusets Bay had in the
preceding year entered into resolutions, and transmitted a petition
to the king and parliament, complaining of a variety of grievances,
and amongst the rest, of the resolution of parliament which announced an intention to impose stamp duties in the colonies. The
same assembly now brought forward another measure of much more
importance in its nature and consequences, as it was the first leading
step towards that confederation amongst the colonies which ultimately separated them from the mother-country. It was no part of
the character of the people of New England to be remiss in any
thing which concerned their interest. They had not been inat-
tentive observers of the discontent which prevailed in the other colonies on account of the stamp act, and they seized upon the present as the critical moment for reconciling the interests, consoli-
dating the grievances, and uniting the complaints, of all the colonies;
a design which we have seen they had in contemplation the preceding year.

In prosecution of this intention the assembly of Massachusets Bay,
on the sixth day of June, entered into a resolution, setting forth the
expedience of holding a general congress, which should consist of
deputies from all the lower houses of assembly on the American
continent, to consult together, and take into consideration the common grievances under which the colonies laboured, in consequence
of the late acts of parliament for imposing duties and taxes, and to
frame and prepare a general petition and address to the king and
parliament, in behalf of all the colonies, setting forth these grievances and praying for redress. They also resolved, that letters
signed by their speaker, by order of the house, should be sent to
                                                          the

the affemblies of the other colonies, communicating this refolution, and requefting fuch other affemblies, if they approved of the propofal, to appoint deputies to meet with thofe which fhould be appointed by the affembly of Maffachufets Bay, in a general congrefs to be held at New York, on the firft day of October following; and they afterwards proceeded to nominate their own deputies, and to vote the fum of four hundred and fifty pounds for defraying their expences. In confequence of thefe refolutions letters were prepared and tranfmitted; and fuch of the other colonial affemblies as were permitted to meet before the month of October, very readily acceded to the meafure recommended by the affembly of Maffachufets Bay, and nominated deputies for the propofed congrefs. Although the leading men in fome of the colonies had not the moft favourable opinion, either of the candour, fincerity, and plain dealing of the people of New England, or of the general courfe and tendency of their politics; yet, fuch is the effect of a common grievance in reconciling differences of opinion and allaying jealoufies, that this proceeding of the affembly of Maffachufets Bay, which certainly had fome appearance of dictating to the reft of the colonies, neverthelefs met with general approbation.

Whilft fuch meafures were purfued in America, an event took place in England which, more than all their own efforts, ferved the caufe of the colonifts, and promoted the fuccefs of their defigns. This was a change of the miniftry. On the 10th of July, Mr. Grenville and his adherents were difmiffed from their offices, to give place to the whig party, under the marquis of Rockingham, a party which we have feen had exerted themfelves ftrenuoufly in oppofing the ftamp act. The vehement declamations of this party againft the minifter within the houfe of parliament, and the active exertions of their friends and partifans amongft the people without; the threats of the Americans to difcontinue the ufe of Britifh manufactures until

3
the

the ftamp act fhould be repealed, and the confequent alarm fpread
amongft the merchants, manufacturers, and fhip owners; the murmurs and difcontents of the lower orders of the people, from the
fcarcity of bread and the high price of provifions, calamities to
which they were expofed during the whole of this year; all thefe
caufes combined had excited fuch a clamour in the nation as greatly
weakened and diftreffed the late adminiftration, and probably con-
duced to their removal. But the immediate caufe of their difmiffion
is faid to have been an affront given to the princefs dowager of
Wales, and through her to the king, by neglecting to infert her
name in a bill introduced by the miniftry into the houfe of lords,
towards the clofe of the laft feffion of parliament, for appointing a
regency in cafe of the death of the king, during the minority of
the prince of Wales; an omiffion which was rectified after the bill
was fent to the houfe of commons. But, whatever was the caufe,
the change which enfued, by placing the whig party in power, gave
to the inhabitants of the colonies a well-grounded hope, that the
act for impofing ftamp duties would be repealed in the next feffion
of parliament.

In America, however threatening the appearances had been, no
actual difturbances took place until the month of Auguft; but in
that month, about the time when intelligence arrived of the change
of the miniftry, the fpirit which had been fo long tumultuoufly gathering, broke forth into open violence, firft at Bofton in Maffachufets Bay, and afterwards in feveral of the other colonies. At
Bofton, the fury of the populace was directed againft the chief-
juftice of the province, who was fuppofed to favour the minifterial
plan for taxing the colonies; againft the officer appointed to diftribute the ftamps, the comptroller of the cuftoms, and the regifter of
the court of admiralty. Previous intelligence of what was in agitation having been conveyed to them by their friends, they were

I   fortunate

fortunate enough to be able to fave their perfons from infult, but their houfes were pillaged, their furniture was burnt or deftroyed, and the records of the admiralty, not lefs odious in that province than the ftamp act itfelf, were committed to the flames. The council of the province were affembled by the governor, but they fhewed no inclination to be active in fuppreffing the riots. The governor attempted to mufter fome companies of militia to affift the civil magiftrate in the prefervation of the peace, but they refufed to obey his orders ; and the ftamp officer, feeing no profpect of protection, foon afterwards refigned his office.

In the other colonies the tumults were not fo violent and outrageous as thofe at Bofton ; but in all of them they were fufficiently alarming to frighten the perfons who were appointed to diftribute the ftamps into a refignation of their offices.

A confiderable interval having been required for preparing the ftamped papers in England, none of them had yet arrived in America ; and the officers to whom they were to have been delivered, having been obliged to refign their appointments, the general care of thefe papers, upon their arrival in the months of September and October, devolved upon the governors of the refpective provinces. In fome of the colonies the ftamped papers were feized and deftroyed by the populace ; in moft of them, through the prudent management of the governors, they were lodged in places of fecurity on fhore, or put on board the fhips of war ; but in none of the thirteen colonies, after fuch riots, was any one found hardy enough to undertake the diftribution of them.

In the month of October deputies from nine out of the thirteen colonies met at New York, to hold a general congrefs. The four colonies not reprefented in this congrefs were, New Hampfhire, Virginia, North Carolina, and Georgia. From the three laft of thefe deputies were not fent, becaufe the letters from Maffachufets Bay

arrived

arrived during the recefs of their affemblies, which were not afterwards permitted to meet till the firft of October had paffed. And
in New Hampfhire, the affembly did not think fit to appoint deputies, although they approved of the holding of a general congrefs,
and fignified an inclination to join in any petition that fhould be
agreed upon by the deputies of the other colonies.   •

The firft feffion of thefe deputies was held on the feventh day of
October; and twelve days having been fpent in debates and deliberations, on the nineteenth they entered into thirteen refolutions, comprehending a declaration as well of the rights as of the
grievances of all the colonies. In thefe refolutions they fet forth,
that the inhabitants of the colonies owe the fame allegiance to the
king as the people of Great Britain, and all due fubordination to
parliament. That they are entitled to the fame rights, privileges,
and immunities, as the people of Great Britain. That no taxes can
be impofed on a free people but by their own confent, or that of
their reprefentatives. That the inhabitants of the colonies are not,
and cannot, be reprefented in the houfe of commons of Great Britain.
That the only reprefentatives of the inhabitants of the colonies are
thofe chofen by themfelves; and that no taxes have been or can be
impofed upon them but by thofe reprefentatives. That all fupplies to
the crown are free gifts from the people; and that therefore it is unreafonable in the parliament of Great Britain to grant the property
of the inhabitants of the colonies. That trial by jury is the right
of a Britifh fubject. That the ftamp act, by impofing taxes, and
extending the jurifdiction of the courts of admiralty beyond their
ancient limits, has a tendency to fubvert the rights and liberties of
the colonifts. That the duties impofed by the late acts of parliament are grievous, and the payment of them impracticable. That,
by the Britifh manufactures which they purchafe, they contribute to
the fupplies granted to the crown. That the reftrictions on trade,

impofed

Impofed by the late acts of parliament, will render them unable to purchafe Britifh manufactures. That the increafe and profperity of the colonies depends on the free enjoyment of their rights and liberties. And laftly, that they have a right to petition the king, or either houfe of parliament.

Thefe refolutions having been entered into, and an addrefs and petition to the king, a memorial and petition to the houfe of lords, and a petition to the houfe of commons, fetting forth, more at large, the grievances mentioned in their refolutions, having been prepared and agreed to; the congrefs diffolved their meeting on the twenty-fifth of October, having fat about eighteen days.

From comparing the refolutions of congrefs with thofe of the affembly of Maffachufets Bay, it is evident that the leading men in the other colonies were not yet prepared to go the full length which the people of New England wifhed. It is true, the congrefs dif-avow the authority of parliament to impofe taxes upon the inhabit-ants of the colonies, and to abridge the trial by jury; but they complain of the other acts of parliament, for impofing duties on merchandize, and reftricting their trade, rather as grievances arifing from an indifcreet and impolitic exercife of a power which they did not call in queftion, than as actual infractions of their conftitutional rights.

Thefe were all the proceedings of this congrefs which were made public. The great temper and moderation manifefted in the papers which were to be tranfmitted to England, were probably intended to counteract the effect of the riots and tumults which had preceded the meeting of the congrefs. The members of this body were aware that all appearance of defiance was carefully to be fuppreffed. Profeffing loyalty to the king, and all due fubordination to par-liament, they endeavoured to exhibit themfelves as patient fufferers,

VOL. I.   G   and

and as dutiful, although oppreffed, fubjects, rather foliciting the compaffion than braving the power of the Britifh nation.

By the meeting of fo many deputies at New York, a communication was opened, an acquaintance was formed, and a correfpondence eftablifhed, between the leading men of all the colonies; and a foundation was thus laid for uniting their common efforts, whenever future circumftances, and the attempts of future adminiftrations, fhould render it neceffary. One effect of the mutual underftanding which took place amongft thefe leading men was indeed immediately difcoverable; for, as foon as they returned to their refpective homes, affociations were fet on foot in all the colonies againft the importation of Britifh manufactures, fuch importation to ceafe after the firft of January following, until the ftamp act fhould be repealed; a meafure which was probably concerted before they left New York.

When the firft of November arrived, the day on which the ftamp act was to take effect, neither ftamps were to be had nor officers to diftribute them. The former had been lodged in places of fecurity, to fave them from deftruction by the populace; and the latter had been either terrified into refignation, or driven away by ill ufage. The courts of law were unable to proceed for want of thofe papers which the act had rendered neceffary; and a total ftop was put to the adminiftration of juftice, except in criminal cafes, in which ftamps were not required. Commerce too was at a ftand, becaufe ftamps were made neceffary in the entry and clearance of veffels at the cuftom-houfes. Some of the merchants ventured to fend their fhips to fea with certificates from the governors that ftamps could not be procured; and in the province of Maffachufets Bay the council and affembly were daring enough to enter into a formal refolution, declaring it to be lawful to tranfact bufinefs, as formerly, without the ufe of ftamps.

Such

Such were the meafures purfued and the fteps taken in America, during the year 1765, for oppofing the ftamp act and procuring its repeal; and the inhabitants of the colonies were not more active and ftrenuous in refifting, than the new miniftry were remifs and backward in iffuing, orders for enforcing its execution. Although the refolutions of the affembly of Virginia were laid before them not long after they came into office, and although, upon the twenty-feventh of Auguft, the board of trade reported thefe refolutions to contain a daring attack upon the conftitution of Great Britain, and to require immediate attention; and although that board recommended orders to be forthwith fent to the executive power, and to all the officers of government in Virginia, to exert themfelves vigoroufly in fupport of the authority of parliament, and to exact a due obedience to all the laws of the land; yet this report of the board of trade, fo urgent in its nature, was not taken into confideration by the privy council until the third of October. On that day indeed, in a very full council, at which lord chancellor Camden affifted, it was determined, that the fubject of the report from the board of trade was of too high a nature for the decifion of the king in council, and that it was proper only for the confideration of parliament: As if it had not been the duty of the executive power to require a prompt obedience to all the acts of the legiflature, and as if that power had a right to deliberate whether an act of parliament fhould be carried into execution or not.

Such was the indecifion of the new miniftry refpecting American affairs; and fo indefinite, and even inexplicable *, was the nature of their difpatches to the American governors, that the laft blow was now given to the little energy which remained in the executive part of the colonial governments. Thofe governors undoubtedly

* See Secretary Conway's letters to Governor Fauquier, of Virginia, dated Sept. 14, 1765.

thought

thought that it was their duty to exact obedience to an act of parliament which extended to America ; but being informed in their
government difpatches that this was a fubject * under the confideration of the privy council, a doubt might arife where there was
none before ; and with fuch information before them, they could
not be certain whether a ftrenuous exertion in compelling fubmiffion
to the ftamp act might not expofe them to the difpleafure of thofe
who now conducted the affairs of government.

· In the party writings publifhed about this time, and in certain
parliamentary fpeeches of a later date, which, from their brilliancy,
gave the tone to public opinion, the ftamp act has been confidered
as the introduction of a new fyftem in the government of the colonies.   But whoever will take the trouble of examining the proceedings of former parliaments, and the various acts which they paffed,
without confulting the inhabitants of the colonies, for confining and
reftricting their trade fo as to make it ferviceable to the mother-country ; for regulating even their domeftic concerns and purfuits, and
for fubjecting both their exports and imports, in certain cafes, to the
payment of duties and taxes, which, when collected, were a part
of the revenue of the kingdom, and applicable to fuch purpofes as
the parliament thought fit to direct †; will fee that the ftamp act was
not the introduction of a new, but the continuation and extenfion
of the old fyftem under which they had always been governed. It
was an application, not of a new, but of the old, principle upon
which former parliaments had acted to the new and improved ftate
of the colonies, which enabled them to contribute more largely than

* Secretary Conway's letter to Lieutenant Governor Fauquier, dated 14th Sept. 1765.
† See the following ftatutes :—

12 Car. II. c. 18.	7 and 8 W. III. c. 22.	9 Ann, c. 17.	5 Geo. II. c. 22.
15 Car. II. c. 7.	3 and 4 Ann, c. 5.	8 Geo. I. c. 15.	6 Geo. II. c. 13.
25 Car. II. c. 7.	6 Ann, c. 30.	5 Geo. II. c. 15.	23 Geo. II. c. 29.

formerly towards raifing a revenue for their own fupport, defence, and protection.

But whatever force there may be in thefe remarks, a clamour had been now raifed in Great Britain as well as America; the mercantile and manufacturing interefts were alarmed; petitions againft the ftamp act, faid to be encouraged by the miniftry *, were tranfmitted from fome of the principal fea-port and manufacturing towns; and in the next feffion of parliament, as had been forefeen, a bill was introduced and fupported by the whole weight and influence of the new adminiftration for repealing the ftamp act. The difturbances in America were by them fpoken of with fome degree of tendernefs. The inhabitants of the colonies were reprefented as an injured people; and the acts of violence which had been committed, were fuppofed to proceed from their defpair. Mr. Grenville and his party ftrongly oppofed the bill, and charged the prefent miniftry with creating the difobedience and refiftance which had arifen in America, by their intemperate and inconfiderate fpeeches whilft they were in oppofition; but it was at length carried and paffed through the houfe by a confiderable majority. The miniftry feem to have wifhed to give fatisfaction to all parties, as well thofe who favoured, as thofe who oppofed, the ftamp act, by introducing at the fame time a declaratory bill, which cenfured and condemned the refolutions of the American affemblies, and contained a formal declaration, that the Britifh parliament had authority to make laws for binding the colonies in all cafes whatfoever. Thefe two bills accompanied each other through the two houfes of parliament, and received the royal affent on the eighteenth of March.

In the bill for repealing the ftamp act, that act was declared to be repealed; not becaufe it was illegal, unconftitutional, or unjuft;

* Mr. Grenville's fpeech on the repeal of the ftamp act.

nor

nor becaufe it was arbitrary or oppreffive; but fimply becaufe it was inexpedient: And it was repealed abfolutely, and free from all terms or conditions.

The principle of the repeal, and the policy of the miniftry in proceeding thus haftily upon it, have been much queftioned, and not without a ftrong appearance of reafon, If the objections of the co-lonial affemblies were deemed of no force or validity, it was the duty of the Britifh parliament, for the prefervation of their own authority, inftead of repealing, to have taken meafures for inforcing the ex-ecution of the ftamp act: On the other hand, if thefe objections were unanfwerable and irrefiftible, it would have been wife, it would have been magnanimous and worthy of the reprefentatives of a great nation, not only to have repealed the ftamp act, but by an open de-claration to have renounced for ever the exercife of fuch an uncon-ftitutional authority; and at the fame time to have devifed fome other expedient for accomplifhing the end propofed by the ftamp act by lefs exceptionable means. Such a declaration would have quieted the minds of the colonifts, and removed all future apprehenfions. But the Britifh parliament purfued neither of thefe courfes. It is true they repealed the ftamp act, but they at the fame time paffed the declaratory act, more arbitrary and more alarming than the other; and by this prepofterous policy kept alive the jealoufy which the ftamp act had excited, whilft they abandoned all the benefits which it was defigned to produce.

The inhabitants of the American colonies had refifted the execu-tion of the ftamp act, becaufe they thought it unconftitutional: The inexpedience of it made no part of their legiflative complaints. They denied the right of parliament to impofe taxes upon them; but they never pretended that the taxes impofed by the ftamp act were greater than they were able to pay.

Here

Here then a favourable occasion presented itself for the exercise of ministerial wisdom, which could not be better employed than in moderating the pretensions of the colonial assemblies, settling the mode of their future contributions, and devising some permanent system or arrangement for reconciling such of their claims as were admissible, with that general and superintending authority which the parliament ought to possess for preserving an union of councils and of interests amongst all the members of an extensive empire. For such a purpose no interval could be more proper than that which passed between the time when the execution of the stamp act was resisted in America, and the time of its repeal; whilst the inhabitants of the colonies remained under the apprehension incident to a consciousness of having for the first time refused obedience to an act of the supreme power of the mother-country—but this opportunity was neglected. It was now become necessary for the ministry, by removing the cause, to allay, as speedily as possible, the storm which they themselves, when in opposition, had assisted to raise. Their credit as a party depended upon it: For after the opposition which they had made to the stamp act, had they proceeded to enforce the execution of it by the power of the mother-country, which was now in their hands, the battery which they had raised against the former administration might have been turned with double effect against themselves. The stamp act was therefore to be repealed at all events; and by this premature and unqualified repeal it has been thought that the interest of the mother-country and the future tranquillity of the colonies were both sacrificed to the convenience of party.

If, in the opinion of the ministry, the stamp act was accounted to be a bold, daring, and rash measure, their opponents thought themselves entitled to say that the act which repealed it was not less marked with the opposite qualities. It is not wise wantonly to provoke a quarrel: But when once a quarrel is begun, from whatever cause it might have originated, the grounds of difference on

both

both fides fhould be inquired into, and fuch a fettlement fhould be made as might prevent future jealoufies and difagreements: To end it in fuch a manner as to leave the pretenfions on both fides open, is weak and daftardly policy;—it is a temporary expedient pregnant with future mifchief.

The repeal of the ftamp act occafioned very general rejoicings in America. The mafs of the people are in all countries led by the few: Looking only at the outfide of things, they eafily take the im_ preffion which is meant to be given: They had been taught to confider the ftamp act as the greateft of all evils, and upon receiving intelligence of its repeal, gave themfelves up to unbounded joy. In this fenfation, even the leading men very cordially joined; they faw in the repeal of the ftamp act, a victory gained by the colonies over the mother-country, and in that victory the firft dawn of future independence, They had experienced the benefits refulting from an union of councils, and a general co-operation in the fame caufe; and confidered the declaratory act, however formidable and offenfive in appearance, as a meafure which was calculated to do them more fervice than harm. They viewed it as a weak and impolitic bravado on the part of the Britifh parliament, which would defeat its own purpofe, by continuing the alarm which had been excited, and by cementing the union which had taken place amongft the colonies.

The courts of juftice now refumed their functions; the affemblies in the different provinces were called; and mutual congratulations paffed between them and their governors. Their late ill-humour gave a poignancy to their prefent enjoyments; and all paft animofities feemed for a time to be forgotten.

But even during this feafon of feftivity, there were not wanting fome, who by publications in the newfpapers cautioned their countrymen againft giving way to intemperate joy; they reminded them, that although the ftamp act was repealed, its principle had not been given

up:

up: That the Britifh parliament perfevered in maintaining their right of taxation, and by paffing the declaratory act affected to poffefs a ftill higher and more arbitrary power than the authors of the ftamp act had ventured to exercife: That the repeal of the ftamp act had rather been extorted than freely granted, and that for this boon they were more indebted to their own wifdom and firmnefs, than to the generofity of the Britifh nation: That future adminiftrations and future parliaments might again attempt to impofe taxes upon them; and that it was therefore incumbent upon the inhabitants of the co- lonies to be vigilant and attentive, and not fuffer themfelves to be lulled into a ftate of thoughtlefs fecurity: That it was their duty, whilft it was in their power, to provide againft the worft that might happen: That with this view they ought to encourage the breeding of fheep, for the purpofe of acquiring a ftock of wool, the culture of flax, hemp, and cotton, and the fabrication of fuch of the coarfer Britifh manufactures as are moft effentially neceffary for the common purpofes of life; by which means they might with lefs inconvenience to themfelves, when future occafions fhould require it, enter into non-importation agreements, and abftain from the ufe and confumption of Britifh manufactures, which they faw was likely to be the moft-effectual mode of oppofition to the illegal ex- ertions of power on the part of the mother-country. By fuch pub- lications, attempts were made to keep alive and nourifh that fpirit of jealoufy and diftruft, which the declaratory act was fo well calculated to infpire.

The fecretary of ftate, in the difpatches fent to the American go- vernors upon the repeal of the ftamp act, took occafion to fet forth the grace and condefcenfion of the king and parliament in liftening to the complaints of the inhabitants of the colonies; and their lenity, tendernefs, moderation, and forbearance, manifefted in the repeal of that act, notwithftanding the provocation which they had received

by the forcible refiftance that had been made to the execution of it;
and intimated that fuitable returns of gratitude, duty, affection, and
fubmiffion, would be expected on the part of the colonies. Thefe
were held forth as themes for the governors to enlarge upon in their
fpeeches to the affemblies. And it muft be confeffed that thofe
affemblies were not backward in voting addreffes of thanks, nor did
they fall fhort of the fecretary's expectations in profeffions of loyalty,
duty, and affection to the king; but in what regarded the parliament
they were far from being explicit: And it very foon appeared that
fome of them, inftead of being eager to give fubftantial proofs of
fubordination to the Britifh parliament, were ftudious to avoid even
the appearance of it.

At the time of repealing the ftamp act, the parliament alfo voted
an addrefs to be prefented to his majefty, requefting that he would
be pleafed to inftruct the governors in America to make requifitions
to the colonial affemblies for granting compenfation to fuch individuals as had fuffered in their private property in confequence of the
tumults. Thefe requifitions were accordingly made in fuch of the
colonies where any lofs of private property had been fuftained, and
particularly in the province of Maffachufets Bay, where the tumults
had been the moft outrageous. But the affembly of that province,
inftead of laying hold of this opportunity to fhew their refpect to the
Britifh parliament, and at the fame time to do an act of juftice, quar-
relled with their governor, under a pretence that he had fet forth the
requifition in ftronger and more peremptory terms than he was warranted to do by the fecretary of ftate's letter; and in an addrefs prefented to him on this occafion, after cenfuring the manner in which
he had communicated the requifition, they coldly tell him, " That
" they will embrace the firft convenient opportunity to confider and
" act upon fecretary Conway's recommendation," without taking the
leaft notice of the refolution of parliament. The governor made
repeated

repeated applications to them, but from various pretences they de- layed paffing an act to compenfate the fufferers for more than fix months; nor was it done until the inhabitants of the town of Bofton inftructed their reprefentatives to vote for it, and informed them that the lords of the treafury in England had refufed to pay the colony the money voted by parliament in the year 1763, until compen-. fation was firft made to thefe fufferers: And when the act was at laft paffed, it contained a claufe of indemnity to the offenders in the riots, which fhewed that thefe were not lefs the objects of that affembly's care and attention, than the unfortunate fufferers. A fimilar backwardnefs appeared in the colonies of Rhode Ifland and New York; but in the province of Maryland the affembly were eager to teftify their refpect for the recommendation of parliament, and without delay voted compenfation to the only individual who had fuffered in that province: And in the other colonies no loffes were fuftained.

In the fame feffion of parliament in which the ftamp act had been repealed, an act was paffed for amending the annual mutiny act, which it had been ufual to pafs, for the government of the troops in America. The intention of the amendment was to provide for the more comfortable fubfiftence of thofe troops by fupplying them with falt, vinegar, and beer or cyder; and the act directed that the ex- pence incurred by the fupply of thefe articles fhould be raifed by the affemblies of the refpective colonies in which the troops were quar- tered. It fo happened, by the accidental march of fome troops into the province of New York, that the governor of that province had occafion, on the day after he had communicated to the affembly the repeal of the ftamp act, to apply to them for quarters for thefe troops, and in his meffage he fpecified the additional articles of falt, vinegar, beer or cyder, which were required to be furnifhed under the

H 2   amended

amended mutiny act of the laſt ſeſſion of parliament. He alſo informed them that the troops were upon their march, and were daily
expected at New York. The aſſembly however was in no haſte to take
his meſſage into conſideration, nor did they preſent an addreſs in anſwer
to it until after the arrival of the troops, who in the mean time were
put to ſome inconvenience for want of quarters. In their addreſs,
the aſſembly avoided noticing the act of parliament: They affected
to conſider the requiſition as coming ſolely from the king; and
agreed to furniſh quarters for the troops with ſuch neceſſaries only
as they had been formerly accuſtomed to furniſh. This anſwer not
proving ſatisfactory to the governor, another meſſage was ſent; and
after various meſſages and addreſſes, the aſſembly at laſt poſitively
refuſed to ſupply the troops with the additional articles required by
the amendment made to the mutiny act, ſeeming to conſider it as
not differing in principle from the ſtamp act, ſo far as it impoſed a
new burthen upon them. A diſinclination to comply with this act of
parliament appeared in ſeveral of the other colonies where troops
were ſtationed; and in no one of them was the act ſpecifically carried into execution. Means, it is true, were fallen upon to ſatisfy the
troops: But the Britiſh parliament was not to be gratified, even at
the ſmall expence of furniſhing the inconſiderable articles of ſalt, vinegar, and ſmall beer.

Such were the returns made in America to the grace and conde-
ſcenſion of the king and parliament in repealing the ſtamp act. But
the Rockingham adminiſtration did not continue long enough in
power to receive official accounts of the effect of their meaſures for
reſtoring peace and tranquillity to the colonies. In the month of
July of the preſent year, they were diſmiſſed from their employments, and a new adminiſtration was formed, at the head of which
was the duke of Grafton, aided by the ſplendid talents, the popular
virtues,

virtues, and energetic powers of Mr. Pitt, now created earl of Chatham, who accepted the office of lord privy feal, and with whofe advice the new arrangements were faid to have been made.

The firſt act of this new adminiſtration which related to America ſerves to ſhew, that although many of the members of it had voted for the repeal of the ſtamp act, yet in reality they differed not much in principle from thoſe who were the authors of it. In the debates which that act had occaſioned in parliament, in ſome of the political pamphlets publiſhed in America, and in the reſolutions of ſome of the colonial aſſemblies, a diſtinction had been taken between external and internal taxation, that is, between raiſing money from the colonies by the impoſition of duties on the importation or exportation of merchandize, and raiſing it internally in the way propoſed by the ſtamp act: And on theſe occaſions it had been ſaid, that although the colonies never would agree to the latter, they had already ſubmitted to the former, which was neceſſary for the regulation of trade; and that the Britiſh parliament ought to be contented with the exerciſe of this acknowledged right, leaving to the colonial aſſemblies the powers of internal taxation, and of regulating the domeſtic policy of the reſpective provinces, which ſeemed to be the objects for which ſuch aſſemblies were originally inſtituted, and of the due exerciſe of which powers, their local information enabled them to be more competent judges than the Britiſh parliament could pretend to be.

The new miniſtry laying hold of this diſtinction, and availing themſelves of the ſuppoſed conceſſion, procured an act of parliament to be paſſed for impoſing certain duties on glaſs, paper, paſteboard, white and red lead, painter's colours, and tea, payable upon the importation of theſe articles into the American colonies; which duties, when collected, were made applicable, in the firſt place, to making proviſion for the adminiſtration of juſtice, and the ſupport

2　　　　　　　　　　　　　　　　　　　　　of

of civil government, in such of the colonies where it should be necessary, and the residue to be paid into the exchequer in England,
and to be applicable to the same uses as the former duties imposed
in the year 1764. The act also contained a clause for discontinuing
the drawback payable on the exportation of china-ware to America,
and made some new provisions for preventing the clandestine running of goods in the colonies. And at the same time another act
was passed for putting these, and all the other customs and duties
payable in America by any former act of parliament, under the
management of commissioners, who were to be resident in that
country.

In the same session too, the dispatches of the governor of New
York, which announced the refusal of the assembly of that province
to comply with the mutiny act, were laid before the parliament:
And timidly indulgent as the members of this parliament had heretofore shewed themselves, in overlooking the rebellious outrages which
had been committed, and the daring insurrections which had appeared in America, in opposition to the stamp act, they now seemed
determined that the assembly of New York should feel the weight
of their displeasure for this recent act of disobedience; and an act
was accordingly passed for suspending them from the exercise of all
their legislative functions, until they should yield obedience to the
act of parliament for quartering the troops. The Rockingham party,
now out of office, could not in decency oppose this coercive measure, the object of which was to enforce obedience to an act of parliament which they, when in power, had procured to be passed.

These acts were all introduced and supported by the influence of
the new ministry. They, like the ministry which had patronized the
stamp act, were conscious that the mother-country, bending under
the weight and pressure of accumulated taxes, with the sinews of
her strength stretched to the utmost possible extent, stood in need of

I   every

every affiftance. Like them too they were convinced that the American colonies were the leaft burthened of all the Britifh dominions ; and that it was the duty of thofe who were entrufted with the adminiftration of government to require them to furnifh a due proportion towards the general expence. It was alfo thought highly probable, that as the colonies had been fo lately gratified with the repeal of the obnoxious ftamp act, they would the more readily fubmit to an act which required their contribution in a fhape and form accommodated in fome degree to the political fpeculations of the time, and to the ideas of fome of thofe friends of the colonies who had efpoufed their caufe in the Britifh parliament. Perhaps too it was thought that the colonies would have been more eafily induced to yield to this mode of taxation, as this would tend to refute the afperfions of their enemies, who charged them with ingratitude, and reproached them with an inclination to avail themfelves of the protection of the mother-country, and of all the benefits which they enjoyed under the Britifh government, without contributing towards its fupport. Such, it may be fuppofed, were fome of the motives which influenced the Britifh miniftry about this period.

But the leading men in the colonies, and their political writers, thought very differently. In the courfe of their fpeculations on the fubject of the ftamp act, they had been led into a train of thought and confequent reafoning that were applicable not only to the act which was the immediate object of their fpeculation, but to all the other acts of the Britifh parliament which extended to America. Some of thefe had exifted for more than a century, and had been fanctioned by time and by conftant and uninterrupted acquiefcence. To have queftioned their validity would have been offering violence to public opinion. Thefe writers therefore were prudent enough for the prefent to avoid pufhing their arguments to fuch a length ; but they were not the lefs anxious to guard their countrymen againft

fubmitting

fubmitting to any farther extenſion of the like authority.   For this
purpoſe, the paſſing of the ſtamp act was to be held out as a new
æra in their political hiſtory, and as the commencement of a new
ſyſtem on the part of Great Britain.   That act had been condemned
as illegal and unconſtitutional.   Thoſe which preceded it, although
upon their grounds of argument not leſs liable to objection, yet having been conſecrated by time, were to be thrown into the back
ground, and the ſtamp act alone was to be put forward as the promi-
nent figure, by a compariſon with which the legality or illegality of
every ſubſequent act of parliament for laying duties or taxes on
America was to be eſtimated.

It required no great reach of thought to perceive that the late act
which impoſed duties on certain articles of merchandize imported
from Great Britain into the colonies, differed not in principle from
the ſtamp act.   The object of both was to raiſe a revenue from the
colonies; in the raiſing of which, and in the diſpoſal of it when
raiſed, the colonial aſſemblies were to have no concern: The articles upon which the duties were impoſed, were become ſo neceſſary
that they could not be diſpenſed with without great inconvenience
to the inhabitants of the colonies; and they were ſuch as either
could not be raiſed in America, or in the raiſing and manufacture of
which it was not the intereſt of the coloniſts to be employed.

On this ground their political writers ſet to work.   They maintained that the new act was a branch of the ſame ſyſtem which had
been introduced in Mr. Grenville's adminiſtration for enſlaving America: That it was in every reſpect as unconſtitutional as the ſtamp
act: That the mother-country, guided by ſuch councils and purſuing ſuch arbitrary meaſures, was rather to be conſidered as a malignant ſtep-mother than an indulgent parent: That ſhe envied the
proſperity of the colonies, and ſeemed determined to cruſh and
keep them down: And that it was therefore a duty which the in-
                                                                        habitants

habitants of the colonies owed not only to themfelves but to their posterity, to withftand fuch illegal exactions; becaufe, if they fubmitted to one, it would afford a precedent for another, and that to a third; until, by the continued renewal and extenfion of fuch impofitions, they would be drained of the little wealth they poffeffed, and be at laft reduced to poverty and diftrefs. Such were the arguments ufed to excite an oppofition to the new act of parliament amongft the people of the colonies; and meeting with no contradiction, the effect which they would have upon the public mind may be eafily conceived.

The inattention of government to thefe publications was one great caufe of haftening the American revolution. For whilft the colonial newfpapers were filled with inflammatory publications, tending to excite jealoufy and promote difcontent, to throw fufpicions on every act of the Britifh government extending to America, and by degrees to leffen that veneration for the mother-country with which the inhabitants of, at leaft a part of, the Britifh colonies were once impreffed; only one or two writerswere employed on the other fide to counteract the effects of fuch feditious publications, to fupport the caufe of the mother-country, and for a time to keep the courfe of public opinion fufpended, until the matters in difpute could be fairly and difpaffionately confidered.

It is to the province of Maffachufets Bay that we are henceforward to look for thofe caufes which had a more immediate influence in accelerating the American revolution. The foundation of this revolution was indeed laid in the meeting of the firft congrefs; not perhaps by any actual agreement to refift the power of the mother-country, but by incorporating and uniting the grievances of all the colonies, and making them the fubject of common complaint. Whence it followed, that whenever afterwards any fingle colony brought upon itfelf the difpleafure of the mother-country, the caufe of that colony was espoused by all the rest; and the refractory un-governable spirit of the inhabitants of Massachusets Bay, for ever running into excesses, and breaking forth into outrages against law-ful authority, and thereby bringing down upon the province the consequent animadversions and chastisements of the mother-country, furnished to the assemblies of the other colonies a never-failing source of disquiet, uneasiness, remonstrance and complaint; until, by successive altercations with government, their passions became in-flamed, resentment was kindled, and all respect for the mother-country being in time thrown aside, the bonds of union which con-nected her with the colonies were at last violently rent asunder. The transactions in this province will therefore occupy a principal part in the following pages, down to the year 1774.

There had been no good agreement between the governor * and the inhabitants of Massachusets Bay from the time of the stamp act. He had on that, and indeed on every other occasion, shewn himself active and zealous in maintaining the authority of the mother-country, as far as it was in his power; and this conduct of itself was sufficient to make him unpopular. He had lived long enough in the province to be fully acquainted with the character of the people over whom he presided, and by his knowledge and experience was enabled to penetrate into their designs, which he did not fail to lay open to the British ministry. The animadversions on their conduct contained in some of the government dispatches, which it was ne-cessary to lay before the assembly, discovered to them the nature of their governor's communications; and they, on their part, charged him with misrepresentation. In the preceding year he had exer-cised the prerogative of putting a negative on some of the violent men of the patriotic party, whom the assembly had elected as coun-

* Sir Francis Bernard.

fellors.

fellors. The excluded members felt this as a gross affront, and became his inveterate enemies. Their influence with the people was great, and they scrupled not to use it in ftirring them up to thwart the governor, gratifying their private resentment at the expence of the public tranquillity: And to the efforts of these restless and discontented men may, in part, be ascribed the perturbed and unquiet state of this province during the whole of the ensuing year.

The first symptoms of a determined opposition to the act of the last session of parliament for imposing duties in America appeared at Boston in the month of October of the preceding year; where the inhabitants, at a meeting held in their town-hall, agreed to enter into associations to encourage manufactures amongst themselves, to discountenance luxuries of all sorts, and to discontinue the importation from Great Britain of all such superfluous articles of dress and clothing as necessity did not absolutely require. But the act which gave them most uneasiness was that which established a board of customs in America. Under the inspection and superintendence of that board they dreaded a more rigorous execution of the laws of trade than they had been yet accustomed to. Their apprehensions were the greater because the residence of this board was fixed to be at Boston: And their chagrin was the more distressing, from a conviction that this, of all the acts which had been passed, was the least liable to be affailed by objections of any considerable weight or importance.

When the affembly of that province met in the month of January of the present year, they entered upon a general consideration of grievances. A petition was prepared, to be presented to the king, complaining not only of the acts of the last session of parliament, but of every other act which had been passed for imposing duties in America fince the year 1763. A very long letter was written to their agent in England, instructing him how to controvert these acts

I 2

upon

upon grounds of natural right, and upon general principles of equity, policy, and commerce; and letters were also tranfmitted to the lords of the treafury, the fecretaries of ftate, the marquis of Rockingham, the earl of Chatham, and lord Camden, pleading the caufe of America, and intreating the exertion of their influence and abilities in furthering the objeᵭt of the petition.

These fteps having been taken for inducing a favourable hearing of their complaints in England, they now had recourfe to the fame kind of policy which had before been fuccefsfully praᵭtifed in oppofing the ftamp aᵭt; thinking the prefent a favourable opportunity for renewing their correfpondence with the other colonial affemblies, and for ftimulating them to prefer fimilar complaints. With this view a circular letter was addreffed to the affemblies of all the other colonies, communicating the deliberations of the affembly of Maffachufets Bay, on the late aᵭts of parliament for impofing duties in America; giving a full detail of the grounds of argument which they had ufed to expofe the evil tendency of thefe aᵭts, in their petition to the king, in the inftruᵭtions to their agent, and in their letters to the great officers of ftate in England; expreffing a hope that meafures of a fimilar nature would be adopted by all the affemblies upon the continent; and intimating a readinefs and a wifh to receive from thefe affemblies a communication of fuch other meafures as might to them appear neceffary to be purfued for the general intereft of the whole.

This letter bore date the 11th of February. A copy of it was without delay fent to England by the governor, and gave much difpleafure to the Britifh adminiftration. They viewed it as a wicked attempt in the affembly of Maffachufets Bay to light up again the flames of difcord in the colonies, and as the commencement of a plan of regular oppofition to the authority of the mother-country. And in order to counteraᵭt its effeᵭts, the fecretary of ftate for

American

American affairs*, on the 22d of April, wrote an admonitory letter to the governors of the colonies, to be by them laid before their assemblies, in which the circular letter of the assembly of Massachusets Bay was condemned as a measure of a most dangerous and factious tendency, calculated to inflame the minds of his majesty's good subjects in the colonies, to promote an unwarrantable combination, to excite an opposition to the authority of parliament, and to subvert the true principles of the constitution: And the colonial assemblies were admonished not to suffer themselves to be led away from their duty, nor to give any countenance to this mischievous effort of the Massachusets Bay assembly for exciting discord; but rather to treat it with the contempt it deserved.

But this administration did not accord with the sentiments of the leading men in the colonies. They maintained that the colonial assemblies had a right to consult together and freely to communicate their observations to each other, on the subject of their common grievances; and they considered the interference of the British ministry, on the present occasion, as an unjustifiable attempt to discourage and prevent the inhabitants of the colonies from exercising the undoubted right of British subjects to prefer their united supplications to the throne whenever they thought themselves aggrieved.

And thus the letter from the secretary of state became the subject of severe animadversion, and gave occasion to some new and angry resolutions in several of the colonial assemblies: Whilst the circular letter from Massachusets Bay was well received and approved of, and produced all the effect which was expected from it. Petitions formed on the model of that of Massachusets Bay were transmitted to England from all the colonies.

* A new arrangement took place at the beginning of the present year, in the secretary of state's office; a third secretary being appointed for the department of the colonies.

I

Those

Thofe fhades of difference which had originally characterized the refolutions of the different affemblies, and which were moft confpicuous in thofe of Maffachufets Bay and Virginia, now began to difappear. The republican notions and high pretenfions of the people of New England were daily gaining ground : And the act of the laft feffion of parliament for impofing duties, although apparently framed for the purpofe of coinciding with the political creed of the fouthern colonies, was now as much condemned in the affembly of Virginia as it had been in that of Maffachufets Bay ; the affembly of Virginia getting rid of their former diftinction between internal taxes, by maintaining that the duties payable by this act, although on the importation of merchandize, were as much internal as thofe of the ftamp act, becaufe they were impofed not for the purpofe of regulation, but of raifing a revenue.

The letter from the fecretary of ftate to the governor of Maffachufets Bay inftructed him to require the affembly of his province to refcind the refolution of the preceding feffion, which had given birth to the circular letter, as it appeared to have paffed near the end of the affembly, and in a thin houfe; and if they fhould refufe, he was directed to diffolve them. This requifition was accordingly made in the month of June; and the affembly, having refufed to comply with it by a majority of ninety-two againft feventeen, was diffolved by the governor, in purfuance of his inftructions.

Previous to the diffolution of the affembly, the ill-humour, difcontent, chagrin, and vexation of the inhabitants of Bofton, aggravated by fome new regulations introduced by the commiffioners of the cuftoms for checking the clandeftine practices of the former, in the landing and fhipping of goods, broke forth into fuch an open and violent refiftance of lawful authority, as threatened fpeedily to involve the whole province in rebellion.

The

The floop Liberty, belonging to John Hancock, one of their principal merchants, had arrived in the harbour of Bofton, laden with wine, and a tide-waiter had been put on board to prevent the cargo from being landed, until fhe fhould be entered at the cuftom-houfe and receive a permit to unlade. On the night after her arrival, and before fhe was entered at the cuftom-houfe, the mafter of the veffel, having in vain tampered with the preventive officer to obtain his permiffion, at laft forcibly locked him up in the cabin, and proceeded to difcharge the wine; taking oil from the fhore in lieu of it, with which the veffel was reladen before the morning. Information of this outrageous proceeding having been given at the cuftom-houfe, the colleftor, on the evening of the following day, being the 10th of June, made a feizure of the floop, and put her for fafety under the protection of the Romney fhip of war. The floop was accordingly removed from the wharf where fhe lay, and moored in the harbour under the ftern of the Romney. This was no fooner feen from the fhore than a mob affembled; the colleftor and controller of the cuftoms were beaten and abufed, and in making their efcape were pelted with ftones: The commiffioners of the cuftoms were threatened, their houfes were attacked, and they themfelves were obliged to take refuge on board the Romney: And finally, the colleftor's boat was carried in triumph, and burnt before the door of the owner of the floop. Such were the riotous proceedings on the evening of the feizure of the floop Liberty.

On the following day the commiffioners of the cuftoms applied to the governor for protection: Their application was by him communicated to the council and affembly, whofe advice and affiftance he requefted; but advice was not given, nor affiftance offered—the commiffioners met with no protection: And the threats againft them being continued, they were at laft obliged to retire for fafety to Caftle William, a fortrefs fituated upon an ifland at the mouth of

the

the harbour. In the mean time, on the 14th of June, a town meeting was held, and fo far were the inhabitants of Bofton from difcountenancing the refiftance which had been made to lawful authority, that they prefented a remonftrance to the governor on the feizure of the floop, and the circumftance of her being put under the protection of a fhip of war; and accompanied it with this ftrange requeft, that he would order his majefty's fhip the Romney out of the harbour. All this happened during the fitting of the council and affembly; and yet no one ftep was taken by them, for affifting the governor in reftoring energy to government, or in protecting its officers in the execution of their duty.

Reprefentations on the fubject of this tumult and infurrection were made not only by the governor but by the commiffioners of the cuftoms to the Britifh miniftry; and troops were ordered to be fent to Bofton to aid the civil power. A rumour of the orders which had been given having reached Bofton before the arrival of the troops, filled the inhabitants with new alarms and apprehenfions; and a town meeting being called on the 12th of September, a petition from the inhabitants was prefented to the governor, intreating him to convene the general affembly. To this petition the governor anfwered, that he had diffolved the affembly in confequence of an inftruction, and that it was not in his power to call another until he received his majefty's orders for that purpofe. The governor's anfwer did not contribute to allay the ferment which the expected arrival of the troops had occafioned; and the people of Bofton, goaded on by their factious and difcontented leaders, conceived and adopted in their prefent ftate of perplexity the new and daring refolution of affembling a convention of the people. For this purpofe the town meeting was adjourned to the following day, when they voted and refolved, that they were under no obligation of fubmitting to laws to which they had not given their confent, either by themfelves or

their

their reprefentatives, that the levying of money within the province for the ufe of the crown, without the confent of the general affembly, is a violation of their charter and of their natural rights as fubjects, declared in the ftatute of the 1 W. & M.; that the fending an armed force amongft them without their confent, would be an infringement of thefe rights, and the employing of fuch a force to aid the execution of laws to which they had not given their confent, an intolerable grievance. And as the governor had declared himfelf unable to call a general affembly for the redrefs of grievances, they refolved it to be expedient that a convention of the people fhould be held. They appointed four perfons to reprefent them in this convention, one of whom was the owner of the floop, the feizure of which had occafioned the tumult. They directed the felect men to write to the felect men of the other towns in the province, to inform them of thefe proceedings at the town meeting of Bofton, and to propofe a convention to be held on the 22d of the fame month. They refolved that the inhabitants of Bofton fhould be requefted to provide themfelves with arms, purfuant to a law of the province which had been too much neglected, affigning as a reafon for this vote, a prevailing apprehenfion of an approaching war with France; and laftly, they requefted that the minifters of the town would fet apart the following Tuefday as a day of fafting and prayer.

In purfuance of thefe votes, letters were written by the felect men; and deputies were appointed to meet in the propofed convention by all the townfhips in the province, that of Hatfield alone excepted; the inhabitants of which not only refufed to appoint deputies for the convention, but wrote an expoftulatory letter to the felect men of Bofton, upbraiding the inhabitants of that town with their riotous behaviour, charging them with being the caufe, by their mifconduct, why troops were to be fent into the province; admonifhing them that their future orderly behaviour was the only way to procure a

removal of the troops, and protesting against the proposed conven‑
tion as a measure that was unconstitutional, illegal, and unjusti‑
fiable, subversive of government, and destructive of the peace of
society.

The convention met on the twenty-second of September, and consist‑
ed of deputies from ninety-eight towns and eight districts. Their first
act was to send a deputation to the governor with a message, in which
they disclaim all pretence to authoritative or governmental acts, allege
that they were met, in that dark and distressful time, only to consult
and advise such measures as might promote the peace of his majesty's
subjects in that province, and conclude with intreating him to call
an assembly. The governor refused to receive their message, and the
next day issued a proclamation in which he warned them of their
danger, if they should proceed to any kind of business, admonished
them to disperse, and threatened, if they did not, to assert the prero‑
gative of the crown in a more public manner.

Whether the members of this convention were disconcerted by
the governor's firmness, or whether they began to think that they
had gone too far in assembling not only without but against his con‑
sent, is uncertain: But their proceedings during their short session
were uncommonly mild and moderate, and did not seem to corre‑
spond with the temper of mind manifested in the votes of the town
meeting at Boston. Their proceedings were only a petition to be
presented to the king against the late acts of parliament, and a report
stating the causes of their meeting, and the objects which they had
taken into consideration. In this report they again disclaimed all
pretence to authority, recommended to the people to pay deference
to government, and wait with patience the result of his majesty's
wisdom and clemency, and promised for themselves to assist the civil
magistrate in preserving the peace. These papers having been pre‑
pared and dispatched to their agent in England, their meeting was
                                                      dissolved

diffolved on the twenty-ninth of September, the day on which the firft divifion of the troops arrived at Bofton.

Upon the arrival of the troops fome difficulties arofe about quartering them; the council propofing that they fhould be fent to Caftle William, where barracks were already erected, inftead of being. quartered in the town, where there were none; but it was neceffary that the troops fhould be quartered in the place where their affiftance was required: And all objections were at laft obviated by hiring fome empty houfes in the town, which were fitted up and converted into barracks. The turbulence of the people being reftrained by the prefence of the troops, peace was thus for a time reftored to Bofton. The commiffioners and other officers of the cuftoms returned from Caftle William; and bufinefs began to be carried on in its ufual courfe.

In the province of New York the affembly having made fubmiffion, and complied with the terms of the mutiny act, were reftored to the exercife of their legiflative functions.

The fuccefs of the circular letter from the affembly of Maffachufets Bay in exciting the other colonial affemblies to petition for a redrefs of grievances has been already noticed. But petitions were not the only means to which they trufted for relief. Affociations were again reforted to for diftreffing the trade of the mother-country, and for influencing the mercantile and manufacturing intereft in England to beftir themfelves in behalf of the colonies. To have reftrained all importation from Great Britain would at that time have diftreffed themfelves more than thofe whom they meant to injure: It was therefore propofed, that the importation of the more neceffary articles of merchandize fhould be continued, and thofe only which were lefs neceffary be prohibited. The concurrence of the merchants was indifpenfable: And as the neceffary articles of merchandize were different in different colonies, it became no eafy matter to adjuft

K 2   their

their jarring interefts; fo that although various attempts had been made to introduce thefe affociations in the beginning of the year, it was not till the end of it that they met with any thing like a general acceptance. The importation of the prohibited articles was to ceafe from the firft of January 1769: And the effect which thefe combinations had upon the commerce of the mother-country will be feen hereafter.

Such were the principal tranfactions in America during the year 1768.

Upon the meeting of the parliament in England, the diforderly and difobedient ftate of the province of Maffachufets Bay was mentioned in the fpeech from the throne, and became the fubject of debate early in the feffion.

The miniftry now feemed determined to act with more than ufual vigour in attempting to fubdue that daring fpirit of refiftance to the authority of parliament, which had fhewn itfelf by this time in fome degree in all the colonies, but moft unjuftifiably in the province of Maffachufets Bay, in the provoking tranfactions of the preceding year. Thefe tranfactions were accordingly made the ground of fundry parliamentary refolutions, in which they were recited with every circumftance of aggravation, and branded with every epithet of difapprobation which could ferve to mark the high difpleafure of the Britifh parliament. The town of Bofton was declared to be in a ftate of diforder and difobedience to law. The difinclination of the council and affembly to affift in fuppreffing the riots was feverely cenfured; and the neceffity of fending a military force to aid the civil power was fully juftified. Thefe refolutions having been agreed to and paffed, a joint addrefs from both houfes of parliament was prefented to his majefty, approving of the fteps which had been already taken for maintaining the authority of the mother-country, and declaring their readinefs to concur in fuch other meafures as might be

I

thought

thought neceffary for that purpofe. The addrefs concluded with recommending to his majefty to bring the authors of the difturbances to exemplary punifhment; to inftruct governor Bernard of Maffachufets Bay to tranfmit to England full information of all treafonable acts committed within his province during the preceding year, together with the names of the offenders; to revive the execution of the ftatute of 35 Hen. VIII. for trying within the realm of England treafons committed beyond the feas; and to iffue a fpecial commiffion for that purpofe, if upon receiving governor Bernard's report fuch a proceeding fhould appear to be neceffary.

Thefe refolutions and this addrefs, although finally paffed by a great majority, were not voted without confiderable oppofition. The Rockingham and Grenville parties united their force to oppofe them, and diftrefs the miniftry. The irregularities and extravagances of the people of Bofton (for in fuch gentle terms were they fpoken of) were either palliated or excufed. It was faid that this fimple and inoffenfive people had been driven to madnefs when they perceived that the taxes of which they now complained were not laid upon them by the influence of their enemies, but of their friends; of thofe friends too who had oppofed the ftamp act, and had totally denied to the Britifh parliament the right of impofing taxes in America. And the oppofition, far from feeming to fhrink from their defence, on the contrary upbraided the miniftry with giving them the appellation of rebellious and difobedient fubjects.

Such fpeeches, whatever might be the intention of thofe who made them, were deftructive of the authority which the parliament wifhed to maintain. They often gave the tone to the fubfequent meafures purfued by the American patriots, who exerted themfelves to verify the predictions which their friends in parliament had previoufly made. They were the means of raifing a party in favour of America, even in Great Britain. And on the prefent occafion they
were

were calculated to encourage the inhabitants of Maffachufets Bay to perfift in their refractory courfe, when they found that even the provoking infults offered to government in the preceding year met with fuch able defenders in the Britifh parliament.

That part of the minifterial plan which advifed the execution of the almoft obfolete ftatute of the 35 Hen. VIII. for the trial of treafons committed beyond the feas, gave the moft ferious concern to all thofe inhabitants of the colonies whofe attachment to the mother-country was yet unfhaken. It was a meafure of feverity which the miniftry probably did not intend to execute; but for that reafon it ought not to have been threatened. To be torn from a man's family and friends, tranfported acrofs an extenfive ocean, landed in a ftrange country as a prifoner and criminal, and tried by a jury not of his vicinage but of ftrangers, unacquainted with him or his character, and whom even the important formality of bringing the prifoner from fuch a diftance to England for trial would be apt to imprefs with an idea of extraordinary guilt—all thefe, with others which might be mentioned, were circumftances of fuch hardfhip as could not fail to arreft the attention of even the moft carelefs and unthinking colonift, and incline him to queftion the foundation of an authority liable to be exercifed in a way fo oppreffive. In fact, the threatened revival of this arbitrary ftatute alienated the affection of the loyal and well-difpofed amongft the inhabitants of the colonies more than any thing which the Britifh parliament had yet attempted. Even thofe who were the moft friendly to government, and who on other occafions were accuftomed to juftify to their neighbours the proceedings of parliament, fhrunk from the defence of it. It was univerfally reprobated as an unjuftifiable meafure, from the practical exercife of which every feeling mind muft revolt with horror.

In

In the province of Maffachufets Bay, where the diforders chiefly
prevailed which this fevere meafure was intended to reprefs, and
where a military force was ready to execute the orders of the civil
power, it produced at firft fome little effect *. The writers of feditious publications for a few weeks defifted from their labours; but
no vigorous meafures being afterwards purfued, their fears were foon
diffipated. The affembly of that province, far from being intimidated, entered into refolutions of an oppofite tendency to thofe of the
Britifh parliament, and maintained, with reafon and juftice on their
fide, that it was the right of every Britifh fubject to be tried in that
country where his fuppofed crime was known to be committed; and
that the fending of perfons into another country for trial was tyrannical and oppreffive, and derogatory of the rights of freemen.
They alfo voted charges againft their governor for mifconduct, which,
with a petition praying for his removal, were tranfmitted to their
agent in England, to be laid before the privy council.

In the other colonial affemblies the addrefs of parliament for re-
viving the execution of the ftatute of 35 Hen. VIII. produced fevere ftrictures on the conduct of the Britifh adminiftration who
could propofe and carry through fuch an arbitrary and tyrannical
meafure. Refolutions were entered into declarative of their rights
in cafes of trials for treafon; and thefe, in fome of the colonies,
were of fo acrimonious a nature, and fo difrefpectful to the Britifh
parliament in the opinion of their governors, that they occafioned
the diffolution of thofe affemblies who had paffed them.

So many altercations happened between the American governors
and their affemblies during the preceding as well as the prefent year,
that diffolutions were now become very frequent: But inftead of
ferving to fupport the authority of the mother-country, they were

* Governor Hutchinfon's Letter, 27th April 1770.

in reality prejudicial to it, by diffusing more widely, upon the return of the members to their constituents, that disrespect to parliament, and that ill-humour, heat, and animosity, the appearance of which in the assemblies had produced their dissolution.

From the time of the arrival in America of the parliamentary resolutions of the present year, those who promoted the associations met with very little farther obstruction. Committees were appointed by the people in all the principal towns, whose business it was to examine cargoes upon their arrival from Great Britain, and make reports to their constituents how far the association had been faithfully adhered to, and in what instances it had been infringed. Meetings of the associators were regularly held for receiving those reports: And at those meetings votes of censure were passed upon delinquents, and their names published in the newspapers to expose them to the hatred of the populace. In some instances goods imported contrary to the association were stored to prevent them from being sold; and in others, in order to prevent them from being destroyed, they were re-shipped to Great Britain.

The effect which such proceedings had on the commerce of the mother-country became very soon perceptible. It was found, that the merchandize exported to America in the year 1769 had fallen short of what had been exported to the same place in the preceding year by the sum of seven hundred and forty-four thousand pounds. It was found too, that the revenue arising from the duties payable in America was yearly decreasing *: And as the associations which had been entered into were not against the use of the prohibited articles, provided they were not of the produce or manufacture of

* The sums applied by parliament out of this revenue in the following years will shew the decrease :

In 1767 applied by parliament £110,000
1768 —————— 70,000
1769 —————— 30,000

Great

Great Britain nor imported from thence, it was manifest that the demand for fuch articles would be transferred to foreign countries; and from them they began to be fmuggled into America, in confiderable quantities. And thus, in confequence of the affociations, the act of parliament, which was the principal ground of complaint, operated in the colonies as a prohibition on Britifh manufactures and as a bounty and encouragement, no only to thofe of America but thofe too of foreign countries. The merchants trading to America were alfo alarmed, and prefented a petition to parliament, praying for a repeal of the act which had given fo much offence in that country, fetting forth the lofs which the mother-country had already fuftained in the declenfion of the colonial trade, and ftating the more ruinous confequences which they ftill apprehended if the repeal was longer delayed.

Influenced by fome or all of thefe confiderations, lord North, now firft lord of the treafury *, as well as chancellor of the exchequer, on the 5th of March moved fundry refolutions in the houfe of commons for difcontinuing all the duties payable in America under the act of parliament of the year 1767, the duty on tea only excepted. The minifter, in moving thefe refolutions, did not hefitate to condemn the act by which thefe duties had been impofed, as a meafure that was at leaft impolitic, becaufe the articles on which the duties were payable being chiefly Britifh manufactures, the exportation of them to the colonies, inftead of being clogged with duties, ought rather to have been encouraged. He alfo admitted that the duty on tea was referved for the fole purpofe of faving the national honour, and maintaining the authority of parliament: A duty which was too infignifi-

* Early in January of this year lord chancellor Camden was difmiffed from his office, and many others of the miniftry refigned. On the 28th of that month the duke of Grafton refigned the office of firft lord of the treafury, but continued to vote with the miniftry. The earl of Chatham, from ill health, had refigned the office of lord privy feal in November 1768.

cant to be noticed by the inhabitants of the colonies, unlefs they were at all events determined to quarrel with the mother-country, the whole produce of it being eftimated at no more than fixteen thoufand pounds per annum.

The members of oppofition, on the other hand, contended that the duty on tea ought to be taken off with the reft; alleging that, unlefs this was done, the difcontinuing of the other duties would be ufelefs, fince the Americans queftioned not fo much the amount of the duties as the right to impofe them. To this the minifter replied, that the Americans could have no reafon to complain, becaufe, at the time when the duty of three-pence per pound payable in America was impofed, other duties upon tea payable in England, and amounting to near one fhilling per pound, were taken off upon its exportation to America; fo that the inhabitants of the colonies, inftead of lofing, actually faved by this impofition nearly nine-pence per pound on all the tea which they ufed. The refolutions were carried as they had been at firft moved by the minifter; and a bill which was introduced in purfuance of them paffed through both houfes of parliament, and received the royal affent on the 22d of April.

Whilft the minifter was thus taking meafures for giving fatiffaction to the colonies, an unfortunate incident happened at Bofton in Maffachufets Bay, which fo exafperated the turbulent and difcontented inhabitants of that province, as to banifh from amongft them all prefent thoughts of a cordial reconciliation with the Britifh government.

So long as the military force which we have feen was fent to Bofton in the autumn of the year 1768, continued refpectable in point of number, fo long the town remained tolerably quiet; but as foon as that was weakened by the departure of two out of the four regiments which had been ftationed there, the former ill-humour of the inhabitants returned. The troops were vilified and lampooned

in

in the newfpapers; the foldiers, when met fingly in the ftreets, were infulted; and every method was taken to degrade them in the opinion, and expofe them to the hatred and contempt of the populace. Daily fcuffles now happened between the lower claffes of people in the town, and the foldiers when not on duty: And fo much animofity had been excited by the virulent publications in the newf-papers, that a defign is faid to have been formed of driving the troops from Bofton by force, in which the people from the country were to have affifted. But if fuch a defign was formed, the execution of it became unneceffary in confequence of the incident which we are now to relate.

On the evening of the fifth of March, the fame day on which the Britifh minifter moved his refolutions in the houfe of commons for difcontinuing the American duties, a quarrel arofe at Bofton between two or three young men of the town, and as many foldiers at or near their barracks. From words they proceeded to blows: And the foldiers having vanquifhed their opponents were feen purfuing them through the ftreets. The alarm to the populace was given by ringing the bells of the churches: And the people of the town affembling in great numbers at the cuftom-houfe, began to crowd round the fentinel who was pofted there, and not only infulted him but threatened his life. Captain Prefton, the officer on duty for the day, who had by this time received information of the tumult, proceeded immediately to the main guard; and hearing that the fentinel placed at the cuftom-houfe had been threatened, fearing too that the cuftom-houfe might be in danger, he fent a party, under the command of a ferjeant, to protect the one and fecure the other; and from greater precaution foon afterwards followed and took the command of the party himfelf. He endeavoured to prevail upon the people to difperfe, but in vain. The mob now became more riotous, not only reviling the foldiers with abufive language, but throwing ftones

L 2

at

at them, and whatever elfe came in their way.   One of the foldiers received a blow from fomething that was thrown, and levelled his mufket: The officer ftretching out his arm to prevent the foldier from firing, was ftruck with a club, and the mufket was difcharged. The attack from the mob became more violent, and the reft of the foldiers following the example of their comrades, difcharged their pieces fingly and in a fcattered manner, by which four of the populace were killed and feveral others wounded.   They were intimidated, and for a moment fled; but foon afterwards collecting, took their ftation in an adjoining ftreet.   The drums beat to arms, the reft of the troops were affembled, and the whole town was in the utmoft confufion;—a town meeting was held, and a deputation was fent to the governor, requefting him to remove the troops from the town.   The governor called together the council, and the council giving it as their opinion, that the removal of the troops from the town would be for his majefty's fervice, the commanding officer promifed to comply with their advice.   Captain Prefton furrendered himfelf for trial; and the foldiers under his command at the cuftom-houfe were taken into cuftody; the mob difperfed, and the following day the troops were removed to Caftle William.

Some days afterwards the bodies of thofe who had been killed in the riot were carried in proceffion through the town, attended by an immenfe concourfe of people, and interred with much funeral pomp.   In this proceffion flags were expofed to view with emblematical devices, calculated to inflame the paffions of the multitude, and infpire them with deadly revenge; and in the newfpapers the tranfactions of the fifth of March were reprefented 'as a deliberate murder on the part of the troops, and as an atrocious maffacre of the unoffending inhabitants.

Whilft fuch unjuftifiable means were ufed to prejudice and poifon the minds of the people, fortunate it was for the officer and foldiers

3   now

now in cuftody that their trials were delayed till the month of October. By that time the ferment which had been ftirred up had in
fome meafure fubfided, and the rancorous hatred of the populace
againft the troops was in part abated. When the trials came on,
the officer, after a moft rigorous inquiry into his conduct and the
examination of near fifty witneffes, was moft honourably acquitted.
The four judges who attended the trial were unanimous in their
opinions upon the facts which were given in evidence; and the laft *
who delivered his fentiments concluded his charge in a few empha-
tical words which did honour to his independence and love of juftice,
and at the fame time furnifhed the beft comment on the whole
tranfaction. " Happy I am," faid he, " that after fuch ftrict exa-
" mination the conduct of the prifoner appears in fo fair a light ;
" yet I feel myfelf at the fame time deeply affected, that this affair
" turns out fo much to the difgrace of every perfon concerned
" againft him, and fo much to the fhame of the town in general."
Six of the foldiers were alfo acquitted, and two only convicted of
manflaughter.

The intelligence of the act of parliament for difcontinuing the
American duties having reached Bofton whilft the minds of the inhabitants were yet agitated with the recent recollection of the melancholy events of the fifth of March, made no impreffion as a ftep
towards reconciliation, but when viewed as a conceffion forced and
extorted from the mother-country, yielded the moft pleafing fatisfaction.

In all the colonies, and in Maffachufets Bay as well as the reft,
the embarraffments and inconveniences arifing from the affociations
had by this time become irkfome to the inhabitants: The want of
fome things which could not ftrictly be called neceffaries, but which
from long ufe and habit were become almoft indifpenfable, had been

* Judge Lyndex.

feverely

feverely felt: And the people had become fo weary of the engage-ments which they had entered into, that upon receiving the intelli-gence of even a partial repeal of the act of parliament which had been the caufe of their complaints, they held the affociations to be no longer binding, except for the fingle article of tea, on which the duty was ftill payable. In reality, thofe affociations, from the tenor of them, ought to have fubfifted in full force until the act for im-pofing the duties had been wholly repealed; and attempts were made in all the colonies to induce the people to conftrue them thus ftrictly But the inconveniences already experienced were fo great, that all the influence of the patriots was infufficient to prevail upon the people to fubmit to a farther continuance of them. The intercourfe with the mother-country was now therefore again opened for every thing but the importation of tea: And during the remainder of this year and the whole of the next, commerce flowed into the American colonies in a tide unufually full.

By the act of the laft feffion of parliament for repealing the Ame-rican duties, introduced by the Britifh minifter, and carried through by his influence, it muft be confeffed that he went a great way to meet the wifhes of the colonial inhabitants: But if entire reconciliation was his object, he did not go far enough. The refervation of the infigni-ficant duty on tea was fufficient to give a fair pretence to the patriotic party * in the colonies to urge, that although the Britifh parliament had now been twice foiled in its attempts to tax the colonies, it ftill made pretenfions to the right, and only waited for a more convenient opportunity to accomplifh this favourite object, the duty on tea being referved for the fole purpofe of eftablifhing a precedent for the ex-ercife of that right. In both thefe unfuccefsful attempts at taxation the colonial patriots faw, or affected to fee, that the Britifh parliament had reluctantly given way, and that the people of the colonies,

-----

* Perhaps by this time it might be called the republican party.

                                                    by

by refiftance and clamour, had worked out their own falvation; and they now renewed their efforts, by frefh publications, to preferve and keep alive amongft the people that jealoufy and diftruft of the Britifh government which they had heretofore been fo fuccefsful in exciting, and the continuance of which they confidered as the beft fecurity for the future maintenance of their rights.

But notwithftanding thefe endeavours to keep up the ball of contention, a general calm now fucceeded to their late agitations amongft the bulk of the people in the middle and fouthern colonies, more efpecially in the latter. If the Britifh parliament had not given entire fatisfaction, nor removed all ground of apprehenfion, the inhabitants of thefe colonies were at leaft willing to give it credit for fo much as had been done, and feemed difpofed to forget their remaining caufes of complaint, provided no new attempt fhould be made to increafe them.

In the New England provinces a very different difpofition of mind prevailed. The act which impofed the duties formed only an inconfiderable part of their complaints. The reftrictions upon their commerce, the powers granted to the officers of the navy to check their contraband practices, the eftablifhment of an American board of cuftoms, and the more fteady execution of the laws of trade, were to them fubjects of as much real concern as taxation. The total repeal of the act of parliament of the year 1767 would not have given them fatisfaction; and the partial repeal of it they received not as a favour conferred, but as a forced and ungracious compliance with only a part of what they had a right to demand. Far from meeting the mother-country in reciprocal acts of reconciliation, they now affumed a higher tone in confequence of her conceffions, and difcovered an inclination to extend their clamour and demands beyond the limits which they had hitherto fet to themfelves. The affembly of Maffachufets Bay, in an addrefs prefented

to

to their governor on the fifth of July in the prefent year, declared " that they knew of no commiffioners of the cuftoms, nor any re- " venue which his majefty had a right to eftablifh in North Ame- " rica ;" and in an indignant ftrain fubjoined, " that they knew and " felt a tribute levied and extorted from thofe who, if they were " allowed to have property, had alfo a right to the abfolute difpofal " of it." In this province too the fame difpofition to obftruct the execution of the revenue laws manifefted itfelf amongft the populace as on former occafions. From the time of the removal of the troops in the preceding year, the officers of the cuftoms were left without protection ; and the populace, not fatisfied with oppofing them in the execution of their duty, proceeded in various inftances to much greater lengths, and inflicted upon their perfons the moft degrading punifhments.

Nor was this impatience under the controul of the laws of trade confined to Maffachufets Bay. It was perceivable in all the New England provinces, and was this year the caufe of a moft outrageous infult offered to government in the deftruction of the Gafpee fchooner, a veffel in his majefty's fervice, ftationed in Providence river, in the colony of Rhode Ifland, to prevent fmuggling, and commanded by an officer * vigilant and active in the execution of his duty.

The Gafpee was boarded at midnight of the tenth of June by two hundred armed men in boats, who, after wounding and abufing her commander, and forcibly carrying him and his people on fhore, fet her on fire.

The caufes of difference between the mother-country and the province of Maffachufets Bay had now fo long fubfifted, and a perverfe fpirit of oppofition had fo intirely poffeffed the inhabitants of

---

* Lieutenant Duddingftone of the navy.

the

the latter, that it would have been no eafy matter to effect a cordial reconciliation between them under any circumftances, however favourable. Thofe which did occur were either of the unfavourable kind, or were wrefted by the fpirit of faction to ferve the infernal purpofe of fanning the torch of difcord; fo that in every fucceeding year, the breach, inftead of clofing, feemed to widen.

A regulation adopted by the Britifh miniftry about the beginning of this year, refpecting the judges and principal officers of the fuperior court in Maffachufets Bay, was fufficient to throw that province again into a ftate of uproar and confufion. The object of this declaration, held forth by the miniftry who framed it, was, to render the judges, and the other officers to whom it extended, more independent: By the republican party in Maffachufets Bay it was faid to be a minifterial plan for rendering them dependent upon the crown. Such oppofite conclufions do oppofing parties deduce from the fame premifes! The real fact, without glofs or comment, was this: By the new regulation, liberal falaries were affigned to the judges, and to the attorney and folicitor general, out of the American revenue, by a grant from the crown, in lieu of the fcanty falaries annually voted to them by the affembly. Such a regulation in the infancy of the colony, inftead of exciting murmurs, might perhaps have been received with fatisfaction and gratitude; but at this time it was worked up into a caufe of alarm almoft equal to that which agitated the province in the year 1768, upon receiving the firft intelligence of the expected arrival of a military force.

It was faid, and impreffed upon the people with much inflammatory declamation, that the Britifh miniftry having in vain attempted to dragoon the inhabitants of that province into a flavifh fubmiffion to the will of parliament by the aid of a military force, were now trying to accomplifh the fame end in a way not fo open, but not lefs dangerous—by influencing the judges with grants of falaries, and

VOL. I. M thereby

thereby corrupting the fource of juftice : And the people were called
upon and conjured to withftand fo infidious and deftructive an innovation.

A town meeting of the inhabitants of Bofton was appointed by
the felect men, and held on the twenty-fifth of October. At this
meeting a petition was prepared and prefented to the governor, fetting forth the evil tendency of the new regulation, with the alarm
which it had occafioned amongft the people, and praying him to
call an affembly. The governor refufed to comply with the prayer
of the petition : And the petitioners having appointed a committee
to confider and propofe what was fit to be . done in that feafon of
danger, adjourned to a future day for the purpofe of receiving their
report. The committee, having taken time to deliberate, drew up
a report containing a new declaration of rights, more extenfive than
any which had been yet framed, and comprehending the rights of
the colonifts as men, citizens, and chriftians. In this report, the
authority of the Britifh parliament to legiflate for the colonies, in
any refpect whatfoever, was completely denied. After enumerating
the rights of the colonifts, it fet forth that thefe had been violated
in various inftances, but more efpecially by the declaratory act of
the year 1766, by which the Britifh parliament affumed to itfelf the
power of legiflating for them without their confent, and under
pretence of that authority had impofed taxes in the colonies, and
appointed new officers to be refident amongft them, unknown to
their conftitution, becaufe unauthorifed by their charter, for the purpofe of fuperintending the collection of thofe taxes, and eftablifhing
what was called an American revenue. And the Britifh miniftry, by
framing the new regulation for granting falaries to the judges and
crown officers out of this odious tribute, were charged with defign-
ing to complete the fyftem of flavery which had originated in the
houfe of commons, affuming a power to grant their money without
their

their confent. At the adjourned meeting of the inhabitants of
Bofton this report was read and agreed to; and fix hundred copies
of it were ordered to be printed and difperfed through all the towns
of the province, accompanied with a circular letter, calling upon the
people " not to doze any longer, or fit fupinely in indifference,
" whilft the iron hand of oppreffion was daily tearing the choiceft
" fruits from the fair tree of liberty."

When the affembly of this province met in the month of January, the governor probably intending to give them an opportunity,
if they were fo difpofed, of doing away the evil impreffions which
might have been made by the unqualified refolutions of the town
meeting at Bofton, took occafion in his fpeech to infift on the fupreme legiflative authority of the king and parliament. But if he
hoped to benefit government by bringing on this difcuffion, he was
entirely difappointed. The affembly, inftead of endeavouring to
moderate and qualify the doctrines contained in the refolutions of
the town meeting, feized the opportunity of the addrefs which was
to be prefented, to fix them more firmly and in their utmoft extent.
They openly denied the authority of parliament, not only to impofe
taxes, but to legiflate for them in any refpect whatfoever; adding,
" that if there had been in any late inftances a fubmiffion to acts of
" parliament, it was more from want of confideration or a reluc-
" tance to contend with the parent ftate, than a conviction of the
" fupreme legiflative authority of parliament." This addrefs alfo recapitulated a number of new grievances which had not heretofore been
complained of: And fuch was its improper tendency, even in the
opinion of the Affembly, upon cooler reflection, that fix months
after, in a letter* to the earl of Dartmouth, fecretary of ftate for
American affairs, they thought it neceffary to apologize for it, im-

* Dated 29th June 1773.

M 2   puting

puting the blame of their intemperate proceedings to their governor, who had unneceffarily brought the fubject of parliamentary authority under their confideration. In this letter they fay, " that their " anfwers to the governor's fpeech were the effect of neceffity, and " that this neceffity occafioned great grief to the two houfes;" and then, in a ftyle truly characteriftic of puritanical duplicity, they exclaim, " For, my lord, the people of this province are true and " faithful fubjects of his majefty, and think themfelves happy in " their connection with Great Britain."

But this was not the only caufe of complaint which that affembly had againft their governor *. Their agent at the Britifh court, Doctor Franklin, a man well known in the philofophical world, had by fome means or other got poffeffion of certain letters written by their governor in former years to official perfons in England, and about this time tranfmitted them to the affembly. The fubject of this correfpondence was fo difpleafing, that it threw the affembly into a violent heat. They fent a deputation to fhew the letters to the governor, without trufting them in his hands, and to inquire whether he acknowledged the fignatures to be his. The fignatures being owned, they prepared a petition and remonftrance to be prefented to the king, charging the governor with betraying his truft, and flandering the people under his government, by giving private, partial, and falfe information; declaring him an enemy to the colony, and praying for his removal from his office.

How the letters which gave occafion to fo much animofity in the affembly of Maffachufets Bay came into the poffeffion of their agent,

---

* Their prefent governor was Mr. Hutchinfon, a native of Maffachufets Bay, a lawyer and a man of learning, who had filled the office of chief-juftice of the province with general fatisfaction, and was appointed governor on the refignation of fir Francis Bernard in the year 1770. Sir Francis Bernard went to England in the year 1769, to defend himfelf from the charges tranfmitted againft him by the affembly; and although he was honourably acquitted by the privy council, he did not chufe to return to a province where he was fo much difliked.

is

is not yet certainly known to the public. But either the manner of his obtaining them, or the ufe which he made of them, or both, gave fo much offence to the Britifh miniftry, that he was difmiffed from his office of joint deputy poftmafter-general for America, under fuch circumftances of marked difapprobation as probably influenced his fubfequent conduct in the American conteft.

Whilft the patriots of Maffachufets Bay were thus active in dif-covering new caufes of complaint, and keeping the province in a ftate of perpetual clamour and agitation; the fouthern and middle colonies were peaceably and quietly advancing in population and profperity, nothing having occurred for fome years to give the re-publican party amongft them (for fuch a party was by this time formed in all the colonies) any new pretence for quarrelling with the mother-country.

But an act of parliament which paffed this year was deftined to revive all the heat of contention, and to bring the difputes between Great Britain and her colonies to their ultimate crifis. This was an act for impowering the commiffioners of the treafury to grant li-cenfes to the Eaft India Company to export tea to all places whatfo-ever free of duty. The affairs of that company had by fome means or other run into great confufion: Being unable to fatisfy their en-gagements, they applied to parliament for relief, and complained that their diftrefs was in part owing to the American difturbances, which had leffened the demand for their tea; in confequence of which, they had then lying in their warehoufes, for want of a mar-ket, near feventeen millions of pounds. One of the regulations adopted for their relief was the act of parliament above-mentioned, for granting them leave, under the fanction of the treafury, to export their teas, duty free, wherever they could find a market for them. The minifter, in procuring this act to be paffed, had probably two objects in view; one, the relief of the Eaft India company, and the other,

other, the increafe of the American revenue, by this new device for
introducing the company's tea into the colonies, where it ftill lay
under a prohibition in confequence of the affociations: And it was
this laft object which gave offence in America. The leading men
forefaw that, if the tea was once introduced and landed in America, it
would be impoffible to prevent its fale and confumption, and thus
the duty would be inevitably levied upon the inhabitants, notwithftanding all their efforts to prevent it. Refiftance to taxation by the
Britifh parliament was become in America a point of national honour which they were determined to maintain. The affociations
againft the importation of tea from Great Britain, which in fome of
the colonies had begun to be difregarded, were now enforced with
rigour: And all thofe means which, we have feen, the leading men
knew fo well how to ufe, were again employed by them to excite
oppofition amongft the people, and ftir them up to refift with force
and violence the landing of fuch cargoes of tea as might be fent
amongft them. Nor were their efforts in any of the colonies ineffectual. But the clamour and threatenings were greateft in the New
England provinces; and in them, as on all former occafions, the firft
forcible refiftance to the act of parliament was made.

As foon as intelligence was received in the month of November,
that three fhips freighted with tea on account of the Eaft India
company were on their paffage to Bofton, that place became again
the feat of tumult, violence, and riot, excited for the purpofe of
frightening the configners of the tea fhips from acting under their
appointments. The populace furrounded their houfes and demanded their refignation, which not being complied with, the windows
and doors of their houfes were broken, and they themfelves narrowly efcaped the fury of the mob by flying from the town and
taking fhelter in Caftle William. The governor in vain iffued a
proclamation commanding the civil magiftrates to fupprefs the riots,

and

and protect the peaceable and well-difposed inhabitants. His proclamation was vilified and contemned, and the fheriff infulted for attempting to read it at one of the illegal meetings. Even the council refufed to advife any meafures for fecuring the tea upon its arrival, or for protecting the confignees.

When the two fhips did arrive, a meeting was held by the inhabitants of Bofton and thofe of the neighbouring towns, and a determination was made that the fhips fhould be fent back without difcharging their cargoes. Notice of this determination was ordered to be given to the confignees of the tea and fuch other perfons in Bofton as were interefted in the fhips; and the meeting was adjourned for the purpofe of receiving their anfwer. In the mean time difficulties arofe about fending away the fhips: A clearance from the cuftom-houfe could not be obtained for them, neither could they pafs Caftle William at the mouth of the harbour, without the governor's permiffion, which he refufed to grant. Thefe difficulties being reported to the adjourned meeting, it was immediately diffolved, with a general cry of, A mob! a mob! And in the evening a number of armed men, difguifed as Mohawk Indians, boarded the fhips and difcharged their cargoes into the fea; the whole value of the tea deftroyed being eftimated at eighteen thoufand pounds.

The outrages committed by the inhabitants of Bofton had been fo many, their oppofition to government fo daring, and their infults fo frequently repeated, that the patience of the Britifh adminiftration was now exhaufted. The intelligence of the deftruction of the tea arriving in England during the fitting of parliament, and being communicated to both houfes by a meffage from the king, was immediately referred to a committee, with the papers which accompanied it: And upon receiving their report it was determined, that the town of Bofton, which had always been the foremoft in refifting the authority of parliament, fhould now be made an example of parliamentary

liamentary vengeance. Two things were apparently neceffary to be infifted on—fatisfaction to the Eaft India company, for the lofs which they had fuftained by the deftruction of the tea; and reparation to the honour of the Britifh nation, wounded by the infult. To effectuate thefe purpofes an act was paffed for fhutting up the port of Bofton, and prohibiting the lading or unlading of all goods or merchandize, except ftores for his majefty's fervice, and provifions and fuel for the ufe of the inhabitants, at any place within its precincts, from and after the firft of June, until it fhould appear to his majefty that peace and obedience to the laws were fo far reftored in the town of Bofton, that trade might again be fafely carried on, and his majefty's cuftoms be duly collected; in which cafe his majefty might by proclamation open the harbour, but not even then until it fhould appear that fatisfaction had been made to the Eaft India company for the deftruction of their tea, and alfo to thofe who had fuffered by the riots at the time of its arrival at Bofton *. This act having been paffed, a fleet of four fhips of war was ordered to be got ready to fail for Bofton, and as a military force might alfo be neceffary to reduce its diforderly inhabitants to obedience, general Gage, commander in chief in America, was appointed governor of Maffachufets Bay in the room of governor Hutchinfon, who had defired leave to come to England: And to general Gage, to whom the execution of this act was to be entrufted, full powers were alfo given, by commiffion under the great feal, to grant pardons for treafon and all other crimes, and to remit all fines and forfeitures to fuch offenders as fhould appear to be fit objects of mercy.

To devife means for preventing the commiffion of future enormities was at leaft as neceffary as to inflict punifhment for thofe which were paft. From the papers laid upon the tables of the two

* This bill was introduced into the houfe of commons on the fourteenth of March, and received the royal affent on the thirty-firft.

houſes of parliament, and from a review of the diſorderly proceedings in the colony of Maſſachuſets Bay for many years paſt, the
weakneſs of civil government in that province, and its total in
ſufficiency for ſuppreſſing tumults and preſerving the peace, were
very apparent; and it was alſo obvious that this inſufficiency and that
weakneſs were in part owing to radical defects in the frame of their government. To provide a remedy for theſe, it was now propoſed to
aſſimilate their conſtitution more nearly to that of the royal governments in America, and to their prototype the government of Great
Britain. For this purpoſe an act was paſſed to deprive the lower
houſe of aſſembly in Maſſachuſets Bay of the privilege of electing the
members of the council, and to veſt that privilege in the crown; to
authoriſe the king or his ſubſtitute, the governor, to appoint the
judges, magiſtrates, and ſheriffs, and to impower the ſheriffs to
ſummon and return juries; and for the prevention of factious aſſemblies, to prohibit town meetings from being called by the ſelect men,
unleſs with the conſent of the governor.

But as it was now determined to proceed with more vigour than
on former occaſions in exacting ſubmiſſion to the authority of the
mother-country, and as reſiſtance might ſtill be made, ſo it was neceſſary that thoſe who were to be employed in enforcing obedience,
ſhould meet with due protection, and be well aſſured of a fair trial, in
caſe they ſhould be queſtioned for any thing neceſſarily done in the
execution of their duty. The caſe of captain Preſton was remembered,
with the clamour then raiſed, and the unjuſtifiable methods taken to
prejudice the people, which might have proved fatal to him had not
his trial been delayed. To obviate ſuch an evil in future, a third act
of parliament was paſſed for the impartial adminiſtration of juſtice in
Maſſachuſets Bay, impowering the governor, with the advice of the
council, where any perſon acting in his duty as an officer of revenue, or as a magiſtrate, for the ſuppreſſion of riots, or in ſupport of

the laws of revenue, or where any perſon acting under the direction of the magiſtrate for any of thoſe purpoſes, ſhould be charged with the crime of murder, or with any other capital offence committed whilſt he was ſo acting, to ſend the perſon ſo charged into any other colony, or to Great Britain, to be tried, if it ſhould appear to the governor and council that an impartial trial could not be had within the province of Maſſachuſets Bay.

During the ſitting of parliament letters were received from all the thirteen colonies, now the United States of America, by which it appeared that in all of them the landing of the tea had been reſiſted. In ſome it had been ſent back in the ſame ſhips which brought it; in others, ſmall parcels of it had been deſtroyed; and in others, where they had conſented at leaſt to the unloading of the ſhips, it was only upon condition that the tea ſhould be ſtored under lock and key, and an engagement that it ſhould not be offered for ſale. Thus it appeared that the inhabitants of all the colonies were involved, although in a leſs outrageous degree than thoſe of the province of Maſſachuſets Bay, in the guilt of having oppoſed the authority of the mother-country.

In this ſtate of theſe provinces on the ſea-coaſt, it was thought neceſſary to give ſatisfaction to the inhabitants of the interior province of Canada, by paſſing an act for the ſettlement of their government. The objects of this act were, to ſecure to the inhabitants of that province the free exerciſe of their religion; and to the Roman Catholic clergy their rights, agreeably to the articles of capitulation at the time of the ſurrender of the province; to reſtore their ancient laws in civil caſes without a trial by jury, as being more acceptable to the French Canadians than the Engliſh laws with the trial by jury; and to eſtabliſh a council, holding their commiſſions from and at the pleaſure of the king, who were to exerciſe all the powers of legiſlation, that of impoſing taxes only excepted. Such a council, compoſed principally

of

of the Canadian nobleſſe, it was ſuppoſed would be more agreeable to the bulk of the people than a houſe of repreſentatives. And the laſt object of the act was to extend the limits of the province, which, reaching far to the ſouthward behind the other colonies, might be made to ſerve as a check upon them if neceſſary.

The firſt of theſe acts, the Boſton port bill, paſſed through the two houſes of parliament without much difficulty, as the conduct of the people of Boſton, in deſtroying the tea, was generally diſapproved of in England, and the cauſe of their loſing many friends. The bill was introduced into the houſe of commons on the fourteenth of March, and received the royal aſſent on the thirty-firſt of the ſame month. But the other three acts, although finally paſſed by a great majority, were not carried through their intermediate ſtages without much oppoſition *. In every thing that reſpected America, the members of oppoſition, and particularly the Rockingham party, hung upon the miniſter, and if they did not prevent, certainly impeded his meaſures and leſſened their effect; and, by their ill-timed prophetic forebodings, ſpirited up the Americans to act what they foretold.

Whilſt the Britiſh parliament were thus paſſing acts for maintaining the authority of the mother-country over the colonies, and for puniſhing paſt and preventing future tranſgreſſions againſt it in the province of Maſſachuſets Bay; the aſſembly of that province, when they met in the beginning of the year, far from taking any ſteps for averting puniſhment, on the contrary, employed themſelves in purſuing ſuch meaſures as had a tendency to provoke ſtill more the Britiſh miniſtry and parliament. The clamour raiſed in Maſſachuſets Bay in the year 1772, in conſequence of the regulation for aſſigning ſalaries to the judges by grants from the crown, has been already noticed; and

* They received the king's aſſent on the twentieth of May.

N 2

this

this year it was revived by the affembly, who fent a meffage to the judges, requiring them to declare whether they meant to receive their falaries from the affembly as ufual, or from the crown, by virtue of the new grants. All the judges, except the chief-juftice, confented to receive their falaries as ufual from the affembly. He alone declared his refolution to receive his falary from the crown, and him the affembly refolved to impeach for this fuppofed unconftitutional proceeding. Charges drawn up in the form of an impeachment were accordingly voted, and carried to the governor and council, whom the affembly judged to be as competent to the trial of an impeachment in Maffachufets Bay, as the houfe of lords is in Great Britain. The impeachment was however fent back with a meffage from the governor, importing, that the governor and council had no authority to try impeachments. The affembly now changed the mode of their accufation, converting the charges contained in the impeachment into a petition of complaint to be prefented to the governor, which concluded with a prayer for the removal of the chief-juftice. The governor refufed to comply with the prayer of the petition; and finding the affembly determined to profecute their complaint againft the chief-juftice in fome form or other, he at laft diffolved them about the end of March.

But the attention of the people of that province was foon to be engroffed by a fubject of higher importance, than a difpute with their governor or chief-juftice; and the inhabitants of Bofton were at laft to feel the weight of the difpleafure of that power which they had fo long provoked with impunity. In the month of May intelligence arrived, that the act for fhutting up the port of Bofton had been paffed by the Britifh parliament; and this intelligence, together with a copy of the act, was immediately publifhed upon a paper with a black border, fymbolical of mourning, and hawked about the ftreets, as a barbarous, cruel, bloody, and inhuman murder.

der. The former riotous preceedings of the town of Bofton had been fo often overlooked, that fuch an act of feverity as the Bofton port bill, was totally unexpected; and upon the firft publication of the intelligence; nothing was to be heard but frantic expreffions of rage and refentment againft the tyranny and inhumanity of the Britifh miniftry and parliament; and vengeance was loudly called for and threatened. But unfortunately for the inhabitants of Bofton, the operation of this act of parliament, as a punifhment, unlike, in this re-fpect, thofe which had preceded it, could not in their prefent circum-ftances be either refifted or eluded. It was doubtful whether the other fea–port towns in the province might not take advantage of the prefent moment, to raife their own commerce upon the ruins of that of Bofton; and it was alfo uncertain whether the other colonies would cordially intereft themfelves in their behalf. Such confiderations had un-doubtedly an influence, as foon as they began coolly to reflect upon their fituation; and to the firft effervefcence of refentment, a ftate of mind feems to have fucceeded, bordering upon defpondence. A town meeting was held, at which a vote was paffed, addreffed to the inhabitants of the other colonies, importing, that if they would come into a joint refolution to give up all intercourfe with the mo-ther-country in the way of trade, until the Bofton port bill fhould be repealed, it would prove the falvation of America and her liber-ties; but if they did not, there was too much reafon to fear that fraud, power, and the moft odious oppreffion, would rife triumphant over right, juftice, focial happinefs, and freedom. Copies of this vote were ordered to be fent to all the other colonies, and the meet-ing was diffolved, every one being bufied in arranging his affairs for the firft of June, the day on which the port of Bofton was to be de-prived of its commerce.

In this ftate of doubt and anxiety the people of Bofton did not long remain without receiving fome confolation. The inhabitants of the

neigh-

neighbouring towns, inſtead of attempting to profit by their diſtreſs, offered them the uſe of their wharfs and warehouſes for the purpoſe of carrying on their trade : And from the other colonies they ſoon received the moſt flattering teſtimonies of condolence and commiſeration.

In all the colonies the landing of tea had been reſiſted, and therefore they all ſhared in the criminality for which the town of Boſton was about to ſuffer ; and on ſuch an occaſion to have deſerted their brethren in diſtreſs would have been unmanly and ungenerous. The aſſembly of Virginia, which was ſitting at this time, ſet the example of making the ſufferings of the inhabitants of Boſton a common cauſe of complaint in all the colonies. In that aſſembly a reſolution was paſſed for appointing the firſt of June, the day on which the Boſton port bill was to take effect, to be ſet apart as a day of faſting, prayer, and humiliation, " to implore the divine " interpoſition, to avert the heavy calamity which threatened deſtruction to their civil rights with the evils of a civil war ; and " to give one heart and one mind to the people firmly to oppoſe " every injury to the American rights." This reſolution, the general tendency of which to excite oppoſition to the mother-country, was ſufficiently obvious, and which at the ſame time encroached on the royal prerogative by enjoining a faſt, occaſioned the diſſolution of the aſſembly : But, before the members ſeparated, a private meeting was held, at which a declaration was drawn up and ſubſcribed by a majority of the aſſembly, ſetting forth that the puniſhment about to be inflicted on the inhabitants of Boſton, in order to compel them to ſubmit to the payment of unconſtitutional taxes, was in truth an attack upon all the colonies, and would ultimately prove deſtructive to the rights and liberties of all, unleſs the united wiſdom of the whole was applied to prevent it. They therefore recommended to the committee of correſpondence to propoſe to the committees of the other colonies,

I

lonies, that an annual congrefs fhould be held for all the colonies, to deliberate on fuch general meafures as the united interefts of America might from time to time require. And they concluded with an intimation, that a regard for their fellow-fubjects, the merchants and manufacturers of Great Britain, prevented them from going further at that time.

The example fet by the affembly of Virginia was followed in the other colonies. Provincial, county, or town meetings were everywhere held, at which refolutions of a fimilar tendency were paffed: And the firft day of June was very generally obferved in America as a day of fafting, humiliation, and prayer.

General Gage arrived at Bofton not many days after the intelligence was received of the act for fhutting up its harbour, and whilft the inhabitants, affembled at a town meeting, were yet deliberating on the melancholy profpect before them. Notwithftanding this inaufpicious entry into his government, he was received with the ufual honours. He had been many years commander in chief in America, was perfonally known at Bofton, and univerfally refpected for his amiable character and manners. But the animofity which had been kindled in the province of Maffachufets Bay againft the Britifh government had rifen to too great a height to be checked by any perfonal confiderations for a governor, however amiable or refpectable. The affembly met according to cuftom, foon after his arrival; and in the fpeech delivered at the opening of the feffion, he gave them notice that they were to remove to Salem on the firft of June, which from that time was to be confidered as the feat of government. This information was far from being pleafing to the affembly, and they prefented a petition to the governor, intreating him to appoint a day of general fafting and prayer. The governor declined complying with the petition, and foon afterwards adjourned the feffion to the feventh of June, then to meet at Salem.

In

In the interval of this adjournment, letters were received from most of the other colonies; and it was perceived that the cause of the inhabitants of Boston was every-where warmly espoused. The leading men in Massachusets Bay, cheered by this intelligence, laid aside their despondency, and resolved to act with more vigour than ever in resisting the claims of the mother-country. When the assembly met at Salem, a resolution was passed declaring the expediency of a general congress to be held for all the colonies, and setting forth at large their reasons for recommending such a measure. Five of their own members were appointed to represent them, all of them zealously attached to the American cause, and violently hostile to the pretensions of the British parliament; and a sum of money was voted to defray their expences. They were sensible that after this proceeding their dissolution would soon follow, and they hastened to prepare another resolution, declarative of their sentiments on the present state of affairs, and recommending to their constituents such measures as they wished them to pursue. In this resolution they lamented their present situation, which obliged them to struggle against the heavy hand of power; they complained that their petitions to the king and parliament had been disregarded; they set forth that it was apparently the design of the British government to destroy the free constitutions of the American colonies, and to erect in their stead the systems of tyranny and arbitrary sway, incompatible with liberty, and totally subversive of their constitutional rights: They called upon the people of the province to obstruct as far as was in their power the execution of such evil designs; and for this purpose recommended to them to give up as much as possible every kind of intercourse with the mother-country, until their grievances should be completely redressed. This declaratory resolution had scarcely been passed, when the governor, receiving

information of their proceedings, put an end to the session by

dissolving

diſſolving the aſſembly; which was the laſt that was held under the

charter of Maſſachuſets Bay.

An attempt was now made by ſome inhabitants of Boſton who were friendly to government to procure reſolutions to be paſſed at one of their town meetings for paying to the Eaſt India company the value of their tea, and for diſſolving the committee of correſpondence; but in this attempt they were defeated by a very great majority.

Rough draughts of the two bills already mentioned for altering the conſtitution, and for the impartial adminiſtration of juſtice in Maſſachuſets Bay, having arrived ſoon afterwards, the clamours of the leading men in all the colonies became louder and more vehement than ever: The calm ſtill voice of the friends of government who remained in any of them was no longer to be heard amidſt the noiſe and uproar of tumultuous fervour: And the cauſe of the inhabitants of Boſton grew more popular, contributions being raiſed for their relief in ſeveral of the colonies.

If thoſe who directed the councils of the people in Maſſachuſets Bay were before reſolved on reſiſtance and oppoſition, they now determined to carry that reſolution to the utmoſt extremity. As a previous ſtep, the recommendation of the aſſembly was immediately acted upon, and an aſſociation was ſet on foot, whereby the ſubſcribers bound themſelves, under the moſt ſolemn obligation, to break off all commercial intercourſe with Great Britain from the laſt day of the month of Auguſt, until the Boſton port bill and the other obnoxious acts of parliament ſhould be repealed, and the colony reſtored to the exerciſe of its chartered rights; and to renounce all dealings with thoſe who ſhould refuſe to enter into this agreement, or who, engaging, ſhould afterwards break through it; and the whole was ſanctioned by an agreement that the names of delinquents ſhould be publiſhed in the newſpapers as enemies to their country, a penalty,

VOL. I.   Q   in

in the prefent lawlefs and perturbed ftate of the province, of the moft dangerous tendency. In order to recommend the affociation more powerfully to the attention of the populace, it was handed to them under the antiquated but impreffive title of a folemn league and covenant, a term of the laft century affixed to an engagement entered into by the Puritans, which was ftill held in great veneration by their defcendants in Maffachufets Bay. To counteract this affoci-
29th June. ation, a proclamation was iffued by the governor, in which it was ftyled an illegal and traiterous combination, contrary to the allegiance due to the king and fubverfive of the authority of parliament; and the people were cautioned againft giving any countenance to it, under the penalties annexed to fuch heinous offences. But the proclamation was difregarded, and the folemn league and covenant was generally fubfcribed throughout New England.

General Gage, foon after he took poffeffion of his government, forefeeing the ftorm which was gathering, ordered fome regiments of foot, with a detachment of artillery, to be fent to Bofton: And thefe, upon their arrival, were encamped upon the common lying between the town and the narrow neck of land called Bofton Neck, which joins it with the continent. When troops were formerly ftationed at Bofton, defertion was much encouraged by the inhabitants; and the fame practice being again revived, a guard was placed upon Bofton Neck to prevent it. This was magnified into an attempt to cut off the communication between the town and the country, and to compel the inhabitants of the former, by famine, to fubmit to fuch terms as might be impofed upon them; and a falfe report to this effect being fpread about in the country, the inhabit-
July. ants of the county of Worcefter affembled in great numbers, and fent meffengers to inquire into the truth of the report. Thefe were charged to give an affurance to the people of Bofton that feveral thoufand armed men were ready to come to their affiftance, fhould it

be

be neceffary; but at the fame time to acquaint them, that if they
fhould lofe their fortitude, fo far as to furrender their liberties, the
people of the country would not hold themfelves bound by their
fubmiffion.

About this time an authentic copy of the act of parliament for
altering the conftitution, and regulating the government of Maffachufets Bay, arrived at Bofton, together with commiffions from
the king to thofe who were to conftitute the new council, in the
room of that elected by the affembly. This council was intended
to confift of thirty-fix members, but twenty-four only accepted their
commiffions; and thefe·having qualified, writs were iffued by the
governor, with their advice, for the meeting of a new affembly in
the beginning of October. But the rage of the populace now again
burft forth, and was directed againft thofe who had accepted feats in
the new council; and the greateft number of them, to fave their
perfons from being torn to pieces by the mob, and their property
from being deftroyed, were obliged to refign their appointments; a
few only who refided in Bofton, and were protected by the troops,
retained their fituations. When the fuperior court fat for the adminiftration of juftice, the juries refufed to be fworn, and the inferior officers of the court, frightened by the threats which were denounced againft them, declined acting under the new regulations; and
fo many obftructions were met with in every department, that from
this time civil government in Maffachufets Bay was entirely diffolved.
Bofton was the only place of fecurity in the province; and that in
confequence of the military force encamped in its neighbourhood.
By means of this force alone was protection afforded to fuch as
differed in fentiment from the popular party. Whofoever rendered
himfelf obnoxious, by difcovering his attachment to the mother-
country, and a wifh to fubmit to her laws, was infulted by the populace; and many were hunted from their dwellings in the country,

O 2   and

and obliged to take refuge in Bofton.   Arms were provided by thofe
who were without them: Ammunition and warlike ftores began to
be collected: And the young men were employed in training themfelves to military difcipline.

Under fuch an appearance of hoftile intention, and fuch preparations going forward, general Gage could no longer refrain from
providing for the fecurity of the troops which he commanded, by
fortifying Bofton Neck; and with the like intent, he removed to
Bofton the powder and other military ftores depofited in the magazines at Charleftown, Cambridge, and the Medford powder-houfe,
left the people fhould have been ftirred up to feize on them.   Thefe
proceedings of the governor, which, in his fituation, were apparently neceffary, gave fo much offence, and created fo great an
alarm, that the people, whofe minds had been worked up to a degree of phrenzy by the machinations of the violent party amongft
them, affembled again from all quarters, and were with difficulty
reftrained from marching to Bofton and attacking the troops.   About
the fame time a falfe report was fpread in Connecticut, that an attack
was begun upon the inhabitants of Bofton by the fhips in the harbour and the troops from the common, when feveral thoufands of
the militia of that province affembled in arms, and marched a confiderable diftance to the fuppofed relief of their brethren at Bofton,
before they were undeceived, and difcovered that the report was
falfe.   Thefe rumours were probably circulated by the contrivance
of the leading men, to try the temper of the people.   But their affairs
were not yet ripe for open hoftilities; and in this ftate of tumult and
commotion it was thought fit to appoint a meeting of delegates from
all the towns in the county of Suffolk, of which Bofton is the capital, to advife fuch a plan of conduct to be obferved by the people
as the prefent pofture of affairs might require.

                                                                This

This meeting was accordingly held, and the complection of its deliberations was fuch as no longer left it doubtful to what lengths the
leading men of this province were determined to go, provided they
met with fupport from the other colonies, and that the difpute between the mother-country and the colonies was faft approaching to
that crifis, when an appeal muft be made to the fword. In the refolutions paffed on this occafion, they refufed all fubmiffion to the
late acts of parliament, and engaged to indemnify fuch as fhould be
profecuted for difobedience to them. They accufed thofe who had
accepted feats in the new council, of violating the duty which they
owed to their country, and threatened them with being treated as
public enemies, unlefs they refigned their appointment. They recommended the holding of a provincial congrefs. They exhorted
the people to perfect themfelves in the ufe of arms, and for that purpofe to affemble once every week. They warned them to be upon
their guard againft the defigns of their enemies, who had determined
to feize upon fome of thofe amongft them, who had deferved well of
their country by a ftrenuous oppofition to the arbitrary meafures of
the Britifh miniftry; and if fuch an attempt fhould be made, they
were exhorted to oppofe it; and fhould their oppofition be ineffectual, they were directed to retaliate, by feizing upon every
Britifh officer they could find: And laftly, they recommended to
the receivers of the public revenue to keep it in their own hands
until the conftitution of the province was reftored, or until it fhould
be otherwife difpofed of by a provincial convention. They alfo
prefented a remonftrance to the governor, complaining of the fortifications carrying on at Bofton Neck, and of the feizure of the
public magazines; and they tell him, that although they have no
inclination to commence hoftilities againft his majefty's troops,
they are yet determined never to fubmit to the late acts of parliament.

This

This was the moſt open aſſumption of power on the part of the people, and the moſt direct and daring interference with the executive authority, that had yet taken place in any of the colonies.

But the attention of all America was now directed to the general congreſs, which had met at Philadelphia on the fifth of this month. During the courſe of the ſummer, preparatory meaſures had been taken in all the colonies, Georgia excepted, for holding this grand aſſembly of colonial repreſentation ; and Philadelphia, from its centrical ſituation, was fixed upon for the place of meeting. In thoſe colonies in which their aſſemblies met, delegates to the congreſs were appointed by them, and reſolutions were paſſed for their government and direction ; and in the others the people elected repreſentatives, as if it had been for an aſſembly ; and theſe repreſentatives meeting together, choſe delegates to congreſs, and gave them inſtructions.

In thoſe inſtructions there was a conſiderable variety, according to the different tempers of the leading men in the delegated aſſemblies. From ſome of the colonies the inſtructions were moderate, and from others more violent; but they all agreed in condemning the Boſton port bill, and the other acts of the laſt ſeſſion of parliament relating to Maſſachuſets Bay, and in denying the right of the Britiſh parliament to tax the colonies. But the moſt material of all their inſtructions, and what in a great meaſure ſuperſeded the uſe of all others, was a power given to their delegates to agree to whatever meaſures ſhould meet with the concurrence of a majority of the congreſs.

This congreſs conſiſted of fifty-one delegates, repreſenting twelve of the colonies lying along the ſhore of the Atlantic, from New Hampſhire to South Carolina incluſive ; the greateſt number of delegates for any one colony being ſeven, and the ſmalleſt two. But this diſparity in the number of delegates did not affect the votes, as it was agreed that each colony ſhould have but one vote, whatever was the number of its delegates. The congreſs ſat with their doors

5   locked;

locked; no one was permitted to be prefent at their deliberations, and all their proceedings, except thofe which they thought fit to publifh, were kept profoundly fecret. Affembled in the caufe of freedom, they neverthelefs thought fit to obferve a form practifed only in the moft defpotic governments. Their proceedings being wrapped up in myftery, and all the intermediate fteps, leading to a conclufion, being hid from the public eye, their decrees, when promulgated, were received like the oracles of ancient times, as the dictates of profound wifdom.

The only proceedings which they publifhed, were, a declaration on the ftate of affairs in Maffachufets Bay ; a letter to general Gage, a declaration of rights and grievances, accompanied with an affociation; a petition to the king; an addrefs to the people of Great Britain; another to the inhabitants of the colonies; and a third to the people of Canada; all of them mafterly compofitions, and well adapted to the purpofes for which they were intended.

In their declaratory refolutions on the ftate of affairs in Maffachufets Bay, which was the firft of their public acts, and bore date the feventeenth of September, they approved of the plan of conduct which had been hitherto purfued by the people of that province, and of the refolutions paffed, and meafures propofed, by the delegates of the towns in the county of Suffolk, and advifed a perfeverance in the fame line of conduct; and for the relief of the inhabitans of Bofton, whofe diftreffes were every day increafing, they recommended that contributions fhould be raifed for them in all the other colonies, to continue fo long as their occafions might require ; and if at laft it fhould be found neceffary to remove the Boftonians into the country, that their loffes in that cafe fhould be compenfated at the charge of all the colonies.

With this firft public act of the congrefs, which was confidered as decifive of the opinions that they held, and the meafures they

meant

meant to purfue, the friends of government (for fuch a party, and a
very confiderable one, there was in all the colonies), and even fome of
the more moderate of the patriotic party, were much chagrined and
difappointed. They had hoped that the congrefs would have adopted only pacific means for obtaining a redrefs of grievances; but in the
unqualified approbation given to the very irregular conduct of the
people of Maffachufets Bay, and particularly to the refolutions of the
delegates of the county of Suffolk, they thought that they faw an
evident determination in the congrefs to oppofe the authority of the
mother-country by force and arms. And their apprehenfions were
rather increafed than allayed by the letter from the congrefs to gen
neral Gage, in which they declared it to be the fixed and unalterable refolution of all the colonies to unite for the prefervation of
their common rights, in oppofition to the late acts of parliament,
and in fupport of their brethren of Maffachufets Bay.

The declaration of rights contained a fummary of all the rights
appertaining to Britifh fubjects, to the free exercife of which they
maintained that they were entitled by the immutable laws of nature, by the Britifh conftitution, and by their feveral charters. All
former diftinctions between legiflation and taxation, between external and internal taxes, were now laid afide. They claimed, in behalf
of the colonies, the fole and exclufive power of legiflating for themfelves in all cafes whatfoever: But from the mere neceffity of the cafe,
were willing to fubmit to fuch acts of parliament as were *bonâ fide*
intended to regulate their foreign commerce, excluding however
every idea of taxation, internal or external, for raifing a revenue from
the people of the colonies without their confent. Their grievances,
they faid, were occafioned by eleven acts of parliament paffed in the
prefent reign, moft of which have been already mentioned in the
courfe of this hiftory; and in the enumerated lift they included the
three acts of the laft feffion of parliament, relating to the colony of

Maffa-

Maſſachuſets Bay, and the act for extending the limits of Canada. The repeal of all theſe acts, they inſiſted, was neceſſary to give them ſatisfaction; and as the moſt effectual meaſure which they could de-viſe, for obliging the mother-country to do them juſtice in theſe re-ſpects, they recommended an aſſociation to be entered into by the inhabitants of the colonies for diſcontinuing all importations from Great Britain, Ireland, and the Britiſh iſlands in the Weſt Indies, after the firſt of December following, and all exportation from the colonies to thoſe countries, after the tenth of September 1775, and for giving up the uſe of tea entirely, from the firſt of March in that year, until the acts of parliament which conſtituted their grievances ſhould be repealed. A formal inſtrument of writing to this effect, and con-taining various other regulations for enforcing the execution of it, having been prepared, was immediately ſubſcribed by all the mem-bers of congreſs; and printed copies of it were forthwith diſtributed through all the colonies for the ſubſcription of the inhabitants.

In their petition to the king, they ſet forth all the grievances re-cited in the aſſociation, and to theſe added many more of leſs im-portance; but at the ſame time gave an aſſurance that if they were relieved from the firſt, the harmony between Great Britain and the colonies, with the uſual intercourſes, would be immediately reſtored, and in that caſe they would truſt in the magnanimity and juſtice of his majeſty and the parliament to grant redreſs in the reſt.

The object of their addreſs to the people of Great Britain was to render the American cauſe in that country more popular than of late it had been; and to apologize for the ſuſpenſion of commerce, a meaſure which, they inſiſted, neceſſity alone, and a regard to ſelf-pre-ſervation, obliged them to adopt.

Their addreſs to the inhabitants of the colonies was deſigned to explain to them in what manner they were all intereſted in the fate of the people of Boſton, and to urge them to a compliance with thoſe

VOL. I. P meaſures

meafures which the congrefs had recommended, until a general redrefs of grievances fhould be obtained.

But the ableft of their compofitions, although the moft malignant in its intention, was their addrefs to the people of Canada; the object of which was to render the inhabitants of that province difcontented . and uneafy under their new form of government, to fow the feeds of difcord between them and the mother-country, and to induce them to join with the other colonies in the general confederacy.

Such were the public proceedings of this congrefs, which, after fitting fifty-two days, diffolved itfelf on the twenty-fixth of October, having firft recommended that another fhould be held in the month of May: And its decrees, although publifhed only in the ftyle of recommendations, commanded greater refpect, and were more im-. plicitly obeyed in all the colonies, than the laws of their own governments.

But we muft now return to the province of Maffachufets Bay, in whofe fate, in confequence of the determination of congrefs, all the colonies felt themfelves deeply interefted, and upon the tranfactions in which depended more immediately the doubtful iffue of peace or war. As the winter feafon approached, general Gage thought it neceffary that barracks fhould be erected, as well for the greater eafe of the inhabitants of Bofton, as for the better accommodation of the troops: But in this necessary arrangement he met with many obftructions, not only from the general difinclination of the inhabitants to afford any affiftance to government, but alfo from the particular interpofition of the felect men, by whofe influence and perfuafion the artificers who had been employed were induced to defift from carrying on the work. Nor were the barracks finifhed till other artificers were procured from New Hampfhire and New York, the two colonies which had hitherto conducted themfelves with the greateft moderation. Throughout the whole province of Maffachufets

chufets Bay every poffible impediment was thrown in the way of government, and every method taken to prevent the troops from being fupplied with fuch things as were neceffary for their accommodation: The people had even proceeded fo far as to burn a quantity of ftraw, and fink a number of boats loaded with bricks coming to Bofton for their ufe. But notwithftanding thefe provocations no offenfive meafures were undertaken, the general having determined to act with the utmoft caution and circumfpection; fo that, if the fword muft at laft be unfheathed, it might appear to be owing to no fault in him. That this muft foon happen there was now indeed the greateft probability, as the violence of the people was daily increafing and breaking out into the moft criminal exceffes againft fuch as were fuppofed to be unfriendly to the American caufe. In confequence of this violence, the commiffioners of the cuftoms and all the officers of government had been obliged to quit Salem, and fly to Bofton for protection; which, inftead of being, as formerly, the feat of tumult and diforder, was now the only place of fafety within the province of Maffachufets Bay.

It may be remembered that foon after the new council had qualified under the act for regulating the government of Maffachufets Bay, writs were iffued by the governor for the election of a new affembly to fit in the beginning of October; but the violence of the patriotic party in the province had increafed to fuch a degree, and fo many of the new council, either from threats or from violence actually committed, had been obliged to refign their appointments, that a fufficient number did not remain to meet the affembly as a feparate houfe. Under fuch circumftances the governor thought fit by proclamation to countermand the execution of the writs of election. But this proclamation was held by the leading men of the province to be illegal, and the elections were made in purfuance of the writs. The reprefentatives who were chofen met at Salem at

the

the time appointed for the return of the writs, and having waited a day for the governor without his appearing, they voted themfelves into a provincial congrefs, and chofe Mr. Hancock for their prefident. This was the fame perfon, the feizure of whofe floop for contraband practices had occafioned an infurrection at Bofton in the year 1768, and the confequences of which infurrection are fuppofed by many to have precipitated the difpute between the mother-country and her colonies towards its prefent alarming crifis. So dangerous is it to provoke a popular character in a republican government!

This felf-conftituted congrefs having chofen their prefident, adjourned themfelves to Concord, a town about twenty miles from Bofton. One of their earlieft proceedings was a remonftrance which they prefented to the governor on the fubject of the fortifications at Bofton Neck, and on the alarm occafioned in the province by the military force collecting at Bofton, which they alleged was now daily increafing by the arrival of troops from all parts of the continent in fuch numbers as tended to endanger the lives, liberties, and property, not only of the people of Bofton but of the province in general. To this remonftrance the governor, however averfe to holding any correfpondence with an illegal affembly, thought it neceffary, in the prefent ftate of the province, to give an anfwer: And in his anfwer he indignantly told the provincial congrefs that the lives, liberties, and property of none but avowed enemies could be in danger from Britifh foldiers, who, notwithftanding the enmity which had been fhewn to them in withholding from them every thing neceffary for their prefervation, had not difcovered that refentment which might have been expected from fuch hoftile treatment. He put them in mind that, whilft they were complaining of alterations made in their charter, they were themfelves fubverting it by their prefent illegal meeting; and he admonifhed them to defift from fuch unconftitutional proceedings.

But

But notwithstanding these admonitions from the governor, the
provincial congress continued to sit, and the situation of the town
of Boston, possessed as it was by the king's troops, engaged much
of their attention. The neck of land which joins it with the continent being now fortified, the people of the town might be kept as
hostages for the behaviour of the inhabitants of the country; and
whilst the inhabitants remained in the town, whom, distressed as they
were, it would have been cruel to prevent from obtaining such things
from the country as they stood in need of, it was not possible entirely to withhold supplies from the troops, an object which the provincial congress had much at heart. Boston too was capable of
being made still stronger; and a garrison placed in it, if things were
brought to extremity, would prove a great annoyance to the rest of
the province. These considerations gave them great uneasiness; but
it was difficult to devise a proper remedy for the evils which they
apprehended. Frequent expresses passed between them and the
general congress which was then sitting, and various plans and
schemes were proposed; but all of them were liable to such insur-
mountable objections, that, after much time spent upon this subject,
nothing was finally determined upon. In other matters they neither
felt any scruples, nor met with any difficulties: They passed resolutions, under the style of recommendations, for regulating and exercising the militia, for collecting and disposing of the public revenue,
and for providing arms and military stores.

These were such daring assumptions of the powers of government, under the mask of advice, that the governor thought it necessary to issue a proclamation warning the inhabitants of the province against suffering themselves to be ensnared by the provincial
congress, or led by their influence to incur the penalties of sedition,
treason, and rebellion; and strictly prohibiting all his majesty's liege
subjects from paying any obedience to the recommendations or re-

solves

folves of fuch an unlawful affembly.   But the governor's proclamation, as on former occafions, was treated with contempt; and the
requifitions of the provincial congrefs were obeyed as laws.   That
affembly appointed another congrefs to be held in the month of
February, and diffolved itfelf towards the end of November.

Previous to the meeting of the general congrefs no hoftile preparations had been made either in the middle or fouthern colonies: But
after the breaking up of the congrefs, and upon the return of its
members to their refpeective colonies, the fame fpirit which actuated
the people of the New England colonies feems to have pervaded
the whole continent.   The militia officers affembled their companies more frequently than had been cuftomary, and were affiduous
in training them.   Arms were provided by thofe who were without
them ; and refiftance to the power of the mother-country by open
force was made the fubject of common converfation.   Soon afterwards a copy of the proclamation arrived, which had been iffued in
England, in the month of October, to prevent the exportation of
warlike ftores; and this prohibition ferved to make the inhabitants of
the colonies more eager to procure fupplies.   Mills for making
gunpowder, and manufactories for arms, were fet up in feveral of
the colonies ; and great encouragement was offered for making falt-
petre.

C H A P. I.

Infurrection in Rhode Ifland—and in New Hampfhire—Confequences of fhutting up Bofton Harbour—Provincial Congrefs at Cambridge, in New England—Hofile Defigns and military Preparations— Preparations in all the Colonies for holding a General Congrefs— Detachment of Britifh Troops fent to deftroy military Stores at Concord—haraffed by the Americans—driven back by the way of Lexington to Bofton—Bofton invefted by an American Army— Meafures refpecting the State of America taken by the Englifh Cabinet—Reinforcement of Troops from Britain arrives at Bofton— Battle of Bunker's Hill.

AS foon as the news of the proclamation reached Rhode Ifland, forty pieces of cannon of different fizes, belonging to the crown, which had been mounted on batteries for the defence of the harbour, were feized by the populace, and removed into the country. They did not hefitate to own that this was done to prevent the cannon from falling into the hands of the king's troops, and that they meant to ufe them againft any power that fhould offer to moleft them. By the affembly of this province refolutions were alfo paffed for procuring at the public expence arms and military ftores wherever they could be obtained, and for training the militia in military exercifes.

In the province of New Hampfhire too, which had been hitherto moderate, the news of this proclamation caufed an infurrection. A number

number of armed men aſſembled, and ſurpriſed a ſmall fort called
William and Mary, garriſoned only by an officer and five men.
They took poſſeſſion of the ordnance, gunpowder, and other military
ſtores that were found in it; and theſe being removed, the fort was
abandoned, and the officer, with his men, releaſed.

Of all the colonies, that of New York ſhewed the greateſt averſion
to giving up an intercourſe with the mother-country in the way of
trade. Such of the aſſemblies of the other colonies as had been
called together ſince the breaking up of the general congreſs, had
approved of its proceedings and confirmed its reſolutions; but the
aſſembly of New York, which met in the month of January of this
year, refuſed to accede to them. That aſſembly nevertheleſs agreed
with the other colonial aſſemblies in all the material points of their
grievances; and, to obtain redreſs of theſe, tranſmitted, during their
preſent ſeſſion, a petition to be preſented to the king, a memorial to
the houſe of lords, and a repreſentation and a remonſtrance to the
houſe of commons.

In the mean time the difficulties which the inhabitants of Boſton
had to contend with were every day increaſing in conſequence of the
inclemency of the winter ſeaſon. Contributions had been raiſed, and
ſupplies of proviſions ſent to them from the other colonies; but theſe
were precarious, and not equal to their wants. In a large trading
town, ſuch as Boſton, where ſo many of the inhabitants were entirely ſupported by commerce and its dependencies, ſcarcely any thing
could befal them ſo ruinous as ſhutting up their harbour. No one
was exempt from feeling its effects in ſome ſhape or other, and many
were plunged in the deepeſt diſtreſs. Their ſufferings they imputed
to the Britiſh miniſtry and parliament, and they felt all the reſentment
that the ills under which they ſmarted were calculated to inſpire.
But the military force now collected at Boſton was ſufficiently re-
ſpectable to prevent them from breaking out into thoſe violences

5   which

which their former refractory conduct gave reason to expect, and
which their present feelings probably dictated. These feelings were
the more grievous for being repressed; and the only consolation
which they received was in knowing that, throughout America, the
inhabitants of Boston were considered as martyrs to the American
cause.

When the new provincial congress met at Cambridge, in the month
of February, they published an address to the people calculated to alarm
them with fresh apprehensions; and in conclusion told them that,
from the information which they had received, they had reason to
apprehend that the British ministry meant to devote to sudden de-
struction that province in particular, for having refused, with the
other colonies, tamely to submit to the most ignominious slavery.
Having thus awakened their fears, they, in the most persuasive terms,
exhorted the militia in general, and the minute-men * in particular, to
perfect themselves without delay in military discipline. They afterwards passed resolutions for the providing and making of arms; and
forbad, in the strictest manner, the inhabitants of the province from
supplying the king's troops with any thing requisite for military
service.

Such hostile intentions being manifested by the provincial congress, whose edicts were obeyed as laws; it became necessary for the
governor to disable them, as far as was in his power, from acting
in a hostile manner, by seizing on such of their military stores as
came within his reach. With this view, on the twenty-sixth of February, he ordered a small detachment of troops, under the command
of a field officer, to proceed to Salem, and take possession of some
brass cannon and field-pieces, which had been brought there for the

---

* Volunteer corps from the militia, who engaged to hold themselves in readiness for service at
a minute's notice.

Q use

use of the provincial congress. The troops sent on this service were embarked on board a transport at Boston, in the morning, and carried by water to Marble Head. Having landed there, they marched to Salem: But the cannon were removed before their arrival, and, according to the best information they could receive, only that morning. The officer, hoping to overtake them upon the road, marched on into the country until he was stopped by a small river, over which there had been a draw-bridge. Upon his approach, the bridge was taken up by a number of people assembled upon the opposite shore, who peremptorily refused to let it down, alleging that the road was not a public one, and the bridge private property, over which he had no right to pass without the owner's consent. The officer, seeing a boat · in the river, was about to make use of it for transporting his men; but some country people, who were near, perceiving his intention, jumped into the boat, and with axes began to cut holes in her bottom. These people were interrupted by the soldiers, and a kind of scuffle now ensued which of them should keep possession of the boat; when a clergyman, who had been a witness of the whole transaction, seeing the officer determined to force his passage, and fearing the consequences that might happen if he met with further resistance, prudently interposed, and by his influence prevailed upon the people on the opposite side to let down the bridge. This was accordingly done; and the detachment passed over. But the day was now so far spent, in consequence of this interruption, that any further attempt to overtake the cannon, it was thought, would be fruitless. The officer marched back his men to Marble Head unmolested, reimbarked with them on board the transport, and returned to Boston.

This incident is of little consequence, except to show on the one hand the strict discipline and cautious conduct of the troops, and on the other, the boldness with which such conduct inspired the people of the province to thwart their operations, and obstruct their movements.

ments. The object of the detachment was defeated by previous intelligence conveyed from Bofton. Although fome of the moft violent of its inhabitants had removed into the country, a great majority of thofe who remained were not lefs hoftile to all the meafures of government. By them every action of the governor and every movement of the troops were narrowly watched: Intelligence was conveyed by expreffes; and the people in the country were previoufly prepared for interrupting, if not defeating, every military operation that was attempted.

Preparations were now making in all the colonies for holding the general congrefs, which was to meet at Philadelphia in the month of May. It has been before obferved, that the inhabitants of the middle and fouthern colonies began to arm themfelves individually towards the end of the preceding year : But the bufinefs of arming and putting the country in a ftate of defence was now taken up by the provincial conventions, which met for the purpofe of appointing delegates to congrefs. By them refolutions were paffed for difciplining the militia, and for inftituting corps of volunteers and minutemen, after the example of the New England provinces : And contributions were directed to be raifed from the people, to be employed in the purchafe of arms and ammunition. Still however the object of thofe preparations was not openly avowed in the public proceedings and journals of thofe conventions; and ftill they profeffed loyalty to the king, and attachment to the mother-country.

But the time was faft approaching, when the mafk was to be thrown off, and when the fubjects of the fame fovereign, marfhalled in oppofing armies, were to imbrue their hands in each other's blood. In the province of Maffachufets Bay the authority of the Britifh parliament had been firft called in queftion ; in the fame province the firft actual oppofition to that authority was made ; and there it was deftined that hoftilities fhould firft commence between the mother-country and her colonies.

Q 2

Information

C H A P
I.
1775.
Detachment
of Britifh
troops fent to
deftroy mili-
tary ftores at
Concord,

Information having been brought to Bofton, that a confiderable quantity of military ftores purchafed by the agents for the provincial congrefs, were depofited at Concord, a town which, as we have already had occafion to mention, was about twenty miles from Bofton; general Gage, in the night between the eighteenth and nineteenth of April, detached the grenadiers and light-infantry of his army, under the command of lieutenant-colonel Smith of the tenth regiment of foot, and major Pitcairne of the marines, with orders to proceed to Concord, and deftroy thofe ftores: And the following morning another detachment, confifting of fixteen companies of foot, with fome marines, was ordered to march, under the command of earl Percy, to fuftain the firft. The detachment under lieutenant-colonel Smith, having embarked in boats, was conveyed up Charles River, as far as a place called Phipps's Farm. Being landed there in the night, the troops proceeded on their march to Concord; every precaution being taken, by fecuring fuch perfons as they met with, to prevent the people of the country from obtaining any intelligence of their march. But, notwithftanding this precaution, they had advanced only a few miles, when it was perceived, by the firing of guns and the ringing of bells, that the country was alarmed.

Upon this difcovery lieutenant-colonel Smith detached fix companies of light-infantry, to march on in all hafte, and fecure two bridges on different roads, leading from Concord, and on the other fide of it. Thefe companies reached Lexington, a town fifteen miles from Bofton, about five in the morning; and as they advanced, faw a body of men affembled under arms on a green adjoining to the road. Upon the near approach of the Britifh troops, who queftioned them as to the caufe of their being fo affembled, and ordered them to difperfe, they retired in fome confufion: But as they went off, feveral guns were fired upon the king's troops from behind a ftone wall, and from fome adjoining houfes, which wounded one

man,

man, and shot major Pitcairne's horse in two places. The British troops now returned the fire, by which some of the people under arms were killed, and others wounded, and the rest disperfed. The light-infantry having been delayed by this unexpected rencounter, were now joined by the grenadiers, and the whole detachment marched on unmolested to Concord.

Upon its approach to that place, another body of armed men, or militia, was seen assembled upon a hill, near the entrance of the town; and the light-infantry were ordered to disperse them, whilst the grenadiers marched on by the direct road to Concord. As the light-infantry ascended the hill, the militia retreated towards Concord, and passed over one of the bridges on the other side of it, which was immediately taken possession of by the light-infantry. In the mean time the grenadiers were executing the purpose of the expedition, by destroying the military stores found at Concord. Whilst this was doing, the militia, who had retreated over the bridge, appeared again, to the number of three or four hundred, and advancing up to it, as if they meant to pass, were fired upon by the British troops. The fire was returned, and a sharp action ensued across the river, in which several on both sides were killed and wounded. But the purpose of the expedition being now accomplished, the light-infantry, posted at the bridge, received orders to retire, and the whole detachment now began their march back to Boston.

The whole country was by this time alarmed: The minute-men, volunteers, and militia, assembled from all quarters, and posted themselves amongst trees, in houses*, and behind walls, along the road through which the British troops were to pass; whilst the

harassed by the Americans.

---

* An officer, on the march of the second detachment to Concord, observed to the commandant, lord Percy, that, in his opinion, the opposition to the king's troops would be very little, for that all the windows were shut, and the houses seemingly deserted. "So much the "worse," lord Percy replied; "for we shall be fired at from those very houses."

militia,

militia, who had been engaged at the bridge, reinforced with others hourly coming in from the country, were ready to prefs upon their rear.

Such was the route by which the Britifh troops had to pafs, fatigued and exhaufted as they were, by conftant exertion from the preceding evening. And as foon as they began their retreat, an inceffant though irregular fire commenced, which was kept up during

Driven back by the way of Lexington to Bofton.
the whole of their march back to Lexington, in which they were driven before the Americans like fheep. At that place they were met by the detachment under lord Percy, with two pieces of cannon. The two detachments refted on their arms, and received fome refrefhment.

Lord Percy now formed his detachment into a fquare, in which he inclofed colonel Smith's party, who were fo much exhaufted with fatigue, that they were obliged to lie down for reft on the ground, their tongues hanging out of their mouths, like thofe of dogs after a chafe. Lord Percy, after refrefhing the troops, moved on towards Bofton, haraffed the whole of the way by the Americans, who, from behind ftone walls and other places of fhelter, kept up on our men an inceffant fire, on either flank, as well as in front and rear. This fire it would not have ferved any purpofe to return; as the Americans were concealed, and kept running from front to flank, and from flank to rear, loading their pieces at one place, and difcharging them at another.

When the united detachments arrived at Bofton river, lord Percy afked information of the country people concerning the moft proper place for croffing it. But, had he followed the advice he received, his troops, in paffing the river, muft have been cut to pieces. Having a general knowledge of the country, he was led to fufpect their intelligence, and paffed the troops at a different place, where the Americans could not with fafety follow him.

In

In war there is nothing that so much avails as secrecy of design
and celerity of execution: Nor, on the contrary, so hurtful as un-
necessary openness and procrastination. General Gage on the evening
of the eighteenth of April told lord Percy, that he intended to send
a detachment to seize the stores at Concord, and to give the command to colonel Smith, " who knew that he was to go, but not
" where." He meant it to be a secret expedition, and begged of
lord Percy to keep it a profound secret. As this nobleman was
passing from the general's quarters home to his own, perceiving
eight or ten men conversing together on the common, he made up
to them; when one of the men said — " The British troops have
" marched, but they will miss their aim." " What aim ?" said lord
Percy. " Why," the man replied, " the cannon at Concord." Lord
Percy immediately returned on his steps, and acquainted general
Gage, not without marks of surprize and disapprobation, of what
he had just heard. The general said that his confidence had been
betrayed, for that he had communicated his design to one person
only besides his lordship.

As soon as the two detachments, after their junction, resumed their
march, they were again annoyed by the provincials, posted as before,
who kept up a continued firing until the British troops reached
Boston, about sun-set, quite spent and worn down with fatigue.
The detachments, together, amounted to somewhat more than
eighteen hundred men; and the whole loss sustained, during this
long and harassing march, on the part of the British, was sixty-five
killed, one hundred and thirty-six wounded, and forty-nine missing.
Several of Smith's party were scalped by the Americans. The loss
of the provincials, as estimated by themselves, amounted to sixty
men, two thirds of whom were killed.

The conduct of colonel Smith in this unfortunate expedition was
generally censured; but lord Piercy gained, on this occasion, what

he

19th April.

he afterwards uniformly fuftained, great reputation as an active, brave, and intelligent officer. Such were the events of the day on which blood was firft fhed in the conteft between Great Britain and her colonies: Events which ferved to fhew, that if the Americans were yet unacquainted with military difcipline, they were not deftitute of either courage or conduct, but knew well, and dared to avail themfelves of, fuch advantages as they poffeffed. The people of the colonies are accuftomed to the use of fire-arms from their earlieft youth, and are, in general, good markfmen. Such men, placed in a houfe, behind a wall, or amongft trees, are capable of doing as much execution as regular foldiers: And to thefe advantages, which they poffeffed during the greateft part of the nineteenth of April, we may attribute the inconfiderable lofs fuftained by them, compared with that of our detachments.

The retreat of the Britifh troops to Bofton, which was always intended as foon as they had accomplifhed the purpofe of their march, was reprefented in the province of Maffachufets Bay as a defeat; and fo much were the people of the province elated with their fuppofed victory, that nothing now was talked of but driving the king's troops out of Bofton. They were irritated too, by the fpreading of a report, that one object of the expedition to Concord was to feize on John Hancock and Samuel Adams, two very popular and leading characters in the provincial congrefs. The militia from all the diftant parts of the province, on hearing what had paffed, poured in fo faft, that an army was foon affembled, amounting to twenty thoufand men, under the command of colonels Ward, Pribble, Heath, Prefcott, and Thomas; officers who had ferved in the provincial regiments during the late war, and who now acted as generals. With this army they formed a line of encampment of thirty miles in extent, reaching from the river Myftic on the left to Roxburgh on their right, and inclofing Bofton in the center. They fixed

An American army, fuddenly raifed, invefts Bofton.

fixed their head quarters at Cambridge, and were soon afterwards
joined by a large detachment of troops from Connecticut, under colonel Putnam*, an old provincial officer of approved experience and
reputation, who had served in the two last wars, and now took such
a position with his detachment as to be able readily to succour such
parts of the line of encampment as were nearest to Boston. By this
force, formidable certainly in point of numbers, was Boston blockaded: But the works erected on the neck of land which joins that
town to the continent, were now so well strengthened and covered
with cannon, that the provincials, numerous as they were, durst not
attack them.

An army being already in the field, the provincial congress, which
now removed to Water-town, a place about ten miles from Boston,
passed regulations for arraying it, and for fixing the pay of the
officers and soldiers. Rules and orders for the government of the
army were also published, and a vote passed for issuing a large sum
in paper currency to defray its expences, for the redemption of
which the faith of the province was pledged. By the same congress
a resolution was passed on the fifth day of May, declaring that general Gage, by the late transactions, had utterly disqualified himself
from acting in the province as governor, or in any other capacity,
and that no obedience was due to him; but, on the contrary, that
he was to be considered as an inveterate enemy.

But it is now necessary to recur to such measures as had been Measures of
taken in England, during the winter, for reducing the colonies to the British cabinet.
obedience. Notwithstanding the union which appeared amongst
them, and their fixed determination not to submit to the authority

---

* Colonel, afterwards general, Putnam, at the conclusion of the war in 1763, retired to
a small farm, to which he annexed a tavern, an œconomy not uncommon in America, particularly in the province of New England.

of parliament in the impofition of taxes, the Britifh miniftry determined to perfevere in their coercive plan, but with fome difcrimination according to the demerits of the refpective colonies. The New England provinces were confidered as the moft deeply reprehenfible; and as thefe had, early in the preceding year, entered into an affociation for giving up all commerce with the mother-country; fo it was thought reafonable by the Britifh miniftry to interdict them on the other hand from all commerce with any other country; and, as a farther punifhment, to prohibit them from fifhing on the Banks of Newfoundland. An act of parliament for thefe purpofes was accordingly paffed. But as it foon afterwards appeared that moft of the other colonies were treading faft in the fteps of the people of New England, it was thought neceffary to include them in the fame prohibition; and another act of parliament was paffed for this purpofe, extending to all the other colonies except New-York, North-Carolina, and Georgia. An addition to the land and fea forces was voted by the houfe of commons, and a large reinforcement ordered to Bofton, under the command of the generals Howe, Clinton, and Burgoyne; all of them officers of reputation.

But whilft the minifter was thus preparing to enforce his coercive meafures, he did not altogether lay afide the hope of reconciliation. With a view to this he moved a refolution in the houfe of commons as the bafis of a future agreement between the mother-country and the colonies, which, after fome debate and oppofition, was carried. The purport of this refolution was, that when any of the colonies fhould propofe, according to their abilities, to raife their due proportion towards the common defence; fuch proportion to be raifed under the authority of the affembly of fuch province, and to be difpofable by parliament; and when fuch colony fhould alfo engage to provide for the fupport of the civil government and the adminiftration of juftice within fuch province; it would be proper, if fuch

proposal

propofal fhould be approved of by his majefty in parliament, to forbear, in refpect of fuch colony, to levy any duties or taxes, or to impofe any further duties or taxes, except fuch as fhould be neceffary for the regulation of trade. It was hoped, that the offer of accommodation held out by this refolution, would be readily accepted by the colonies, in order to avert the calamities impending over them in confequence of the prohibitory acts of the prefent feffion of parliament already mentioned: And had fuch an offer been made by the Rockingham adminiftration previous to the repeal of the ftamp act, there is fcarcely any doubt that it would have been then gladly accepted by at leaft a majority of the colonies, and prevented that union amongft them fo fatal to the authority of the mother-country. But it was now too late. The feafon for reconciliation was paft. The minds of the colonial inhabitants had become foured in the profecution of the difpute; and every propofition now made by the Britifh miniftry was viewed with jealoufy and received with diftruft. A kind of military furor, too, had by this time feized the inhabitants of the colonies, and rather than make any fort of conceffion to the Britifh parliament, they were willing to rifque the confequences of oppofing in the field their juvenile ardour to the matured ftrength of the parent ftate; and in this refolution they were encouraged to perfift by recollecting the events of the nineteenth of April, by which it appeared, according to their manner of reafoning, that in fuch a country as America, abounding with dangerous paffes and woody defiles, the Britifh troops, with all their valour, difcipline, and military fkill, were not, when oppofed to the Americans, fo formidable as had been generally apprehended.

Copies of this conciliatory propofition were tranfmitted by the miniftry to America; and as foon as thefe arrived, the different affemblies

blies were convened, before whom they were laid for their confideration. But this parliamentary refolution was accepted by none of them as a ground for reconciliation. By fome it was viewed only as a minifterial fcheme for dividing and difuniting the colonies: By others it was held not to be fatisfactory, becaufe the amount of the contribution was not left to the difcretion of the colonial affemblies, but was to be determined by the king in parliament: And by all the affemblies it was agreed to be referred to the general congrefs, which, they held, was alone competent to decide upon it. A reference to the general congrefs was the fame thing as a rejection; for it was well known that the Britifh miniftry would hold no communication with the general congrefs on that or any other fubject. Such was the fate of the minifter's conciliatory propofition for terminating the difpute between the mother-country and the colonies.

Towards the end of May, and in the beginning of June, the expected reinforcements arrived at Bofton, with the generals appointed to command them. From the time of the expedition to Concord the Britifh troops had continued blockaded in Bofton, the force then under general Gage being too fmall for any other purpofe than defence. But this force, now increafed by the troops lately arrived, was become refpectable, not fo much indeed for its numbers, as the excellence of the troops of which it confifted.

As a ftep preparatory to offenfive meafures, general Gage on the twelfth of June iffued a proclamation, offering, in his majefty's name, a free pardon to all thofe who fhould forthwith lay down their arms, John Hancock and Samuel Adams only excepted, and threatening with punifhment all fuch as fhould delay to avail themfelves of the proffered mercy. By the fame proclamation alfo, martial law was declared to be in force in the province, until peace and order fhould be fo far reftored that juftice might be again adminiftered in the civil courts.

courts. But this proclamation, like others which had been issued before, produced no beneficial effect, and was as much disregarded as
they had been.

Adjacent to the peninsula of Boston, on the north, is another of
similar form, called the Peninsula of Charlestown. They are separated from one another by Charles River, which is navigable, and
nearly the breadth of the Thames at London bridge : And on the
northern bank of this river, over-against Boston, lies Charlestown,
a spacious well-built town, which gives name to the peninsula. The
peninsula of Charlestown, being bounded on the north by the river
Medford or Mystic, and on the east by Boston harbour, is entirely
surrounded by navigable water, except where it is joined to the main
land by an isthmus, somewhat wider, and more accessible than Boston
Neck. In the centre of the peninsula rises an eminence, called
Bunker's Hill, with an easy ascent from the isthmus, but steep on
every other side ; and at the bottom of this hill towards Boston
stands Charlestown. Bunker's Hill was sufficiently high to overlook any part of Boston, and near enough to be within cannon-
shot.

Why a situation, from which the town of Boston was so liable to
be annoyed, was so long neglected, it is not easy to assign a reason *.
But, about this time, the provincials receiving information that general Gage had at last come to a determination to fortify it, were resolved to defeat his intention if possible, by being the first to occupy
it ; and their resolution was executed without delay. About nine
in the evening of the sixteenth of June, a strong detachment of provincials moved from Cambridge; and passing silently over Charlestown Neck, reached the top of Bunker's Hill unobserved. Having

---

* It is said that general Gage was repeatedly advised to occupy and fortify this commanding post.

previously

previously provided themfelves with intrenching tools, they imme-diately fet to work, and threw up an intrenchment, reaching from the river Myftic on the left, to a redoubt on their right, both of which they had nearly completed by the morning; their works being in many places cannon-proof. Although the peninfula was almoft fur-rounded with fhips of war and tranfports, the provincials worked fo filently that they were not difcovered till the morning; when, at break of day, the alarm was given at Bofton, by a cannonade begun upon the provincial works, from the Lively fhip of war. A battery of fix guns was foon afterwards opened upon them from Cop's Hill, in Bofton; and, about noon, a detachment from the army was landed upon the peninfula of Charleftown, under the command of major-general Howe and brigadier-general Pigot, with orders to drive the provincials from their works. The troops were formed without op-pofition as foon as they landed; but the generals perceiving that the provincials were ftrongly pofted on the heights, that they were al-ready in great force, and that large columns were every moment coming in to their affiftance, thought it neceffary to apply for a rein-forcement. When the reinforcement arrived, the whole detachment, confifting now of more than two thoufand men, formed in two lines, moved on towards the enemy, with the light-infantry on the right wing, commanded by general Howe, and the grenadiers on the left by brigadier-general Pigot; the former to attack the provincial lines, and the latter the redoubt. The attack was begun by a fharp cannonade from fome field-pieces and howitzers, the troops advancing flowly, and halting at intervals to give time for the artillery to produce fome effect. The left wing, in advancing, had to contend with a body of provincials, pofted in the houfes in Charleftown, and in this con-flict the town was fet on fire and burnt to the ground. The pro-vincials upon the hill, fecure behind their intrenchments, referved their fire for the near approach of the Britifh troops, when a clofe

and

and unremitting difcharge of mufketry took place, the provincials in the works, as foon as they difcharged their pieces, being furnifhed with others ready loaded. So inceffant and fo deftructive was this continued blaze of mufketry, that the Britifh line recoiled, and gave way in feveral parts. General Howe, it is faid, was, for a few feconds, left nearly alone; moft of the officers who were about him, being either killed or wounded: And it required the utmoft exertion in all the officers, from the generals down to the fubalterns, to repair the diforder which this hot and unexpected fire had produced.

At this juncture, general Clinton, who had arrived from Bofton during the engagement, was moft eminently ferviceable in rallying the troops; and by a happy manœuvre almoft inftantaneoufly brought them back to the charge. The Britifh foldiers, ftung with the reflection of having given way before an enemy whom they defpifed, now returned with irrefiftible impetuofity, forced the intrenchments with fixed bayonets, and drove the provincials from their works. The latter, thus driven, fled with precipitation; but as no purfuit was ordered, they were fuffered to retire unmolefted, except in paffing Charleftown Neck, which was enfiladed by the guns of the Glafgow floop of war, and fome floating batteries; and here the provincials fuftained their greateft lofs.

This deftructive, although fuccefsful attack, coft the Britifh, in killed and wounded, nearly one-half the whole detachment. The total lofs amounted to one thoufand and fifty-four, of which two hundred and twenty-fix were killed, and eight hundred and twenty-eight wounded, nineteen commiffioned officers being amongft the former, and feventy amongft the latter. The lofs on the fide of the provincials, as eftimated by themfelves, was four hundred and forty-nine; of thefe one hundred and forty-five being killed or miffing, and three hundred and four wounded. Amongft the flain on the

5   fide

fide of the Britifh, were lieutenant-colonel Abercrombie, and majors Pitcairne and Williams; all of them officers of experienced bravery and diftinguifhed merit, who had fignalized themfelves on this fatal day, in an eminent degree; as alfo did major Spendlove, who died of his wounds fome days after. Amongft the provincials, fome officers of rank were alfo killed, but the lofs of doctor Warren, who commanded in the redoubt, was moft lamented.

If any thing had been wanting to fhow the bravery and difcipline of the Britifh troops, the action at Bunker's Hill furnifhed an ample proof of both. Twice they were ftopped, and twice returned to the charge. In the middle of a hot fummer's day, incumbered with three days provifions, their knapfacks on their backs, which, together with cartouche-box, ammunition, and firelock, may be eftimated at one hundred and twenty-five pounds weight, with a fteep hill to afcend, covered with grafs reaching to their knees, and interfected with the walls and fences of various inclofures, and in the face of a hot and well-directed fire, they gained a complete victory over three times their own number (for fuch was the Britifh general's eftimate) of provincials ftrongly pofted behind a breaft-work, and defended by a redoubt. But, whatever credit may be due to the valour of the troops, the plan of the attack has been feverely cenfured.

Had the Symmetry tranfport, which drew little water, and mounted eighteen nine-pounders, been towed up Myftic channel, and been brought to, within mufket-fhot of the left flank, which was quite naked; or one of our covered boats, mufket-proof, carrying a heavy piece of cannon, been towed clofe in; one charge on their uncovered flank, it was faid, might have diflodged them in a moment. It has been alfo faid, that the Britifh troops might have been landed in the rear of the provincial intrenchment, and thereby have avoided thofe difficulties and impediments which they had to

encounter

encounter in marching up in front. By fuch a difpofition, too, the
breaft-work of the Americans would have been rendered ufelefs, and
their whole detachment, being inclofed in the peninfula, muft have
either furrendered at difcretion, or attempted, in order to get back to
the main land, to cut their way through the Britifh line. Further
ftill, it has been faid, that the fuccefs of the day was the lefs brilliant,
from no purfuit being ordered, after the provincials had begun to take
to flight.

Few engagements are free from unfortunate accidents and miftakes:
And fome which occurred in the action at Bunker's Hill, are fuppofed to have rendered that day more difaftrous than it would have
otherwife been to the Britifh. During the engagement, a fupply of
ball for the artillery, fent from the ordnance department in Bofton,
was found to be of larger dimenfions than fitted the calibres of the
field-pieces that accompanied the detachment—an overfight which
prevented the farther ufe of the artillery: But a difadvantage, perhaps,
ftill greater, was the unneceffary load already mentioned, under which
the Britifh troops marched to the attack; and by which they were
greatly exhaufted before they came to the fcene of action. This
circumftance was univerfally cenfured as unmilitary and abfurd.
Another error certainly was, that, inftead of confining our attack to
the enemy's left wing only, the affault was made on the whole front.
Their left was covered with nothing more than a breaft-work of
rails and hay, eafy to be fcrambled over; and behind it, was an open
hill which commanded their redoubt and lines.

CHAP. II.

Defigns of Congrefs on Canada—Capture of Ticonderoga and Crown Point—Fort Chamblée—St. John's—and Montreal—Siege of Quebec.

ALL the colonies, now united, vied with each other in profeffions of invincible attachment to the common caufe; and
the congrefs beheld their power acknowledged, in a very great degree,
from Nova Scotia to Georgia. And as it was now evident that the
mother-country was as refolutely determined to maintain, as they were

Defigns of
congrefs on
Canada.

to refift, her authority, they began to concert meafures for fupporting a war, and, in the firft place, to confider where that authority was moft vulnerable. With thefe fentiments they caft their eyes
on the province of Canada.

Canada, furrounded by rivers and lakes, and ftretching from
Nova Scotia, in an oblong direction, almoft to. the fouthern extremity of Penfylvania, was conveniently fituated for hoftile invafion, and would, if reduced, prove a moft important acquifition:
Nor were various moral circumftances wanting to encourage the
Americans to commence hoftilities by an attack on that extenfive
region. They were not unacquainted with that general odium that
attended the Quebec act among the Canadians, who faw that it intended, by eftablifhing the French laws, to introduce arbitrary power.
Neither were they ignorant that the rejection of the petition prefented
againft that offenfive law, had weakened the attachment of the inhabitants to the mother-country; by which country they conceived that they

had been treated with injuſtice and oppreſſion; inaſmuch as, though C H A P.
ſubject to her power, they were deprived of the chief bleſſings re- II.
ſulting from her conſtitution. The ſupporters of the American 1775.
cauſe failed not to place thoſe arguments in as forcible a light as
poſſible: Nor were their repreſentations without effect. The congreſs however did not wait for the full reſult of thoſe diſcontents
and reaſonings to which they gave birth, but came to a reſolution
to attack our province while they might do it with advantage.

Ticonderoga and Crown Point, the former ſituated at the north
end of Lake George, and the latter near the ſouthern extremity of
Lake Champlain, form the gates on that quarter of Canada. Theſe
poſts had already been ſecured in the following manner: A volun- 3d May.
teer, of the name of Ethan Allen, aſſembled, of his own accord,
about fifty men, and proceeded immediately to the environs of the
firſt-mentioned fortreſs, commanded by captain De la Place of the
twenty-ſixth regiment, who had under his command about ſixty men.
Allen, who had often been at Ticonderoga, obſerved a complete
want of diſcipline in the garriſon, and that they even carried their
ſupine negligence to the length of never ſhutting the gates. Having
diſpoſed his ſmall force in the woods, he went to captain De la Place,
with whom he was well acquainted, and prevailed on him to lend
him twenty men, for the pretended purpoſe of aſſiſting him in
tranſporting goods acroſs the lake. Theſe men he contrived to make
drunk; and, on the approach of night, drawing his own people
from their ambuſcade, he advanced to the garriſon, of which he Capture of
immediately made himſelf maſter *. As there was not one perſon Ticonderoga,
awake,

---

* The ſtores taken at Ticonderoga were between 112 and 120 iron cannon, from 6 to 24
pounders; 50 ſwivels of different ſizes, 2 ten inch mortars, 1 howitzer, 1 cohorn, 10 tons of
muſket balls, 3 cart-loads of flints, 30 new carriages, a conſiderable quantity of ſhells, a ware-
houſe full of materials to carry on boat-building, 100 ſtand of ſmall arms, 10 caſks of very

S 2 indifferent

CHAP.
II.
1775.

and of Crown
Point.

awake, though there was a fentry at the gate, they were all taken prifoners. On the commandant's afking Allen, by what authority he required him to furrender the fort, he anfwered, " I demand " it in the name of the Great Jehovah, and the continental con- " grefs." The reduction of Crown Point, which had neither guard nor garrifon, became a matter of courfe. Allen alfo furprifed Skenefborough, belonging to major Skene, who, with his fon and negroes, were taken prifoners. About the fame time, an American officer, afterwards highly diftinguifhed, feized the only fhip of the royal navy on the Lake Champlain. Benedict Arnold, at the commencement of the difference between Great Britain and America, was placed at the head of a company of volunteers by the inhabitants of Newhaven. As foon as he received intelligence of the affair at Lexington, he affembled his company, and declared his intention of proceeding to Bofton. Having obtained their confent, he applied to a committee, to which general Woofter belonged, for ammunition. After fome demur they fupplied him, and he marched off with his company to the American head-quarters, which he reached on the twenty-ninth of April.

The whole military force of Canada, at this period, did not exceed two regiments, the feventh and the twenty-fixth, containing together about eight hundred men : For fo much did general Carleton rely on his influence with the Canadians, and the reprefentations of the clergy, that in the preceding year affurances were fent to general Gage at Bofton, that a corporal's command was fufficient for the defence of the province. Immediately however on the reduction of Crown Point, Ticonderoga, and the king's fhip on the Lake

indifferent power, 2 brafs cannons, 30 barrels of flour, and 18 barrels of pork. The prifoners were 1 captain, 1 gunner, 2 ferjeants, and 44 rank and file, befides women and children. Captain de la Place, notwithftanding his fhameful conduct, was not brought to a court-martial, but was fuffered to fell out.

Champlain,

Champlain, the two regiments were ordered to St. John's, a fort
about twelve miles from Montreal, which was ſtrengthened by two
redoubts, that were ordered to be conſtructed on their arrival.

No ſooner was intelligence of the ſucceſs of the Americans received at Boſton, than general Gage diſpatched brigadier-general
Preſcott, and two officers of inferior rank, with two ſhips to Montreal, where they arrived in July. About the ſame time alſo colonel
Guy Johnſtone arrived at that place with ſeven hundred of the warriors of the Five Nations, who propoſed to general Carleton to retake Crown Point and Ticonderoga, alleging that theſe places
were but weakly garriſoned by the Americans. This project was
not adopted by the general.

In purſuance of the reſolutions of congreſs to attack Canada, the
generals Schuyler and Montgomery were diſpatched with three
thouſand men to Lake Champlain, acroſs which flat-bottomed boats
were to convey them down the Sorrel. And, in order that their
paſſage might not be obſtructed, they took poſſeſſion of an iſle called the Iſle aux Noix, commanding the entrance into the lake.
Hence they marched to St. John's, where they arrived on the ſixth
of September. The moment they landed they were attacked by a
party of Indians, who obliged them to retreat to their boats, and to
return to Iſle aux Noix.

General Schuyler having fallen into an indiſpoſition of body, the
command of the detachment devolved of courſe on general Montgomery, who being joined by ſeveral parties of Indians, offended at
their rejection by general Carleton, and the remainder of the troops
deſtined for this expedition, reſolved to advance immediately and lay
ſiege to St. John's.

The whole military force of Canada being thus concentered in
one point, colonel Allen, the ſame Allen to whom the Americans
were indebted for the reduction of Crown Point and Ticonderoga,

and

and who knew the weak ftate of Montreal, refolved to add, if pof-fible, this important place to his other conquefts.

With a party of about one hundred and fifty men, compofed of Americans and Indians, he marched to the banks of the river St. Laurence, which he croffed in the night, about three miles below Montreal. Intelligence however by this time had been received of their approach; and the town's-people, with about thirty-fix of the twenty-fixth regiment, being embodied under the command of major Campbell, attacked and beat back colonel Allen's detachment, and took the colonel himfelf prifoner.

On this an order was difpatched to colonel Maclean, a brave, indefatigable, and experienced officer, then at Quebec, to procure as many recruits as he could, and haften to that part where the river Sorrel difcharges itfelf into the Gulph of St. Laurence. The colonel, by unwearied diligence, raifed a force of three hundred and feventy Canadians, with whom he marched to the poft to which he was ordered, where he was reinforced by about two hundred more of the natives. Here he remained waiting for orders, and expecting to be joined by general Carleton, who intended to crofs the river at Montreal, and march to the relief of St. John's.

But it unfortunately happened that at the place where the general attempted to land, his boats could not be brought nearer than within a mufket fhot of the fhore, where, too, the enemy had planted two pieces of cannon, which annoyed them feverely. It was a fubject of general animadverfion, that he had attempted to land at the only place where oppofition might be expected, and contrary to the advice of the moft experienced inhabitants. There were other places where he might have landed in fafety. Several of our men were killed: The few who landed were inftantly taken prifoners; and the general, with the fmall remainder of his detachment, was forced to return to Montreal.

In

In the mean time, general Montgomery had taken Fort Chamblée, a fmall fortrefs, five miles above St. John's, and commanded by major Stopford, of the feventh regiment, at the head of about one hundred and fixty men, with a few artillery. The whole of the detachment headed by Montgomery did not exceed, when greateft, two thoufand five hundred men; nor the force fent againft Chamblée, under a lieuteuant colonel, three hundred. For at leaft fifteen days there was no breach made in the wall, nor at any time any impreffion made that deferved that name; for the enemy, who had only two fix-pounders, and next to no ammunition, had never formed a regular battery *. The garrifon did not want powder and other ammunition; but they were poorly clothed, and otherwife ill-provided. On the third of November they furrendered to the Americans, on the condition of being allowed to go out with the honours of war. It was generally and deeply regretted that this fort was not timeoufly reinforced, as it might have been, and alfo that the ammunition was not deftroyed; as there was a fally-port through which it might have been thrown, even in day-light, and without the knowledge of the enemy, into the river.

The ammunition found in Chamblée † enabled the American general to purfue the fiege of St. John's, which, for want of provifions and ammunition, was under the neceffity of furrendering unconditionally on the thirteenth of November §. The works of St.

C H A P.
II.
1775.
Capture of
Fort Chamblée.

Nov. 3.

Capture of St
John's,

---

* A fmall hole was made in the wall, but not within lefs than twenty-five feet from the ground.

† Amounting to 80 barrels of flour, 11 of rice, 7 of peafe, 6 firkins of butter, 134 barrels of pork, 124 barrels of gunpowder, 300 fwivel fhot, 1 box of mufket fhot, 6564 mufket cartridges, 150 ftand of French arms, 3 royal mortars, 61 fhells, 500 hand grenades, 83 royal fufileer's mufkets, 83 accoutrements, and rigging for 3 veffels. As the affailants were reduced to their laft round of fhot, if it had not been for the furrender of Chamblée, they muft have abandoned their attempt on Canada.

§ In this fort were found 17 brafs ordnance from 2 to 24 pounders, 2 eight-inch howitzers, 7 mortars, 22 iron ordnance from 3 to 9 pounders, a confiderable quantity of fhot

St. John's had been fuffered to remain in bad order, and without fufficient ftores, although the governor had long been informed that a defcent on Canada was in contemplation. Ammunition might, in good time, have been thrown in from Chamblée, only twelve miles diftant. It is but juftice here to mention that the garrifon, confift-ing of upwards of five hundred regulars, and above one hundred Canadian volunteers, behaved with great fortitude and perfeverance, though, from the difadvantages juft mentioned, they were forced to furrender. Immediately on the furrender of St. John's, general

and of Mont-
real.

Carleton quitted Montreal, as it was incapable of making any defence. It fell of courfe into the hands of the American general.

Apprehenfions were now entertained for the fafety of Quebec, and not without reafon; for at this period it was ill provided with men, and its fortifications were in a ruinous condition. The garrifon contained but one captain, two fubalterns, and fifty men of the feventh regiment, one lieutenant-colonel, fix captains, twelve fubal-terns, and three hundred and fifty of colónel Maclean's corps then raifing, five companies of Britifh militia, containing each about forty men, fix companies of Canadian militia, about fifty men each, a bat-talion of feamen, under the command of captain Hamilton of the Lizard frigate, amounting to two hundred and fifty men, and a few of the artillery. There were no other works than a wall, furround-ing the town; the parapets were broken down in feveral places, and

fhot and fhells, and about 800 ftand of fmall arms, with a few naval ftores. The cap-ture of St. John's muft undoubtedly be attributed to the fhameful furrender of Chamblée by major Stopford, and to the reprehenfible negligence of the commanding officers at Montreal and Quebec. It was well known that St. John's poffeffed neither a fufficient quantity of ftores nor provifions; yet no affiftance was afforded them in either of thefe articles, though both of them could have been procured with fufficient eafe from Chamblée and Montreal, from the former place even by land carriage. The fort however, notwithftanding thefe difadvan-tages, was moft gallantly defended, and was furrendered only on account of the want of pro-vifions and ammunition.

there

there was neither glacis nor covered-way. The majority of its in-habitants were but ill affected to the British caufe; and the Quebec act, with the rejection of their petition againft it, had in a manner alienated their affections from the mother-country, as already ob-ferved. At this period general Carleton was not very popular; for when the Quebec act was in contemplation, he had taken an active part in the framing of it, and, on his examination before the houfe of commons, had caft fome reflections on the conduct of the British merchants of that province. His manners, befides, were not conci-liating, and he had always attached himfelf to the Canadian nobleffe. The Americans were not ignorant of thefe circumftances, which, with good reafon, they flattered themfelves would operate in their favour.

Colonel Maclean in the mean time, with his detachment, which decreafed daily by defertion, ftill remained in expectation of receiv-ing orders at Sorrel; which place, however, he was at length, without waiting for orders from fir Guy Carleton, determined to quit on the following account : On the fifth of November, an exprefs was tranfmitted to him, acquainting him that colonel Arnold had unex-pectedly arrived at a place called Point Levy, oppofite Quebec, and that the city was in the moft imminent danger.

At the time when the provincial army was encamped before Bof-ton, colonel Arnold laid before general Wafhington the following plan: About one hundred and thirty miles to the northward of Bofton, a river called the Kennebeck, ftretches from the fea as far northward as the lake St. Pierre, which is at no great diftance from the city of Quebec. The colonel propofed to fail up the river with a de-tachment of one thoufand five hundred men, and penetrating through the fwamps, forefts, and hilly land that feparate New England from Canada, beyond the fources of the Kennebeck, to furprife Quebec; which being unprepared for fuch an attempt, would fall an

VOL. I. T eafy

eafy prey. General Wafhington having teftified his approbatio of the propofal, the colonel fet out on his expedition. Extreme were the difficulties and dangers he encountered and furmounted with the moft aftonifhing fortitude and perfeverance. The Kennebeck is full of rocks and fhoals, which often obliged this gallant detachment to carry their boats and rafts on their backs for miles along the fhore. Nor when they had traverfed the length of the Kennebeck were their difficulties diminifhed. The fwampy grounds, added to the fatigue already endured, produced a variety of diforders; provifions began to fail, and a third part of the detachment, on fome trivial pretence, deferted with a colonel at their head. Difficulties however feemed only to invigorate Arnold: Neither difpirited by the defertion of a part of his army, nor by the difeafes under which many of the remainder laboured, the colonel left the fick behind him, and marched on. Six weeks after his departure from Bofton he arrived on the plains of Canada, and immediately encamped oppofite to Quebec, at a fpot called Point Levy.

The confternation occafioned by his unexpected arrival, and by the intrepidity of the atchievement, was univerfal; and had not the fmall-craft and boats been fortunately removed before his approach, he would doubtlefs, in the general confternation, have made himfelf mafter of the city. The removal of thefe produced a delay of fome days, to which Quebec owed her fafety; for colonel Maclean, with his fmall detachment, having quitted Sorrel, after having informed fir Guy Carleton by letter of his intention, advanced by forced marches to Quebec, where he arrived in the evening of the thirteenth of November. On the fucceeding day, Arnold, by the help of a dark night, having landed his men on the other fide of the river, and being totally ignorant of colonel Maclean's arrival, attacked the city at the gate of St. Louis, but was repulfed with flaughter; the city being ftrengthened by fome pieces of cannon that were landed from a frigate in

the

the river. Arnold receiving intelligence from several Canadians residing in Quebec, that it was proposed to attack him early in the morning of the nineteenth, removed his men to Point au Tremble, twenty miles distant from Quebec.

On the twentieth, general Carleton, who had made his escape through the enemy's craft in a whale-boat, arrived in the city, and immediately began to make vigorous preparations for its defence. At the same time he expressed his entire approbation of colonel Maclean's conduct, and publicly thanked him for his very judicious and gallant conduct.

Arnold, who had brought no artillery with him, and who now discovered the impossibility of taking the city without that advantage, contented himself with returning to the spot he had formerly occupied, where he could intercept all supplies and communications, and where he resolved to wait the arrival of Montgomery. Montgomery, after the capture of Montreal, employed himself in constructing flat boats to attack the British armaments, which, consisting of eleven armed vessels, on board of which were general Prescot, and some other officers of rank, together with a large quantity of military stores, was obliged to surrender to his victorious arms. Proceeding immediately to Quebec, he arrived there on the fifth of December, and summoned the city to surrender. The summons was treated with contempt, and general Carleton refused all correspondence with him. Batteries were then immediately opened, which did little damage, and were demolished almost as soon as they were erected. The whole artillery and fortifications of the city were committed to the management of colonel Maclean (whose indefatigable diligence and intrepid demeanour during the whole of the siege acquired him infinite honour), and every possible preparation was made to defend the city to the last extremity.

T 2

Mont-

CHAP. II. 1775.

Montgomery and Arnold were now in a moſt critical ſituation from the want of proper artillery, for they had none heavier than twelve pounders. They ſaw themſelves unable to make any impreſſion on the fortifications of Quebec; and from the malcontents they had nothing now to expect, becauſe each had thought it moſt prudent to join the common cauſe for the preſervation of his own private property. Winter was approaching faſt, and to conſume it on the plains of Canada was a proſpect moſt dreary and unpromiſing; yet, on the other hand, it was eſſentially neceſſary that the firſt campaign ſhould be cloſed with a brilliancy that ſhould prevent the public ardour from experiencing any diminution.

Thus ſituated, it was reſolved to ſtorm the city. Forlorn indeed were the hopes of ſucceſs; but forlorn, at any rate, was the proſpect before them; and the reſolution was not abandoned. It was ſuppoſed that Montgomery was averſe to this meaſure, but he was under the neceſſity of giving his aſſent, becauſe a large number of his men, whoſe time of ſervice had nearly expired, threatened to leave him immediately if the attempt were not made. The neceſſary diſpoſition for ſtorming the town was accordingly put in execution, and Montgomery reſolved to lead the forlorn hope. Four attacks were to be made at the ſame time—two falſe ones, by Cape Diamond and St. John's Gate; and two real, under Cape Diamond, by Drummond's Wharf and the Potaſh. The attacks were to be begun at break of day on the thirty-firſt of December 1775, and the firing of rockets was to be the ſignal. By ſome miſtake however, the attacks on Cape Diamond and St. John's Gate were begun firſt, and the Engliſh diſcovering them to be merely feints, poſted only a ſlight force to defend thoſe points, and conveyed the greater part of their ſtrength to the lower town, where with good reaſon they imagined the real attacks were to be

 made.

made. Montgomery headed one of thefe attacks, Arnold the other. Montgomery, with nine hundred men, had to pafs a dangerous part, where he was between two fires. He led his men however to the attack with that coolnefs and intrepidity which never forfook him. Captain Bairnsfeather, the mafter of a tranfport, who defended this poft, fuffered the enemy's detachment to advance within fifty yards before a gun was fired. A dreadful difcharge of cannon was then poured upon them, and almoft the firft who fell was Montgomery. The Americans, deprived thus of their gallant leader, paufed a moment, but did not retreat. They marched onward to the attack with firmnefs, and for half an hour fuftained a moft galling difcharge of cannon and mufquetry. Finding then that their attempts could not be attended with fuccefs, they withdrew from the attack, and retreated.

Arnold, who at the head of feven hundred men attacked the city at the Saut des Matelots, was rather more fuccefsful. The Canadian guard, appointed to defend it, ran away after the firft fire; and of the feamen who managed the guns, all were either killed or wounded. Arnold having the misfortune to receive a wound in the leg early in the engagement, was obliged to retire; but the next in command continued the attack with unabated vigour. The firft and the fecond barriers were taken, after an obftinate refiftance, and againft the third a ladder was already placed to convey the enemy into the town, when a detachment of colonel Maclean's regiment under captain Nairn, and a party with colonel Caldwell at their head, fortunately arrived. Captain Nairn immediately feized the ladder, and by his refolute conduct drove the enemy from the houfe againft which they had fixed it. They were then driven from the barrier, after a moft defperate attack, and purfued to fome diftance. In thefe attacks

the

the lofs on the part of the Englifh was but trifling, nor did the Americans lofe above fifty men.

Colonel Arnold, though thus difappointed in his endeavours againft Quebec, refolved not to withdraw from the province. He ftill remained encamped on the heights of Abraham, whence he could intercept any fupplies that might be attempted to be conveyed into the city, and where he hoped to increafe his fmall detachment by ingratiating himfelf with the Canadians.

Such was the iffue of the expedition againft Canada, and fuch the termination of the firft campaign, in which the Americans had acquired great military diftinction; yet brilliantly (though certainly unfuccefsfully) as the firft campaign was concluded, the Americans thought their military glory dearly purchafed with the lofs of the gallant Montgomery.

Montgomery, at the conclufion of the laft war, retired to America, where he married. Here his character was fo univerfally refpected, that at the commencement of the difturbances he was invited by congrefs to defend their caufe, and honoured with the rank of brigadier-general. His manners were eafy and conciliating, and he poffeffed in a peculiar degree the art of acquiring the confidence of thofe whom he commanded. In his perfon he was tall and flender, but well limbed. The day after the attack his body was found, and upon examining it, a wound was difcovered in each thigh, and one on his head.

C H A P. III.

Situation of Affairs in Virginia, North and South Carolina, and at Boston.—1775, 1776.

C H A P.
III.

1775.
Situation of
affairs in Vir-
ginia.

THE fatal effects of diforder and tumult were not felt, however, folely in the northern provinces. In the fouth the fituation of affairs was equally critical and alarming. The governor of Virginia at this period was the earl of Dunmore, a man of fufficient firmnefs and refolution, and who had been formerly very popular. His popularity, however, was now rapidly declining; for, at the commencement of the difturbances in the other colonies, he had tranfmitted to the government of Great Britain an account of the ftate of the province of Virginia. The particulars of this ftatement, by fome means becoming known, highly incenfed the planters, to whom it chiefly related. It reprefented them as encumbered with debts, of which they feemed anxious to rid themfelves by encouraging rebellion. It accufed them of impeding the operations of juftice, in order to procure temporary advantages by fuch delays; and it concluded by deducing from their conduct a prediction that they would foon attach themfelves openly to thofe who oppofed the mother-country.

The planters were more highly enraged on account of the truths which this reprefentation contained. They poured upon the governor the fouleft torrents of invective and abufe, and infinuated that his lordfhip, in conjunction with adminiftration, had formed a defign of affaffinating the fpeaker of their affembly, Mr. Randolph.

In

In order to add to the effect of this infinuation, the corporation of Williamfburg prefented an addrefs to Mr. Randolph, who returned an anfwer, not at all calculated to difappoint the wifhes of thofe with whom it had originated. While the public mind was thus ftimulated, an event occurred which was made a pretence for taking up arms.

Lord Dunmore, forefeeing the confequences of this ftate of fermentation, and unwilling to place the means of violence within the power of the planters, had early in May removed the gunpowder from the public magazine at Williamfburg. The motives of this meafure being eafily penetrated, an armed force affembled under the command of a Mr. Henry, a man poffeffed of great influence and popularity, in order to compel a reftitution of the powder. This detachment, however, proceeded no further than within fifteen miles of Williamfburg, where they were met by the magiftrates of the city, who prevailed on them to depart, after having entered into an agreement that the receiver-general of the province fhould become fecurity for the payment of the gunpowder.

But the reign of temperance and moderation was now at an end; public meetings and military affociations were univerfally encouraged; and the affembly of the province, approving the conduct of Mr. Henry, ordered a guard to be provided for the fafety of the magazine, without fubmitting this ftep to the confideration of the governor.

In confequence of lord Dunmore's intimations to the government of Great Britain, feveral conciliatory propofitions were tranfmitted to his lordfhip, who, early in June, laid them before the council of Virginia. The council acceded to them; but the affembly unanimoufly refufed their acquiefcence. Scarcely had this rejection been conveyed to his lordfhip, when, from a private channel, he received intelligence of a defign upon his life. It is probable that this was

only

only a falfe alarm, conveyed by the malcontents to the governor, in
order to induce him to retire from the province. Whether it was
or was not, his lordſhip certainly adopted the moſt prudent line of
conduct: For immediately on receiving this intimation, he abandoned his houſe and property, and with his lady and children retired on board the Fowey man of war. The motives for this ſtep
he tranſmitted to both houſes, who immediately united in addreſſing
his lordſhip ; aſſuring him that his fuſpicions were ill-founded, and
befeeching him, for the fake of the public peace, to return to the capital. But his lordſhip, unwilling to commit himſelf in a manner to
their cuſtody, declined complying with the contents of the addreſs.
Nevertheleſs, he ſubmitted to their confideration the fubſequent propoſition : That he would either correſpond with the council and
aſſembly from the Fowey, or adjourn them to York, about twelve
miles from Williamſburg, where he had no objection to refide, and
terminate the bufineſs of the feſſion. This propoſal, however, was
rejected, and both houſes continued fitting. After having, on a trivial pretence, increaſed the military eſtabliſhment, by the addition of
a company of riflemen, they proceeded to inveſtigate the conduct of the governor. In the courſe of this inveſtigation feveral propoſitions and meſſages were tranſmitted to his lordſhip, the purport
of which was, that he ſhould return to Williamſburg, to give his
aſſent to feveral bills ; replace the powder he had removed from the
magazine ; and depoſit an additional quantity of military ſtores for
the uſe of the colony. To theſe propoſitions his lordſhip returned
for anſwer, that, as his fuſpicions relative to his perſonal fafety were
by no means allayed, he could not return to Williamſburg, but that
if the council and aſſembly choſe to bring the bills to him, he would
give his aſſent to them. With reſpect to the powder, the colony had
no right to claim it, becauſe it belonged to the Rippon man of war.
To the laſt propoſition his lordſhip returned no anſwer. Immedi-

ately on receiving this determination, the affembly entered the following refolution on their journals; viz. "That their rights and
" privileges had been invaded ; that the conftitution of the colony
" was in danger; and that preparation ought to be made accord-
" ingly." Having paffed this refolution, both houfes adjourned to
October.

The greateft part of the members having now retired to their plantations, and tumult and diforder having fomewhat fubfided, lord
Dunmore, with feveral officers of the Fowey, ventured to a farm belonging to his lordfhip on the banks of York river, about two miles
from Williamfburg. Many minutes, however, had not elapfed after
their arrival, before intelligence was received of a party of riflemen
being on their march to feize his lordfhip. He was therefore under
the neceffity of retreating immediately to the boats, which were ready
to receive him. Several fhot were fired at them, but happily they
were at too great a diftance to receive any injury. Lord Dunmore,
now fully convinced that moderate meafures would be feeble and
ineffectual, difpatched his lady and family in a fchooner to England,
and repaired immediately to Norfolk, a town advantageoufly fituated
at the mouth of Chefapeak Bay. In the mean time, the colony
proceeded to the election of deputies, who, on their meeting, affumed
the appellation of the provincial convention. After juftifying their
conduct, by afferting that their liberties and poffeffions were en-
dangered by the machinations of the mother-country, they increafed
the military eftablifhment, and impofed taxes for the maintenance
of it.

At this period the refources poffeffed by lord Dunmore were very
inadequate to oppofe or counteract the proceedings of the convention.
His lordfhip had ravaged thofe parts which were contiguous to the fhore,
and had made an attempt to burn the town of Hampton. In this however, though well fupported by the fhipping, he was unfuccefsful. A
body

body of riflemen coming to the affiftance of the town, compelled him to retire with the lofs of one of his veffels. In order to remedy this infufficiency of refources, his lordfhip adopted a meafure which was certainly not very politic, and which ftimulated the minds of the Virginians almoft to a degree of phrenfy. He iffued a procla- mation, declaring martial law to be in force throughout the colony. He erected the royal ftandard, to which he commanded his majefty's fubjects to repair, and he emancipated all the flaves who fhould take up arms in defence of the Britifh caufe. By this means his lordfhip obtained a confiderable increafe of ftrength, but far from adequate to his expectations. He had already fecured the poffeffion of all the country fituated between Norfolk and the fea; when the provincial meeting, in order to prevent the defertion of the flaves, and to arreft his lordfhip in his career, refolved to fend a confider- able force againft him. About the beginning of November, a de- tachment, confifting of one thoufand men, was difpatched from the weftern fide of Virginia to Norfolk, in the neighbourhood of which they arrived early in December. The river Elizabeth running be- tween them and the town, they were under the neceffity of making a circuit of ten miles to a village called the Great Bridge, where the river is fordable: Previoufly, however, to their arrival, the bridge had been removed, and fome works thrown up, which were defended by a body of provincials and negroes, in order to impede their croffing the river. Thus fituated, and convinced that the loyalifts would foon be obliged to abandon their poft, the Americans contented themfelves with intrenching on the oppofite fide of the river. Lord Dunmore, though he poffeffed a confiderable degree of military experience, was impetuous and impatient. He refolved to adopt a fcheme which was certainly not defenfible on the grounds of prudence, and which was far from receiving the approbation of thofe who were under his command. The fcheme was, to attempt to diflodge the enemy from

U 2

their

their intrenchments on the other fide of the river. On the eighth of December a detachment of one hundred and twenty men, under the command of captain Fordyce of the fourteenth regiment, a brave officer, departed from Norfolk at midnight, and arrived at the Great Bridge before day-break. The planks of the bridge were replaced as filently as poffible, and every proper difpofition made for the attack. The Americans, however, apprifed of the fcheme, had prepared themfelves accordingly. A caufway extended from the bridge through a fwampy bottom, almoft as far as the enemy's works, which were fituated on a rifing ground. The right fide of this caufway was fkirted by a thicket, within the diftance of mufket-fhot. At break of day captain Fordyce croffing the bridge proceeded along the caufway, and was fuffered to advance very near the intrenchments without oppofition. A heavy fire was then poured at the fame moment upon him, both from the thicket and the works, which did great execution. Difconcerted, but not daunted, he ftill continued to advance. A fecond difcharge from the enemy proved fatal to him. He fell within a few feet of the breaft-work of the intrenchments. Thirty of the hundred and twenty, including the leader, being now killed or wounded, the detachment retreated from the attack, and retired acrofs the bridge.

On the fucceeding night, the Englifh abandoned their poft between the Elizabeth and Norfolk, which laft place it was thought prudent alfo to relinquifh, on account of the increafing ftrength of the Americans. Lord Dunmore therefore, with fuch of the inhabitants as were attached to the Britifh caufe, retired on board the fhipping in the river, and the Americans took poffeffion of the town.

The loyalifts were now in the moft pitiable fituation: Provifions were fcarce, and fuch of the boats as ventured on fhore to obtain a frefh fupply, were in the moft imminent danger from the riflemen, who had taken poffeffion of the wharfs, which projected a great

way

way into the river. To remedy this inconvenience, it was refolved by lord Dunmore to fet thefe wharfs on fire. This was performed accordingly, on the firft of January 1776. The other parts of the town were at the fame time fet on fire by the Americans; and thus was the town of Norfolk levelled with the duft. Norfolk, at the commencement of the difturbances, was one of the moft flourifhing towns on the fhores of the Chefapeak. It contained eight thoufand inhabitants. Its proximity to the fea, the excellence of the timber that grew in abundance near it, the capacioufnefs and fafety of its harbour, and the falubrity of its fituation, had rendered it the moft defirable place of refidence in the extenfive province of Virginia. The damage computed to be done by the deftruction of this place was near four hundred thoufand pounds.

After the conflagration of Norfolk, the Americans, in order to prevent the fhipping from procuring provifions, deftroyed all the plantations contiguous to the river, forcing the poffeffors of them to remove with their effects into the interior parts of the province. Experiencing now the greateft diftrefs, the fhips were obliged to put to fea, and lord Dunmore, leaving a confiderable body of the loyalifts and negroes who had joined the royal ftandard, proceeded with the remains of his army to New York, and joined the army under the command of general Howe.

In ftating the fituation of affairs in Virginia at this period, it may not be thought anomalous to mention the particulars of an enlarged and daring fcheme that was projected by a Mr. Connelly, a native of Penfylvania, and communicated to lord Dunmore while he was on the coaft of Virginia. The plan was, to invade that and the other fouthern colonies on their back and inland parts, where it was known that the people were ftrongly attached to the Britifh government. Thefe, it was not doubted, would take up arms in its defence; and it was alfo fuppofed that feveral of the Indian tribes might be induced

to

to join them. With this force it was intended to open a paffage into the very heart of the colonies. The projector, Mr. Connelly, was peculiarly fitted for the conduct of fuch an enterprife. He was active, enterprifing, patient of fatigue, and he poffeffed that which is the foul of enterprife, unconquerable perfeverance.

The fcheme having received the approbation of lord Dunmore, was immediately put into execution. Notwithftanding the variety of difficulties and dangers that furrounded him, Mr. Connelly traverfed the province of Virginia from Chefapeak Bay to the Ohio, a journey of between three and four hundred miles, negotiated a treaty with the Indians on that river, and brought over to his purpofe the white people fituated in thofe diftant fettlements. Returning to lord Dunmore, he was immediately difpatched to general Gage, who appointed him leader of the enterprife, and promifed him his countenance and fupport.

It was determined that Mr. Connelly, as early as poffible in the enfuing fpring, fhould collect as many men as Detroit and the neighbouring forts could fpare, and proceed with them to Pittfburg, fituated beyond the Allegany mountains, where he was to remain until he had procured a fufficient number of perfons attached to the Britifh caufe. He was then to crofs the Allegany mountains, and penetrate into Virginia: Then leaving a ftrong garrifon at Fort Cumberland, he was to fail down the river Potomack, and feize upon Alexandria, where lord Dunmore was to join him with as many fhips as poffible. Strong fortifications were immediately to be conftructed, in order that at all times the friends of government might declare themfelves and form a junction, and that all communication might thus be cut off between the northern and fouthern colonies, divided from each other by the Potomack, which ftretches from an arm of Chefapeak Bay to the Allegany mountains. It is broad, rapid, and not eafily to be forded. The only town of any confequence

quence on its banks was Alexandria, equidiftantly fituated between the fea and the Allegany mountains. But the fcheme was fruftrated by one of thofe caufes which, trifling as they appear, produce often the moft important effects.

Already had Mr. Connelly penetrated to the back fettlements of Maryland, and had congratulated himfelf on having fortunately efcaped almoft every danger, when a tradefman, who knew him, met him on the road, and immediately communicated his fufpicions to the neareft committee. In confequence of this information, he was feized, thrown into prifon, his papers taken from him, and tranfmitted to congrefs. Thefe difcovered the whole fcheme, which was thus entirely overthrown; Mr. Connelly was fent prifoner to Philadelphia, where he was put in irons, and treated with the moft rigorous feverity.

While lord Dunmore was thus driven from his government of Virginia, the governor of North Carolina, Mr. Martin, was not more peaceably fituated. The fame complaints were advanced againft him as had been adduced againft his lordfhip, viz. of having attempted to ftir up the negroes againft their mafters. The replication of Mr. Martin, couched in the form of a proclamation, was fo fpirited and fevere, that the provincial convention voted it to be a moft outrageous libel, and ordered it to be burnt by the public executioner.

Ten or twelve pieces of old difmounted cannon, which had been for many years ufed only on joyful occafions, lay on the banks of the river near governor Martin's houfe at Newburn. On the firft of June 1775, the governor's fervants being employed in examining them (probably for the purpofe of ufing them on his majefty's birth-day), were obferved by the malcontents, who fpreading the alarm, the inhabitants immediately affembled, chofe a perfon of the name of Nafh for their fpeaker, and went in a body to the

the governor's houfe. On being afked what he meant to do with the guns, he replied, that they belonged to his majefty, and that he fhould ufe them in any manner he pleafed. This firm reply fome-what daunted the malcontents, and they retired without continu-ing the inquiry relative to the guns. Newburn, where Mr. Martin refided, was fituated in fuch a manner, that it could derive no affiftance from the navy. On this account, and intelligence having been received that the malcontents had embodied themfelves, the governor

thought it moft prudent to retire on board a fhip off Cape Fear. Si-milar difturbances arofe about the fame time in South Carolina, the inhabitants of which compelled lord William Campbell, the governor, to retire on board a man of war.

As foon as his lordfhip had departed, proper meafures were ufed to prevent an invafion from the inhabitants of the back fettlements, by concluding a treaty with them, and to put the province in an adequate ftate of defence.

At Bofton no events of importance occurred at this period, except the refignation of general Gage, who departed for England, leaving the command of the Britifh forces to general Howe. The befiegers of Bofton, and the befieged, remained in a fituation of equal inacti-vity.

C H A P. IV.

Proceedings of the British government—Deputies arrive in London from Congress—State of Commerce—Meeting of Parliament—Effect of its Resolutions in the Colonies.

ABOUT the latter end of August, two deputies from congress, Messrs. Richard Penn and Arthur Lee, arrived in London with a petition, which they were ordered to present to his majesty. The petition pointed out the flourishing state of the colonies previous to the present disturbances, and reminded his majesty of the assistance they had afforded him during the continuance of the late glorious war. As a recompense for this assistance, it had been expected that they would have been permitted, with the rest of the empire, to share in the blessings of peace, and the emoluments of victory and conquest. How were they disappointed, when, in place of this reward, a new system of statutes and regulations was adopted for the administration of the colonies, equally injurious to their prosperity, and to the welfare of the mother-country? The petition then animadverted in a pointed manner on the conduct of his majesty's ministers, who, by persevering in their obnoxious system, and by proceeding to open hostilities in order to enforce it, had compelled them to arm in their own defence. But as they were not ignorant of the consequences of civil discords, they thought themselves required by indispensable obligations to Almighty God, to his majesty, to their fellow-subjects, and themselves, to stop the further effusion of blood. After expreffions of duty and attachment to his majefty, they folemnly affured him, that they not only moft ardently defired that the former harmony between Great Britain and her colonies might be reftored, but that concord might be eftablifhed between them upon fo firm a bafis as to perpetuate its bleffings, uninterrupted by any future diffenfions, to fucceeding generations in both countries. But this reconciliation they did not wifh to procure at the expenfe either of the dignity or welfare of the mother-country. In conclufion, it was earneftly recommended to his majefty, to direct the adoption of fome mode which fhould have for its tendency the repeal of thofe ftatutes that were injurious to the interefts of the colonies.

Such were the particulars of this celebrated petition, which was figned by John Hancock, prefident of the congrefs, and every one of the members. On the firft of September it was delivered to lord Dartmouth, and on the fourth of the fame month, Meffrs. Penn and Lee were informed, " That no anfwer would be given to it."

The fate of this petition, and the acrimony of argument ufed by thofe who fupported and thofe who oppofed it, revived that party diftinction of Whig and Tory, which had been dormant fince the reign of queen Ann.

State of commerce.

Hitherto the commercial part of the nation had experienced but trifling inconveniences from the lofs of the trade to America : For the Americans had tranfmitted large fums to difcharge the debts due to their Englifh correfpondents. Demands for goods to a confiderable amount were alfo received from Turkey and Ruffia; and Great Britain herfelf, by contracts and fupplies for the army and navy, prevented commerce from drooping, on account of the deprivation of a free intercourfe with her colonies. But in the middle of the year, however, the trading part of the nation received a fevere and an unexpected blow. The profits derived from the Newfoundland

fifhery

fifhery are, in the knowledge of every one, immenfe. The ufual number of veffels were fent this year to the banks of Newfoundland, where, on their arrival, they found themfelves unable to proceed in their operations, on account of a decree made by congrefs, which prevented their being fupplied with their former neceffaries. This decree owed its origin to the act paffed by Great Britain, for depriving the people of New England of the benefits of the fifhery at Newfoundland. In confequence of this prohibition moft of the fhips, in order to avoid the miferies of famine, made the beft of their way home; and the decreafe in the profits of this branch of commerce this feafon, was computed at very little lefs than half a million. This was a fevere ftroke which, while it afforded the oppofers of the American war additional arguments againft it, increafed the anger of thofe who confidered the inhabitants of the colonies in no other light than that of rebels.

On the twenty-fixth of October, the feffion of parliament was opened with a fpeech from the throne, in which his majefty ftated that the fituation of America was the caufe of his affembling both houfes of parliament fo early. Adverting to the particulars of this fituation, he declared, that his revolted fubjects had raifed troops; affembled a naval armament; feized the public revenue; affumed legiflative, executive, and judicial powers, which they exercifed in the moft defpotic manner over their fellow-fubjects. Till they had arrived at this poffeffion of power, they had endeavoured to deceive and amufe the mother-country by vague expreffions of attachment to her, and of proteftations of loyalty to her fovereign. His majefty next reminded each houfe, that though it was known laft feffion that a rebellion exifted within the province of Maffachufet, yet even that fingle province it was endeavoured rather to reclaim than fubdue. The fame mode of conduct had been purfued with refpect to the other revolted colonies, and though certainly proper

Meeting of parliament.

X 2

meafures

measures were taken to enforce authority, yet, at the same time, conciliatory propositions had always preceded those coercive measures. America, however, had rejected all these propositions, and prepared herself to oppose force by force. Hence it was visible, that she aimed at the establishment of a separate government, and an independent empire. After pointing out the injurious consequences that would ensue to the parent state from the success of such a plan, his majesty declared that it was absolutely, necessary to adopt the most decisive measures. Under the impression of this idea, he informed both houses that he had increased the naval and military establishments, and that he had it in contemplation to engage some foreign troops offered him. Nevertheless he assured them that he should be ready to receive the misled with tenderness and mercy, whenever they should become sensible of their error. In conclusion, the parliament was informed, that the proper estimates for the necessary supplies were ordered to be submitted to their consideration.

In answer to this speech, the ministry proposed that an address should be presented to his majesty, assuring him that both houses concurred in admitting the necessity of adopting vigorous measures against the colonies; and that they would assist him with supplies necessary to carry such measures into effect. This proposition met with severe and violent opposition; and instead of such an address, it was moved by a member in the minority, that a declaration should be adopted; the purport of which should be, that the parliament were convinced that the means which had been adopted to allay the ferment in the colonies, had rather increased it. From which they were led to suppose that those means were not properly adapted to secure the end proposed: That they were satisfied that the present disturbances originated in the want of adequate information relative to the true state of the colonies, which had been the cause of obnoxious measures having hitherto been carried into execution. The

declaration;

declaration then proceeded to assure his majesty that his parliament would proceed to review, in a most solemn manner, the whole of the late proceedings, in order to avoid the alarming necessity of shedding the blood of fellow-subjects, and the dreadful expedient of arming a Briton against a Briton. The ministry carried their point with respect to addressing his majesty; but the above-mentioned declaration occasioned long and important debates.

The arguments used by those who supported the declaration, and opposed the adoption of coercive measures, were copiously answered by the supporters of government, who asserted that the representations of the opposition were unfounded, and only calculated to intimidate and repress the national vigour and spirit. From the conduct of the Americans, it was absurd and ridiculous to infer that they aimed at less than unconditional, unqualified, and total independence. In all their proceedings they had considered themselves as entirely separated from Great Britain; and though their professions and petitions breathed peace and moderation, their actions and preparations denoted war and defence. Whether it was more wise to infer intentions from words than from deeds, remained with the opposition to determine. Every attempt that could be made to soften the colonists had been put in practice without effect. Their obstinacy was inflexible, and in proportion as the parent state acceded to their wishes, their conduct became more insolent and overbearing. The right of taxation had in a manner been given up by parliament, for they had allowed the Americans the right of taxing themselves. Yet with this permission they were not contented, refusing to contribute any thing towards the expenses of that state which had nursed them with such tenderness and fostered them with such care. Every hope of accommodation was now at an end. Only two alternatives remained for the British nation to adopt, coercion or contempt.

To

To this effect were the arguments adduced in support of the ministry. A whole night was spent in debating upon the royal speech,
and it was not till five o'clock in the morning that a division took
place, when the declaration proposed by the opposition was rejected
by a majority of one hundred and seventy; the numbers being, for
it, one hundred and eight; against it, two hundred and seventy-
eight.

The colonies in the mean time waited with anxious impatience
for the determination of Great Britain. That hostilities were resolved did not much surprise them, but the idea of having foreign
troops employed against them stung them to the quick. They considered the adoption of this measure as an avowal of the mother-
country having shaken off all former considerations, and of her having banished from her memory every idea that reminded her of both
having originated from the same source.

The consequence of this indignation in the colonies may be easily
conceived. Their resolutions to oppose the measures of the mother-
country were fortified more strongly. Preparations were continued
with additional eagerness and impetuosity; and those of the Americans who had wished hitherto that moderate measures should be
adopted, felt no longer that inclination. And indeed, it must be
confessed that the idea of introducing foreign troops was not
reprobated solely by the Americans and the colonies: Many of
the firm friends of the minister conceived it to be derogatory
to the constitution, and contrary to law. Thus, though they ac-
quiesced in the necessity of decisive and vigorous measures, they
absolutely refused their assent to this proposition, and refused him
every assistance which it was in their power to give, either by their
eloquence or their votes.

The minister however remained firm to his purpose. Hitherto,
he said, Great Britain had been unsuccessful through delay. Immediate

diate meafures were to be ufed, and the fupplies neceffary to
carry on the war ought to be tranfmitted to America as early as poffible. That the introduction of foreigners was illegal he denied in
the moft pofitive manner, affirming it to have been adopted in times
not very diffimilar to the prefent, viz. in the rebellion of 1745.
In the midft of debates on this fubject, the miniftry received information from America that the inhabitants increafed in ftrength daily;
that moft vigorous preparations were carrying on both by fea and
land; and that they had made overtures to feveral foreign nations,
who did not feem averfe to afford them every affiftance and fupport.
In confequence of this information, it was propofed that the naval
eftablifhment fhould be augmented this year to twenty-eight thoufand men and eighty fhips; and that the military eftablifhment in
America fhould confift of twenty-five thoufand of the flower of the
Englifh forces. This propofal was condemned by the oppofition, who tried their ftrength a fecond time in moving, with a view
to render fuch warlike operations no longer neceffary, an addrefs to
his majefty, requefting him to authorife the commiffioners alluded
to in his fpeech from the throne, to receive conciliatory propofitions
from congrefs, or any collective body that fhould be formed to convey the fentiments of one or more of the colonies, without inquir-
ing into the legality of fuch an affembly, or the forms under which
they might be difpofed to treat. This condefcenfion, it was ftrongly
infifted, would fmooth the way to confequences moft beneficial and
advantageous to the mother-country. Nor were condefcenfions of
this nature uncommon. Monarchs, wifely confidering that formal
diftinctions fade away before fubftantial powers, had often treated
with their fubjects who had affembled without any legality of form.
John offered no objection to the informality of the barons' affembly; and fubfequent monarchs, deriving no claim to the crown from
lineal defcent, had owed it folely to the will of a popular affembly.

Befides,

Besides, it was contended, that if forms had always been attended to, none of those revolutions which have contributed to the happiness of mankind, and the advancement of arts and sciences, would have been accomplished. Prudent policy always accommodated itself to the exigencies of events.

The ministerial party, in replying to these arguments, agreed that peace and reconciliation were generally preferable to war and opposition; but, at the same time, that there were circumstances which rendered the former even more desirable than the latter. Great Britain had sufficiently receded. It was her duty now to advance. At all events it was totally inconsistent with her dignity and her character to acknowledge the congress to be a legal assembly. After every possible argument had been marshalled on each side, the proposal made by opposition was negatived, and the minister carried his point.

Indispensable business had hitherto prevented any formal notice being taken of the petition presented to his majesty by the deputies from congress, in either house of parliament. At length however a copy of it having been laid before the house of lords, a motion was made that Mr. Penn should be examined at the bar of the house relative to its contents. In order to induce the ministry to comply with this motion, it was stated that Mr. Penn, who had been formerly governor of Pensylvania, was well acquainted with the real interests of the colonies, and could communicate such information to the house as would tend, perhaps, to heal the breach between the contending powers: Besides, he was personally acquainted with every member of the congress. To this motion the ministry acceded, and Mr. Penn was examined. In his examination he positively, and in the most explicit terms, denied the charge brought against the Americans, viz. that they aimed at independence. Congress had not been elected in any other manner than what was

warranted

warranted by the conftitution of Great Britain. They were chofen
by the voice of their conftituents, and entrufted by them with almoft
unlimited power. With a view to determine what number of men
would be fufficient for carrying on the war, he was particularly
queftioned relative to the population of Penfylvania. This he reprefented to have increafed fo much, during a very fhort period,
as to afford a militia of fixty thoufand men. Of thefe, twenty
thoufand, before his departure, had attached themfelves to the common caufe, arming themfelves at their own expence, and receiving
no pay for their fervices. Congrefs had purchafed in abundance
materials for iron cannon, which they had already caft at Philadelphia, as well as fmall-arms, fully adequate to prefent and future
exigencies. He likewife ftated that fanguine hopes were entertained
of the fuccefs of the petition he had brought over; fo fanguine indeed, that it was called the olive-branch. The confequences of the
rejection of it he feared would be fatal. The moft vigorous preparations would be adopted; and he had every reafon to fuppofe that
the Americans would not want the affiftance of foreign powers poffeffed of ample refources. Such was the effect of Mr. Penn's examination, and fo fatisfied were the oppofition with the information
it contained, that a motion was immediately made for declaring that
the petition from the continental congrefs to the king, afforded fufficient ground for reconciling the unhappy differences fubfifting between Great Britain and her colonial poffeffions. Though the oppofition however were fatisfied with Mr. Penn's evidence, it muft be
confeffed that that gentleman had overftated feveral circumftances.
It cannot be denied that the object of the Americans, from the commencement of the difturbances, was unqualified independence. It
is alfo true that congrefs had not been chofen by more than one third
of the people, and that the militia did not amount to above half the
number at which Mr. Penn had ftated it. In debating on the motion

VOL. I.   Y   made

made by the oppofition, various arguments were adduced on each fide. The blood that would be fhed, the treafures that would be wafted by proceeding to hoftilities, were again infifted on and again anfwered by the minifterial party, with the arguments of the duplicity and deceit of congrefs; the contradiction that exifted between their words and their actions, their profeffions and their preparations; and the obftinacy with which they had rejected every propofition that Great Britain had found it confiftent with her dignity to offer.

After a long debate the houfe divided, and the motion in favour of the petition was rejected by a majority of fifty-three.

Mr. Burke's
conciliatory
bill.

Much about the fame period Mr. Burke, who at that time patronized the republican principles, and maintained an intimate correfpondence with the prime movers of the revolution in America, brought forward a bill in the houfe of commons, which, on account of its tendency, was called the conciliatory bill. It reprobated every idea of a war that propofed for its ultimate object either conqueft or treaty; and it propofed peace and immediate conceffion. In order that fuch a meafure might not wear the appearance of innovation, the bill was modelled on a ftatute made in the thirty-fifth year of Edward the Firft. The neceffity which occafioned that ftatute to be framed was fimilar to the exigencies of the prefent times. It originated in a difpute between that monarch and his people relative to taxation. The latter were victorious; obtaining this important privilege, that no taxes fhould be impofed on them without the confent of the parliament. The prefent bill was intended to procure a fimilar advantage for the Americans. On this account the bill, in the firft place, renounced the exercife of taxation, waving the confideration of the queftion of right. Great Britain however referved to herfelf the power of levying commercial duties, which were to be applied to thofe purpofes that the general affembly of each province

I   fhould

fhould judge to be moft falutary and beneficial. The mother-country alfo referved to herfelf the power of affembling the colonies in congrefs. The bill then propofed to repeal all the laws complained of by the Americans, and to pafs an immediate act of amnefty.

Againft the provifions of this bill it was objected, that though they gave too much away from Great Britain, they would not fatisfy the demands of America: That after what had been propofed by his majefty, any other conciliatory plan would be difrefpectful to him; and that, finally, nothing now remained for Great Britain but coercion. After an important debate, in which both fides difplayed uncommon abilities and eloquence, the bill was rejected, two hundred and ten dividing againft it, and one hundred and five for it.

The rejection of this bill was immediately followed by the introduction of a prohibitory bill, to reftrain all intercourfe with the colonies. This paffed both houfes, not however without violent oppofition. Notwithftanding the fate of Mr. Burke's propofition, another conciliatory bill was fubmitted to the confideration of the lower houfe by Mr. Hartley. The end propofed to be attained by it was the fame as that intended by Mr. Burke's bill, but the means were varied. It propofed that hoftilities fhould be immediately fufpended, and that the colonies fhould be enjoined to eftablifh a trial by jury in favour of their flaves in criminal cafes. If they complied with this injunction, all the obnoxious laws fince the year 1763 were immediately to be repealed, and an act of indemnity paffed. Subfequently to the adoption of thefe meafures the colonies were to be required to furnifh only thofe fupplies which were neceffary for their own fupport and defence. The fame anfwer was given to this propofition by the miniftry, as had been before given to Mr. Burke's bill; and it met with the fame fate.

In confequence of the conciliatory propofition agreed to laft feffion of parliament, the colony of Nova Scotia tranfmitted, about this

The prohibitory bill.

Mr. Hartley's conciliatory bill.

Petition from Nova Scotia.

Y 2
period,

period, a petition to government, the contents of which were, that a revenue fhould be raifed in that colony, under the direction of Great Britain : The manner in which this revenue was to be raifed, was by a ftipulated fum in the hundred on the importation of foreign goods. The petition was granted, and all the other taxes and duties, except thofe which regarded commerce, were, in confequence, immediately repealed.

Foreign
troops.

About the latter end of February 1776, the minifter fubmitted to the confideration of both houfes that part of his majefty's fpeech which related to the engagement of foreign troops. The meafure was oppofed with the united abilities and eloquence of oppofition ; neverthelefs, after feveral debates, it was carried by the minifter, in the houfe of peers, by a majority of fixty-eight, and in the houfe of commons by a majority of one hundred and fifty-four.

Conciliatory
motion by
the duke of
Grafton.

Though oppofition had hitherto been unfuccefsful in every conciliatory propofition, another attempt was made to put a period to the differences between Great Britain and her colonies, by the duke of Grafton, on the fourteenth of March. This nobleman, at the commencement of the difturbances, poffeffed a fhare in the adminiftration, which he foon after refigned in difguft. His grace moved that an addrefs fhould be prefented to his majefty, intreating him, in order to put an end to the effufion of blood and treafure, and to evince to the world the wifh of the fovereign and the parliament to reftore peace and tranquillity, to iffue a proclamation, declaring that, if the revolted colonies would prefent a petition to the commander in chief of his majefty's forces in America, or to the commiffioners fent out with powers adequate to the purpofes of making peace or war, fetting forth their grievances, hoftilities fhould be immediately fufpended, and the petition fhould be referred to the parliament, by whom it fhould be

confidered

considered with the moft folemn and ferious attention., In order
to ftrengthen this propofition, it was alleged that the Americans
would immediately be joined by foreign powers; for, from undoubted authority, it was known that two French gentlemen had
been difpatched to America, where, on their arrival, they had inftantly repaired to congrefs.   In reply to the affertions of the
oppofition, it was alleged that no dependence could be placed
on the affurances of the colonifts with refpect to peace : That
they had never difcuffed any terms of pacification, and that they
feemed to think that the mother-country either poffeffed not fufficient power to compel them to obedience, or that, if her abilities
were adequate to fuch a tafk, fhe was afraid to exert them.   On
this account therefore it was abfolutely neceffary that the colonies
fhould be convinced of their error ; and that government fhould no
longer, by delay, furnifh them with an opportunity of accomplifhing their preparations, and completing their hoftile intentions.
With regard to the intimation of their receiving affiftance from
foreign powers, that was only vague and uncertain; for nothing
had yet tranfpired relative to the bufinefs which had conveyed
the two French gentlemen to America.   But granting even that
the fuggeftions held out by oppofition, on this head, were true,
they afforded only an argument for immediate and vigorous preparations.

The debate on the duke of Grafton's motion was long and
violent.   It was at length negatived by a majority of fixty ; and
thus ended all attempts to reconcile the unhappy diffenfions between
the two contending powers..

CHAP. V.

Blockade and Evacuation of Boston—Siege of Quebec—Defeat of Loy-
*alists at Moore's Creek—Attack of Charlestown.—*1776.

WHILE Great Britain was engaged in these parliamentary dif-
cussions, the British troops blockaded in Boston suffered incredible hardships and fatigue. They had been closely invested
ever since the affair at Lexington; provisions were scarce; and
though they sent to the West Indies for a fresh supply, they could
not obtain any, on account of the dearth subsisting in that quarter.
In addition to these hardships, general Washington began to prosecute the siege with redoubled vigour, in order that the place might
be captured before the arrival of reinforcements from Great Britain.

On the second of March 1776, a battery was opened on the
western side of the town, whence it was dreadfully annoyed by a
furious discharge of cannon and bombs; and on the fifth another was
opened on the eastern shore: Nevertheless the British troops acquitted themselves with the most surprising fortitude, and for fourteen
days endured this bombardment with the most undaunted courage.

No alternative remained now for the besieged, but to dislodge the
provincials from their new works, or evacuate the town. To suc-
ceed in the former was impossible, for the British troops must
have ascended an almost perpendicular eminence, on the top of
which the Americans had prepared hogsheads chained together in
great numbers, and filled with stones, to roll down upon them as
                                                        they

they marched up : A curious provifion, by which whole columns would have been fwept off at once. This fpecies of preparation will exemplify, in a ftriking manner, that fertility of genius in expedients, which ftrongly characterized the Americans during the war. This would effectually have deftroyed all order, and have broken the ranks. It was therefore determined to evacuate the town : This meafure required a fortnight to carry it into execution, on account of the numbers to be removed, many of whom were fick and wounded. At length, however, it was effected, and the brave garrifon, with thofe attached to the Britifh caufe, in number about two thoufand, embarked for Halifax in Nova Scotia, where, on account of the favourablenefs of the weather, they foon arrived *. Thus was the capital of Maffachufet added to the American caufe.

* The Britifh troops left behind them at the Caftle-Ifland and at Bofton, 250 pieces of cannon, half of which were ferviceable, 4 thirteen and a half inch mortars, 2500 chaldrons of fea-coal, 25,000 bufhels of wheat, 2300 bufhels of barley, 6co bufhels of oats, 100 jars of oil, and 150 horfes. This large fupply was of the utmoft importance to the enemy, who were labouring under the greateft want both of ftores and provifions. It ought not, however, to be omitted, that fir William Howe might have carried with him the greateft part of the ammunition, and all the provifions ; it may alfo be neceffary to mention that the fortifications of Bofton were fo excellent, that it would have been extremely difficult for the Americans to have forced them. The Britifh troops left the houfes of Bofton in good condition, and in a ftate of cleanlinefs, which was foon abolifhed by the refidence of the American troops. The evacuation of Bofton afforded alfo another moft important advantage to the enemy. Many ftore-fhips from Great Britain configned to Bofton, and ignorant of the Britifh troops having abandoned it, entered the harbour, and were of courfe captured ; of thefe, the fhip Hope was the moft valuable—She had on board 1500 barrels of powder, befides carbines, bayonets, travelling-carriages for heavy cannon, and all forts of tools neceffary for the army and artillery : Befides thefe, there were other articles, thofe of bedding and clothing particularly, of which the enemy ftood greatly in need. Thefe goods fir William Howe might have diftributed among the army and navy, trufting to government to make payment to the individual proprietors. At any rate, they fhould not have been left in Bofton, but have been deftroyed, as they were articles of which the Americans ftood in the greateft need ; and which enabled them to bear up under the feverities of that winter.

As

As foon as general Wafhington had taken poffeffion of the town, he detached feveral regiments to the defence of New York, imagining that the Britifh troops might have departed for that place, on their feceffion from Bofton.

Colonel Arnold, in the mean time, remained encamped near Quebec : Though unable to capture the town, he reduced it to great diftrefs, on account of having cut off all communication between the inhabitants and the adjacent country. But the feafon now approaching when reinforcements would arrive from England, he was under the neceffity of recommencing the fiege in due form. On the fhores of the river St. Laurence, batteries were erected to burn the fhipping. Thefe attempts, however, were unfuccefsful. While the attention of the befieged was engaged in thefe endeavours on the fhipping, Arnold had prepared fcaling-ladders to ftorm the town: The fcheme was plaufible, but it failed in part: The Americans obtained admittance into the fuburbs, where they burned feveral houfes, and compelled the garrifon to pull down the reft, in order to prevent the fire from fpreading. While the Americans were employed in this fiege, the fmall-pox broke out among them with great violence, and many of the foldiers deferted, in order to fave themfelves from the confequences of a diforder fo fatal, and fo much dreaded in that country. On this account, and certain that fuccours would foon arrive from England, Arnold thought proper to retire, The Englifh fquadron, making its way through the ice, arrived unexpectedly before Quebec. Though, at the time when Bofton was evacuated, it was underftood that this fquadron, with reinforcements, were at fea, no care was taken to leave a fufficient force off the harbour, to prevent them from running into the throat of the enemy: In confequence of which neglect, lieutenant-colonel Archibald Campbell, with feven hundred men, ran

right

right into Bofton harbour, not knowing but that place was ftill in our hands. He was treated in a cruel and favage manner *. Commu-

* Copy of a letter from the late fir Archibald Campbell to fir William Howe.

" S I R,   " *Concord Gaol*, 14th *February* 1777.

" Scarce eight days had elapfed after the period of my firft addrefs, when I found my-
" felf ftripped of half my property, the very neceffaries of life; and I have been lately informed
" that the fide-arms of my officers have actually been difpofed of, notwithftanding they were
" honourably reftored to them by the captors. I was, however, fent upon my parole of honour
" to Reading, where I refided till the firft of this month, during which time it was even be-
" yond the power of malevolent afperfion to charge my conduct juftly with impropriety.

. " On the firft of February I was committed, by an order of congrefs, through the council
" of Bofton, to the common gaol of Concord, intimating for a reafon, that your excellency
" had refufed to exchange general Lee for fix field officers (of whom I happened to be one),
" and that your excellency had put that officer under cuftody of the provoft. How far it may
" be confiftent to ill treat an officer becaufe his commander does not chufe to accept of prof-
" fered barter of that nature, is left to reafon and future confequences to decide, efpecially
" when it is confidered, that there is no perfonal charge againft that officer, and the public
" faith and honour of America was pledged for his being treated as a gentleman.

" With refpect to your excellency's treatment of general Lee, I can fcarcely think it fimilar
" to mine; but that you may be able with more precifion to decide on that point, I fhall
" briefly ftate my prefent unmerited condition.

" I am lodged in a dungeon of twelve or thirteen feet fquare, whofe fides are black with
" the greafe and litter of fucceffive criminals; two doors, with double locks and bolts, fhut me
" up from the yard, with an exprefs prohibition to enter it, either for my health or the ne-
" ceffary calls of nature: Two fmall windows, ftrongly grated with iron, introduce a gloomy
" light to the apartment, and thefe are at this time without a fingle pane of glafs, although
" the feafon of the froft and fnow is actually in the extreme. In the corner of the cell, boxed
" up with the partition, ftands a neceffary-houfe, which does not feem to have been emptied
" fince its firft appropriation to this convenience of malefactors. A loathfome black-hole, deco-
" rated with a pair of fixed chains, is granted me for my inner apartment, from whence a felon was
" but the moment before removed, to make way for your humble fervant, and in which his litter
" and excrement remain to this moment. The attendance of a fingle fervant is alfo denied
" me, and every vifit from a friend pofitively refufed: In fhort, fir, was a fire to happen in
" any chamber of the gaol, which is all of wood, the chimney-ftacks excepted, I might
" perifh in the flames before the gaoler could go through the ceremony of unbolting the doors;
" although, to do him juftice in his ftation, I really think him a man of humanity; his houfe
" is fo remote, that any call from within, efpecially if the wind is high, might be long of
" reaching him effectually.   " I have the honour to be, &c.

                                    " ARCHIBALD CAMPBELL."

nication

nication between the forces that lay on each fide of the river was
thus prevented, and Arnold found it impoffible to put his intentions
of the day before into execution.

On the fixth of May 1776, the reinforcement being landed, general Carleton fallied out upon the provincials, who fled with the
utmoft fpeed, leaving behind them all their artillery and military
ftores. Their veffels were at the fame time attacked and taken by
the light-armed veffels of the Englifh. Thus was the fiege of Quebec raifed, after a duration of five months. The prifoners taken by
general Carleton were treated with the greateft lenity; while, on the
other hand, the Americans, by their mifconduct, entirely loft the
affections of the Canadians: A circumftance to which we are in
fome meafure to impute the failure of their defigns.

Expedition
againft the
Cedars.
Early in the fpring of this year, an expedition, by command of
fir Guy Carleton, was undertaken againft a place called the Cedars
by captain Forfter, who commanded the poft of Ofwagatchie. The
Cedars is fituated about thirty miles from Montreal, to the weftward,
on the river St. Laurence, about a mile from the Cafcade. This
place is naturally ftrong: On the fouth the land ftretches fo far into
the river as to render the eaft and weft points inacceffible: The north
part is the only one on which an attack can be made with any probability of fuccefs.

11th May.
On the eleventh of May captain Forfter departed from
Ofwagatchie with two lieutenants, thirty-eight privates, ten volunteers, and about one hundred and twenty Indians. Arriving on the fourteenth at the village of St. Regis, he convened a
council of the warrior chiefs, and endeavoured to prevail on them to
afford him their affiftance in his intended expedition. The chiefs,
who had been tampered with by the enemy, at firft refufed to accompany him, but at length permitted their young men. On the feventeenth of May, having received intelligence that the Americans, to
                                                              the

the number of four hundred, were pofted at the church of the Cedars, but that they were ignorant of his expedition, he embarked his troops, and landed at ten o'clock at night at Point au Diable, a place about fix miles from the Cedars. A party was immediately difpatched to reconnoitre the fituation of the enemy. On the eighteenth captain Forfter proceeded, under cover of a thick wood, within a mile of the fort, where he made the following difpofition: One company of privates, the volunteers, and one hundred Indians, were ordered to take poffeffion of the wood, and to penetrate it as near as poffible to the enemy. Another body of one hundred Indians was at the fame time difpatched to the Falls at the entrance of the Cafcade, in order to cut off all communication with the ifland of Montreal. This body on their march fell in with a detachment of the garrifon, who were returning with provifions from the Cafcade. At fight of the Britifh troops they fled to the fort, with the lofs of one man. This was the firft certain intelligence received by the enemy of the approach of captain Forfter.

A flag of truce was then fent to the fort, ordering the enemy to furrender themfelves prifoners of war. Major Butterfield, who commanded it, requefted four hours confideration. Conceiving that this requifition originated only in a wifh to gain time, and being informed that a colonel Biddel had been fent to obtain a reinforcement from Montreal, captain Forfter fent a fecond flag, faying that the Indians were at prefent perfectly under his command, and that if the garrifon furrendered immediately, he had no doubt but that they would agree to any thing he wifhed; but if the fort did not furrender, and any of the Indians fhould be killed, captain Forfter could not anfwer for the confequences. In reply to this requifition, the commanding officer of the garrifon agreed to a furrender, on condition of being allowed to retire to Montreal. To this, captain Forfter

would

CHAP.
V.
1776.

would not consent. In the evening of the eighteenth a redoubt was thrown up at the edge of the wood, within five hundred yards of the fort. In the morning of the nineteenth captain Forster advanced within one hundred and twenty yards of the fort, and commenced a heavy fire of musketry, which continued till twelve o'clock, when the fort was surrendered, on condition of the lives of the enemy being preserved, and their baggage prevented from being plundered. In this attack one Indian was killed on the part of the English. The number of prisoners taken amounted, officers included, to three hundred and ninety *. On the twentieth of May, captain

* Articles of Capitulation for surrendering the Cedars.

" After the maturest deliberation on the customs and manners of the savages in war, which " I find so opposite and contrary to the humane disposition of the British government, and to " all civilized nations, and to avoid the inevitable consequence of the savages custom in former " war (which by their threats and menaces I find is not changed), that of putting their pri- " soners to death, to disencumber themselves in case of their being attacked by their enemy; I " have therefore, in compliance with the above disposition in government and the dictates of " humanity, thought fit to enter into the following articles of agreement with brigadier- " general Arnold, in the name of the power he is employed by, and of the officers and sol- " diers who shall be released by this agreement, whose rank and number shall be endorsed " on this cartel.

" 1st, That there shall be an exchange of prisoners faithfully made, returning an equal " number of his majesty's troops of the same rank of those released by this agreement, as " soon as possible, within the space of two months, allowing a moderate time for casualties " that may render the performance of this article impracticable.

" 2d, That the prisoners shall be conducted with safety, and all possible convenience and " dispatch that circumstances will permit, to the south shore of the river St. Laurence, from " which they are to repair to St. John, and return to their own countries immediately, with- " out committing any waste or spoil on their march thither, allowing ten or twelve to go to " Montreal, to transact their private affairs.

" 3d, That the prisoners so returned shall not, under any pretext whatsoever, either in words, " writing, or signs, give the least information to government-enemies, or to their adherents " now in arms, in the least prejudice to his majesty's service.

" 4th,

captain Forfter being informed that a party of the enemy were advancing from Montreal to the fort, ordered one hundred Indians to
take poffeffion of the woods on both fides of the road through
which they were under the neceffity of paffing. This detachment
foon fell in with a party of the enemy, which, after a fhort con-
flict, in which one Indian was killed and three wounded, furrendered at difcretion. The Indians immediately returned with their
prifoners to the fort. On their arrival at the outfide of the works
they halted, for the purpofe of putting them to death. Captain
Forfter however, by his fpirited conduct, prevented them from putting this inhuman determination into execution, and, rifking the

" 4th, That the batteaux, or other conveniencies made ufe of to tranfport the prifoners to
" the fouth fhore of the faid river, or the neceffary people to conduct them, fhall return un-
" molefted.

" 5th, That hoftages be delivered, for the performance of articles to the full, according
" to the fenfe and fpirit of the agreement, without any equivocation whatfoever.

" 6th, That the fecurity of the fubfcribers be given to the inhabitants for all the wafte and
" fpoil committed by the detachment under colonel Biddel, on fair account attefted and figned
" being delivered, for which the hoftages are not to be anfwerable.

" It being our full intention to fulfil the above articles, we mutually fign and interchange
" them as affurances of performance.

" Given under our hands this 27th day of May, A. D. 1776.

(Signed) " GEORGE FORSTER,

" At Vaudreuil. " Captain, commanding the king's troops."

" Article 2d, The prifoners fhall be fent to the fouth fhore of St. Laurence, within
" one league of Caughnawaga, and from thence to St. John's to their own country, except
" twelve who have liberty to go to Montreal, for which purpofe fix days fhall be allowed, and
" hoftilities to ceafe on both fides.

" 4th, Four captains fhall be fent to Quebec as hoftages, and remain there until prifoners
" are exchanged.

" 6th, The continental troops, from principle, have ever avoided plundering. Upon proof
" being made of any wafte committed by colonel Biddel's detachment, reparation fhall be
" made.

" Given under our hands this 27th day of May 1776.

(Signed) " B. ARNOLD,

" St. Ann's. " Brigadier-general of the continental troops."

2   fafety

fafety of his own men, depofited the prifoners in the fort, hav-ing fatisfied his Indians by making them fome prefents. On the fucceeding day he advanced to Vaudreuil, fituated about fix miles to the northward of the Cedars. On the twenty-fourth of May, hav-ing received intelligence that the enemy, under colonel Arnold, had pofted themfelves at Lafhine, nine miles from Montreal, captain Forfter marched to attempt to diflodge him from it. He had ad-vanced within three miles of Lafhine, when he was informed that the number of the enemy amounted to fix hundred, which would be increafed to near treble that number on the fucceeding day. On this account he thought it prudent to retire to Vaudreuil. On the twenty-fixth of May colonel Arnold advanced up the river, with feven hundred men, to attack him. Captain Forfter immediately formed his men into three divifions, which were placed on three points of land that ftretched a little way into the river. The left point was occupied by the favages. The ground in that point was rather fwampy, and covered with wood almoft to the water's edge. The central point, which was open ground, was poffeffed by cap-tain Forfter; and the right point, fituated at the head of a danger-ous rapid, was defended by a body of Canadians: Another body of Canadians was alfo fituated on the ifle of Perrault, oppofite to the right point. The enemy firft made an attempt on the left point, but were repulfed. They next endeavoured to land in the central point, but were prevented. An attempt againft the third point was attended with the fame fuccefs. The enemy therefore relinquifhed their intentions, and returned to St. Ann's, on the ifland of Mont-real. Captain Forfter finding himfelf now much encumbered by the number of his prifoners, and having received no intelligence of ge-neral Carleton's arrival at Trois Rivieres, judged it expedient to enter into an exchange of prifoners with colonel Arnold. This cartel was afterwards broken by congrefs, on a pretence that captain Forfter had conducted himfelf towards the prifoners taken at the Cedars in a

I   cruel

cruel and inhuman manner. This pretence however, it fhould be mentioned in juftice to captain Forfter, had not the fmalleft foundation. And in confirmation of the affertion, and of captain Forfter's humanity, captain Sullivan, who had been taken prifoner, in a letter to his brother general Sullivan, expreffed his furprife at hearing that congrefs, inftead of redeeming him and the other hoftages, according to the cartel, had demanded captain Forfter to be delivered up. At the fame time he declared, in the moft folemn manner, that no man could behave with more humanity than that gentleman did after the furrender of the party to which he belonged *.

General

* Letter from E. Sullivan to major-general John Sullivan, member of congrefs.

"DEAR SIR,   *Montreal, Aug. 4, 1776.*

" I AM permitted by his excellency, which is a favour I did not expect to obtain, to inform
" you I am well, as are the hoftages that are with me. I am much furprifed to hear that the
" congrefs, inftead of redeeming us according to the cartel, have not only refufed to do it,
" but have demanded captain Forfter to be delivered up to anfwer his conduct in what they
" are pleafed to term the maffacre at the Cedars. I would fain flatter myfelf that the con-
" grefs would never have thought of fuch unheard-of proceedings, had they not had a falfe
" reprefentation of the matter. I do not think that I am under any reftraint when I fay,
" and call *that* God who muft judge of all things to witnefs, that not a man living could have
" ufed more humanity than captain Forfter did after the furrender of the party I belonged to;
" and whoever fays to the contrary, let his ftation in life be what it will, he is an enemy to
" peace, and a fallacious difturber of mankind. What reafon they can give for not redeem-
" ing us I cannot conceive; if they are wrongly informed that the affair of the Cedars was a
" maffacre, why do not they rather fulfil the cartel than let their hoftages remain in the hands
" of a mercilefs enemy; or do they regard their troops only while the heavens make them
" victorious?

" Were we in the hands of a rigorous power, as they would intimate, have they not
" every colour of juftice, after fo enormous a breach of faith, laden with chains, to
" caft us into fome horrid place, and tell us to languifh out our days under a fentence
" paffed by our own people? If they fay that there is fome hidden reafon far beyond
" the reach of policy to find out, for could they fuppofe it policy to diftrefs his
" majefty's troops by retaining fuch a number of men from them, it would not only
" be the breach of their faith that would threaten them; for confider the number of
" prifoners already in the hands of the Britifh army, and alfo confider the chance of war

" that

The Ameri-
cans attack
Trois Ri-
vieres.

General Carleton, now reinforced by an additional number of troops from England, haftened to Trois Rivieres, fituated half-way between Montreal and Quebec. That place, however, the Americans had deferted, and retreated as far as the river Sorrel, a diftance of one hundred and fifty miles. Here they halted, and were joined by reinforcements fent by congrefs. On the ftrength of thefe they refolved to make an attempt on Trois Rivieres. On this expedition two thoufand men were difpatched under the command of general Thomfon. Coafting the lake St. Peter's on the fouth fide, they proceeded to the river Nicolet, which commences at the extremity of the lake, and difcharges itfelf into the river St. Laurence. The banks of the Nicolet are covered with a thick wood. Here they remained all day. At night they croffed over to a place called Point

" that may yet throw greater numbers into their hands. Will people reft content when they
" find their own rulers willing to let them remain prifoners in the hands of what they them-
" felves term (though unjuftly) a mercilefs people; or will they not, fired with refentment for
" fuch inhuman treatment, take arms to fupprefs the power that regards them no longer than
" while their blood is fpilling in their fervice? If this, which appears too probable, fhould
" happen, confider whether thofe perfons will not be followed by a number of their friends,
" which muft naturally make a great divifion in the colonies. Then take a view of Grea
" Britain and her allies pouring on you, and let the moft fanguine expecter in America there
" judge how long the colonies, thus divided, can ftand the fury of the combat. I know your
" influence has been great, and for that reafon have written, that you may, if poffible, yet pre-
" vent America from being branded with the name of injuftice. If you fufpect I write this
" for the fake of getting my own liberty, your fufpicions wrong me; it is not my confine-
" ment, but the breach of a treaty, which even favages have ever held facred, that caufes me
" to write.

    " You will be fo kind as to convey the inclofed to my wife, and if ever I had fo much of
" your love as to demand any favour of you, let this be the time I may implore your affiftance
" for my diftreffed wife and helplefs orphans. May God grant that I may once more fee them;
" till when,   " I am

            (A true copy.)   " Your affectionate brother,

                                              " EBEN. SULLIVAN."

    " To the hon. general John Sullivan, in Durham county,
        " in New Hampfhire, near Portfmouth."

du Lac, where they landed, and immediately proceeded to Trois Rivieres. A Canadian peasant, however, as soon as they had landed, hastened before them to general Frazer at Trois Rivieres, to inform him of their operations. General Frazer immediately landed a body of troops and some field-pieces, and prepared to receive them. General Nesbit, at the same time, posted his detachment in the enemy's rear, and effectually cut off a retreat by the common road, while major Grant taking possession of the bridge, rendered their escape over the river De Loup impracticable.

On the arrival of the enemy at Trois Rivieres, a furious attack was commenced, which proved unsuccessful. General Frazer repulsed them with great loss; and their commander, general Thompson, with about two hundred of his men, were taken prisoners. A large body, under the command of colonel Allen, who afterwards commanded a provincial regiment in his majesty's service, knowing that their retreat by the common road had been cut off, retired into a wood on their left, which was full of deep swamps. Here they remained in great distress till next day, when sir Guy Carleton, who had arrived from Quebec, ordering major Grant to relinquish the possession of the bridge over the river De Loup, they fortunately effected their escape. The enemy, however, were pursued by water, but for some unknown reason the pursuit was discontinued on the arrival of the British troops at Sorrel. It was generally believed that if, instead of coming to anchor, general Carleton had continued the pursuit, which he might have done, as the wind was as favourable as it could possibly be, he would undoubtedly have arrived at Chamblée ten or twelve hours before general Sullivan, who was encumbered with heavy cannon and baggage. In this case Sullivan would have been compelled to lay down his arms; general Arnold would have been intercepted at Montreal, where he remained till the sixteenth of June;

Repulsed with great loss.

C H A P.
V.
⌣⌣⌣
1776.

June.

and Ticonderoga, alfo, would have been taken, as no troops had been ftationed there for its defence.

General Burgoyne, who had arrived with the laft reinforcements from England, now proceeded, in purfuit of the continental army, up the river to St. John's, but under orders from general fir Guy Carleton, not to rifk an engagement, until he fhould be fuftained by another column on his right, directed to proceed to Montreal. This great precaution of the commander in chief gave the Americans an opportunity of making their efcape.

The Americans driven from Canada.

The Americans had now entirely quitted Canada, having in their retreat from Montreal and St. John's, croffed the lake Champlain, and ftationed themfelves at Crown Point; which poft it was not judged expedient by the Britifh commanders, at prefent, to attack.

Efforts on the fide of the Britifh government in North Carolina.

It has already been mentioned that Mr. Martin, governor of North Carolina, had been obliged to flee for fhelter, like the governors of other provinces, to a fhip. In this fituation, however, he was not inactive: He had, by means of his emiffaries, formed a junction between fome Scotch emigrants, and a band of refolute unruly men, called Regulators, who had long lived in a wandering ftate of independence, their chief occupation being that of hunting. The command of thefe parties was given to the colonels Macdonald and Macleod, who, by the governor's direction, erected the king's ftandard, to which he fummoned all perfons to repair. This force was intended to act in conjunction with a body of troops expected early in the fpring, which, however, did not arrive in time for co-operation. The Highlanders were to march down the northernmoft branch of Cape Fear to Wilmington, a town about twenty-four miles from the Fork, where they were to be met by the king's troops, and fuch veffels of war, of eafy draught of water, as could come up there: A plan which, if it had been adhered

to,

to, bid fair to fecure the allegiance of the inhabitants of Cape Fear, and of confequence extending more or lefs influence over the other parts of this province. In the mean time thofe who had ufurped the government, directed that fix regiments of continental troops fhould be raifed in North Carolina; one of which was to be ftationed at Wilmington, under the command of colonel James Moore, a man of the moft juft fame in that part of the province, who had formerly been lieutenant-colonel of provincials, under his majefty's government; a man of an active, humane, and gallant difpofition, but little acquainted with military operations. On the other hand, the loyalifts were by no means inactive; a number of the inhabitants in the counties of Orange and Chatham, many of whom were formerly diftinguifhed by the name of Regulators, agreed to act in concert with the Highlanders: In confequence of which, a council was formed of fome of the leaders of the back-country men, and the chiefs of the Highlanders. The governor appointed Mr. Macdonald to the command, with the rank of brigadier-general, and gave a lieutenant-colonel's commiffion to Mr. Macleod, who was to be fecond in command. The other officers were nominated by the council, fuch as were moft agreeable to their leaders: It happened unfortunately, however, that general Clinton did not arrive as foon as was expected; and in the month of January 1776, it was neceffary to embody the loyalifts, as the only chance of keeping them fteady in their intentions, and which was to take place on a certain day, at the town of Crofs Creek, which they had fixed upon as their head-quarters and place of rendezvous. Thefe operations, however fecretly they were intended to be carried on, did not elude the vigilance of the popular leaders; and as foon as it was known that the loyalifts were embodying, the continental regiment at Wilmington, and fuch of the rebel militia as could be collected, were ordered to march under the command of colonel James Moore, to intercept their

A a 2   progrefs

progrefs from Crofs Creek to Wilmington. The troops collected on this occafion amounted to between eight and nine hundred, and they marched up the north-weft of Cape Fear, without meeting any of the loyalifts, who remained embodied at Crofs Creek. The rebel troops croffed Rock-Fifh, which is a creek with very high banks, and there is a bridge over its end, which is about fix miles from Crofs Creek; upon the weftern fide of this bridge the rebels encamped, and remained there for three days, during which time nothing took place but meffages by flags of truce, relative to fuch perfons as were occafionally taken prifoners by each party.

It unfortunately happened that there were great divifions in the councils of the loyalifts. That unanimity, neceffary to vigorous and decided meafures, was wanting; and it may be prefumed they did not mean to act offenfively, unlefs impelled to it by neceffity; or otherwife the infecure and unfoldierly pofition that the rebels had taken, which was with a deep morafs and fwamp on their left, the north-weft river on their right, and the deep creek of Rock-Fifh in their rear, added to the dread that at that period they entertained of the broad-fword, as well as of the ufe the Highlanders had on former occafions made of it, were circumftances too inviting to be neglected by any who were in the leaft acquainted with military operations.

The loyalifts had certainly nothing elfe in view but to fmuggle themfelves down to Wilmington, regardlefs of what force they left in the rear, provided they met none in front to oppofe their progrefs; and, with this view, after wafting their time in fruitlefs intercourfe with the rebel party at Rock-Fifh, they croffed the north-weft river at Cambleton and Gibfon's ferries, intending to proceed to Wilmington, through a neck of land thinly inhabited, which is called Black River Road, and feparated by that river and the north-weft, and which leads to a place, fituated on the conflux of the north-

eaft

eaſt and north branches of Cape Fear, within half a mile of Wilmington, and called Negro-Head Point.

In the mean time, the embodying of the loyaliſts had ſpread abroad
through the province; and as ſoon as colonel Moore's party had marched from Wilmington, a colonel Caſwell, who commanded one of the
continental regiments in the neighbourhood of Newburn, collected
about four or five hundred men, and with one two-pounder and two
ſwivels marched to the north-weſt of Cape Fear, to act as occaſion
might require. Colonel Caſwell, who was a ſenſible diſcerning man, and
was reckoned one of the beſt woodſmen in the province, readily fore-
ſaw that, if an engagement had taken place between the loyaliſts and
rebel party on the north-weſt ſide of Cape Fear, that their route would
be by the Black River Road; and for that purpoſe he marched to the
road leading to Negro-Head Point, and croſſed Moore's Creek, which
is about twelve miles from thence.

In order to arreſt the progreſs of the loyaliſts, at the ſame time, colonel Moore, finding that the loyaliſts had taken the other ſide of the
river, returned with his troops the ſame way he went up, and
croſſing at the lower ferries, on the north-weſt, effected a junction
with colonel Caſwell, who was at that time encamped on the north
ſide of Moore's Creek bridge. The loyaliſts had proceeded without
interruption within half a mile of the rebel camp; and the night before they intended to attack it, they ſent a flag of truce, by way of
getting intelligence of their ſituation, and which was nearly as hazardous a one, as that which colonel Moore had placed himſelf in
at Rock-Fiſh; but the inſecurity of their poſition did not eſcape the
vigilance of Mr. Caſwell; for as ſoon as night came on, he lighted
up all his fires, which he left burning, in order to deceive the
loyaliſts, retreated over Moore's Creek, took the planks off the bridge,
and greaſed the ſleepers, which are only paſſable by one man at a
time, and placed his men about fifty yards from the banks of the
creek,

creek, behind trees, and such little intrenchments as in the course of the night they were able to throw up.

The loyalists, on the other hand, flushed with the accounts that their flag of truce brought them, determined to attack the rebels in their camp the next morning; and accordingly colonel Macleod, who commanded the attack, seeing the fires in the rebel camp burning, and nobody there, concluded that the rebels had evacuated it through fear, and with about twenty-two of the Highlanders he got over the bridge, intending to attack them sword in hand. But he had no sooner reached the top of the bank than he received two or three bullets, and almost instantly expired; the remainder of the advanced party were all killed and wounded, except colonel Thomas Rutherford and captain Frafer, who escaped unhurt. The loyalists, dismayed at seeing a leader fall in whom they had so much confidence, after firing off some of their firelocks (which were levelled too high to do any execution), broke and disperfed, every one taking the nearest way he could through the woods to his own home. Those from the back country were more successful in their retreat, as being better woodsmen than the Highlanders, the leaders of whom were almost all taken, together with general Macdonald, and sent off under a guard to different prisons at the northward. The rebels had one or two slightly wounded; the loyalists, about eight killed and fourteen wounded, of whom the greater part died. And thus unfortunately ended the first enterprise in the Carolinas in support of his majesty's government.

Colonel Moore was afterwards a major-general in the rebel service, and colonel Cafwell was one of their governors; and both behaved with great lenity and moderation towards the loyalists while they continued in power. The army of the loyalists consisted of about eighteen hundred.

The

The governors of the several colonies, in their representations to the government of Great Britain, had adduced many reasons on which they founded the following suppositions: That on account of the insufficiency of strength in the different provinces, those who were well affected to Great Britain were restrained from taking an active part against the Americans; but that, if the mother-country would provide a respectable force to countenance and co-operate with them, they would immediately attach themselves to her cause. In consequence of these representations, the fifteenth, twenty-eighth, thirty-third, thirty-seventh, fifty-fourth, and fifty-seventh regiments, with seven companies of the forty-sixth regiment, embarked from Cork, on the twelfth of February 1776, under the command of lord Cornwallis, in several transports under the convoy of sir Peter Parker. This is the force above alluded to, intended to co-operate with the loyalists in North Carolina. After a long voyage of near three months, occasioned by the improper lateness of their departure from Great Britain, all the fleet, except some few ships, arrived at Cape Fear, in North Carolina, on the third of May. General Clinton, who had quitted Boston in December, immediately took the command of the troops, and issued a proclamation, in which he invited the inhabitants of the several colonies to return to their allegiance, and to place themselves under the protection of the British government.

The effect produced by this proclamation was trifling, and the cause of Great Britain acquired by it but a small addition of adherents.

The remainder of the fleet being not yet arrived, general Clinton resolved to make a small diversion, the principal object of which was to obtain a supply of cattle, sheep, and vegetables. Four companies of light infantry, with the thirty-third and thirty-seventh regiments, embarking in flat-bottomed boats, proceeded to the town of

Brunswick,

Brunfwick, fituated on a fmall river to the north-weftward of Cape Fear. On the approach of the troops the inhabitants abandoned their habitations, and after furprifing a party of the Americans, and fecuring a quantity of provifions, the detachment returned on board their refpective fhips. It was expected that the troops from Ireland would have arrived two months earlier than they did. General Clinton's orders were to try if any of the fouthern provinces would take up arms in favour of Britain; in which cafe he was to have left a body of troops to affift thofe loyalifts; but he was inftructed to repair with the remainder of the troops to New York harbour, by fuch time as it was probable that the commander in chief would arrive there, from Halifax, to begin the great operations for that campaign. The arrival of the troops at Cape Fear was fo tardy, that it was obvious that no time could be fpared fufficient to make a proper trial of the affections of any of thofe provinces. General Clinton, however, thought he might avail himfelf of the force collected under his command to attempt a fecondary purpofe, fuggefted by the information which reached him during his ftay in Cape Fear river, and which it was hoped might be completed within the time allowed him by his inftructions. The trade carried on from the harbour of Charleftown was the great fupport of the funds for the warlike preparations of the fouthern colonies. A fort built on Sullivan's Ifland protected and commanded the channel of the harbour. The capture of that fort was the object of the expedition to South Carolina. The poffeffion of that fort would give to the Britifh the entire dominion of the harbour of Charleftown. It was therefore projected that, if the fort fhould be taken, a fufficient garrifon fhould be left for its defence; but that operations, for the prefent, in this quarter, fhould be carried no farther.

General Clinton having waited till the thirtieth of May for the fhips he expected, refolved to wafte no more time, but to fet fail for

3   South

South Carolina. Fortunately however thofe fhips joined him off Cape Fear, and the whole fleet now proceeding to Charleftown, arrived there on the fourth of June. The general immediately taking poffeffion of Long Ifland, the loyalifts of which had been difarmed by the Americans in January, encamped the troops upon it.

Half a mile from Charleftown harbour the Americans had conftructed a ftrong fortification on Sullivan's Ifland, which confifted of twenty-two thirty-two pounders, and was garrifoned by three hundred men. As it commanded the harbour, general Clinton refolved to attempt the reduction of it. Lee, the American general, who had watched with the utmoft anxiety every operation of general Clinton, and who had followed him through the feveral provinces he had vifited, was at this period encamped on a fpot northward from Sullivan's Ifland, with which he held a communication by a bridge of boats. Two batteries of cannon and mortars, conftructed on the point of Long Ifland to anfwer thofe of the enemy, and to co-operate with the floating batteries deftined to cover the landing of the troops on Sullivan's Ifland, being completed, it was determined to commence the reduction of the fort on the twenty-eighth of June. At half paft ten o'clock in the morning fir Peter Parker, in the Briftol, made the fignal for action to the following fhips—the Experiment of fifty guns; the Active, Solebay, Actæon, Syren, and Sphynx, frigates; the Thunder bomb, and the Friendfhip armed fhip of twenty-four guns. At a quarter paft eleven, all the fhips having got fprings upon their cables, began a moft tremendous fire upon the fort. Three of the frigates, the Actæon, Syren, and Sphynx, got aground. The two laft however hove off, but the firft ftuck faft, and was fet on fire on the fucceeding morning, in order to prevent her falling into the hands of the enemy.

Vol. I.   B b   At

At the same time that the fleet began firing, the batteries on Long Island opened. At twelve o'clock the light-infantry, grenadiers, and the fifteenth regiment, embarked in boats, the floating batteries and armed craft getting under way at the same time to cover their landing on Sullivan's Island. Scarcely, however, had the detachment proceeded from Long Island, before they were ordered to disembark, and return to their encampment: And it muft be confeffed that, if they had landed, they would have had to ftruggle with difficulties almoft infurmountable. The ground on which the fort ftood was infulated by a broad and deep trench cut acrofs the ifland, and this canal under the immediate command of the guns of Fort Sullivan.

In the mean time the ships continued an unremitting fire upon the fort. Between one and two o'clock the fire of the enemy flackened for a fhort time, owing to a want of ammunition. Having obtained however a frefh fupply, their fire was renewed, and ceafed not till between nine and ten o'clock. In this day's attack the Briftol and Experiment fuffered moft; the fire of the enemy being principally directed againft them, they were left almoft wrecks upon the water. Early on the morning of the twenty-ninth, the light-infantry, grenadiers, and the fifteenth regiment, were again embarked, and almoft immediately afterwards ordered to difembark. In this inactive ftate did affairs remain till the fifteenth of July, when orders were iffued to the troops to embark on board the tranfports. Sir H. Clinton had been greatly deceived in his information. The paffage was not fordable in the rear of the fort; for fir Henry and feveral other officers waded up to their fhoulders, and then, on finding that the depth of water increafed, returned. On putting the boats, in which were the artillery, into the water, it was found that they let in the water fo faft that they muft fink. The officers and men of the artillery who were in them had nearly been loft. The ships kept at too great a diftance: They might have gone

2   much

much nearer, and, if they had, would have done great execution by pouring broadfides into the fort; but their diftance was fuch that they did little or no damage to the fort. The Americans were much elated upon this fuccefs, which confiderably inflamed the fpirit of revolt.

On the twenty-firft, the army failed for New York, under the convoy of the Solebay frigate, the reft of the fleet being under the neceffity of remaining to refit. Thus ended an expedition from which the friends of government had predicted the moft beneficial confequences.

B b 2

CHAP. VI.

Proceedings of Congrefs—Declaration of Independence—Arrival of. Lord Howe from England—Battle of Long Ifland—Overtures on the part of the Britifh Commanders for Peace.—1776.

IT will be remembered that early in the fummer of 1775 congrefs had voted that the affemblies of the feveral colonies fhould give inftructions to their delegates relative to the independence of America. However premature fuch a vote might be thought at that period by moderate men, the fubfequent fuccefs of the American arms had entirely overcome their objections to its tendency, and had paved the way for another vote more open and more ample in its nature.

Acts of the American congrefs.

On the fifteenth of May 1776 it was refolved " to recommend to the various affemblies and conventions in the United States of America, where no form of government adequate to the exigencies of affairs had yet been adopted, to eftablifh fuch a conftitution as fhould be moft conducive to the public welfare and fecurity." This vote was immediately publifhed in the Penfylvania Gazette, with a preamble, ftating that, as " his Britannic majefty had, with the concurrence of his parliament, excluded the inhabitants of the colonies from his protection," it was deemed neceffary and expedient to fupprefs and abolifh the power and conftitution which had been derived from that fource.

The affemblies of the colonies readily complied with the recommendations of congrefs, except Maryland, whofe delegates, together
with

with the Penfylvania affembly, feceded from congrefs. Virginia, however, feemed to poffefs more of the fpirit that animated the congrefs than the other provinces; for on the day on which the above refolution paffed at Philadelphia, the affembly of Virginia, which was then fitting at Williamfburg, inftructed their delegates to propofe a refolution of a fimilar tendency to that of congrefs; appointing at the fame time a committee to prepare the plan of a new conftitution. They alfo publifhed the following declaration of rights:

1. That all men are born equally free, poffeffing certain natural rights, of which they cannot by any compact deprive their pofterity.

2. That all power is vefted in the people, from whom it is derived.

3. That they have an unalienable indefeafible right to reform, alter, or abolifh, their form of government at pleafure.

4. That the idea of an hereditary firft magiftrate is unnatural and abfurd;—and,

5. That no government, independent of, or feparated from, the government of Virginia, ought to prevail within the limits of Virginia.

In purfuance of the recommendation of congrefs, moft of the provinces had inftructed their delegates on the fubject of independence. The cataftrophe was now at hand, and on the fourth of July 1776, America was fevered for ever from Great Britain by a refolution, which, after enumerating the feveral grievances already ftated, declared, " that, on account of the king of Great Britain having refufed to redrefs them, the inhabitants of the United Colonies were thereby difcharged and abfolved from all allegiance and obedience to him."

Declaration of independence.

Previoufly

Previoufly to the paffing of this refolution it had been difpatched to the different provincial affemblies, in order that it might be ratified immediately after it had paffed the congrefs. No oppofition was made on this account in any of the provinces, except in Maryland, where the ratification was rejected by the affembly, who ordered their delegates to fecede from congrefs. A body of the people however obliged them to return immediately, and the affembly were compelled to ratify the important refolution. This unanimity was in a great degree produced by the numerous publications that appeared about this period. Of thefe the moft diftinguifhed was a work entitled Common Senfe, the author Mr. Thomas Paine, who has fince rendered his name fo famous on the theatre of Europe, and of the world. Such were the meafures which America had adopted previoufly to the arrival of lord Howe from England.

Arrival of a
fleet under
lord Howe
from England.

The army having now fufficiently recovered from the fatigue and ficknefs produced by their confined fituation in Bofton, departed from Hallifax on the eleventh of June, and proceeded to Sandy Hook, to wait for the arrival of the reinforcements from Europe. It may not be unneceffary to mention here, that it was the general opinion that fir William Howe fhould have gone to Long Ifland inftead of Hallifax; the foldiers might then have been fupplied from the ifland with cattle in abundance, and if there had been no tents they might have been hutted, as the Americans were, and by that means have been enabled to have opened the campaign much earlier. The army reached Sandy Hook on the twenty-ninth of June. General Howe, who had been there for fome time, had received from major-general Tryon, the governor of New York, who had been obliged to take refuge on board a man of war, the following account of the fituation of the Americans in that province:

Having

Having obtained undoubted information that the Britifh armaments were to be directed againft New York, they were endeavouring, by ftrong entrenchments, both there and on Long Ifland,
to obftruct the paffage of the fleet up the north and eaft rivers. To
increafe thefe impediments, chains of funken veffels were laid in
various parts of the channel. They had alfo magazines of warlike
ftores, and a large train of artillery. In confequence of this information, and certain that fuccours from England would foon arrive,
general Howe refolved to wafte no more time at Sandy Hook, but
to proceed with the army to Staten Ifland, fituated oppofite
to Long Ifland, where he could watch the operations of the
enemy. Accordingly, on the third of July, he landed the troops on
the Ifland without oppofition, the enemy abandoning it on his approach. The troops thus landed, confifted of two battalions of
light-infantry, two of grenadiers, the fourth, fifth, tenth, feventeenth, twenty-fecond, twenty-third, twenty-feventh, thirty-fifth,
thirty-eighth, fortieth, forty-fecond, forty-third, forty-fourth, forty-
fifth, forty-ninth, fifty-fecond, fifty-fifth, fixty-third, and fixty-fourth
regiments of foot, and part of the forty-fixth and feventy-firft regiments, and the feventeenth regiment of light dragoons. There were
befides two companies of volunteers raifed at New York, confifting of
one hundred men each. The total amount was nine thoufand men.
It had been determined to land on Long Ifland; but upon further
confideration it was thought more advifable to wait for the arrival
of the troops from Europe, and to land in the mean time upon
Staten Ifland.

On the firft of July lord Howe, and the long-expected fuccours
from England, arrived at Sandy Hook, and thence proceeded to
Staten Ifland. The reinforcement brought from England amounted, with the troops already in America, to near thirty thoufand
men. The late arrival of this reinforcement is to be particularly
                                                              lamented,

lamented, becaufe, for fome time before this period, general Wafhington's army did not amount to nine thoufand men fit for duty;
two thoufand of whom were entirely deftitute of arms. It muft
therefore be fufficiently apparent, that moft important advantages
would have accrued to the Britifh caufe if the campaign had commenced two months earlier than it did. The American army muft
then have been inevitably overwhelmed by the fuperiority of numbers and of difcipline oppofed to it. So well convinced was colonel
Jofeph Read, the American adjutant-general, of this fuperiority,
that, in a letter to a member of congrefs, he ftated the amount of
the American army to be lefs than eight thoufand men, " all of
" whom, from the general to the private, were exceedingly difcou-
" couraged." Lord Howe had been appointed to the command of
the fleet deftined to co-operate with his brother general Howe,
with the unanimous approbation of the people of England. Whatever may be thought of lord Howe as a naval commander, there
was a certain hauteur and frigid referve in his deportment that but
ill qualified him for the office of a foother and a mediator between
two contending parties, irritated againft each other almoft to a degree
of madnefs. His lordfhip brought with him a commiffion
fanctioned by parliament, empowering him and his brother
to treat with the Americans. Their powers were ample
and extenfive. They were invefted with the ability of making
peace or of continuing the war—of receiving the fubmiffion of
all or any one of the colonies—of pardoning or of punifhing
delinquents.

At this period, the celebrated Dr. Franklin, who had for many years
refided in England as agent for the colonies of Maffachufets and Penfylvania, retiring to America foon after his difmiffion from his office
of joint poft-mafter-general of America, was a leading member of the
congrefs. To him lord Howe addreffed a letter foon after his arrival. In

it

it he informed him of the nature of his commiffion; expreffing, at the fame time, hopes that he would find in America the fame difpofition for peace that he brought with him, and concluding with requeft-ing his aid to accomplifh this defired end. Dr. Franklin, in anfwer, informed his lordfhip, that, preparatory to any propofitions of amity or peace, it would be required that Great Britain fhould acknow-ledge the independence of America, defray the expences of the war, and indemnify the colonies for burning their towns. This, how-ever, he ftated to be only his own opinion, and that what he had faid was not authorifed by thofe in whom the Americans had invefted the power of peace or war. Lord Howe alfo addreffed a circular letter, accompanied with a declaration, to feveral of the late governors of the provinces, acquainting them with the power with which he was invefted. Thefe letters and the declaration were forwarded to con-grefs, and publifhed in the different newfpapers: At the fame time his lordfhip opened a correfpondence with general Wafhington, which produced no beneficial confequence to the Britifh caufe.

Lord Howe and his brother, unwilling to accede to thofe condi-tions which had been ftated by Dr. Franklin to be the only terms that would be accepted, and feeing, from the declaration of independ-ence, and the vigorous preparations of the enemy, that nothing lefs would be accepted, refolved to commence hoftilities immediately.

The troops under general Clinton, from the fouthward, having joined the grand army, the campaign opened on the twenty-fecond of Auguft. A divifion of four thoufand men, under the command of general Clinton, landed without oppofition in Gravefend Bay, Long Ifland, to the right of the Narrows, their difembarkation be-ing covered by three frigates and two bomb-ketches: This divifion having landed without refiftance, the reft of the army and artillery were alfo landed. The advanced party of the enemy fled at the ap-proach of the army, fetting fire, on their retreat, to all the houfes and

Vol. I.   C c   granaries,

granaries, and feeking refuge in the woody heights that commanded the way which the Englifh were under the neceffity of paffing. The Englifh poffeffed an extent, reaching from the Narrows through Gravefend and Utrecht. The Americans, to the number of fifteen thoufand, were pofted on a peninfula, between Mill Creek, a little above Red Hook, and an elbow of the river, called Wallabach Bay. They had conftructed ftrong fortifications oppofite to New York, from which they were feparated by the Eaft River, at the diftance of a mile. A line of intrenchment from the Mill Creek enclofed a large fpace of ground, on which ftood the American camp. This line was not only fecured by abbatis, but flanked by ftrong redoubts, and lined with fpears or lances provided againft affault. From this poft ten thoufand men, under the command of general Putnam, were detached. Their object was to occupy the heights which obliquely interfected the ifland, and to defend againft the progrefs of the Englifh, the defiles which led through thofe hills.

Oppofite the centre of Putnam's line ftood, in the plain, the village of Flat Bufh. To this town the Heffians, under general De Heifter, were advanced, occupying entirely the attention of the Americans, and frequently fkirmifhing with their patroles. In the mean time fir Henry Clinton and fir William Erfkine, having reconnoitred the pofition of the enemy, faw that it would not be a difficult matter to turn their left flank, which would either oblige them to rifk an engagement, or to retire under manifeft difadvantage. This intelligence being communicated to fir William Howe, he confented to make the attempt. Accordingly the right wing of the Englifh army moved, confifting of a ftrong advanced corps, commanded by general Clinton, fupported by the brigades under lord Percy. The commander in chief himfelf marched with this corps, which quitted its camp at nine o'clock at night on the twenty-fixth of Auguft, croffing the country, by Flat Lands, in order to fecure

2   a pafs

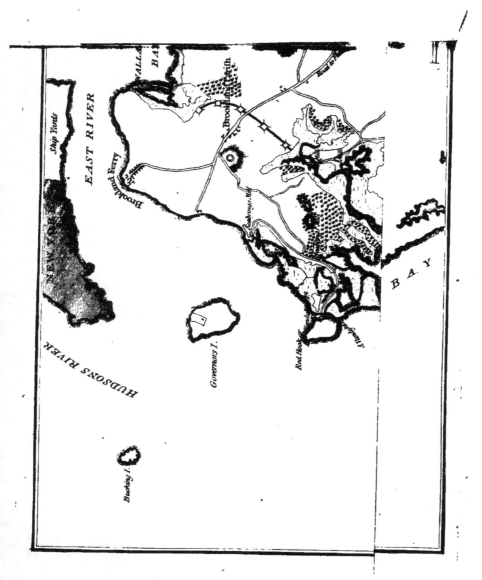

a paſs over the heights of Guiana, on the road to Bedford. This páſs the enemy had neglected to ſecure by detachments, on account of its great diſtance. In order to watch it, however, they ſent out occaſional patroles of cavalry: But one of theſe being intercepted by a Britiſh advanced guard, the paſs was gained without any alarm being communicated to the Americans. At nine o'clock in the morning the Britiſh paſſed the heights and reached Bedford. An attack was immediately begun on the enemy's left; they made but a feeble reſiſtance, and retired from the woody grounds to their lines, into which they threw themſelves in evident confuſion. It is to be lamented that this advantage was not purſued; for in the confuſion into which the enemy were thrown by the rapid march of the Engliſh army, a moſt deciſive victory would have undoubtedly accrued to the Britiſh arms. The works of the enemy could not have reſiſted an attack, when it is conſidered that it might have been made by that part of the army under ſir William Howe, which had not been engaged, and which therefore poſſeſſed a manifeſt ſuperiority over troops fatigued by conteſt, exhauſted by hard labour, and diſheartened by partial defeat.

As ſoon as the firing on the enemy's left was heard, general De Heiſter, with a column of Heſſians from Flat Buſh, attacked the centre of the Americans. After a warm engagement the enemy was routed and driven into the woods, with the loſs of three pieces of cannon. The left column, led by general Grant, advancing from the Narrows by the edge of the bay, in order to divert the attention of the enemy from the principal attack on the right, about midnight fell in with their advanced guard, ſtationed at a ſtrong paſs, which, however, they immediately abandoned, and retired to a very advantageous poſt, where they kept their ground. On the advancement of the Engliſh, a furious cannonade commenced on both ſides, which was continued with unceaſing perſeverance till the enemy heard the firing at Bed-

C c 2
ford.

ford. The Americans in this quarter did not attempt to retire until they received news of the total rout of the rest of their army. Apprehensive then of being unable to regain their lines, they made a sudden movement to secure a retreat, by crossing a morass to Mill Creek, which covered the right of their works. But this movement was made in much disorder and confusion; general Grant, however, did not take adequate advantage of it, for had he moved rapidly to the edge of the morass, through which, and over a mill-dam, the principal part of them escaped, the greatest number of the detachment, as well as of those who fled from Flat Bush, must have either been drowned or taken prisoners.

Thus ended the operations of the day : Victory was certainly on the side of the English; but it was not so decisive as it might have been, owing to the restrictions imposed by the commander in chief. The loss of the Americans was great. Two thousand were either killed on the field, drowned, or taken prisoners : And among the latter, generals Sullivan, Udell, and lord Sterling. The Maryland regiment suffered most severely, having lost upwards of two hundred and sixty men ; which was much regretted, as that regiment was composed of young men of the best families in the country. The royal army took six pieces of brass ordnance. The loss on the part of the English did not exceed three hundred in killed and wounded ; of which number between sixty and seventy were killed. Among the killed was lieutenant-colonel Grant, of the fortieth regiment; among the wounded, lieutenant-colonel Monckton. The British troops, on this occasion, displayed great activity and valour : So impetuous was their courage, that it was not without difficulty that they could be restrained from attacking the American lines ; and had they been permitted to go on, in the judgment of most men, including sir William Howe himself, they would have carried them.

August.

" But," says the general, " as it was apparent that the lines must

" become

" become ours, at a very cheap rate, by regular approaches, I
" would not rifk the lofs that might have been fuftained in the
" affault, and ordered them back to a hollow way, out of the
" reach of the mufquetry."

On the evening of the twenty-feventh, our army encamped in
front of the enemy's lines; and on the twenty-eighth broke ground
about fix hundred yards from one of the redoubts on the left. The
Americans, finding that it was impoffible to maintain their poft on
Long Ifland, evacuated their lines on the twenty-ninth, and made
good their retreat to New York. At firft the wind and tide were both
unfavourable to the Americans; nor was it thought poffible that
they could have effected their retreat on the evening of the twenty-
ninth, until about eleven o'clock, the wind fhifting, and the fea becoming more calm, the boats were enabled to pafs. Another remarkable circumftance was, that on Long Ifland hung a thick fog,
which prevented the Britifh troops from difcovering the operations
of the enemy; while on the fide of New York the atmofphere was
perfectly clear. The retreat was effected in thirteen hours, though
nine thoufand men had to pafs over the river, befides field artillery,
ammunition, provifions, cattle, horfes, and carts.

The circumftances of this retreat were particularly glorious to the
Americans. They had been driven to the corner of an ifland, where
they were hemmed in within the narrow fpace of two fquare miles.
In their front was an encampment of near twenty thoufand men; in
their rear, an arm of the fea, a mile wide, which they could not crofs,
but in feveral embarkations. Notwithftanding thefe difficulties, they
fecured a retreat without the lofs of a man. The pickets of the
Englifh army arrived only in time to fire upon their rear-guard, already too far removed from the fhore to receive any damage. Sir
William Howe had early intelligence fent him of the retreat of the

3   Americans;

Americans; but a confiderable time had elapfed before a purfuit was ordered. Sir William Howe at length, however, defired lord Percy to order a purfuit; but it was too late. The enemy had effected their retreat, which was rendered lefs hazardous from the want of frigates in the Eaft River between Long Ifland and New York. Had any armed fhips been ftationed there, it would have been impoffible for them to have made their efcape. The Eaft River is deep enough for a feventy-four gun fhip to ride at anchor. Wafhington thought himfelf happy in getting fafe with his papers from Long Ifland, having croffed to New York in a fmall boat. Had two or even one frigate moored as high up as Red-Hook, as the Phœnix and Rofe men of war had done before, the one carrying forty-four guns, and the other twenty-eight, the retreat of the Americans would have been cut off moft completely; and indeed fo decided were the Americans themfelves in this opinion, that, had only a fingle frigate been ftationed in the Eaft River, they muft have furrendered at difcretion. It is to be obferved, that in the very fame boats in which the Americans croffed from New York to Long Ifland, they re-croffed after their defeat from Long Ifland to New York, the boats having lain for three days on the Long Ifland fhore in readinefs to carry them off. Now it is evident that this fmall craft, by the above precaution, might have been effectually deftroyed.

In reviewing the actions of men, the hiftorian is often at a lofs to conjecture the fecret caufes that gave them birth. It cannot be denied but that the American army lay almoft entirely at the will of the Englifh. That they were therefore fuffered to retire in fafety, has by fome been attributed to the reluctance of the commander in chief to fhed the blood of a people fo nearly allied to that fource from whence he derived all his authority and power. We are rather
inclined

inclined to adopt this idea, and to fuppofe motives of miftaken
policy, than to leave ground for an imagination that the efcape
of the Americans refulted from any want of exertion on the
part of fir William Howe, or deficiency in the military fcience.
He might poffibly have conceived that the late victory would
produce a revolution in fentiment capable of terminating the
war without the extremity which it appeared to be, beyond all
poffibility of doubt, in his power to enforce.

About this time a reinforcement arrived under the command of
fir George Collier, after a very long paffage, occafioned by their
too late departure from England.

The Englifh army, being now in poffeffion of Long Ifland, commanded New York; and Governor's Ifland, being of courfe no
longer tenable by the enemy, was alfo evacuated on the night of
the thirtieth of Auguft. Two brigades of Heffians, and one Britifh
brigade, being left at Bedford, the reft of the army was pofted at New
Town, Hell Gate, Bufhwick, and Flufhing. On that part of Long
Ifland oppofite Horan's Hook, where the enemy had thrown up a
ftrong work, two batteries were erected. This work commanded
Hell Gate, a paffage between the iflands of Buchanan, Montrefor,
and the Two Brothers, into the Sound which feparates Long Ifland
from New York and the Connecticut fhore. The Englifh batteries in a fhort time not only filenced the fire of the enemy
from the work, but broke it up entirely, and rendered it utterly in-
defenfible.

In the Sound are three fmall iflands, Barren, Montrefor, and
Buchanan, which are only ufeful inafmuch as they can awe
veffels paffing through the Sound. Of thefe the Englifh took
poffeffion; and thus was all communication with New York prevented by fea.

Whilft

C H A P.
VI.

1776.
Overtures on
the part of
the Britifh
commanders
for peace.

Whilſt theſe operations were carrying on, general Sullivan, who had been taken priſoner on Long Iſland, was difmiſſed on his parole, and difpatched to Philadelphia at his own requeſt, in order to ſubmit ſome propoſitions to congreſs. In thoſe propoſitions lord Howe expreſſed a wiſh to enter into conferences with ſeveral moderate members of congreſs, not as deputies from an independent ſtate, but as private gentlemen of influence in the different colonies. In theſe conferences preliminaries were to be ſettled, on which an accommodation of the differences between the two countries was to be founded. As an inducement to congreſs to comply with theſe propoſitions, it was ſtrongly infiſted that ſo favourable a criſis as the preſent would not again occur; inaſmuch as neither party had been reduced to a ſtate of humiliation by compulſory means, nor to a ſituation where aſſent or ruin was the only alternative.

The congreſs, in reply to this meſſage, acquainted his lordſhip that it was inconfiſtent with their dignity to ſend any of their members to confer with him in a private capacity; and requeſted that they would depute a committee to learn whether his lordſhip had authority to treat with perſons commiſſioned by congreſs, and that they would receive what propoſals he was commanded to offer. Accordingly a committee, confiſting of Dr. Benjamin Franklin, Meſſrs. John Adams and Edward Rutledge, was appointed to wait on lord Howe at Staten Iſland. No advantage could be expected to accrue to the mother-country from ſuch a committee; the members of it being men whoſe principles were violent in the extreme, and who ſought every opportunity of reducing the parent-ſtate to humiliating and mortifying ſituations. In the outſet of the conference lord Howe ſtill adhered to the contents of the meſſage carried to congreſs by general Sullivan, viz. " that though his powers did not " extend ſo far as to treat with the above gentlemen, as a committee
" deputed

" deputed by congrefs, yet he was empowered to enter into a con-
" fultation on the means of reconciling the differences between Great
" Britain and America with any gentleman of influence and im-
" portance." As foon as his lordfhip had made this declaration, the
committee informed him that they fhould not act in any other
character than that with which congrefs had invefted them : Neverthelefs they wifhed to hear any propofals he might have to make.
His lordfhip then informed them that the moft ardent wifh of the
king and government of Great Britain, was, to put an end to the
diffenfions at prefent exifting between the parent-ftate and the colonies. To accomplifh this defire, every act of parliament which had
been thought obnoxious to the latter fhould undergo a revifal, and
every juft caufe of complaint fhould be removed, if the latter would
declare her willingnefs to fubmit to the authority of the Britifh government.

In reply to this offer the committee declared, that an acknowledgment of the fuperiority of Great Britain could not now be expected. They recalled to his lordfhip's remembrance the many petitions that had been prefented by the colonies to parliament and the
king, all of which, particularly the laft, had been treated with dif-
refpect and contempt. They reminded him that it was not America that had fevered herfelf from Great Britain ; but Great Britain
that had feparated herfelf from America. The latter had never declared herfelf independent till the former had denounced war againft
her, and thereby rendered fuch a declaration indifpenfably neceffary.
Befides, even if congrefs wifhed to replace America in her former
fituation, fhe could not carry thefe wifhes into execution; for the
declaration of independence had been made in confequence of the
congregated voice of the whole people, by whom alone it could be
invalidated and abolifhed. But though the Americans defired not

VOL. I.   D d   to

to return under the domination of England, yet they were willing to enter into any treaty that fhould be deemed advantageous to both countries. From this declaration of the committee, it required very little penetration to difcover that America was refolved to enter into no accommodation; but to procure the acknowledgment of her independence by force. Immediately therefore on being furnifhed with this anfwer, lord Howe put an end to the conference.

When the deputies returned to congrefs they made the following report :—" That it was their opinion that lord Howe's commiffion " did not contain any other powers than thofe of granting pardons, " and of receiving all, or any one, of the colonies into the protection " of the Britifh government, upon fubmiffion. With regard to treat- " ing with congrefs, the commiffioners were totally filent, on account " of their being forbidden to acknowledge the authority of that af- " fembly, and empowered only to treat with the members of it in " their private characters, as men of abilities, weight, or importance." The commiffioners being therefore thus limited in their powers, no firm reliance could be placed on any terms they might propofe or accede to *. Though lord Howe had been thus unfuc- cefsful in his propofitions to the congrefs committee, he thought it neceffary to publifh a declaration to the people of America, wherein, after glancing at the anfwer returned by that committee to his offers of reconciliation, he acquainted them that the parent-ftate was willing to receive into its bofom and protection all who might be willing to return to their former fubmiffion and obedience. His lordfhip was certainly induced to adopt this meafure from the con- viction that a majority of the inhabitants of America were decided-

* It was confidently afferted at Philadelphia that Mr. Rutledge, upon his return, declared that the whole of what had paffed between lord Howe and the committee had not been made public, i. e. the whole of what had been offered by lord Howe.

ly

ly in favour of entering into an accommodation of the differences between the two powers; and this conviction was by no means ill-founded. This declaration however produced but little effect, for thofe who refolved to accede to nothing fhort of an acknowledgment of the independence of America had acquired the fole management of affairs, and had concentered in themfelves all the powers and refources of the country.

C H A P.
VI.
1776.

. D d 2 .

C H A P. VII.

The Americans retreat, and the Englifh Army takes poffeffion of New
York—The Americans greatly difheartened—Defign to burn New
York partly executed—Various Skirmifhing—Battle of White Plains.

C H A P.
VII.
1776.

CONVINCED now that all pacific meafures would be ineffectual, lord Howe refolved to adopt other meafures. It has been before faid that when the provincial forces retreated from Long Ifland they took fhelter in New York. Here they employed themfelves in erecting batteries, and throwing up intrenchments, in order to annoy the Britifh fhipping. Both armies were divided by the Eaft River, the breadth of which, at this part, was about thirteen hundred yards. After a long and fevere cannonade it was refolved to make a defcent on the ifland on which New York ftands. To prevent their intentions from being difcovered by the enemy, five fhips of war moved higher up the Eaft River, while, on the fifteenth of September, feveral flat-bottomed boats were employed in landing the troops.

The firft divifion, confifting of four thoufand men under general Clinton, landed on New York ifland, at a place called Kipp's Bay, about three miles from the town, and took poft on a height called the Inclenberg. The enemy were at this time in poffeffion of very advantageous ground and powerful intrenchments: Neverthelefs, they not only refrained from oppofing the Englifh, but abandoned their works on account of the furious cannonade of the five men of war

I   appointed

appointed to cover the difembarkation of the troops. As the different divifions, landed they pofted themfelves on the high grounds
that ftretch in an afcending direction from the fea-fhore.   At the
fame time a detachment of Heffian troops advanced to New York,
and in their way fell in with a party of the enemy retreating by
the pafs at Blooming Dale.   A fkirmifh enfued, in which the Britifh were victorious, and the Americans loft a brigadier-general and
feveral other officers.   About the fame time another detachment of
the Britifh troops made a movement to the right, in order to attack
a large body of the enemy, who, however, on the approach of the
Englifh, retreated to the main body of the American army pofted on
Morris's Heights.   No attempt being made to defend New York, it
was taken poffeffion of by the Englifh. General Wafhington's army,
at this period, amounted to twenty-three thoufand men, but moft of
thefe, raw, undifciplined, and ill provided with neceffaries.

New York is fituated in an ifland about fifteen miles in length,
but not more than two in breadth; on which account the Englifh
were enabled to extend their camp quite acrofs the ifland, on the
part fartheft from the town.   The enemy were pofted oppofite to
them, and in fuch an advantageous manner that any attack upon
them would have been dangerous and imprudent.   General Wafhington had ftationed four thoufand five hundred men in New York,
which he withdrew on the approach of the Britifh army; fix thoufand five hundred at Haerlem; and twelve thoufand at a place called King's Bridge, which he had fortified in order to fecure a retreat, in cafe he fhould be under the neceffity of relinquifhing his
prefent fituation, to the continent.   And indeed it was peculiarly
fortunate for the enemy that they were thus, in a manner, fecure
from attack, as their ardour had vifibly declined fince their defeat
on Long Ifland.   A paufe was neceffary in order to enable them to
recover their former fpirit.

The

C H A P.
VII.

1776.
The Ameri-
can army
greatly dif-
heartened.

The check at Long Island, and the expulsion from New York, dispirited the American troops greatly. They apprehended every thing, and were in great despair. The militia were impatient to return, and totally disobedient to orders. They went off by half, and in some instances by whole, regiments. What was called their flying camp was literally so. Ravages were committed not only by privates, but, among the New Englanders, by officers. " Almost " every villany and rascality," a gentleman of the army * wrote to his friend, " was daily practised with impunity. Unless some " speedy and effectual means of reform are adopted by congress, our " cause will be lost. As the war must be carried on systematically, " you must establish your army upon a permanent footing, and give " your officers good pay, that they may be, and support the character of, " gentlemen, and not be driven, by a scanty allowance, to the low and " dirty arts which many of them practise, to filch the public of more " money than all the amount of the difference of pay. It is not " strange that there should be a number of bad officers in the con- " tinental service, when you consider that many of them were " chosen by their own men, who elected them, not from a regard to " merit, but from the knowledge they had of their being ready to " associate with them on the footing of equality. It was sometimes " the case, that, when a company was forming, the men would " chuse those for officers who consented to throw their pay into a " joint stock with the privates, from which captains, lieutenants, " ensigns, serjeants, corporals, drummers, and privates, drew equal " shares. Can it then be wondered at, that a captain should be tried " and broken for stealing his soldiers blankets? or that another " officer should be found shaving his men in the face of characters " of distinction ? With an army of force before, and a secret one

* General Read, in a letter to a member of congress, dated July 4th, 1776.

" behind,

" behind, we ftand on a point of land with fix thoufand old
" troops, if a year's fervice can entitle them to that name, and
" about fifteen hundred new levies of this province; many dif-
" affected, and more doubtful.   In this fituation we are. Every man
" in the army, from the general to the private (acquainted with
" our true fituation) is exceedingly difcouraged.   Had I known the
" true pofture of affairs, no confideration would have tempted me
" to have taken an active part in this fcene : And this fentiment is
" univerfal.   General Howe is fufficiently ftrong, confidering the
" goodnefs of his troops, to make a fuccefsful attempt on the
" Americans; but being in daily expectation of reinforcements
" from Europe, he will undoubtedly remain inactive until their
" arrival."

The greateft animofities, too, prevailed between the northern and
fouthern troops. Their reflections on each other were mutual and
equally illiberal.   Their variances were fo great, that the Penfylva-
nians and New Englanders would as foon have fought each other as
the enemy.   Officers of all ranks were indifcriminately treated with
the greateft fcurrility and abufe, for no other reafon than that they
were born on this or that fide of Hudfon's River; juft as formerly,
in England, violent difputes were carried on between the inhabitants of the fouth and thofe of the north fide of the Trent.

As foon as the Englifh had taken poffeffion of New York, general Howe, and fome other general officers, repaired to the houfe of
a Mrs. Murray, with whom they remained in converfation fo long,
that general Putnam, with three thoufand five hundred men, was
enabled to make good his retreat to the main body of the American
army.   But delay is not the only error imputable to the commander in chief in this tranfaction.   It has been mentioned that the
American army was pofted at Haerlem and King's Bridge : Its pofition at this little place was for the purpofe of fecuring a retreat

to

to the continent, fhould the preffure of affairs render fuch a meafure neceffary. Inftead, therefore, of directing his attention to New York, fir William Howe ought to have thrown his army round King's Bridge, by which means he would have hemmed in the whole American army; and fuch a ftep was not at all impracticable, when we confider the extent of the military and naval refources fubfervient to his will.

September.

On the morning of the fixteenth of September, a detachment was fent out from the main body of the Americans to a wood facing the left flank of the Englifh army. Three companies of our light-infantry were difpatched to diflodge them. The enemy, with a feeming intention of retreating to the main body, retired into the interior parts of the wood, where they were reinforced by another detachment; which made it neceffary that the remainder of the light-infantry, with the forty-fecond regiment, fhould be fent to fupport the companies that were engaged. The action was carried on by reinforcements on both fides, and became very warm. The enemy, however, poffeffed a great advantage from the circumftance of engaging within half a mile of their intrenched camp, whence they could be fupplied with frefh troops as often as occafion required. Victory, neverthelefs, was on the part of the loyalifts; and the Americans retreated with the lofs of three hundred killed and wounded.

The Englifh encampment, it has been faid, extended acrofs the ifland, on each fide of which were ftationed fhips of war, in order to fecure the right and left flanks. The enemy faw the advantage of this difpofition of the fhipping, and attempted to make fome impreffion on it by fending down four fire-fhips, which, however, by the fkilfulnefs of the commanders of the Englifh veffels, were prevented from doing any damage. It had been refolved by the Americans, in cafe the Englifh fhould obtain poffeffion of New York, to fet fire to it in feveral places, previous to the evacuation of it by the

Defign to burn New York partly executed.

the enemy. The fpeed, however, with which they were obliged to quit it, had rendered it impoffible for them to put their defigns into execution: Neverthelefs, feveral perfons having purpofely fecreted themfelves in the deferted houfes, contrived to fet fire to the town, on the morning of the twenty-firft of September, in feveral places. One-third of the town was thus deftroyed; and had not the military exerted themfelves in a moft extraordinary manner, the whole would have been levelled with the ground. The flames firft broke out at fome wooden ftore-houfes, at the fouthern-moft or windward part of New York, near the Whitehall-ftairs, juft by the battery, and foon became general up the Broadway, &c. by the violence of the wind blowing burnt fhingles from the houfes on fire to others, and fetting them on fire in rapid fucceffion. The wind was fo ftrong, that it was almoft impoffible to face it, for fmoke and flakes of fire. The next day (Saturday) a great many cart-loads of bundles of pine fticks, dipped at each end for five or fix inches in brimftone and other combuftible matters, were found concealed in cellars of houfes to which the incendiaries had not had time to fet fire. Between one and two hundred men and old women were taken up during the night, and fent to gaol on fufpicion, and three or four men detected with matches and combuftibles were killed by the enraged foldiers. Moft, if not all the men and women put into gaol, were releafed in a few days, after having their names taken and examined by a committee. The old Englifh church, and a German church, near it, with about eleven hundred houfes, were burnt. The rebels at Paulus Hook gave three cheers when the fteeple of the old Englifh church fell down, which; when burning, looked awfully grand.

The American army, with ftrong ground in their front, and ex-tenfive fortifications in their rear towards King's Bridge, feemed to

Vol. I.   E e   think

think themselves perfectly secure, and almost invulnerable. The British troops knew the strength of situation which the enemy possessed, and therefore employed themselves in throwing up a chain of redoubts on Macgowan's Hill to cover New York, and render it capable of a vigorous defence, even after the bulk of the army should be engaged in more remote operations. As soon as the redoubts were completed it was determined to attempt the enemy's rear, by the New England road, from which they received most of their supplies. This arrangement would either force them to hazard a battle, or reduce them to the necessity of suffering themselves to be surrounded and confined in York Island. It has been asserted that as soon as the English had taken possession of New York, they should have attacked the Americans, as the different positions which they had taken between the city and Fort Washington, afterwards called Fort Knyphausen, might have been forced without great difficulty or danger. In consequence of the determination just mentioned, three brigades of British and one of Hessians being left to guard New York, the rest of the troops embarked on the twelfth of October in flat-bottomed boats and batteaux, and passing through an intricate and dangerous passage, called Hell Gate, to the Sound, landed the same morning at Frog's Neck, not far from West Chester, on the continent towards Connecticut. This was thought to be an error on the part of the commander in chief: Frog's Neck being really an island connected with the main by a bridge, easy to be broken down (as happened in fact) by the enemy. The mistake, when discovered, should have been remedied instantly, by pushing along some other route to King's Bridge, which would undoubtedly have reduced the enemy to the necessity either of defending the island or of forcing their way through the English army, in order to gain the territory of New England. All possibility of their retiring to the Jerseys was cut off by the British ships, which had now, with incredible difficulty

I   and wi

was
culty
and

and danger, paffed Fort Wafhington, and taken their ftations in the North River. Thus it is fufficiently apparent that the Americans could not poffibly have effected a retreat without hazarding a battle, unlefs, indeed, they were to be permitted to retire to the continent in as fecure and uninterrupted a manner as they did from Long Ifland to New York. The Americans themfelves began to entertain ferious alarms for their fafety; for on the day the Englifh landed, their main body moved off, in order to avoid being blockaded in the ifland. This movement originated with general Lee, who had recently arrived from South Carolina, and whofe abilities and fuccefs had rendered his opinion of great weight and importance. But this meafure, to which the American army undoubtedly owed its fafety, was adopted contrary to the original plan of general Wafhington. The circumftances of it are as follow:—When the Britifh army landed at Frog's Neck, Wafhington harangued his officers, and told them, that they muft retreat no farther, but decide the fate of America on that ground. The ground on which they were then entrenched, extended in front of King's Bridge. General Lee came up foon after, and having learnt what had paffed, remonftrated againft fo abfurd a determination. He reprefented that the Britifh would infallibly hem Wafhington's army round with fuch a chain of works, as would reduce him to the neceffity of furrendering through famine, without expofing them to the hazard of a battle. Lee's reprefentations fucceeded; and the American army immediately refolved to quit fo dangerous a pofition.

On the eighteenth of October, the Britifh troops re-embarking October 18. proceeded along the coaft to Pell's Point, where they ought to have landed originally; and difembarked there without difficulty. Soon after their landing a fharp fkirmifh happened in an attempt to diflodge the enemy from a narrow pafs, at which they had taken poft with a ftrong corps. Notwithftanding their advantageous fituation,

the

the Americans retired with confiderable lofs. Thirty-two were killed and wounded on the fide of the Englifh.

On the twenty-firft of October the main divifion of the Britifh army moved to New Rochelle, fituated on the found that divides Long Ifland from the continent. Here they were joined by the fecond divifion of foreign troops that had arrived from England, under the command of general Knyphaufen. The American army was now in a difagreeable fituation. The foldiers were very poorly clothed, and a fcarcity of provifions among them had been followed by much illnefs. Nor, amidft thefe difadvantages, was their pofition either fecure or eligible in other refpects. Their fole refource was to avoid action: For which reafon it was determined in a council of war that they fhould extend themfelves into a long line behind the Brunx, well fecured by works thrown up in front, to command every ford. The provincial army, in confequence of this determination, ftretched along the ground parallel to that on which the Britifh troops were marching; from King's Bridge on the right, to White Plains on the left. The two armies were feparated by a deep river called the Brunx, already mentioned. The rear of the Britifh was covered by the Sound, not far diftant. With this relative arrangement the armies moved flowly towards the White Plains, where, on the eaftern fide of the Brunx, a detachment had been fortifying a camp for the Americans, which camp they occupied with their whole army on the twenty-fixth.

Oct. 28.   The royal army, in two columns, marched from its encampment near Ward's Houfe, on the banks of the Brunx; fir William Howe accompanied the left column, fir Henry Clinton commanded the right. As they approached the White Plains, the right column fell in with feveral bodies of the enemy: And thofe bodies, fharply driven back, propagated a confiderable alarm in the enemy's camp. When our troops arrived within about three quarters of a mile of the Americans,

The battle of White Plains.

Americans, they had a diftinct view of their whole pofition. They were encamped on a long ridge of hill, the brow of which was covered with lines haftily thrown up. A bend of the Brunx protected their right flank, and by another turning in its courfe enveloped alfo the rear of their right wing. Farther ftill, the point of the hill on the enemy's right, exceedingly fteep and rocky, was covered by a ftrong abbatis in front of the entrenchment. The left of the enemy was rather refufed to the line in which the Britifh troops approached them, fo that they could not judge of it with great accuracy; but it appeared to be pofted in very broken ground, difficult to be affailed, and furnifhing a fecure retreat. The weakeft part was the centre. The flope of the hill was very gradual in the direction of the road by the Court Houfe. The lines were by no means formidable, not being fraized; and the rockinefs of the foil prevented the ditch from being made of any troublefome depth. The Britifh had in the field thirteen thoufand effective men. The enemy's force was faid to exceed twenty thoufand, but was not probably above feventeen or eighteen thoufand: Nor was a great part of this force any other than a loofe militia; nor had the continental regiments yet acquired the character which they afterwards attained from continued and more fuccefsful fervice. Had an affault been made on the centre of the enemy's works, defeat would have been deftruction to the Americans. The whole of their right wing muft have fallen into the power of the Britifh army; for the Brunx not being paffable in that part, cut off their retreat, and victory was to be reafonably expected, not only from the valour of our troops, but from the confufion of the enemy. This indeed was obvious beyond example. When our army came in fight their tents were ftanding. The hurry of ftriking them, and of loading the waggons with the baggage, together with the movement of troops backward and forward, in evident uncertainty of purpofe, gave an extraordinary picture of alarm.

During

During this time the Americans kept up a cannonade on our army, who returned it, but the diftance was fo great that there was little effect on either fide. Part of the Britifh columns formed behind fome rifing ground, nearly parallel to the enemy's front; but the right wing of the Britifh did not extend beyond the centre of the American army. That part of the enemy's pofition did not feem to be confidered; all the attention of the Britifh commander being fixed on another part of the field. Four thoufand of the enemy were pofted on a hill in a line with the right of their camp, but feparated from it by the Brunx. The reafon of their occupying this pofture is inexplicable, unlefs it be that they could not be contained within the works of their camp. The poffeffion of that hill would not enable the royalifts to annoy their camp, for it rofe fo gradually from the Brunx that its creft was not within random cannon fhot; as was proved by many of our battalions lying upon it on their arms the whole evening after the action: Nor had the enemy to apprehend that, from that quarter, an attack might be made on their rear, fince the Brunx, deep and impracticable, would have been ftill between the two armies. It feems to have been a blunder of general Wafhington's to have placed fo confiderable a corps entirely out of the capability of fupporting the reft of the army; for two battalions and two pieces of cannon could effectually prevent them from croffing either a ford or a bridge near their right flank, for the purpofe of annoying our troops, whilft they affailed their camp. Poffibly this error might lead fir William Howe to imagine this hill to be of more importance than it immediately appeared to be from its fituation. However, againft this hill all the efforts of the Britifh army were directed. A part of our left wing paffed the ford, which was entirely under command of our cannon. They then mounted the hill, and very gallantly drove the enemy from the ftrong heights on which they were pofted. It was an

attack

attack little lefs rough than what an affault on the enemy's lines
might be conceived to be: And victory, being obtained, was not
followed by a fingle advantage.   The Americans remained tranquil
in their entrenchments.

On the part of the Britifh, it became neceffary to fuftain the troops
which had taken poffeffion of the hill; and as this occafioned a difficulty of co-operation between the left and right wing of our army,
it was obvious that the latter could no longer expediently attempt
any thing againft the enemy's main body.   When, three days after,
preparations were made for attacking the enemy's camp, doubts
were entertained concerning the wifdom of carrying the meafure
into execution; as the Americans had recovered their fpirits, and
had affiduoufly ftrengthened their works.   A rain of uncommon violence, during the whole night, made the ground fo flippery that it
was thought it could not be poffible to mount the face of the hill:
And, for that profeffed reafon, the intended affault was laid afide.

On the night of the twenty-eighth of October the Britifh troops
lay on their arms, and encamped next day with the left wing in the
field of battle, and the right extending from the ôther fide of the
Brunx; which pofition enabled them to make a front parallel to a
certain extent with that of the enemy.   In the mean time the Americans, who ftudioufly avoided being reduced to the neceffity of a
pitched battle, employed themfelves in ftrengthening their lines.
On the thirtieth, four battalions from York Ifland, and two from
the Maroneck Poft, having reinforced the Britifh army, a difpofition
was made for the attack of the enemy's lines on the fucceeding
morning.   This refolution, however, was abandoned, on account
of rainy and tempeftuous weather, as already mentioned.   On the
thirty-firft, the weather proved fine about noon, but the commander
in chief did not think proper to put his former intentions in execution.   The enemy had rendered their lines fufficiently ftrong to
refift

refift an attack, but being informed by a deferter that the Britifh army would march againft them the next morning, they evacuated their lines on the morning of the firft of September, and retired acrofs the Crotton river to North Caftle, fetting fire, in their retreat, to all the houfes on White Plains. Their pofition was now fo advantageous, that any attack on them muft have proved unfuccefsful, for the river Crotton ftretched along their front, and their rear was defended by woods and heights. Convinced that it was part of the enemy's fyftem ftudioufly to avoid an action, and that their knowledge of the country enabled them to execute this fyftem with advantage, general Howe refolved to ceafe an ineffectual purfuit, and employ himfelf in the reduction of King's Bridge and Fort Wafhington. This laft poft was of the utmoft importance, inafmuch as it fecured an immediate intercourfe with the Jerfey fhore, to Fort Lee, and effectually obftructed the navigation of the North River. It was fituated on the weftern fide of New York Ifland, at a fmall diftance from King's Bridge, and almoft oppofite to Fort Lee. The fortifications were in good order, but its principal ftrength confifted in its fituation; for it could not be approached without expofing the befiegers to a heavy fire from the garrifon, and the works and lines by which it was furrounded. · Senfible of the importance of this poft, the Americans had garrifoned it with three thoufand men, under the command of colonel Magaw, a gentleman peculiarly fitted for the truft repofed in him. He was brave, generous, and humane; his manners engaging, and his education liberal. He was a native of Penfylvania; and the former part of his life had been fpent in the profeffion of the law. As foon, however, as the difturbances commenced, he offered his fervices to congrefs; whom he ferved with zeal and fidelity, that could refult only from a conviction that the caufe for which he fought was the caufe of liberty and independence. On the fifteenth of November,

the

the Englifh batteries being completed, a fummons was fent to the garrifon to furrender, on pain of being put to the fword. Before this fummons was fent, it was objected to the general by an Englifh officer of rank, that this menace would determine Wafhington to withdraw the garrifon or reinforce it, which latter he did; and returned for anfwer, that he would defend it to the laft extremity. It was determined therefore to commence a vigorous attack upon it next morning. The army was divided into four parts. The firft, on the fide of King's Bridge, under general Knyphaufen, confifted of five thoufand Heffians. The fecond contained the guards and light-infantry, under general Matthews, together with two battalions of grenadiers and the thirty-third regiment, commanded by lord Cornwallis: This divifion was to land at Haerlem Creek, in thirty flat-bottomed boats, which, for that purpofe, had paffed up the North River in the night. The third divifion, comprifing the forty-fecond regiment, was intended to make a feint in batteaux upon the left, between the enemy's lines, towards New York. The fourth divifion, under the command of lord Percy, was to attack in front of the lines above Haerlem Plain. Lord Howe attended the operations of the laft body. Soon after day-break, on the fixteenth, the cannonading began, and continued with great fury on both fides till noon. The Heffians, under the command of ge- neral Knyphaufen, then filed off in two columns; one of which, led by colonel Ralle, afcended a hill circuitoufly, not without much toil. They gained however the fummit of it, and penetrating through the advanced works of the enemy, formed within a hundred yards of the covered-way of the front. The fecond column, commanded by general Knyphaufen, climbed the hill in a direct line. They had to pafs an almoft impervious wood, which was rendered more dangerous by abbatis of brufh-wood and felled timber, covering both fides of the declivity: Neverthelefs, after great labour,

VOL. I. F f they

they penetrated through the wood, and fixed themfelves on the top of the afcent. The fecond divifion was equally fuccefsful: The light-infantry made good their landing, and forced the enemy from their rocks and trees up a fteep and rugged mountain. The third divifion was much galled in croffing the lower part of Haerlem Creek. Colonel Sterling, the commander of the forty-fecond, had to encounter a heavy fire before he landed, and he had then to afcend a woody promontory, the ground of which was very uneven: Neverthelefs he fucceeded in his attempt, and, though the poft was obftinately defended, he carried it, making two hundred of the enemy prifoners. The laft divifion was not lefs fortunate in the advances they made through the enemy's lines. Lord Percy, with his ufual gallantry and good conduct, having furmounted incredible difficulties, carried the advanced works of the enemy. The garrifon, finding that it was not poffible to defend the fort longer, furrendered prifoners of war. The lofs of the royal army, in killed and wounded, amounted to about eight hundred: That of the garrifon, including killed, wounded, and prifoners, about three thoufand three hundred. It was a great error in colonel Magaw, that he fuffered his troops to crowd into the fort, after quitting their lines: For had they been pofted on the brow of the hill, facing the north and fouth, the conteft would have been prolonged, and the affailants have fuftained a heavier lofs: But the grand error was on the part of the American general; who, as if he had entertained a predilection for a poft, no longer ufeful, did not withdraw the garrifon on the evening preceding the affault.

On the morning of the attack, general Wafhington had been at the fort, in order to give directions to colonel Magaw: He had, however, repaffed over to the Jerfey fhore long before the heat of the action. On the other fide of North River, oppofite to Fort Wafhington, lay Fort Lee, which occupied next the attention of the commander

mander in chief; inasmuch as its reduction would secure the command of the river, and open a communication with the Jerseys.

On the eighteenth of November, lord Cornwallis landed on the Jersey shore, eight miles above Fort Lee, with two battalions of British and three of Hessian grenadiers, two of light-infantry, the guards, the chasseurs, the royal Highlanders, the thirty-third regiment, and a detachment of the queen's light dragoons. The sailors of the fleet were employed in dragging the artillery up a rocky road to the summit of the river's bank, which stretches, in an almost perpendicular direction, half a mile from the river. As soon as the detachment had landed, lord Cornwallis began his march with great secrecy and dispatch. In all probability he would have surprised the fort and made the enemy prisoners of war, had not a deserter informed them of his approach. In consequence of this information the garrison retreated in the utmost confusion, leaving their tents standing, and all their provisions and military stores. The next day major-general Vaughan, with the dragoons, grenadiers, and light-infantry, was detached to New Bridge, on the Hakensack river, which runs into New York Bay. The enemy retreated before them with evident confusion, leaving behind them, on the roads, a great quantity of stores and artillery.

Lord Cornwallis now penetrated into the remotest parts of East and West Jersey without opposition. On the twenty-fourth of November, being reinforced by two brigades of British troops and a battalion of Highlanders, his lordship proceeded to New Bridge, thence to Hakensack, Newark, Elizabeth Town, and Brunswick: At this last town he was commanded to remain; an order, which saved the panic-struck and fleeing army of the Americans from utter ruin. The Raritan is fordable at that place in every recess of the tide, and had this noble general been left to act at his own discretion, if we may form a conjecture from that activity and good sense

n()   F f 2   which

which diftinguifh his ufual conduct, he would have purfued the weakened and alarmed enemy to the Delaware, over which, without falling into his hands, they never could have paffed. At Brunfwick the Britifh army halted near a week; the Americans, to the number of three thoufand, with all their heavy cannon and baggage, at Prince Town, feventeen, and at Trenton, on the Delaware, twenty-nine miles diftant. On the feventeenth of December, our army marched from Brunfwick at four o'clock in the morning, and about the fame hour in the afternoon arrived at Prince Town. This place general Wafhington, in perfon, with Stirling's brigade, left not one hour before the Britifh arrived. At Prince Town the Britifh general waited feventeen hours, marched at nine o'clock in the morning of the eighth, and arrived at Trenton at four o'clock in the afternoon; juft when the laft boat of general Wafhington's embarkation croffed the river, as if he had calculated, it was obferved, with great accuracy, the exact time neceffary for his enemy to make his efcape.

The winter now beginning to fet in, the army went into winter-quarters. The Britifh troops were placed between the Delaware and the Hakenfack, the latter of which runs near New York. Trenton, the moft important poft and the barrier, was occupied by a brigade of Heffians, under the command of colonel Ralle; and Bordenton, which formed the angle neareft the enemy, was placed under the command of count Donop and four battalions of Heffians. The enemy, in the mean time, were fuffered to make good their retreat acrofs the Delaware.

While lord Cornwallis was thus fuccefsful in the Jerfeys, an expedition was undertaken againft Rhode Ifland by general Clinton and fir Peter Parker. At their approach the provincials abandoned the ifland, and the Englifh took peaceable poffeffion of it. An unlucky meafure, as it had no ufe but to keep a great body of troops unemployed during three years.

On

On account of the fuccefs of this expedition, the American
fquadron, commanded by commodore Hopkins, was under the
neceffity of retiring up the river Providence, where it remained
blocked up and inactive. When the expedition was difpatched
to Rhode Ifland, fir Henry Clinton ftrongly urged that he might
rather be permitted to conduct it to the Delaware. Poffibly, had
that counfel been adopted, the blow might have been irre-
coverable to the Americans: But it is faid lord Howe infifted
on the poffeffion of Rhode Ifland for the fleet.

CHAP. VIII.

Tranfactions in the Jerfies—Apparent Errors of the Britifh Commander—Defpondence of the Revolters—Vigour of Congrefs—Encouragement to enlift in the American Army—Congrefs appeal with Effect to the American People.—1776.

FROM the fuccefs that had attended the Britifh army, very beneficial confequences were expected to refult. And indeed, when we confider the comparative fituation and ftrength of both armies at this period, fuch expectations will neither appear too fanguine nor unreafonable.

The American army had been raifed and embodied on the following principle:—Each man enlifted only for a twelvemonth; after which period, he was at liberty to quit the fervice. Congrefs began now to be convinced that this principle was erroneous; for the fhortnefs of the term induced many to inlift at firft, but it was now become neceffary to form a fettled and permanent military eftablifhment: Such an eftablifhment, however, could not at prefent be accomplifhed. Thofe who had fulfilled the term of their engagement retired from the fervice, alleging, as a reafon for their conduct, that it was incumbent on their fellow-countrymen to bear an equal fhare in the defence of the common caufe. Thus the places of thofe who had acquired a degree of military experience, were filled by perfons who were totally ignorant of the duties of their new fituation, and who were very inadequate to refift the attacks of the veterans, of which the Britifh army was compofed. In confequence

of

of the fuccefs of the royalifts, fupplies of men were acquired by
congrefs but flowly.   On the other hand, prodigious numbers retired from the fervice, and the actual ftrength was reduced from thirty
thoufand, of which it confifted when general Howe landed on
Staten Ifland, to fcarcely three thoufand.   The Britifh army, at this
period, amounted from twenty to thirty thoufand.   The men
were all healthy and in good fpirits; fuccefs had increafed their military ardour, and they poffeffed every thing that could contribute
either to their comfort or their convenience.   The greateft expectations were accordingly formed, from fo great a degree of health, animation, and courage, heightened by fuccefs: Advantages which, if
rightly improved, would naturally lead the way to ftill farther fuccefs
and glory.   The reduction of Forts Wafhington and Lee opened to
the Britifh general a free ingrefs into the Jerfeys.   The enemy, pa-
nic-ftruck, flew before him, and yet he would not fuffer them to be
purfued; ordering lord Cornwallis to proceed no further than
Brunfwick.   By this tendernefs of operation, the enemy were
enabled to make good their retreat, and to crofs the Delaware in
fafety.   He thus neglected the opportunity of making the remnant
of the American army prifoners of war: Yet, even fubfequent to
this period, his conduct was equally inexplicable.   The Americans,
though they had thus croffed the Delaware, were far from feeling
themfelves in fecurity; and had the commander in chief paffed over
the river after them (which he might have done a little above Cor-
rell's Ferry), the confequences would have certainly been fatal to the
American caufe.   The panic ftruck by the feveral defeats of the
Americans at Long Ifland, New York, and the White Plains, with
the progrefs of the army through New Jerfey, had extended itfelf
from the military to all the civil departments of the new ftates, and
particularly in the middle colonies.   The governor, council, affem-

Blunders of
the Britifh
commander.

5   bly,

bly, and magiftracy of New Jerfey had deferted that province.
The felf-created ftate in Philadelphia had difperfed, and the congrefs
itfelf, giving up all as loft, had fled with great precipitation into Maryland. Repeated attempts were made to raife the militia of Penfylvania in vain. Three of the principal citizens of Philadelphia, in
behalf of the reft, waited on congrefs before their flight, and boldly
informed them, that they intended to meet fir William Howe, and
throw themfelves on his protection. The principal city of North America, and at that time the feat of the new government, only waited
for the arrival of the Britifh army, to fubmit to the mother-country.
Other parts, which had, from the commencement of the difturbances, followed the example of Philadelphia, would have purfued
the fame conduct. In this manner advantages, which, in all probability, would have put a period to the war, were neglected :
Nor were thefe the only errors of which the commander in chief
was guilty. The great and principal error in fir William Howe's
conduct at this period, was, his dividing his army into fmall
detachments ; and thofe at fuch a diftance from each other, as, in
cafe of attack, not to be capable of receiving immediate affiftance
from the main army : And it was owing to this injudicious arrangement, that the Britifh army, when in the Jerfeys, were, as we fhall
fee hereafter, cut up in detail. The manner in which he difpofed the
army into winter cantonments, was particularly blameable. In the firft
place, the chain of communication which the Britifh troops occupied
from the Delaware to the Hakenfack was too extenfive, and the cantonments too remote from each other ; for the fpace between the two
rivers was not lefs than eighty miles. In the next place, foreign
troops ought not to have been ftationed either at Trenton or Bordenton ; for they were the barriers to the Jerfeys, and lay neareft
to the enemy. The light-infantry fhould have occupied thefe pofts;

                                                              for

for the Heffian troops, underftanding nothing of the language of the country, were unable to obtain proper intelligence, and, inftead of conciliating the affections, made themfelves particularly difagreeable to the natives, by pillaging them, and taking from them the neceffaries of life, without making them an adequate compenfation. It was farther obferved, that the four frontier cantonments at Trenton, Bordenton, White Horfe, and Burlington, were the weakeft, in refpect of number of troops, in the whole line of cantonments. The poft at Trenton, oppofite to which Wafhington lay with the main body of his army, and with boats prepared to crofs the Delaware at his pleafure, was defended only by twelve hundred Heffians; and thofe of Bordenton, White Horfe, and Burlington, by no more than two thoufand. In this weak ftate, the frontier pofts, the pofts of moft danger, were left by the commander in chief; while the other pofts were made ftronger and ftronger, in proportion to the decreafe of their diftance from the enemy, and their confequent danger; nor were thefe frontier cantonments fecured from the attacks of the enemy by any works of art, but left without a fingle redoubt or intrenchment, to which, in cafe of a furprife, the troops, until they fhould be relieved from the other pofts, might retreat.

The affairs of congrefs, in the mean time, continued to droop daily. As foon as the Britifh troops had been difperfed into winter-quarters, the commander in chief iffued a proclamation in the name of his brother and himfelf, in which pardon was offered to all perfons, who, within the fpace of fixty days, fhould take the oath of allegiance, and fubmit to the authority of the Britifh government. The good effects of this proclamation were foon apparent. People from all quarters crowded to take the benefit of it. Whole diftricts threw down their arms: Nor was this all the diftrefs that con-

grefs fuffered. In addition to their misfortunes, they incurred the following unfortunate lofs :—General Lee, to whom, on the departure
of general Wafhington, the command of the troops at Croton's
Ferry had devolved, receiving information of the perilous fituation of general Wafhington, and the defencelefs condition of the
banks of the Delaware on the fide of Philadelphia, refolved, notwithftanding the defertion in his army, occafioned by thofe whofe
terms of fervice were expired, to crofs the North River, and form a
junction with him. Accordingly, on the fixth of December, he
croffed the North River at King's Ferry, with three thoufand men
and fome pieces of cannon. He continued his route through Morris
County, intending to crofs the Delaware to the northward of Trenton.

Capture of
general Lee.

On the thirteenth of December, while his army was encamped in
Morris County, he quitted the camp, in order to reconnoitre. In
the courfe of this employment he proceeded to the diftance of three
miles from his army, where he ftopped at a houfe to breakfaft.

In order to obtain information of the movements of the army under
general Lee, colonel Harcourt had been difpatched with a detachment of light-horfe: Collecting information, as he advanced into
the country, the colonel was induced to proceed farther. In his
progrefs he intercepted a countryman, charged with a letter from
general Lee, by which he underftood where he was, and how
flightly he was guarded. He immediately formed a refolution of
carrying him off; and for that purpofe made the proper difpofitions
to prevent his efcape. He then galloped up to the houfe where the
general was at breakfaft, furprifed the centinels placed to guard it,
forced open the door, and made him a prifoner, as well as a French
lieutenant-colonel, who had accompanied him. The general was
immediately mounted, and, notwithftanding the extent of country
                                                             through

through which he was to be carried, conveyed in fafety to New York, where the commander in chief then refided.

The lofs of general Lee was a fevere blow to the American caufe. His military knowledge was great, and he had been a foldier from his infancy: He had formerly poffeffed the rank of lieutenant-colonel in the Britifh fervice, and had ferved all the laft war in America and Portugal with reputation. His abilities were extenfive, and his knowledge improved by an intimate acquaintance with every nation in Europe. His difpofition was reftlefs and romantic, and the poffeffion of an eafy fortune enabled him to indulge it. Having received fome affront from the individuals who compofed the Britifh adminiftration, he emigrated to America on the commencement of the prefent difturbances, and offered his fervices to congrefs. His abilities and his profeffional reputation being well known, his offers were accepted with joy, and he was honoured with the rank of major-general. He had been eminently ufeful in difciplining the American troops, and by his activity and fkill had greatly contributed to the fuccefs of the common caufe. To thefe qualifications, however, the impartiality of hiftory requires us to add, that he was a man of moft abandoned principles; that he laughed at every attribute of the Divinity, and turned into ridicule every tenet of religion. No prifoner of equal rank with general Lee being in the hands of the provincials, general Wafhington offered in exchange for him fix field officers: General Howe, however, replied, that general Lee, having deferted from the fervice of Great Britain, could not be confidered as a prifoner of war. To this general Wafhington rejoined, that, having on the commencement of the troubles refigned his commiffion as a Britifh officer, general Lee could not be fuppofed to be a deferter. The commander in chief, however, refufed to releafe him; which occafioned the Americans to treat feveral of their prifoners with an unufual degree of feverity and rigour.

G g 2

Notwith-

Vigour of
congrefs.

Notwithftanding the perilous fituation of their affairs, congrefs were not difpirited. They proceeded with the utmoft vigour and activity to repair their loffes, and to remedy the defect in their military fyftem. They ordered a new army to be raifed, the foldiers of which, inftead of ferving one year, fhould be bound for three, or during the continuance of the prefent difturbances. This army was to confift of eighty-eight battalions, to be furnifhed and maintained by the refpective colonies, according to the following proportion : Virginia and Maffachufet were to furnifh fifteen battalions each ; Penfylvania, twelve—North Carolina, nine—South Carolina, fix—Connecticut, eight—Maryland, eight—Rhode Ifland, two— Delaware, one—New Hampfhire, three—and Georgia, one. New York and Jerfey being partly in the enemy's poffeffion, were only affeffed at four battalions each.

Encourage-
ment to enlift
in the Ame-
rican army.

As an inducement to men to enlift, the following liberal offers were made : Each foldier was to have a bounty of twenty dollars, befides an allotment of lands at the end of the war to all who furvived, or to the families of thofe who fhould fall in the fervice. The allotment of a common foldier was to be one hundred acres— of an enfign, one hundred and fifty—of a lieutenant, two hundred —a captain, three hundred—a major, four hundred—a lieutenant-colonel, four hundred and fifty—and a colonel, five hundred. This allotment, however, was not to extend to thofe who enlifted only for three years. In addition to thefe offers, congrefs forbad any one to purchafe the allotment of lands belonging to another, in order that by this prohibition each foldier might procure for himfelf a decent maintenance when the public fhould no longer want his profeffional affiftance. In order to provide for the fupport of fuch a large body as was propofed to be raifed, congrefs borrowed a loan of five millions of dollars at four per cent. intereft.

The

The Britiſh troops at this period were maſters of the Jerſeys, and ſeparated from Penſylvania, and the capital Philadelphia, only by the Delaware. In this critical ſituation, congreſs thought it adviſable to publiſh an appeal to the inhabitants of the ſeveral colonies, in order to·remind them of their aſſurances of protection and ſupport. In this appeal they were entreated not to forget that activity and unanimity were abſolutely neceſſary to enſure welfare and ſucceſs to the common cauſe. They travelled over the ſame grounds they had formerly done, with reſpect to a recapitulation of the grievances they had ſuffered, and the manner in which they had been ·treated by the mother-country. They inſiſted that nothing ſhort of an abſolute ſubmiſſion would ſatisfy the demands of their enemies, and they deſired an anſwer to this queſtion: Which of the two alternatives was preferable—reſiſtance or ſlavery? The appeal next adverted to recent tranſactions, and contended that the ſucceſs of the Britiſh arms had been greatly exaggerated, and dearly purchaſed. In concluſion, congreſs aſſured them of the aſſiſtance of foreign powers, and exhorted them to prepare for a vigorous defence of thoſe objects which muſt be dear to every man. This appeal produced the deſired effect. The people of America determined to contribute every poſſible aſſiſtance to the common cauſe; and for that purpoſe exerted themſelves with aſtoniſhing activity in procuring reinforcements of men for the army under the command of general Waſhington.

Winter was now approaching faſt. The Delaware was expected to be ſoon frozen, and it was not doubted but that the Britiſh troops only waited for this event in order to croſs it and attack Philadelphia. The friends of congreſs, therefore, with good reaſon, began to entertain apprehenſions for the ſafety of that body, which on this account retired to Baltimore in Maryland. The city of Philadelphia by their departure was thrown into confuſion. As long as congreſs reſided

there,

there, thofe who were attached to Great Britain were under the neceffity of fubmitting to a power which they could not refift. The
operation of this caufe had no fooner ceafed than they avowed their
attachment openly, and ufed every endeavour to acquire frefh adherents to the Britifh caufe. Their attempts were not unfuccefsful.
Many of the inhabitants quitted Philadelphia, and claimed the benefit of the proclamation recently made by the commiffioners.
Others, who, though well affected to Great Britain, did not think
proper to leave the city, made ufe of every artifice to prevent its
being put into a proper ftate of defence, according to the directions
of congrefs before their departure. Thefe attempts occafioned violent animofities and difturbances; to put an end to which, general
Wafhington was reduced to the neceffity of difpatching a confiderable detachment of the trivial force which now remained under his
command.

The fituation of the Americans was now almoft defperate. General
Wafhington, though reinforced by the junction of general Lee's
army, had not five thoufand men under his command; many of
whom were raw and inexperienced, and all were difpirited by difappointment and defeat. An hoftile army, flufhed with conqueft and
fuccefs, lay on the oppofite fide of the Delaware, within twenty
miles of him. Winter was approaching faft. The Delaware would
be frozen; and the only obftacle that prevented the enemy from attacking him would then be removed. Thus fituated, he refolved to
adopt a defperate expedient; and indeed the neceffity of the cafe
left him only the alternative of adopting fuch a meafure, or of
fubmitting to the enemy. He knew the manner in which the
Britifh army was difpofed; that it was ftationed in extenfive cantonments; and therefore could not eafily be condenfed, in a fhort
period, into one body capable of refifting the attack of the men under
his command. Befides, he wifhed to obtain for Philadelphia a temporary

porary fecurity, by inducing the enemy to quit the vicinity of the
Delaware.

It has been already faid that the barriers at Trenton and Borden-ton were defended by Heffian troops under the command of colonel Rhalle and count Donop. Thefe pofts general Wafhington deter-mined to attack. But in order to draw colonel Donop from his poft at Bordenton, and to prevent him from affording any fupport to Colonel Rhalle, at the time of the intended affault, he fent a corps of four hundred and fifty militia, many of whom were boys picked up in Philadelphia, and the counties of Gloucefter and Salem, to Mount Holly, with orders not to fight, but to take to flight the moment when the effect of the manœuvre fhould take place. The plan fucceeded. Colonel Donop marched againft this infignificant detachment of the American force, with the whole of his party, to the number of two thoufand men, with the exception of eighty, left at Borden-ton, down to Mount Holly, twelve miles from his own ftation, and eighteen from Trenton, the poft he ought to have been near, for the pur-pofe of fupporting it in cafe of danger. The fmall American party, on his approach, immediately fled and difperfed; and yet Donop, in-ftead of returning ftraight to fupport colonel Rhalle, loitered two days in the neighbourhood of Burlington, without the fmalleft femblance of neceffity. Wafhington difcerned the fit moment for enterprife, and embraced it. He divided his troops into three parts, which were to affemble on the banks of the Delaware on the night of the twenty-fifth of December. Two of thefe divifions were led by ge-nerals Irwing and Cadwallader. The third, which was the principal divifion, was commanded by himfelf in perfon. It confifted of two thoufand five hundred men, and was furnifhed with a few field-pieces. General Wafhington was attended by generals Sullivan and Green. The firft divifion was ordered to pafs the river at Trenton

2

Ferry,

Ferry, a mile below the town—the fecond near Bordenton—and the third at Mackenzie's Ferry, nine miles above Trenton. The Delaware had already begun to be frozen, and the boats that carried this laft divifion found it difficult to make their way through the ice. Other inconveniencies which the men encountered after they landed delayed their march fo long, that they did not arrive at the deftined place before eight o'clock on the morning of the twenty-fixth of December. As foon as general Wafhington had landed he divided his men into two detachments, which were ordered to proceed to Trenton by the two roads that led to it; the upper, or Pennington road; and the lower, or River road.

The Heffians, fince they had been quartered at Trenton, had given way to a laxity of difcipline, and an inattention that proceeded from a knowledge of the enervated fituation of the enemy, and of the improbability of their adopting any offenfive meafures againft them. It is not therefore wonderful that they negle&ed the means of fecuring themfelves from a furprife, nor that the Americans were fuffered to proceed on their march without moleftation. The firft intelligence that the Heffians received of their approach was from an advanced poft in the upper road, and the out-guards on the lower road, both of which were under the neceffity of retreating into the town with the utmoft celerity. Rhalle, with all poffible fpeed, endeavoured to colle& his troops during the night; but many of his men were abfent on pillaging parties, and thofe who were on the fpot were more bufily employed in fecuring their plunder in waggons than in putting the town in a proper ftate of defence. The enemy took advantage of this confufion, and poffeffed themfelves of the different avenues, where they placed their fieldpieces, and thence began to pour a heavy fire upon the difmayed and aftonifhed Heffians. By a&ivity and diligence Rhalle
assembled

affembled the beft part of his three regiments, with which he charged the enemy with great courage, but receiving a mortal wound in the commencement of the engagement, his troops refufed to continue it, and endeavoured to retreat to Prince Town. Being difappointed, however, in this attempt, they were under the neceffity of furrendering prifoners of war. The number of killed and wounded on both fides was inconfiderable. The number of prifoners amounted to near one thoufand. The two other divifions of general Wafhington's army were not fo fuccefsful. The quantity of ice in the Delaware was fo great, where they attempted to crofs it, that they found the tafk impracticable. Had this not been the cafe, their fuccefs would have been complete; for thefe divifions would have prevented the chaffeurs and light-horfe from efcaping to Bordenton, and alfo have made themfelves mafters of all the cantonments on the fide of the river. General Wafhington, in confequence of this failure in the other divifions, judged it improper to profecute his intentions further. He therefore repaffed the Delaware on the evening of the twenty-fixth, carrying with him his prifoners, and all the artillery of which he had made himfelf mafter at Trenton.

The Americans had hitherto beheld the Heffians with fear and difmay. They knew that they were veterans, and in the higheft ftate of difcipline. This victory, however, gained over thofe ftrangers, animated them to a furprifing degree, and revived that fpirit which had for fome time been decreafing. The Heffians were difpatched to Philadelphia, and carried through the different ftreets of that city, in order to convince the inhabitants that the fuccefs of the American arms was not, as many induftrioufly fuggefted, pretended or fictitious. The lofs of Trenton was very generally imputed to the mifconduct of the commander in chief. It was al-

VOL. I. H h leged

leged that the principal barrier fhould not have been committed to the care of foreigners; that it was extremely reprehenfible to neglect throwing up fome defenfible works in order to prevent a furprife; and that the extent of the cantonments was fo enlarged, as already obferved, as to render every idea of conveying affiftance from one cantonment to another totally impracticable. Rhalle, though brave, was totally unfit for the ftation he held. He was obftinate, paffionate, and inceffantly intoxicated with ftrong liquors. The commander in chief affected to throw the blame of the appointment of Rhalle to the command at Trenton on general De Heifter.

Sir William Howe has been very feverely cenfured for having given the command of this poft to a foreigner, unacquainted with the language, cuftoms, or manners, of the people. He was liable to be impofed on by the country people in any information he might want; and little could be expected from colonel Rhalle in the way of conciliation accompanying that of armed force, the only way in which final fuccefs was to be expected. For whoever cafts his eye on the map of the vaft continent of America muft readily perceive that force of arms alone, unaccompanied by conciliatory meafures, muft be wild and chimerical. When the enemy had arrived in the town the troops in the Britifh fervice were folely occupied in fecuring their plunder in waggons, and many of them were actually made prifoners while engaged in this fhameful avocation.

Though the fuccefs of general Wafhington, in his attack on Trenton, had furpaffed his moft fanguine expectations, he yet dreaded every moment the approach of the troops under general Leflie, from Prince Town, and of colonel Donop from Mount Holly, and fled with the utmoft precipitation to his winter-quarters on the weft

I

fide

fide of the Delaware. Of taking up quarters in New Jerfey he never entertained a thought: Not doubting but the Britifh commander, with a force fo greatly fuperior to his own, would reoccupy the important pofts on the Delaware, and fortify them fo ftrongly as to put it out of his power to retake them. Nor was Wafhington, as yet, fufficiently acquainted with the character of fir William Howe, to fuppofe it poffible that this commander might purfue a different line of conduct. To recover and fortify his chain of pofts on the Delaware was neceffary, in order to keep alive the panic already diffufed throughout all the colonies, and fupport the fpirits of the well-affected to government. It was neceffary to the prefervation of Weft New Jerfey, juft conquered: It was neceffary, in order to convince the enemy that the Britifh troops, although they might be furprifed, were not to be intimidated or difcouraged from action: And, finally, it was practicable without danger, as thofe troops were, at that crifis, fix times more in number, as well as fuperior in point of military difcipline and experience, to the feeble force that oppofed them. But inftead of an immediate movement of the two neareft corps, to regain what had been fo ftrangely loft, colonel Donop abandoned his poft, and haftened to join general Leflie at Prince Town. Thefe officers, united, were much fuperior in force to general Wafhington: Yet, though there was no enemy in New Jerfey to difturb them, they were permitted to remain for fome time wholly inactive. The two main barriers of the Britifh power on the Delaware being left unguarded and defencelefs, and the conduct of the Britifh commander betraying manifeft irrefolution, if not infatuation, general Wafhington, after an interval of eight days, was encouraged again to crofs the Delaware, and march to Trenton at the head of four thoufand men.

The

The Britifh commander in chief was now ferioufly alarmed. The
Britifh and auxiliary troops, with the forces at Brunfwick under general
Grant, advanced to Prince Town; and lord Cornwallis, who was
on the point of failing for England, was immediately ordered to
leave New York, and take the command of the Jerfey army. As
foon as his lordfhip joined general Grant, he marched to attack
the enemy at Trenton. General Wafhington, on his approach, retired from the town, and croffing a rivulet at the back of it, pofted
himfelf on fome high grounds, feemingly with a determination of
defending them. Both armies immediately commenced a fevere
cannonade, which continued till night. Lord Cornwallis determined
to renew the attack next morning, but general Wafhington refolved

not to hazard a battle. About two in the morning of the third of
January he retreated with profound filence, leaving his fires burning, his pickets advanced, and feveral fmall parties for the purpofe
of guarding the paffage of the rivulet. Quitting the main road, he
took a large circuit through Allenftown, and proceeded to Prince
Town, which place he intended to furprife. When lord Cornwallis
quitted Prince Town, he left lieutenant-colonel Mawhood to defend
it with the feventeenth, the fortieth, and the fifty-fifth regiments.
On the third of January however, orders were tranfmitted him to
march with the feventeenth and fifty-fifth regiments to Maidenhead,
a village midway between Prince Town and Trenton. General
Wafhington had ufed fuch expedition in his march, that at fun-rife
his van came up with colonel Mawhood's detachment, which had
juft begun its march. The morning was fo foggy, that the enemy were at firft fuppofed to be Heffians: Colonel Mawhood
foon difcovering that it was part of the American army, immediately conjectured that general Wafhington had retreated from lord
Cornwallis, and was on his march to Prince Town. A brook feparated

rated the two armies. By cutting away a bridge over it, the detachment might have avoided an engagement, and fecured their paffage
to Maidenhead. The commanding officer however, conceiving
that fome advantage might refult from delaying the enemy, refolved to hazard an action. The fogginefs of the morning, and the
woods, prevented him from difcovering, at firft, the number of the
enemy. Poffeffing himfelf of fome high ground that led to Prince
Town, he ordered the waggons to return to that place, and directed
the fortieth regiment to come to his affiftance. When the enemy
advanced he poured a heavy difcharge of artillery upon them, which
did confiderable execution, on account of their not having yet
formed in a regular line. For a fhort fpace of time a brifk cannonade was carried on on both fides. The van of the enemy beginning then to be in fome diforder, the feventeenth regiment
rufhed forward with fixed bayonets, and drove them back to a ravine
which feparated them from their rear. Great flaughter enfued in
the endeavour of the enemy to repafs this line. It was faid that,
had the fifty-fifth regiment fupported the feventeenth with a proper
degree of fpirit, and had the fortieth regiment obeyed the orders
tranfmitted them to march to the affiftance of the other two regiments, the enemy would have totally failed in their defigns. But
thefe feem to have been only the excufes with which it was attempted to cover the want of a regular combined difpofition for the
attack : A neglect naturally imputable to the unexpectednefs of fuch
a meeting with the American army. The feventeenth regiment, fevered by their ardour from the reft of the Britifh detachment, cut
their way through the enemy, and purfued their march to Maidenhead. This was one of the moft gallant exploits during the
whole war. Captain Scot, who led that regiment, received very
deferved applaufe for his conduct on that occafion. The Englifh fuffered confiderably in killed and wounded, and the Americans

ricans much more. Among the killed, on the part of the latter, was a general Mercer, whofe lofs was extremely lamented. The fortieth and fifty-fifth regiments being unable to make good their way to Maidenhead, effected a retreat to Brunfwick, with the lofs of near one half their number. The Americans at the fame time took poffeffion of Prince Town. As foon as daylight appeared, on the third of January, lord Cornwallis difcovered the retreat of the American army, and entertaining apprehenfions for the fafety of Brunfwick, which was in a defencelefs fituation, refolved to march inftantly to its relief. On the approach of his lordfhip, general Wafhington retreated from Prince Town, and proceeded to Brunf-wick. Brigadier Matthews, the commanding officer of the garrifon, being informed of his approach, took the precaution to fend away the immenfe quantity of ftores that had been placed there for the ufe of the army, and with his fmall detachment pofted himfelf on fome high grounds commanding the town, intending to check the pro-grefs of the enemy, in order to cover the retreat of the ftore-wag-gons, which were hurrying along the Rariton to a bridge about two miles diftant from the town. The captive general Lee, who was confined in Brunfwick, was at the fame time difpatched acrofs the Rariton in company with thefe waggons.

Notwithftanding the expedition that general Wafhington ufed in his march to Brunfwick, yet his rear was hard preffed by the van of the Englifh army. He therefore refolved to relinquifh his de-figns on Brunfwick, and croffed the Millftone river, breaking down the bridge at King's Town to evade a purfuit.

The army under lord Cornwallis, haraffed and fatigued, declined purfuing the enemy, and proceeded to Brunfwick. Whilft Cornwallis, for the neceffary refrefhment of his troops, remained in this town, general Wafhington over-ran both Eaft and Weft Jerfey, fpreading his army over the Rariton, and penetrating into Effex County, where he made

made himfelf mafter of the coaft oppofite to Staten Ifland, by feizing Newark, Elizabeth Town, and Woodbridge. His head-quarters he fixed at Morris Town. This place is fituated amongft hills which are difficult of accefs. A fine country was in his rear, whence he could draw fupplies, and through which he could at any time fecure an eafy paffage over the Delaware.

By fuch judicious movements did general Wafhington not only fave Philadelphia and Penfylvania, but recover the greateft part of the Jerfeys, in defiance of an army infinitely fuperior to his, in difcipline, refources, and numbers. Of all their recent extenfive poffeffions in the Jerfeys, the Englifh retained now only the pofts of Brunfwick and Amboy; the firft fituated on the banks of the Rariton; the fecond on a point of land at its mouth. Both places have an open communication with New York by fea.

Inactivity of the Britifh army.

In all thefe tranfactions there was fomething inexplicable, to the rational part of mankind. They could not, by any well-founded arguments, defend the manner in which the troops were cantoned. They could not account for fo flender an eftablifhment being left on the two barriers of Trenton and Bordenton. At the firft place Rhalle had only twelve hundred Heffians; at the fecond, count Donop's force exceeded not two thoufand. The neglecting to fortify thefe pofts neareft the enemy, and moft in danger, feemed to them unpardonable: The placing the Britifh in the greateft numbers fartheft from the enemy; the not retaking the pofts on the banks of the Delaware, which pofts covered the whole province of Jerfey: All thefe circumftances were generally animadverted on with much feverity. Men of plain fenfe could not underftand why the commander in chief, at the head of thirty thoufand veteran troops, fhould fuffer an undifciplined army, not amounting to a fixth part of his own numbers, to remain in a province fo lately in his firm poffeffion; and not only to remain there, but to compel him to abandon that province. When the

the adherents of adminiſtration reflected on the dreadful conſequences that muſt ariſe from this erroneous conduct, they were reduced to a ſituation of grief and deſpair.

General Waſhington, with his uſual ſagacity, perceived that, during the winter of 1776, his ſituation required enterpriſe. and daring expedients; which, while they haraſſed the Britiſh army, would keep his little force in action, and prevent the minds of his men from yielding to the fatal effects of deſpondence. Small as his force was, he always poſted himſelf near the Britiſh army. He was inceſſantly inſulting, ſurpriſing, and cutting off their pickets and advanced guards ; firm and undaunted amidſt want, inclemency of weather, and difficulty and danger of every kind. Amboy and Brunſwick were in a manner beſieged. In this unfavourable and indeciſive warfare it is ſuppoſed that more of the Britiſh were ſacrificed than would have been loſt in an attack on general Waſhington's whole force, which, at this period, was leſs than four thouſand men, moſt of them undiſciplined and inexperienced, and ſuch as might have been defeated and diſperſed by a fifth part of the Britiſh army.

Sir William Howe ſuffered ſuch an enemy, ſo greatly inferior to his own, as then oppoſed him, to remain for ſix months within twenty-five miles of his head-quarters, without moleſtation, and without taking any means to revenge the inſults that were offered daily to the army under his command.

It has been alleged in defence of ſir William Howe's inactivity and paſſive demeanour, that he had to attack an enemy, poſted in a country containing numberleſs inacceſſible poſts, and ſtrong natural barriers formed by the various combinations of woods, mountains, rivers, lakes, and marſhes ; and that theſe circumſtances might be ſaid to fight the battles of the inhabitants of ſuch countries in a defenſive war. Allowing the validity of this argument, ſtill it will neither acquit
the

the commander in chief of the charge of impolicy, in not croffing the Delaware after the capture of Forts Lee and Wafhington, nor in the feveral other inftances already mentioned.

Thefe fuccefsful operations on the part of the Americans were immediately followed by a proclamation, in the name of general Wafhington, abfolving all thofe who had been induced to take the oaths of allegiance tendered by the Britifh commiffioners, and promifing them protection on condition of their fubfcribing to a form of oath prefcribed by congrefs. The effects of this proclamation were almoft inftantaneous. The inhabitants of the Jerfeys, who had conceived a violent hatred to the Britifh army, on account of their unchecked courfe of plundering, inftantly renounced their allegiance to Great Britain, and attached themfelves to the caufe of America. Several who were refolved to avenge their wrongs, joined the army under general Wafhington, while others rendered equal fervice to the fide to which they attached themfelves, by fupplying the American army with provifions and fuel, and by conveying intelligence of the operations of the Britifh army at Brunf-wick and Amboy.

Well-timed proclamation by general Wafhington.

In confequence of their affiftance, general Wafhington was enabled to harafs the Englifh greatly. The excurfions which the garrifon of Brunfwick made for forage, were often attended with fatal con-fequences; and as the American army had extended their line of cantonments from Morris Town to Woodbridge, within three miles of Amboy, the provifions that were forced to be conveyed by land to Brunfwick were often cut off by parties of the enemy, who were always on the watch, and to whom intelligence was regularly conveyed by thofe perfons who inhabited the fpace of ground be-tween Amboy and Brunfwick. General Howe too, as has been obferved, had iffued proclamations, calling upon the inhabitants to join him, in fupporting his majefty's government, and promifing

Howe's con-duct contraft-ed with that of Wafhing-ton.

I i them

them protection in both perfon and property. But no fooner had the army entered the Jerfeys, than the bufinefs (we fay bufinefs, for it was a perfect trade) of plunder began. The friend and the foe, from the hand of rapine, fhared alike. The people's property was taken, without being paid for, or even a receipt given, which would have been evidence that fuch property was taken; leaving the payment or non-payment to be determined by the iffue of the war, and the political merit of the parties. The Britifh army foraged indifcriminately, procuring confiderable fupplies of hay, oats, Indian corn, cattle, and horfes; which were never or but very feldom paid for. Neverthelefs the expences of the extraordinaries of the army were rapidly increafing, and ultimately fwelled to a moft unparalleled and alarming amount.

Before the difafter at Trenton, the people of the Jerfeys were well affected to his majefty's government. Numbers joined the royal army; and two brigades of provincials were raifed for the Britifh fervice, who, on many fubfequent occafions, difcharged their duty with all the zeal of good fubjects, and the bravery of veteran foldiers. But when the people found that the promifed protection was not afforded them; that their property was feized, and moft wantonly deftroyed; that, in many inftances, their families were infulted, ftripped of their beds, with other furniture—nay, even of their very wearing apparel; they then determined to try the other fide, trufting that they would at leaft, at one period or other, receive compenfation for the fupplies taken from them for the ufe of the American army. And it is but juftice to fay that the Americans never took any thing from their friends, but in cafes of neceffity; in which cafes they uniformly gave receipts for what they did take, always living, as long as they could, upon their enemies; and never fuffering their troops to plunder their friends with impunity. But at the fame time it is to be noticed, that the American troops

I   were

were fuffered to plunder the loyalifts, and to exercife with impunity every act of barbarity on that unfortunate clafs of people ; frequently inflicting on them even fcourges and ftripes.

In this manner ended the campaign of 1776 ; in the courfe of
which it has been fufficiently feen, how advantages were neglected on the one part, and trivial occurrences rendered highly beneficial on the other; and, what activity and perfeverance can effect,
even with inferiority of ftrength, when oppofed to negligence and
inertnefs.

C H A P. IX.

*Proceedings of Congress—They determine to renounce all Dependence
on Great Britain—Sketch of a new American Government.*

CHAP.
IX.

1776.

IN the midft of thefe operations in the Jerfeys, congrefs were not
idle. Though they could not afford at prefent much affiftance to
general Wafhington, they refolved to ftrengthen the band of union
between the thirteen colonies, by putting the laft hand to the famous fyftem of confederacy.

Hitherto their fyftem of conduct had proceeded upon certain fup-
pofitions of a reconciliation with the parent ftate. Thofe fuppo-
fitions, however, were now fuperfeded by the determination that
had been made to renounce all dependence upon Great Britain, and

American
congrefs de-
termine to re-
nounce all de-
pendence on
Great Bri-
tain.

to erect the colonies into fovereign ftates. In confequence of this
determination, a permanent form of government, relinquifhing every
idea of a fubordinate connection with the parent ftate, was abfolutely
neceffary to be fettled. A committee appointed to prepare a new form
of government, in the outfet of their compofition, made the following
alteration in the appellation of the colonies: Whereas they had hitherto ftyled themfelves the United Colonies; they now affumed the
name of the United States of America. The conftitution propofed
by this committee, was in fubftance as follows:

Sketch of a
new Ameri-
can govern-
ment.

1. That each colony fhould bind itfelf to affift the reft, and to re-
pel the attacks that might be made upon them on any pretence
whatever.

2. That

2. That each ſtate ſhould poſſeſs the power of regulating its own internal government, and of making laws in all caſes; provided they did not interfere with the general ſafety and welfare of the common cauſe.

3. That all negotiations, alliances, and treaties, ſhould be ſubmitted to the conſideration of the United States aſſembled in general congreſs; and that no ſtate in particular was to infringe the proviſions of this article on any pretence whatever.

4. That it ſhould be criminal in any perſon, poſſeſſing authority under the United States, to accept preſents, gratuities, employments, or titles, from any foreign power.

5. That no titles of nobility ſhould be conferred by the general aſſembly of the United States, or the aſſembly of any particular ſtates.

6. That none of the ſtates were to form alliances or private treaties among themſelves, without the conſent of the United States.

7. That no duties or impoſts were to be eſtabliſhed in any ſtate, which might tend to infringe the proviſions of any treaty which the general aſſembly might think proper to enter into with any foreign power.

8. That no particular ſtate was to increaſe its naval eſtabliſhment beyond the number preſcribed for each ſtate by the general aſſembly. That the military eſtabliſhment ſhould be governed by the ſame regulation. That a well-diſciplined militia was to be kept up in every ſtate, adequately armed and equipped; and that the public magazines ſhould always contain a ſufficient number of field-pieces, tents, and other neceſſary implements of war.

9. That all officers of the rank of colonel, and under, ſhould be appointed by the legiſlative body of each ſtate.

10. That the expences of war ſhould be defrayed out of the general treaſury of the United States.

11. That

11. That in order to conftitute a public fund, adequate to any particular exigencies, each of the ftates fhould contribute a certain fum, in proportion to the number of its inhabitants (Indians excepted). That this number might be now precifely determined, it was provided that the inhabitants of each ftate fhould be numbered every three years. This enumeration was then to be fent to the general affembly of the United States.

12. The affeffment determined on by this enumeration was to be paid by taxes levied by the authority of the legiflative body of each ftate.

13. When any queftion was fubmitted to the decifion of the general affembly, by any particular ftate, that decifion was to be binding.

14. War was not to be commenced without the confent of the general affembly, except in cafes of invafion, or where it was known that an invafion was intended, and the danger was too preffing to obtain the confent of the general affembly.

15. Commiffions to veffels or letters of marque and reprifal were not to be granted by any particular ftate, till after a declaration of war by the general affembly.

16. For the general intereft of the United States, each ftate was to nominate a certain number of delegates, who were to meet at Philadelphia on the firft Monday in November of each year.

17. To each ftate was to be attached the power of recalling their delegates, at any part of the year, and of appointing others in their room. The delegates of each ftate were to be maintained at the expence of that ftate, during the fitting of the general affembly, and alfo as long as they were members of the council of ftate.

18. Each ftate was to have a vote for the decifion of queftions in the general affembly.

19. To

19. To the general affembly alone was to belong the right of deciding on peace and war; to determine in all cafes of capture, whether by fea or land; to conftitute tribunals for the trial of piracies; to appoint and receive ambaffadors; to negotiate treaties; to decide the differences between each ftate; to coin money; to regulate commerce; to treat in all matters concerning the Indians; to appoint general officers of the land and naval forces; and to direct the operations of both in time of war.

20. A council of ftate was to be appointed by the general affembly, and alfo fuch committees and civil officers as fhould be neceffary to difpatch the public bufinefs during their fitting. The public affairs were to be under the direction of the council of ftate, after the rifing of the general affembly.

21. The prefident and other officers were to be appointed by the general affembly, to which were to belong the right and power of fixing the fums neceffary to be raifed for the public defence, and of determining the application of thofe fums; of borrowing money and of creating bills; of building and fitting out fleets; of deciding on the number of troops neceffary to be raifed; of calling upon each ftate for its proportion of military affiftance, and of requiring it to arm and equip the forces raifed in obedience to this requifition, in a proper manner.

22. The general affembly was to be allowed the power of demanding of any particular ftate more than its juft proportion; and compliance with this power was not to be refufed, unlefs the legiflative body of the ftate fhould deem fuch compliance to be injurious to its fecurity and fafety.

23. The general affembly was not to exercife any of the powers contained in the twenty-firft article, unlefs nine of the thirteen ftates fhould confent to it. On every point whatever, a decifion fhould be made by the majority of the United States.

24. No

24. No delegate was to be chosen for more than three years out of six.

25. No person possessed of any employment, or receiving a salary, or wages, was eligible to the office of a delegate.

26. The general assembly was to publish, monthly, a journal of their proceedings, except what might relate to treaties, alliances, or military operations, which it should be deemed necessary to keep secret.

27. The council of state was to consist of one delegate of each state, chosen by the other delegates of the said state.

Article 28th related to the powers of the council of state, which, during the adjournment of the general assembly, were similar to those allowed to the general assembly.

29. If Canada should be willing to accede to the present system of confederation, it was to be allowed all the benefits of it, and to be admitted into the union. No other colony, however, was to be admitted but by the consent of nine of the United States.

The foregoing articles were to be submitted to the legislative bodies of each state. If they approved of them, they were to authorise their delegates to ratify them in the general assembly: Thus ratified, the provisions of them were to be implicitly obeyed by all, and an eternal union was thus to be established. Such were the conditions of this celebrated treaty of union. After they had been prepared by the committee, they were submitted to congress, and solemnly discussed. Having received the approbation of congress, they were transmitted to the different colonies, and then ratified by all the delegates, who signed them on the fourth of October 1776.

October.

Such cool, deliberate, and resolute conduct was the more remarkable, that congress had now to contend with an additional enemy. This enemy was the Indians.—It has been shewn how unsuccessful every attempt had hitherto proved to detach the southern colonies
nies

nies from the fupport of the common caufe to their own immediate defence, by involving them in civil war through the means of the Regulators and Highland emigrants in the Carolinas, or of the negroes in Virginia. It has alfo been fhewn that the provincials adduced thefe attempts as charges againft their feveral governors. Unfuccefsful, however, as thefe endeavours had hitherto been, the confequences that would refult from fuch a plan of operations were too important to be neglected. Britifh agents were again employed in engaging the Indians to make a diverfion, and to enter the fouthern colonies on their back and defencelefs parts. Accuftomed to their difpofitions and habits of mind, the agents found but little difficulty in bringing them over to their purpofe by dint of prefents, and hopes of fpoil and plunder. The plan of action that was to be adopted in confequence of this confent, on the part of the Indians, was as follows : A large body of men was to be fent to Weft Florida, in order to penetrate through the territories of the Creeks, Cherokees, and Checkefaw Indians. The warriors of thefe nations were to join the body, and the Carolinas and Virginia were immediately to be invaded. At the fame time the attention of the colonifts was to be diverted by another formidable naval and military force, which was to make an impreffion on the fea-coafts.

But this undertaking was not to depend folely on the Britifh army and the Indians. It was intended to engage the affiftance of the white inhabitants of the back fettlements, who were known to be well affected to the Britifh caufe. Circular letters were accordingly fent to thofe perfons by Mr. Stuart, the principal agent for Indian affairs, requiring not only the well-affected, but alfo thofe who wifhed to preferve their properties from the miferies of civil war, to repair to the royal ftandard, as foon as it fhould be erected in the Cherokee country, with all their horfes, cattle, and provifions, for which they fhould be liberally paid. They were likewife required, in order to infure their fafety, and to diftinguifh them from the king's enemies, to fubfcribe a written declaration of their allegiance. Thefe operations were conducted with fuch plaufibility, that confiderable hopes were entertained of their fuccefs. Already had a large number of the Indians declared in favour of the Englifh; and even the Six Nations, who had fworn to the obfervance of a ftrict neutrality, violated their oaths, and committed feveral acts of hoftility. Matters were not yet ripe for execution, when the Creeks, a bloody and cruel race, eager to partake of the expected plunder, refolved not to await the arrival of the Britifh troops, but to commence the infurrection immediately. They proceeded in the execution of their intentions with incredible barbarity; but finding that they were not fupported, and beginning to confider that they fhould be overpowered if they acted fingly, they paufed in their career, and, in a confultation among the chiefs, it was determined to defift from hoftilities, and to fue for a peace with the colonifts. In the prefent fituation of affairs their requeft was eafily complied with, and they returned to their native poffeffions.

The Cherokees, ignorant of the determination of the Creek Indians, fent them word, as foon as they had completed their preparations, that they were going to march againft the enemy, and intreated their affiftance. The Creeks, however, returned for anfwer, " that the Cherokees had plucked the thorn out of their foot, " and were welcome to keep it." The Cherokees, notwithftanding this repulfe, proceeded to invade the back fettlements of Virginia and the Carolinas with inconceivable fury and barbarity; but their career was foon checked. The inhabitants of the provinces of Carolina and Virginia immediately affembled a large militia, which marched with great expedition to the relief of the back fettlers. The Cherokees were foon driven from the places of which they had poffeffed themfelves, and purfued into their own

country,

country, where their towns, their habitations, and their fields were
laid wafte, and a prodigious number of their warriors deftroyed.
In this dreadful dilemma they were glad to accept of any terms the
conquerors chofe to impofe on them. The Checkefaws, who, fortunately for them, had not completed their preparations, as foon as
they heard of the ill fuccefs that had attended their neighbours, the
Creeks and the Cherokees, determined to remain quietly within their
own confines. Thus, for the prefent, ended the defigns of the Englifh
on the back fettlements of America. The event was peculiarly
fortunate for congrefs; for it made them formidable to the Indians,
and attached feveral of the back fettlers to their caufe, convincing
them that they had now nothing to hope from a continuance of their
attachment to the government of Great Britain.

The congrefs, relieved from any apprehenfions of an invafion
on their frontier fettlements, and the grand fyftem of confederation being now ratified, were enabled to concentrate their attention
upon general Wafhington, whofe army they laboured with uncommon activity and diligence to fupply with the neceffaries it wanted,
and with new levies of men, in order that the enfuing campaign
might be commenced with a proper degree of vigour.

CHAP. X.

Situation of Affairs in Canada—General Carleton sends an Armament against Crown Point and Ticonderoga—Force opposed to this by the Americans.

General Carleton equips an armament against Crown Point and Ticonderoga.

THE Americans, though they were under the necessity of relinquishing their designs on Canada, still possessed Crown Point and Ticonderoga, and were masters of Lake Champlain. To dispossess them of these posts was an arduous and a difficult task, inasmuch as the British had not a vessel on Lake Champlain to oppose the American fleet. Difficult however as it was, general Carleton resolved to use every effort to procure a naval force adequate to the importance of the object in view. Thirty vessels were necessary to acquire a superiority of force on the Lake. The largest were sent from England; but it was found necessary to take them to pieces. It was also requisite to transport over land, and drag up the rapid currents of St. Therese and St. John's, with thirty long boats, a number of flat boats of great burthen, a gondola, weighing thirty tons, and above four hundred batteaux.

In spite of the fatigue of the undertaking, and the complexity of difficulty that attended it, the task was completed in about three months. Dispatch indeed was rendered absolutely necessary; for the winter season was approaching, and it was wished that the object should be attained before the severities of the season should render

2   any

any attempts of the kind impracticable. The difficulty of the scheme may be conceived from the following relation : The Eng_ lish had to pass two inland seas, to subdue an unknown force on each, and to make themselves masters of Crown Point and Ticonderoga.

In addition to these impediments, the communication between Lakes George and Champlain would not admit the passage of those vessels of force, which, after being successful on one lake, might be wanted on the other. Should, however, all these difficulties be overcome, then the army would still have to march through intricate forests, deep morasses, swamps, and a country still in a state of nature, before they could arrive at Albany, the first post southward. But the magnitude of the object rendered all these difficulties and dangers light : For general Carleton, in dispossessing the enemy of Crown Point and Ticonderoga, and in securing the possession of Lakes George and Champlain, had not only in view the clearing the frontiers of Canada, but of opening a communication with the northern and middle colonies, which he conceived he could then invade at will. Besides, by possessing Hudson's River, he knew that he should be able to co-operate with general Howe, and to afford him assistance in case of emergency. Added to these advantages, should success attend the present undertaking, the southern would be separated from the northern provinces. The latter would, of course, be under the necessity of sustaining the attacks of two armies, or of yielding to such terms as should be imposed upon them, leaving the southern colonies to continue the war alone. Nor could general Washington then hold the possession of the Jerseys, unless he chose to expose himself to the disadvantageous predicament of encountering a superior army in front, and the Canadian forces in his rear.

About

About the beginning of October the English fleet was ready to oppose the enemy on Lake Champlain. It confisted of the following veffels: The Inflexible, mounting eighteen twelve-pounders; which veffel had been re-conftructed at St. John's in twenty-eight days after her keel had been laid down; one fchooner, mounting fourteen, and another twelve, fix-pounders; a flat-bottomed batteau, carrying fix twenty-four, and the fame number of twelve-pounders, befides howitzers; and a gondola, with feven nine-pounders. Twenty fmaller veffels, called gun-boats, carried either brafs fieldpieces, or howitzers. Some long-boats were furnifhed in the fame manner. An equal number of large boats ferved as tranfports for the troops, baggage, warlike ftores, provifions, and all the other neceffaries for the army, that, under convoy of the fhipping, was to be conveyed acrofs the lakes. This fleet was commanded by captain Pringle, an active and brave officer, who had under his command feven hundred feamen. The army embarked in the batteaux, which were ordered to keep in the rear as foon as they had entered Lake Champlain, in order that the fleet might reconnoitre the fituation of the enemy.

The force oppofed to the British armament by the Americans

The force which the Americans had to oppofe to this armament was in every refpect unequal to it. Their veffels were neither fo well conftructed nor furnifhed with neceffaries as thofe of the English; befides, they were inferior in point of number, the fleet amounting only to fifteen veffels of different kinds, confifting of two fchooners, one floop, one cutter, three gallies, and eight gondolas. Colonel Arnold, who had acquired fuch fame before Quebec, was honoured with the command of it. On the eleventh of October the British fleet difcovered that of the enemy, very advantageoufly pofted off the Ifland Valicour, with an intention of defending the paffage between that ifland and the weftern main. A
                                                                fchooner

schooner and some gun-boats, being confiderably a-head of the reft C H A P. X. of the fleet, began the engagement, which was continued for fome hours on both fides with great intrepidity. Unfortunately the Inflexible, and the other fhips of force, could not advance near enough to take a part in the engagement, on account of the unfavourableneſs of the wind: For this reaſon captain Pringle, having conſulted general Carleton, thought it adviſable to order thoſe that were engaged to ſheer off, and, for the preſent, diſcontinue the action. In this attack the largeſt of the enemy's fhips was forced a-ſhore, defeated. and one of their gondolas funk. Night coming on, the enemy retired into Cumberland Bay, and captain Pringle, in order to prevent their retreat, formed the Britiſh fleet into a line as near the entrance of the bay as poſſible.

Arnold, who was fully fenfible of the infufficiency of his ſtrength, determined to take advantage of the darkneſs of the night, and retreat to Crown Point. This determination, notwithſtanding the proximity of the Britiſh fleet, he was enabled to execute in part. He retired out of the bay undiſcovered, and on the morning of the twelfth of October was out of fight. The Britiſh fleet immediately followed him, and the wind proving favourable on the thirteenth, he was overtaken a few leagues from Crown Point. Unable to avoid an engagement, Arnold reſolved to conduct it with his wonted intrepidity and reſolution. About noon the engagement commenced on both fides, and continued with great fury for two hours. Several of Arnold's fleet then left him, and retreated with great ſpeed to Ticonderoga. Arnold, however, refuſed to follow their puſillanimous example, and, with the remnant of his fleet, ſtill continued to reſiſt the attack of the Britiſh with unabated intrepidity. At length victory decided againſt him. His ſecond largeſt galley, called the Waſhington, commanded by bri-

gadier-

gadier-general Waterby, after a defperate refiftance, was at length forced to ftrike her colours. Finding then, that all his efforts would be ineffectual, he refolved to retreat. But even in this fituation he difplayed a magnanimity of courage that was aftonifhing. Though reduced to the neceffity of bending under fuperior power, he refolved that neither his men nor his veffels fhould be taken. The Congrefs galley, which he commanded, and five other gondolas, were run a-ground by his orders, and as foon as the men were landed, burnt down to the water's edge. He remained himfelf on board his own fhip till fhe was fet fire to in feveral places, in order that his flag might not be ftruck by the Englifh.

This victory on the Lakes was obtained without much lofs on the fide of the Englifh, two gun-boats only being loft, and not more than fifty men killed and wounded. On the fifteenth of October the Britifh fleet anchored off Crown Point, which the enemy immediately evacuated, retiring to their main body at Ticonderoga. General Carleton difembarking the army at Crown Point, remained there till the third of November. As the winter was advancing faft, he did not think it advifable to attempt the reduction of Ticonderoga. His opinion, however, did not coincide with that of other officers. Ticonderoga is but fifteen miles from Crown Point. It was well known that the fortifications were in no condition to withftand an attack; and indeed, general Gates, convinced of this fact, was prepared to evacuate it, as foon as any meafure fhould be adopted for the inveftiture of it. With refpect to the advanced ftate of the feafon, they thought that to be not a very ftrong argument, becaufe eight days would have been fully fufficient for the attainment of the defired object. The reduction of it would certainly have forwarded the operations of the enfuing campaign, and would have increafed the number of loyalifts, a body of

perfons

perfons from Albany, well affected to Great Britain, having
prepared themfelves to join the commander in chief as foon as
he fhould arrive àt Ticonderoga. General Carleton remained not
long at Crown Point, but returned to St. John's, and placed the
army in winter-quarters, Ifle aux Noix, being the frontier poft,
and the cantonments extending through different parts of the
country.

CHAP. XI.

Inevitable Neceffity of War in the general Opinion of the Britiſh Nation—Diſtreſs of the Weſt Indies—Capture of American Pri-vateers—Conduct of France and Spain—Meeting of Parliament— Debates in both Houſes.

CHAP.
XI.

1776.

Inevitable ne-
ceffity of war.

May 14.
1776.

Diftrefs of
the Britiſh
Weſt India
iſlands.

WAR, in the opinion of a great majority of the people of Great Britain, was now inevitable. There was, indeed, a kind of paſſion for it that pervaded the whole nation; nor could the depredations of the American cruizers, the capture of many richly-laden Weſt India veſſels, and the conſequent failure of ſeveral large houſes in the city, retard its operation, or arreſt its effect. Such a diſpoſition could not but be extremely agreeable to adminiſtration, becauſe it procured them a degree of ſtability that ſeemed to defy the attacks of an oppoſition ill connected, and proceeding on no regular or given line of conduct. In both houſes of parliament the force of government was fully adequate to every deſire that adminiſtration could entertain; neverthelefs, a few days before the recefs, the upper houſe received an addition of ten new peers. In every preceding debate on the American war, thoſe who oppoſed it had always predicted that it would involve the Britiſh Weſt India iſlands in great calamity and diſtreſs. Such predictions were then treated as chimerical.

In July, accounts were received of a ſcarcity in the iſlands of the neceſſaries of life, which, on that account, had, within a ſhort period, riſen to four times their uſual price. Other wants began to multi-ply; but as they did not immediately relate to a ſcarcity of neceſſary

ſuſtenance,

fuftenance, they were felt lefs fenfibly than otherwife they would have been. In addition to thefe diftreffes, the negroes in Jamaica had meditated an infurrection, which, however, was happily crufhed before it had attained any dangerous height. Our military ftrength in Jamaica was but weak, on account of the drafts that had been made for the American fervice. The naval force was on the point of being employed in convoying home a large fleet of merchantmen, which had completed their homeward-bound inveftments. Their departure was to be the period at which the infurrection was to commence. By fome fortunate event the plan was difcovered. The naval force, of courfe, was detained, and the merchantmen remained a month beyond the time fixed for their departure. After the mutinous fpirit of the negroes had been fufficiently quelled, the merchantmen were fuffered to depart; but the delay produced the moft ruinous confequences. The Americans thereby gained time to equip their privateers, and bad weather feparating the fleet, many of our merchantmen, whofe cargoes were extremely valuable, fell into their hands. The Britifh nation, by thefe captures alone, during the year 1776, loft property to the amount of above a million fterling.

It was about the middle of this year that France and Spain began to manifeft a hoftile difpofition towards Great Britain. Their ports in Europe were open to the American privateers, and Englifh prizes were fold without any attempts to make fuch fales fecret. Government remonftrated againft fuch proceedings; but their remonftrances were attended but with little effect: For though the open difpofal of prizes was checked, yet the practice ftill continued in fecret. In the French Weft India iflands, the countenance given to the Americans was much more avowed. French veffels accepted American commiffions, and carried on hoftilities againft the commerce of Great Britain, even without any American feamen on board. Thefe

Conduct of France and Spain.

L l 2   doings

doings were not unknown to the adminiftration of Great Britain; but it was judged neceffary that, for a time, the affertion of the national dignity and character fhould be fufpended.

In confequence of thefe captures by the American cruizers and the French veffels with American commiffions, the price of infurance was confiderably increafed; but that upon veffels bound from the Weft Indies amounted to the enormous fum of twenty-three pounds per cent.

It was now apparent to all, that Great Britain would not have only one enemy to contend with. Spain and France were bufily employed in making warlike preparations; the object of which, it was reafonably fuppofed, was to co-operate with America. Befides, the hoftile difpofition of each of the two powers was fufficiently difcernible from their treatment of the ally of Great Britain, Portugal. Thefe circumftances were fufficient to infufe into the mind of adminiftration a confiderable degree of difquiet and alarm: Neverthelefs they prepared to meet the impending ftorm with refolution, in which, it has been faid, and generally believed, they were encouraged and confirmed from a very high quarter. Nor, indeed, is there any thing more natural than that the auguft perfonage, now alluded to, confcious of a juft caufe, breathing the courage of his royal anceftry, and animated by the general vows of his people, fhould be willing to call forth all the refources, in order to maintain the glory, with the individuality, of the empire; refources which, in fpite of all our enemies, would have ultimately led to fafety and triumph, if they had been as prudently employed as they were liberally opened. About the middle of October fixteen additional fhips were put into commiffion, and feamen were invited to enter into the fervice, by a bounty of five pounds per man. A proclamation was iffued, commanding all Britifh feamen, who were employed in any foreign fervice, to return to England: A fecond and a third were

iffued,

iffued, laying an embargo on the exportation of provifions from Great Britain and Ireland ; and the fourth commanded the obfervance of a faft..

On the thirty-firft of October 1776, both houfes of parliament affembled, and the following is the fubftance of the fpeech delivered to them from the throne: It began by affuring them, that it would have afforded his majefty much fatisfaction to have been able to inform them that the difturbances in the revolted colonies were at an end, and that the people of America, recover͏ing from their delufion, had returned to their duty; but fo mutinous and determined was the fpirit of thofe who led them, that they had openly abjured and renounced all connection and communication with the mother-country, and had rejected, with the utmoft contempt, every concilitory propofition that had been fubmitted to them. After alluding to the late declaration of congrefs, in which they had erected the colonies into fovereign and independent ftates, it was contended that much mifchief would accrue, not only to the commerce of Great Britain, but to the general fyftem of Europe, if this rebellion and revolt were fuffered to take root. Neverthelefs it was afferted, that this benefit would refult from the open declaration of the rebellious colonies—that their intentions being now clearly underftood, would produce unanimity at home, becaufe every one muft be convinced of the neceffity of the meafures propofed to be adopted. The fuccefs of the Britifh arms in Canada, and on the fide of New York, was adduced as a good reafon for fuppofing that the moft beneficial confequences would arife from it. Another campaign, however, muft be prepared for, and the fupplies neceffary for carrying it on, procured as foon as poffible.

The conduct of Spain towards the Britifh ally, Portugal, was next adverted to; and it was ftated that, though a continuance of the general tranquillity in Europe was hoped, yet it was thought moft advifable viſeable to increaſe the defenſive reſources at home. The diſpoſition of other European powers was declared to be pacific. After expreſſing a conviction of the cheerfulneſs with which the neceſſary ſupplies would be granted, the ſpeech in concluſion aſſured both houſes that his majeſty had no other end in view, by his preſent ſyſtem of conduct, than to reſtore the revolted colonies to their former ſituation of proſperity and ſecurity under the dominion of Great Britain. The addreſſes in anſwer to this ſpeech were couched in the uſual form : Amendments, however, were propoſed in both houſes.

In the houſe of commons lord John Cavendiſh moved an amendment to the following effect : It included an enlarged view of the conduct of adminiſtration with reſpect to America, and expreſſed great regret at beholding the hearts of a large, and hitherto loyal, portion of his majeſty's ſubjects alienated from his government. This event, it was contended, could not have been produced without great miſconduct on the part of thoſe who poſſeſſed the direction of the affairs of government; the particulars of which miſconduct were ſtated, at great length, and with much animation, in the houſe of lords. A ſimilar amendment, propoſed by the marquis of Rockingham, was defended by ſimilar arguments. The miniſter however, as uſual, was ſupported by a large majority. In the houſe of commons the amendment propoſed by lord John Cavendiſh was rejected by two hundred and forty-two, and ſupported by only eighty-ſeven. The original addreſs was then put and carried. In the upper houſe the friends of the miniſter were equally numerous. The marquis of Rockingham's motion was negatived by ninety-one lords to twenty-ſix. The propoſed amendment, however, was entered in the Journals of the houſe, in form of a proteſt, and ſigned by fourteen peers. Yet was not the miniſter ſupported by a large majority in parliament only : The obſtinate and unvarying oppoſition which the Americans

had

had fhewn towards the mother-country, and the arguments that
had been adduced by the adherents of adminiftration, had, in a
great manner, eftranged the hearts of the people from their brethren
in the colonies. Perhaps too, from national pride, which it is not
my intention to condemn, they were induced to fupport the war,
from a wifh that the mother-country might convince the world
that fhe poffeffed the means of fubduing all who were hardy enough
to oppofe her.

C H A P. XII.

Proclamation iffued by Lord and General Howe—Debates upon it—
The American Laws propofed to be revifed by Lord John Cavendifh—
This Motion rejected—The Propriety of a partial Seceffion confidered
—Seamen voted—Naval Affairs—Supplies for the Military and
Naval Service—Recefs of Parliament.—1776.

CHAP.
XII.
1776.

SCARCELY had the addreffes from both houfes been prefented
to his majefty, when the proclamation iffued by lord Howe and
his brother, fubfequently to the capture of New York, was publifhed
in one of the morning papers. This was conceived to be extraordinary, becaufe, although two gazettes had been publifhed the preceding day, no notice had been taken of fuch a proclamation in
either of them. On the day on which the proclamation appeared in the morning paper, lord John Cavendifh fubmitted it
to the confideration of the houfe of commons, though he affected not to confider it in any other light than as a forgery,
and an impofition on the people, which required exemplary
punifhment.

Nov. 6.

In reply to this fpeech, the minifter acknowledged that fuch a proclamation had been made, and that the paper now produced contained an authentic copy of it. Lord John Cavendifh, on receiving
this information, immediately rofe with great warmth and indignation. He reprobated the conduct of adminiftration, contending
that they had grofsly infulted the houfe by withholding fuch an important

portant piece of intelligence, and by fuffering it to come to the knowledge of the public through the medium of a common paper. But this treatment was not different from that which the minifter had thought proper to fhew to parliament from the commencement of the American difturbances; a treatment that, whilft the fhadow of a conftitution remained, and minifters continued to be refponfible for their conduct, could not be defended on any grounds or by any arguments whatever. Adminiftration, on the other hand, and their adherents, contended that the promife held out in the proclamation by the commiffioners was not novel. It was only purfuing that mode of conduct which had been adopted by parliament at the commencement of the difturbances, viz. the reftoration of peace to America. With regard to the infulting treatment with which adminiftration had been charged in not publifhing the proclamation in the gazette, it was faid, that it feemed not to be of fufficient importance, becaufe it was neither a treaty, nor part of one; it only formed a preliminary, which might eventually lead to one. If, therefore, this preliminary were even important enough to be laid before parliament, minifters were juftified in not purfuing fuch a meafure by precedent. The negotiation between Mr. Pitt and M. De Buffy was not laid before the houfe of commons during its pendency. The motion for a committee was oppofed in the moft ftrenuous manner. It was contended that it would tend rather to impede than accelerate the negotiations of the commiffioners, and to infufe into the minds of the Americans improper jealoufies and apprehenfions. Befides, it would be impolitic to feem too fond of conceding; for the Americans would then demand more than they might originally intend. Another, and moft forcible, objection to the motion was, that it would be abfurd to confider of the revifal or repeal of laws, the authority of which was denied in the moft unqualified manner. America had declared herfelf inde-

VOL. I. M m pendent.

pendent. The firſt point therefore to be ſettled, preliminary to any negotiation, was the queſtion of independence. As long as ſhe perſiſted in this independence, no treaty could be begun, and all conceſſions would be diſhonourable. If ſhe conſented to give it up, and to acknowledge the authority of the mother-country, then would be the proper ſeaſon to reviſe and repeal obnoxious laws, and to eſtabliſh regulations conſonant with the rights of thoſe who were to be bound by them. From the approaching campaign much was to be expected. The tyranny of the congreſs would operate in favour of the Britiſh cauſe, and the acknowledged ſuperiority of the Britiſh troops, both in number and in diſcipline, would produce conſequences favourable to the mother-country, and likely to put a ſpeedy termination to the war. After a very long and intereſting debate, the motion was put, and the houſe divided: Forty-ſeven ſupported the motion, and one hundred and nine voted againſt it.

The rejection of this motion produced an extraordinary effect. Several members of the minority withdrew themſelves whenever any queſtions relative to America were diſcuſſed. They did not wholly refrain from attending the houſe; but as ſoon as the private buſineſs of the day was diſpatched, they made their uſual obeiſance to the ſpeaker, and retired. Thus, for ſome time, all debates upon important ſubjects were avoided, and vaſt ſupplies were granted without a ſingle obſervation with reſpect to their tendency, or the purpoſes to which they were to be applied. The members who ſeceded adduced the following reaſons in juſtification of their conduct: As affairs were at preſent ſituated, all oppoſition to the propoſitions of government, with reſpect to American affairs, was not only fruitleſs, but contemptible, on account of the numbers that ſupported the miniſter on every queſtion. They were tired with oppoſing reaſon and argument to ſuperior power and numbers. This conduct, however, of the ſeceding members, did not receive the approbation

· of

of the oppofition in general. Several contended that a partial feceffion was inconfiftent with the duties attached to the fituation of
a member of parliament. A collective feceffion had been fanctioned
by a precedent in the reign of the firft Charles, but it ought always
to be general.

The difunion occafioned by this, difference of opinion, added
greatly to the ftrength of adminiftration, and contributed not a
little to increafe the number of thofe who fupported the continuance
of the war. When the minifter, in a committee of fupply, propofed
that forty-five thoufand feamen fhould be voted for the fervice of
the enfuing year, Mr. Luttrell, a member in oppofition, feized the
opportunity of reprobating, in very fevere terms, the conduct of the
peer who poffeffed the rank of firft lord of the admiralty. He
charged him with wilfully impofing on the parliament and the nation
by a fallacious account of the ftate of the navy both with refpect to
the fhips and the feamen. The minifter, in reply to thefe obfervations, vindicated the conduct of the peer alluded to, and contended that it was improper to attack a perfon who, from his ſtation, could not defend himfelf in that houfe. He alfo alleged, that
the introduction of the accufation, without any previous notice, was
diforderly, and inconfiftent with the rule of parliament.

Mr. Luttrell, however, infifted that, as a member of parliament,
he had a right to make fuch obfervations on the conduct of minifters
as appeared to him to be well-founded. With refpect to the want of
a formal accufation, he would remove all objections on that head
when the houfe fhould be refumed. Accordingly he took the
earlieft opportunity of moving for feveral returns of the navy.
Thefe, he contended, would eftablifh the charges he had adduced
againft the noble lord, and convince the houfe what was the real
ftate of the naval refources of the country. Thefe returns, however, were refufed by adminiftration, and their refufal was fupported

on

on the following grounds: It was contended that a difclofure of the naval ftrength or weaknefs of the country would be attended with injurious confequences, inafmuch as, if Great Britain were fuperior to other powers, they would be induced to be more eircumfpect in their defigns, and if fhe were weaker than them, they would thereby be encouraged to take advantage of our defencelefs fituation.

The fupplies for the navy, granted this year, amounted to three millions two hundred and five thoufand five hundred and five pounds; including the ordinary, at four hundred thoufand pounds; and the expences of building and repairing fhips, at four hundred and fixty-two thoufand five hundred pounds. In this account, however neither the fum voted to Greenwich hofpital, nor the million granted at the clofe of the feffion for the difcharge of the navy debt, were included. The fupplies for the military eftablifhment amounted to a fum little lefs than the fupplies for the navy—the amount was three millions. The extraordinaries, however, of the preceding year, amounting to one million two hundred thoufand pounds, with frefh contracts for German forces, expences of half-pay and Chelfea hofpital, were not included in the grofs fum. All the neceffary public bufinefs being difpatched on the thirteenth of December, both houfes adjourned to the twenty-firft of January.

Adjourn-
ment of par-
liament.

CHAP. XIII.

Letters of Marque and Reprifal Bill—Bill for fecuring Perfons charged with High-Treafon—Debates upon it—Amendment propofed by Mr. Dunning—Agreed to—The Bill carried through both Houfes—Extraordinary unprovided Expences of the War voted—Motion for an Addrefs to the Throne by the Earl of Chatham—Rejeincluded— Prorogation of the Parliament.—1777.

AS foon as the parliament met after the recefs, a bill was paffed, authorifing any owners or captains of private merchant-fhips to make prizes of all veffels belonging to the thirteen American colonies.

On the fixth of February, the minifter moved in the houfe of commons for leave to bring in a bill, to fecure and detain perfons charged with, or fufpected of, the crime of high-treafon, committed in America or on the high feas, or the crime of piracy. In fupport of his motion he obferved that, during the prefent difturbances, prifoners had been made in the actual commiffion of the crime of high-treafon; others, fufpected of the fame crime, could not be fecured, on account of the want of fufficient evidence. Formerly, in cafes of rebellion and revolt, and when an invafion was apprehended, parliament granted this power to the crown; but in the prefent period, as neither rebellion at home, nor invafion from abroad, were in danger of being experienced, he fhould not requeft that power in its full extent. The law now did not empower government officially to apprehend the moft fufpected perfon, nor could the crown confine rebel prifoners or pirates in any other place than in the com-

mon

3

mon gaols. To remedy thefe inconveniences, and to empower his majefty to confine fuch perfons in the fame manner as other prifoners of war, until criminal proceedings could be inftituted againft them, were the objects propofed to be attained by the prefent bill. Leave was given for the introduction of the bill: On the queftion for the fecond reading of it, it appeared that the enacting claufe rendered all perfons taken in the act of high-treafon, or fufpected of it, liable to be committed to prifon without bail or trial, during the continuance of the law. When the queftion was put, a gentleman of great eminence in his profeffion (Mr. Dunning) animadverted feverely on the conduct of the minifter, in attempting, when the houfe was thinly attended, to introduce and precipitate the paffage of a bill, which was to undermine that bulwark of the conftitution, the Habeas Corpus act. Time, he contended, ought to be given to the nation to confider whether they would furrender the foundation and corner-ftone of all the rights which they poffeffed. For thefe reafons, and in order to prevent the fecond reading of the bill, he moved that it fhould be printed; in which the minifter was under the neceffity of acquiefcing. The introduction of this bill recalled feveral of thofe members who had feceded from the houfe. In every ftage through which the bill paffed, it was violently oppofed by the minority, who contended that no reafon exifted for invefting the crown with fo dangerous a power; that it would tend to widen the breach between the mother-country and the colonies, and cut off all hopes of a conciliation of the differences between them. Befides, it was contended, that the power might be extended to innocent perfons, and would thereby become an inftrument of tyranny and oppreffion. Several amendments were propofed, all of which were rejected, except one on the third reading, propofed by Mr. Dunning. The amendment was contained in the following claufe: " Provided alfo, and be it hereby declared, that nothing herein

" contained

Debate upon it.

Amendment propofed by Mr. Dunning,

" contained is intended, or fhall be conftrued to extend to the cafe
" of any other prifoner or prifoners, than fuch as have been in fome
" one of the colonies before mentioned, or on the high feas, at the
" time or times of the offence or offences wherewith he or they
" fhall be charged." . The amendment, with fome trifling alteration,
was agreed to. The acceptance of this claufe afforded great. joy to agreed to.
the minority, who confidered the bill as divefted thereby of the
moft dangerous tendency. Neverthelefs they ftill continued to oppofe the principle of the bill with undiminifhed vigour and unwearied perfeverance. In this, however, they were unfuccefsful, and
the bill was paffed without a divifion.

In the houfe of lords, no oppofition was made to it, all the peers The bill car-
in the minority having abfented themfelves, except the earl of ried through
Abingdon.   both houfes.

About the latter end of February, the feveral extraordinary un- Extraordina-
provided expences of the war, to the amount of two millions one ry unprovided
hundred and feventy thoufand pounds, were defrayed by the houfe the war voted.
of commons. No debates of any importance relative to the American
war occurred in either houfe, till the end of May. An addrefs to
the throne was then moved in the houfe of peers, by the venerable
earl of Chatham. At this period his lordfhip laboured under many
bodily infirmities. Neverthelefs his intellectual vigour remained un-
impaired, and, in his zeal to ferve his country, the enfeebled ftate
of his body was forgotten. His lordfhip had in former periods repeatedly endeavoured to reconcile the differences between the colonies and the mother-country, and though his attempts were not attended with the defired effect, yet he refolved to make one effort more.

The lords being accordingly fummoned on the thirtieth of May, his
lordfhip moved that an addrefs fhould be prefented to his majefty, Motion for an
reprefenting that the houfe of lords were fenfible of the ruin that throne by the
threatened the country from a continuation of the unnatural war with earl of Chat-
                                                                    ham.
                                                           the

the Britifh colonies in America, and advifing that the moft fpeedy and effectual meafures fhould be taken for putting a period to fuch fatal hoftilities, upon the only juft and folid foundation, namely, the removal of the accumulated grievances ; with an affurance, that the houfe would enter upon that great and neceffary work with cheerfulnefs and difpatch, in order to open to his majefty the only means of regaining the affections of the Britifh colonies, and of fecuring to Great Britain the commercial advantages of thofe valuable poffeffions; fully perfuaded that to heal and to redrefs would be more congenial with the goodnefs and magnanimity of his majefty, and more prevalent over the hearts of generous and free-born fubjects, than the rigours of chaftifement, and the horrors of civil war, which hitherto had ferved only to fharpen refentment and confolidate union, and, if continued, muft finally end in diffolving all ties between Great Britain and her colonies.

Such was the purport of the addrefs. In commenting on the neceffity of an affent being given to it, his lordfhip declared, that under the words *accumulated grievances*, he meant to convey every tranfaction, with refpect to America, fince 1763, and the redrefs of all their grievances, including more particularly the right of difpofing of their own money. This fpirit of conduct would pave the way for treaty and negotiation; it would teftify the amicable temperament of the parliament; and thus the chief obftacle being removed, all other matters would follow as things of courfe. The preffing and immediate neceffity of acquiefcing in the addrefs he infifted on, from the danger to which Great Britain was expofed from France.—A few weeks, and the fate of the country, as a nation, might be decided by a treaty between the houfe of Bourbon and the Americans. His lordfhip proceeded to ftate the immenfe advantages that the mother-country would lofe from the commerce of the colonies being turned into another channel, and

                                                        fuffered

fuffered to flow into the hands of the natural enemies of Great Britain. Trade, he faid, was rapidly declining, inafmuch as it was now carried on in French and other bottoms ; the conqueft of America was impracticable; and if it were not, it would be attended with the moft ruinous confequences. To ufe the words of this great man, "America," he declared, " was contending with Great " Britain, under the mafked battery of France, which would · open " upon this country, as foon as fhe perceived that we were fufficiently " weakened for her purpofe, and fhe found herfelf fufficiently " prepared for war."

In reply to his lordfhip's obfervations, and to thofe who fupported him, adminiftration oppofed the addrefs on the old grounds that independence was the primary object of the Americans, that their prefent conduct was but the effect of the premeditation of feveral years, and that all conceffions on the part of Great Britain would be equally ridiculous and impolitic. The danger held out from France was again denied, and it was contended that the affiftance afforded the Americans in that quarter, originated, not in the government, but in private individuals, and in that fpirit of enterprife for which that nation had always been remarkable. After an animated debate, the queftion was put, when rejected. there appeared, on a divifion—for the propofed addrefs, twenty-eight —againft it, ninety-nine.

The money bills *, a vote of credit, and the other public bufinefs being difpatched, his majefty thought proper to prorogue both houfes of parliament on the fixth of June. In his fpeech from the throne, he declared his entire approbation of the meafures that

had

---

* The fpeech of the fpeaker of the houfe of commons, fir Fletcher Norton, afterwards lord Grantley, to his majefty, on the feventh of May 1777, in the houfe of peers, on prefenting a bill for the better fupport of his majefty's houfehold, which made a great noife at

had been adopted during the continuance of the feffion; teftified his thankfulnefs for the liberality and cheerfulnefs with which the extraordinary fupplies for the fervice of the current year had been

that time, and was a fubjed of various refledion, together with a confequent refolution and vote of the houfe of commons, we here lay before our readers.

Moft Gracious Sovereign,

THE bill, which it is now my duty to prefent to your majefty, is intituled, " An ad for " the better fupport of his majefty's houfehold, and of the honour and dignity of the crown " of Great Britain :" To which your commons humbly beg your royal affent.

By this bill, fir, and the refpedful circumftances which preceded and accompanied it, your commons have given the fulleft and cleareft proof of their zeal and affedion for your majefty. For in a time of public diftrefs, full of difficulty and danger, their conftituents labouring under burthens almoft too heavy to be borne, your faithful commons poftponed all other bufinefs; and with as much difpatch as the nature of their proceedings would admit, have not only granted to your majefty a large prefent fupply, but alfo a very great additional revenue;—great, beyond example; great, beyond your majefty's higheft expence.

Butt all this, fir, they have done in a well-grounded confidence, that you will apply wifely what they have granted liberally; and feeling, what every good fubjed muft feel with the greateft fatisfadion, that, under the diredion of your majefty's wifdom, the affluence and grandeur of the fovereign will refled dignity and honour upon his people.

[Copied from the Votes of the Houfe of Commons, 7th May 1777.]

Ordered, Nem. Con.

That Mr. Speaker be defired to print the fpeech by him made to his majefty in the houfe of peers, this day, upon his prefenting to his majefty the bill for the better fupport of his majefty's houfehold, and of the honour and dignity of the crown of Great Britain, which then received the royal affent.

9th May 1777. Some allufions having been made, in the debate on the laft queftion, to the fpeech of Mr. Speaker, delivered at the bar of the houfe of peers, on Wednefday laft, Mr. Speaker, as foon as the faid queftion was determined, called the attention of the houfe to this fubjed, and defired that a copy of the fpeech then made by him, might be read at the table. And the fame being read accordingly, Refolved, That the fpeaker of this houfe, in his fpeech to his majefty at the bar of the houfe of peers on Wednefday laft, and which was defired *nemine contradicente,* by this houfe to be printed, did exprefs, with juft and proper energy, the zeal of this houfe, for the fupport of the honour and dignity of the crown, in circumftances of great public charge.

Ordered,

That the thanks of this houfe be returned to Mr. Speaker, for his faid fpeech to his majefty.

voted;

voted; and finally expreffed his hope that, by a well-concerted C H A P. and vigorous exertion of the great force entrufted to his hands, XIII. the operations of the prefent campaign would effectually tend to 1777. the fuppreffion of the rebellion in America, and to the re-eftablifh-ment of that conftitutional obedience which all the fubjects of a free ftate owed to the authority of the law. The parliament was Prorogation proqued to the twenty-firft of July. of parlia-ment.

N n 2

C H A P. XIV.

Opening of the Campaign—Expedition to Peek's Hill—To Danbury —Veffels and Provifions deftroyed at Saggy Harbour—The Commander in Chief takes the Field—Endeavours to bring Wafhington to an Action—The Britifh Troops relinquifh the Jerfeys— General Prefcot carried off—Commander in Chief proceeds to Chefapeak Bay—Lands at the Head of the Elk—Proclamation iffued—General Wafhington moves to the North Side of the Brandywine River, in order to defend Philadelphia—Action at the Brandywine—General Wayne defeated—Royal Army paffes the Schuylkill—Lord Cornwallis takes poffeffion of Philadelphia.

CHAP.
XIV.

1777.

IT has been already fhewn what hardfhips the Britifh army endured at Brunfwick and Amboy during the winter, and till the commencement of the fpring. The weather was particularly fevere; the duty unremitting and hard; the enemy watchful; and provifions and forage were not obtained without repeated fkirmifhes. Neverthelefs the foldiers endured thefe hardfhips with a fortitude and a perfeverance that acquired them infinite honour.

At the opening of the feafon a body of provincial troops, amounting to feveral thoufand men, was embodied under the direction of the commander in chief. Thefe men were difciplined by thofe who had been under the neceffity of relinquifhing their poffeffions, and of flying from their habitations, on account of their attachment to the Britifh caufe. Thefe troops were allowed the fame pay as the regulars, with a further advantage of receiving an allotment of lands

3

at

at the conclusion of the disturbances. Such a large body of strength drawn from the heart of the country with which the British were waging war, was a most fortunate circumstance. It decreased the resources of the country, and it enabled the veteran troops to adopt. more active operations than they would otherwise have been enabled. to undertake. These provincial forces, it is true, were inexperienced, and unacquainted with military discipline, but they were extremely well fitted for garrison service, and for the defence of a town. Accordingly they were immediately sent to New York, from which the regulars were drafted in order to join the grand army. Governor Tryon, who had been very active in raising and disciplining these new forces, was raised to the rank of major-general of the provincials, by which he was enabled, on any emergency, to unite the divided bodies of these troops, and to condense them into one body *.

CHAP. XIV.
1777.

The natural strength of the tract which the Americans possessed, and which has been before described, and its fertility in resources, had induced them, notwithstanding the severities of the winter, to employ themselves in adding as much as possible to this natural strength, by erecting forts and building mills and magazines. Of this tract of land, the most mountainous, and of course the most advantageous, was a place which bore the appellation of the Manor

Opening of the campaign.

* About this time the royalists in the counties of Somerset and Worcester, in the province of Maryland, became so formidable that an insurrection was dreaded: And it was feared that the insurgents would, in such a case, be joined by a number of disaffected persons in the county of Sussex in the Delaware state. Congress, to prevent this evil, recommended the apprehension and removal of all persons of influence, or of desperate characters, within the counties of Sussex, Worcester, and Somerset, who manifested a disaffection to the American cause, to some remote place within their respective states, there to be secured. From appearances, congress had also reason to believe that the loyalists in the New England governments and New York state had likewise concerted an insurrection. See Gordon's History of the American Revolution, vol. ii. p. 461, 462. By the same authority we are informed that general Gates wrote to general Fellows for a strong military force, for the prevention of plots and insurrection in the provinces of New England and New York.

of

of Courland. This was in a manner converted into a citadel, and large quantities of provisions, forage, and stores of every kind, were deposited in it. About fifty miles from New York, up the North River, was a place called Peek's Hill, which served as a port to Courland Manor, and by which stores and provisions were received and conveyed either to the army or to the numerous erections situated in the more interior parts.

Convinced of the importance of this place, and the distrefs to which the Americans would be driven if they should be deprived of it, the commander in chief determined to open the campaign by an attack upon it. An attempt upon the Manor of Courland was deemed unadvisable, on account of its great natural and acquired strength, and the consequent disadvantage of a battle in such a place. Besides, even if such an attempt had not been judged improper, it would have been absolutely necessary, preliminary to it, to have secured the poffeffion of Peek's

Expedition
to Peek's
Hill,
Hill. In pursuance of this resolution, a detachment of five hundred men, under the command of colonel Bird of the fifteenth regiment, was ordered to proceed from New York about the latter end of March, on this service. This detachment embarked on board two tranfports, which conveyed them to the place of their deftination the day after they left New York. On their approach a body of between feven and eight hundred men drew up at a diftance, under the command of a colonel Macdougal, with a feeming determination of oppofing the British armament. On the nearer advancement, however, of colonel Bird, they thought proper to retire from Peek's Hill, and being unable to remove the ftores and provifions it contained, fet fire to the barracks and ftore-houfes. Unable, on this account, to bring off the different articles that were contained in the magazine, the British thought proper to complete the conflagration; after which they returned to New York.

The

The confequences that had refulted from the fuccefs of this ex- C H A P.
pedition were not fo important as had been expected. The com- XIV.
mander in chief had received falfe intelligence of the fituation of 1777.
Peek's Hill, which did not contain that quantity of ftores and provifions he had been led to expect. Neverthelefs it was abfolutely
neceffary that the ftrength of the enemy fhould be impaired and
weakened as much as poffible, by cutting off their refources, and
curtailing the means by which they were enabled to convey fupplies to the troops ftationed in different parts of the Manor of
Courland.

The commander in chief having received intelligence of a large
quantity of ftores having been depofited on the borders of Connecticut, in the town of Danbury, and other parts on the confines of
Courland Manor, refolved to undertake another expedition againft and to Dan-
thofe parts. Two thoufand men, drafted from different regiments, bury.
were employed in this fervice, which was entrufted to the command of major-general Tryon, who had accepted of the rank of
major-general of provincials, and who panted for a military command. Sir William Howe very prudently appointed general Agnew,
and fir William Erfkine, to accompany governor Tryon, in his new
character of general on this fervice. On the twenty-fifth of April
this detachment embarked from New York in tranfports, under the
convoy of two frigates. They proceeded up the Eaft River, as far
as Camp's Point, where they landed. At ten o'clock at night they
began their march to Danbury, where, about eight o'clock the next
day, they arrived. The enemy, entertaining no apprehenfion of the
intentions of the Englifh, and unprepared to refift them, retired on
their approach, and fuffered them to enter the town without oppofition.
Convinced of the impoffibility of carrying off the ftores that were contained in the town, and indeed having brought with them no carriages
neceffary for this purpofe, the Englifh were under the neceffity of fetting

ting fire to the place *. The conflagration was not completed till the next morning. The detachment immediately set out on their return to the transports. The enemy, however, during the time occupied in the burning of Danbury, had assembled from all quarters, and posted themselves, under the command of general Arnold, at a tcwn called Ridgefield, through which it was necessary for the English to pass. In order to render their situation more secure, Arnold had thrown up intrenchments.

The British troops did not expect to meet with any resistance ; nevertheless, on their arrival at Ridgefield, they attacked the American intrenchments with great spirit, and carried them in a short space of time. The troops were by this time extremely fatigued from want of rest and their late hard service. As the day was on the wane, they lay on their arms till morning, having first taken the precaution to form themselves into an oblong square. As soon as they began their march at day-break, the enemy, who, during the night, had received a considerable increase of strength, assailed them from all quarters ; and from the houses and stone walls, with which that country abounds, did considerable execution on the shipping as the British retreated. The route of the British troops lay over a bridge, of which the enemy took possession, as well as some strong ground that commanded the pass beyond the bridge. They were in possession of some field-artillery, which had been brought by general Wooster, and the front they presented to the English was extremely formidable. Fortunately, however, the guide whom the English had engaged conducted them to a part of the river, three

* The British destroyed at Banbury 1600 barrels of pork and beef, 600 barrels of flour, upwards of 2000 barrels of wheat, rye, and Indian corn, a very considerable quantity of military clothing, and 2000 tents ; a loss which, from their scarcity, was severely felt by the Americans. The British, in their return, destroyed about 70 barrels of flour, and 112 hogsheads of rum.

miles

miles above the bridge, which they forded, and which the enemy had neglected to fecure, having deemed the paffage of it impracticable. This manœuvre fomewhat difconcerted them; neverthelefs they continued their fkirmifhes and attacks on the Britifh troops till they had arrived within half a mile of the fhipping. Two diftinct bodies of the enemy now appeared, making a fhew of attacking the detachment, which by this time was almoft exhaufted with fatigue. The men had had no reft for three days and nights, and feveral of them dropped on the road with fatigue. Difpirited however and exhaufted as they were, brigadier-general Erfkine putting himfelf at the head of four hundred of the moft able of the detachment, attacked and broke the two columns, and put them to flight. So great was the panic among them, occafioned by this fpirited attack, that they did not attempt any further annoyance on the troops, though they might have done them confiderable damage on account of the numerous rocks that fkirt the fhore. The Englifh, embarking in the tranfports, returned to New York. It may be reafonably doubted, whether the lofs which the Britifh fuftained in this expedition, did not more than counterbalance the advantage derived from the complete attainment of their object.

In this expedition near two hundred men, including ten officers, were killed and wounded on the part of the Britifh. The lofs of the Americans was much greater, and general Woofter, with fome field-officers, was numbered amongft the flain.

The enemy feized every opportunity of annoying the Englifh by fkirmifhes, and the thirty-third regiment, and a battalion of the feventy-firft Highland regiment, who were pofted at Bonham Town, between Amboy and Brunfwick, loft a great many men, the enemy conftantly attacking their pickets.

On the twelfth of April lord Cornwallis, with a confiderable detachment, effected a furprife upon the enemy's advanced pofts at

VOL. I.   O o   Bondwick,

Boudwick, feven miles from Brunfwick, where the American general Clinton was ftationed with about twelve hundred men. The
furprife would have been more complete had not fome chaffeurs,
who were in the van, given the alarm too foon, by firing on the
centinels; neverthelefs the enemy were routed, and retired from the
town, leaving fome field artillery behind them, and about one hundred prifoners.   On the nineteenth of April, an attempt was made
by general Vaughan, with the garrifon at Amboy, to cut off the
enemy's advanced pickets at Woodbridge.   His intentions, however, were prevented, on account of the Americans having received
intimation of his defigns.

On the eighth of May, an attempt was made on the poft of
Pifcataway, by the American general Stevens, who had two thoufand men under his command.   The forty-fecond regiment, which
was cantoned there, fuftained the attack with great refolution, and
forced the enemy to retreat, after a furious engagement, with confiderable lofs.

About the middle of this month, the Americans having received
intelligence that a large quantity of provifions and forage were depofited in Long Ifland, at a place called Saggy Harbour, refolved to
attempt the capture of them.   In this defign they were encouraged
by the diftance of the place from New York, and the weaknefs of
it, being defended only by an armed fchooner of twelve guns.   Neverthelefs fome danger attended the execution of the fcheme, on account of the neceffity of croffing the Sound, which was full of Britifh
cruizers.   This expedition was entrufted to colonel Meigs, an active
officer, who had been trained under Arnold, and had been taken
prifoner in the attempt to ftorm the city of Quebec.   The colonel,
with his detachment, traverfed the Sound in whale-boats, landed on
the north branch of the ifland, and after carrying the boats over an
arm of land, embarked again, and landed on the fouth branch of the
                                                            ifland,

ifland, within four miles of Saggy Harbour. At this place they arrived before break of day, and immediately commenced the attack. The place was vigoroufly defended by the crews of the merchant-veffels and the fchooner, which kept up a very heavy fire upon them; neverthelefs they fucceeded in their intentions, having burnt a dozen brigs and floops that lay at the wharf, and deftroyed every article of provifion and ftores that was depofited on the fhore. In this attack ninety of the Englifh were made prifoners, viz. the officer who commanded the harbour, and his men; the commiffaries, and the crews of the veffels which they had burnt.

There is a circumftance in this expedition, which, if it be true, is curious. The Americans relate, that colonel Meigs, with his detachment, returned to Guildford in Connecticut, within twenty-five hours after his departure. In this fpace of time, he had paffed and repaffed the Sound, and traverfed a fpace not lefs than ninety miles.

About the latter end of May, congrefs were enabled to fend fupplies of men from the different provinces to general Wafhington, who, on receiving this large reinforcement, relinquifhed his encampment at Morris Town, and removed to a ftrong place, called Middle Brook. Here it was not thought advifable to attack him, for his camp extended along feveral hills, and was ftrongly fortified by intrenchments and artillery. In the front the approach was difficult, on account of the natural ftrength of the ground. Every movement of the Britifh on the Brunfwick hills was eafily difcernible; as alfo any operation that might be carried on in the intermediate fpace between Brunfwick and Amboy. In his rear, general Wafhington had a plentiful country, from which he drew vaft fupplies; and he was enabled, if the fituation of affairs fhould render fuch a ftep neceffary, to fecure a fafe retreat over the Hudfon and the Delaware rivers.

The

The tents and other neceſſaries, together with a freſh ſupply of
troops, being at length arrived from England, in the beginning of
June the commander in chief left New York, and croſſed over to
the Jerſeys, with an intention of opening the campaign immediately.
The Britiſh troops were, as uſual, greatly ſuperior in point of number to the Americans ; and perhaps it may not here be deemed improper to ſtate the number of the troops on each ſide, from the
beginning of 1776, to the commencement of the campaign in the
following year.

BRITISH and REBEL FORCE in 1776.

Dates.		Britiſh.	Rebel troops.
Auguſt	——	24,000	16,000
November	——	26,900	4,500
December	——	27,700	3,300

In 1777.

March	——	27,000	4,500
June	——	30,000	8,000

Endeavours
to bring Waſh-
ington to an
action.
Sir William Howe was thoroughly ſenſible of the impracticabi-
lity of making an attack on general Waſhington in his preſent ſituation.   He therefore made uſe of every poſſible effort to induce him
to quit his poſition, and to hazard an engagement.   The American
general, however, eaſily penetrated into the deſigns of the commander in chief, and eluded them by his cool, collected, and prudent
conduct.   Finding that all his endeavours hitherto to provoke him
to battle were unſucceſsful, general Howe reſolved to adopt an expedient, which in part ſucceeded.   On the nineteenth of June he
ſuddenly retreated from his ſituation in front of the enemy, with
marks of ſeeming precipitation.   He ordered the whole army to
relinquiſh Brunſwick, and retire to Amboy.   This manœuvre deceived

ceived the Americans, who, in feveral large bodies, under the command of generals Maxwell and Conway, and lord Sterling, purfued them. The commander in chief fuffered himfelf to be purfued to fome diftance. He threw a bridge over the channel that feparates Staten Ifland from the continent, over which he paffed his heavy baggage, and a fmall number of men. General Wafhington, conceiving this retreat to be real, immediately relinquifhed his encampment on the hills, and removed to a place called Quibble Town, in order to be able to co-operate with that part of his army which had been detached in purfuit of the Britifh. As foon as the Britifh commander in chief had fucceeded in drawing the American general from his faftneffes, he marched the Englifh army back by different routes, in order to bring general Wafhington to an engagement, to cut off his advanced parties, and, if both thofe fchemes fhould fail, to fecure fome paffes in the mountains, which would reduce the Americans to the neceffity of relinquifhing their former encampment on the hills. For this laft purpofe, lord Cornwallis was detached with a confiderable body of troops. On the twenty-fixth of June, his lordfhip began his march, and about feven o'clock in the morning, fell in with an advanced body of the enemy, amounting in number to about three thoufand, under the command of lord Sterling and general Maxwell; they were ftrongly fituated and well provided with artillery. The ardour, however, of the Britifh troops was irrefiftible—after a furious attack, the enemy gave way on all fides, and retreated with great precipitation. They were purfued as far as Weftfield, when, on account of the intenfe heat of the day, and the woods, his lordfhip thought proper to difcontinue it. In this action, the Americans loft two hundred men, killed and wounded, befides three pieces of brafs cannon. Convinced of his error, in removing to Quibble Town, general Wafhington immediately regained

C H A P.
XIV.

1777.

The British
troops relin-
quish the Jer-
feys.

gained his station on the hills, and at the same time secured those
passes, of which it was in the contemplation of lord Cornwallis to
have possessed himself.

Sir William Howe, being now sensible that every scheme of
bringing the Americans to an engagement would be unattended with
success, resolved to retire from the Jerseys. Accordingly, on the
twenty-eighth of June, he returned with the army to Amboy, and on
the succeeding day crossed over to Staten Island. A short cessation
of course occurred on each side.

General Pref-
cot carried
off.

During the continuance of this, a spirited determination was made
and executed by an American colonel of the name of Barton; it was
to carry off the commander of Rhode Island (general Prescot), and in
consequence to procure the enlargement of general Lee, by exchanging
him for general Prescot. The British general's head-quarters were on
the west side of the island, near the Narraganset Bay, about a quarter
of a mile from the shore. He was guarded by only one centinel at a
time, and his quarters were above a mile from any body of troops.——
No patroles were posted on the shore, and the general depended
solely on a guard-ship that lay in the bay, opposite to his quarters.
Colonel Barton being acquainted with these circumstances, set out
from Providence, with some officers and soldiers, in two boats, keeping near the island of Providence, till he came to the south end, which
was not more than two miles and a half from the general's quarters.
Here he remained till dark, when he proceeded across the bay un-
perceived, and landed about midnight. The centinel was surprised
and properly secured—two other soldiers ran away; the general was
taken out of bed, and, without being suffered even to put on his
clothes, was hurried on board one of the boats. The boat passed
under the stern of the British guard-ship without being perceived,
and conveyed the general in safety to Providence. The general was

2   much

much and defervedly blamed for his imprudence, in trufting himfelf
fo far from the troops under his command, and for not adopting
proper means to fecure his fafety. The commander in chief had
hitherto fteadily refufed to relieve general Lee on any conditions
whatever; neverthelefs, the capture of general Prefcot obliged him
to relinquifh his refolution; and general Lee was, in a fhort period,
reftored to the American caufe.

Until the beginning of June, the numbers of general Wafhington's
army did not exceed eight thoufand men, militia included; a circumftance which naturally pointed to the expediency of an early
campaign; but the Britifh commander conceiving it impoffible to
make any confiderable movements till the green forage was on the
ground *, did not take the field with the main army till the twelfth
of June, when he affembled the troops at Brunfwick. General
Wafhington was encamped on a hill above Quibble Town, about
nine miles from that place, on the north fide of the Rariton, with
a force under fix thoufand, and thefe undifciplined and badly appointed; which, with a corps under general Sullivan of two thoufand men at Prince Town, compofed his whole force. His camp
was not inacceffible, either through nature or art; it was ftrong,
and capable of defence in front, being guarded by the Rariton;
and the hill in that quarter was fteep and difficult of accefs; but in his
rear towards the mountains, and on his right towards the Delaware,
it was by no means impracticable. There were large and good roads
around it, leading from Brunfwick on either fide of the river. In
this ftate Wafhington remained, as if he had been perfectly acquainted with the intended movements of the Britifh army. The
Britifh commander marched his army in two columns, to Middle

* Yet the country was full of grain, hay, and dry forage, much to be preferred to green,
which would rather fcour and weaken his horfes, than add to their ftrength. This kind of
forage he had, or might have had in his magazines, or might, as in the laft campaign, have
procured in his march through the country.

Bufh

Bufh and Hillfborough, two villages lying in a low level country, completely overlooked by the Americans, and on the fouth fide of the Rariton, keeping that river, which was not at that time fordable, between his army and the enemy. Provifions for a few days only were taken from Brunfwick; the pontoons and flat-bottomed boats were left at that place, and the fleet lay ready at Staten Ifland to receive the army. General Wafhington, probably judging from the circumftances that fir William Howe did not mean to crofs the Delaware, remained in his camp, contenting himfelf with frequently haraffing the Britifh by his advanced parties.

General Sullivan, on the approach of the troops towards Prince Town, fled in a panic towards the Delaware. He had begun to embark his men, but was ftopped by an order from general Wafhington, and took poft at Flemingtown. In thefe pofitions the two armies remained from the fourteenth to the nineteenth of June; when the Britifh general returned to Brunfwick, and on the twenty-fecond to Amboy. In his march to both thefe places, his army was infulted and haraffed by fmall parties of the rebels. On the thirtieth the troops croffed Staten Ifland, in order to embark for the Chefapeak. Thus the Britifh general retreated before an enemy greatly inferior in force; and, after obtaining great advantages, altered the plan of operation which he himfelf had propofed, and the Britifh minifter for war had approved *. Why (it was afked) did he make fuch expenfive preparations for croffing the Delaware, without making ufe of them? Why did he pafs on the fouth fide of the Rariton, and take pofitions in which he could neither affail his enemy nor the enemy him, if difpofed to do fo? Why did he not march round either on the north or fouth to the rear of that enemy, where he might have been affaulted without any other hazard than

---

* In a letter to lord George Germaine, dated the twentieth of January 1777, he declared his intention of penetrating with the main body of the army into Penfylvania by the way of Jerfey.

fuch as muft, in the common courfe of war, be unavoidably incurred ? If the enemy was, in his judgment, fo ftrongly pofted as
to render an attack on his camp a meafure too bold and defperate,
why did he not intercept his convoys, cut off his fupplies of provifions, and reduce him under his power by famine ; or crofs the
Delaware, and deftroy his pofts and magazines ? It could not be
fuppofed that general Wafhington would fuffer the Britifh army to
pafs the Delaware, and feize his magazines and other places of
ftrength, without a ftruggle. Had that been attempted, he muft
have quitted his camp and fought the Britifh army, or have loft his
magazines, and the capital and moft important city in North America ; a facrifice which, as was demonftrated by his fubfequent conduct, he would never make without meafuring arms.

Notwithftanding thefe and many other confiderations that, in
the general opinion, fhould have moved our force in another
direction, the Britifh troops, confifting of thirty-fix Heffian and
Britifh battalions, including light-infantry and grenadiers, a corps
called the queen's rangers, and a regiment of light horfe, on the
fifth of July embarked in tranfports, where both foot and cavalry remained pent up, in the hotteft feafon of the year, in the holds of
the veffels, until the twenty-third, when they failed from Sandy
Hook ; but meeting with contrary winds, did not arrive at the
Capes of the Delaware till the thirtieth. At New York were left
feventeen battalions, the new provincial corps, and a regiment of
light-horfe, under the command of general Clinton, and feveral
battalions were ftationed on Rhode Ifland. There were many who
blamed the commander in chief, and with apparent reafon, for not
proceeding up the North River to Albany, inftead of going to Philadelphia, in order to have effected a junction with general Burgoyne, and it was the general opinion that, had he adopted fuch a
meafure, he would not only have prevented the fatal confequences

*British com-
mander in
chief pro-
ceeds to
Chefapeak
Bay.*

July 23.

that enfued, but would have effected the reduction of America. Befides, the delays incident to any expedition to the fouthward at a feafon of the year when the foutherly winds ufually blow nineteen out of twenty days, might have proved exceedingly injurious to the men fo clofely ftowed in the tranfports, and could not but be ruinous to the horfes. The commander in chief at firft intended to have gone up the Delaware, but having received intelligence that the enemy had rendered the navigation of that river difficult, he gave up his original intention, and proceeded to Chefapeak Bay. The winds proved fo contrary, as every one acquainted with the climate had predicted, that the fleet did not enter the Chefapeak till the middle of Auguft. As foon as they arrived in the Bay they proceeded up the Elk, the head of which river fir William Howe gained in fafety on the twenty-fourth of Auguft.

Lands at the head of the Elk.

Proclamation iffued.

As foon as the army was landed, the commander in chief publifhed a proclamation, in which he offered pardon and protection to all who would furrender themfelves to the Britifh troops; and at the fame time he affured the inhabitants that the ftricteft order and difcipline fhould be preferved by the troops in marching through the country. On the twenty-eighth of Auguft the army moved forwards to a village at the head of the Elk, where the head-quarters were fixed. On the third of September a farther progrefs was made by a part of the army, which moved forwards about five miles; difperfing the advanced guards of the enemy, and taking poft on Iron Hill, a place that commanded a view of the Delaware. Generals Grant and Knyphaufen having joined the commander in chief with the troops under their command on the eighth of September, the whole army moved onwards in two columns on the route to Philadelphia. After they had proceeded about thirteen miles they halted, on receiving intelligence that the enemy were in motion.

On

On the eleventh of September the Britiſh army moved forwards; the enemy, to the number of fourteen thouſand, retiring before them to the other ſide of the Brandywine river. Here the Americans halted, and poſted themſelves on ſome very ſtrong ground under cover of woods with intervals of open ground between them. Their advanced corps was ſtationed at Red Clay Creek. The Brandywine Creek runs into the Delaware at Wilmington, and it was indiſpenſably neceſſary for the Britiſh army to paſs over it in their route to Philadelphia. The enemy therefore ſecured, and reſolved to defend, the principal fording-places.

At Chad's Ford, the ſpot where it was judged moſt probable that the royal army would make an attempt, batteries were erected on the banks of the rivulet, with intrenchments that commanded the paſs.

While the enemy were occupied at Chad's Ford, lord Cornwallis, with one column of the army, conſiſting of two battalions of grenadiers, as many of light infantry, the Heſſian grenadiers, part of the ſeventy-firſt regiment, and two Britiſh brigades, made a circuit of ſome miles, and croſſed the forks of the Brandywine on the thirteenth of September, with an intention of gaining the enemy's rear. At the ſame time general Knyphauſen, with the ſecond diviſion, conſiſting of two Britiſh brigades, the Heſſians, and Wemys's corps of rangers, marched in a direct line to Chad's Ford; and attacked a detached body of the enemy that had croſſed the river, and were poſted on the ſouth ſide of it. This body, after ſome reſiſtance, was forced to repaſs the Brandywine under cover of their batteries.

Several pieces of cannon having been brought up and placed on the moſt commanding eminences, a ſharp cannonade enſued, which was anſwered by the enemy's batteries on the other ſide of the river. The attention of the Americans was thus amuſed, in order that lord Cornwallis might make his paſſage good. As ſoon as this was known, by the firing of cannon in that quarter, and the evident confuſion of

the

C H A P.
XIV.

1777.
General Waſhington moves to the north ſide of the Brandywine river, in order to defend Philadelphia.

the enemy, general Knyphaufen, with his divifion, began to pafs the ford, and with great bravery foon carried the batteries and intrenchments; the enemy relinquifhing them, and leaving behind five pieces of cannon and an howitzer. Lord Cornwallis, on the other hand, as foon as he had croffed the two branches of the river, took the road to Delworth, which led him upon the enemy's right.

Action at the Brandywine.

General Wafhington being informed of lord Cornwallis's movements, detached general Sullivan, with a confiderable force, to oppofe him. The general took poffeffion of the heights above Birmingham church, his left reaching towards the Brandywine, his artillery judicioufly placed, and his flanks covered by woods. About four o'clock in the afternoon lord Cornwallis formed the line of battle, and began the attack. The Americans fuftained it with confiderable intrepidity, but the impetuofity of the Britifh troops was not to be refifted. They rufhed upon the enemy, and, in fpite of a very fpirited oppofition, drove them into the woods on their rear. Neverthelefs the enemy pofted themfelves a fecond time in one of the woods, from which they were, after a defperate refiftance, diflodged and forced to retire. A general rout took place. A confiderable part of the American army fled with precipitation, in fmall and confufed parties, by different roads, towards Philadelphia, Lancafter, and Reading, while general Wafhington, and the corps he was able to keep together, fled with his cannon and baggage to Chefter ; where he remained, within eight miles of the Britifh army, till next morning, when he marched by Derby to Philadelphia. Here he ftaid three days, collecting as many of his troops as he poffibly could, and recruiting from his magazines the ftores he had loft in battle. On the third day after the engagement he affembled his troops, and marched up the north fide of the Schuylkill, which he croffed at Sweed's Ford, and paffed on to the road to Lancafter. Meantime the Britifh army under fir William

I

Howe

Howe remained on the field of battle. The Americans fuffered confiderably in this action. Three hundred were killed, fix hundred
wounded, and near four hundred taken prifoners ; they alfo loft feveral pieces of artillery. The lofs on the part of the Britifh was
by no means in proportion to that of the enemy. Not above one
hundred were killed, and four hundred wounded.

It may not be improper to mention here fome circumftances that
evince the opinion which feveral European nations entertained of
the prefent difturbances. In the action at Brandywine the celebrated marquis de la Fayette, at that time a young man of fpirit
and enterprife, and a warm partifan of the Americans, bore a command in the American army. Infpired by enthufiaftic notions of liberty,
he purchafed and freighted a fhip with military ftores, and proceeding
in it with feveral of his friends to America, prefented it to congrefs.
His age was not more than nineteen, and when he departed from
Paris he informed his wife that he was going to pay a vifit to his
aunt in Italy. Several other French noblemen were officers in the
American army, and two Polifh noblemen exhibited in the battle of
Brandywine, great proofs of bravery and attachment to the caufe
they had efpoufed. On the evening after the battle, a party of the
Britifh was fent to Wilmington, who took the governor of the Delaware ftate, Mr. Mackenlie, out of his bed, and feized a fhalloop
lying in the creek, loaded with the rich effects of fome of the inhabitants, together with the public records of the county ; a large
quantity of public and private money ; all the papers and certificates belonging to the loan office and treafury office ; articles
of plate, &c.

The victory does not feem to have been improved in the
degree which circumftances appeared to have admitted. When
the left column of the Britifh had turned Wafhington's right
flank, his whole army was hemmed in: General Knyphaufen
and

and the Brandywine in front; fir William Howe and lord Cornwallis on his right; the Delaware in his rear; and the Chriftiana
river on his left. He was obliged to retreat twenty-three miles to
Philadelphia, when the Britifh lay within eighteen miles of it. Had
the commander in chief detached general Knyphaufen's column in
purfuit early next morning, general Wafhington might with eafe
have been intercepted, either at the heights of Crum Creek, nine
miles; at Derby, fourteen; or at Philadelphia, eighteen miles, from
the Britifh camp; or the Schuylkill might have been paffed at
Gray's Ferry, only feventy yards over; and Philadelphia, with
the American magazines, taken, had not the pontoons been
improvidently left at New York as ufelefs. Any one of thefe
movements, it was thought, might have been attended with the
total deftruction of the American army. For fome reafon however, which it is impoffible to divine, the commander in chief employed himfelf for feveral days in making flight movements, which
could not by any poffibility produce any important benefits to the
Britifh caufe.

On the twentieth of September intelligence was received that
general Wayne had concealed himfelf in the woods on the left wing
of the army with fifteen hundred men, with an intention of haraffing the rear of the Britifh army. Major-general Grey was accordingly difpatched at night to furprife him. The Britifh general proceeded in this expedition with great fecrefy and difpatch, and in
order that the furprife might be complete, he gave ftrict orders that
bayonets alone fhould be ufed, and that not a gun fhould be fired.
This manœuvre had the defired effect. General Wayne's outpofts
were furprifed about one in the morning, and the Britifh troops
rufhing immediately on the enemy's encampment, made a dreadful
flaughter. Three hundred were killed and wounded, and one hundred taken prifoners. The reft contrived to make good their retreat

General
Wayne de-
feated.

with

with the lofs of all their baggage. On the part of the Britifh the
lofs was too trifling almoft to be mentioned.   One officer was killed,
and feven privates were killed and wounded.   The fkill and energy
of general Grey were very confpicuous in this enterprife.

CHAP.
XIV.
1777.

On the twenty-third of September, fir William Howe having fecured the command of the Schuylkill, croffed it with the whole army,
advanced, on the twenty-fixth, to German Town, and on the fucceeding day lord Cornwallis, at the head of a ftrong detachment, took
peaceable poffeffion of Philadelphia.

Royal army paffes the Schuylkill. Lord Corn- wallis takes poffeffion of Philadelphia.

German Town confifts in one ftreet two miles in length ; and is
diftant from the capital of Penfylvania about feven miles.   The
Britifh army, in their line of encampment, interfected this village
near the centre, and almoft at right angles.   The Schuylkill covered
the left wing ; in the front of which were the German chaffeurs.   A
battalion of light-infantry and the queen's American rangers covered
the right wing in front ; and at the head of the village, the fortieth
regiment with another battalion of light-infantry were ftationed.
Three regiments detached under colonel Sterling, for the purpofe
of conveying ftores and provifions, lay at Chefter ; and a confiderable body of troops, as already mentioned, under lord Cornwallis, at Philadelphia.   The poffeffion of this place was a moft
important acquifition, as it opened a communication between
the northern and fouthern provinces ; and, if the Delaware were
opened, between the army and the navy.   So fenfible were the
Americans of its importance, that they had formerly refolved,
if ever it fhould be in real and imminent danger of falling into the
hands of the Britifh, to commit it to the flames.

But, although German Town and Philadelphia had been for
fome time occupied by the Britifh troops, the communication was
not yet free down the river to the fleet.

3.

CHAP. XV.

*American Batteries and other Means of Defence—Attacked—Action
at German Town—At Red Bank—Mud Island and Red Bank
taken—American Fleet burnt—Removal of the royal Army to
Whitemarsh.*

CHAP.
XV.
⌣⌣⌣⌣
1777.

American
batteries and
other means
of defence,

AS the Delaware is navigable to Philadelphia and even beyond it,
the congress, whose residence was at that city until it was
taken by sir William Howe, very early endeavoured to render it in-
accessible to the British fleet. In devising contrivances for this purpose, Dr. Franklin is said, before his departure for France, to have
assisted. Three rows of chevaux de frize, composed of immense beams
of timber bolted and fastened together, and stuck with iron pikes
fastened in every direction, were funk across the channel, a little
below the place where the Schuylkill empties itself into the Delaware.
The lower line of chevaux de frize was commanded by some works,
erected on the Jersey shore, at Billing's Port; and the upper by an
inclosed fort, mounting heavy cannon, and situated on a marshy island,
called Mud Island, being formed by an accumulation of fand and
vegetable mould, near the Pensylvania shore; and on the opposite
shore, by a redoubt and intrenchment, at a place called Red Bank;
the redoubt being constructed on high and commanding ground,
served also as a protecton for the provincial water force, which might
occasionally retire under the guns of that work for safety. This
water force, which was stationed between the two forts, consisted of
fourteen row-gallies, carrying each one piece of heavy ordnance—
two floating batteries, carrying nine guns each—and a number of
fire-

fire-fhips and rafts. Towards the end of September, a detachment
from the Britifh army, confifting of three regiments under colonel
Sterling, had been paffed over from Chefter to the Jerfey fhore,
for the purpofe of reducing the provincial works of Billing's Port,
which, on the approach of that detachment, were abandoned by the
garrifon, and immediately difmantled. The lower line of chevaux
de frize being thus left without defence from the fhore, an attempt
was made to remove it by captain Hammond of the Roebuck, who
commanded the Britifh naval force in the Delaware; in which he fo
far fucceeded, notwithftanding the oppofition made by the enemy's
row-gallies and floating batteries, as to make an opening fufficient
to admit the largeft fhips of the fleet ; but ftill the two other rows
of chevaux de frize remained; and the forts which defended them
were yet in the poffeffion of the Americans. Things were in this
fituation, when lord Howe arrived with the fleet from the Chefapeak.
Lord Howe, as foon as he received intelligence of the fuccefs of the
army at Brandywine, left the Elk river, and quitting the Capes of
Virginia on the twenty-third of September, fteered his courfe towards the Delaware, where he arrived on the eighth of October.
As the paffage to Philadelphia was yet impracticable, the fleet was
brought to anchor, on the weft fhore, from the town of Newcaftle
down to Reedy Ifland.

The voyage from the Capes to the Delaware was boifterous;
and the attempt to get up that river required great abilities,
caution, and prudence; for the obftructions that had deterred the fleet from entering the Delaware before, had been
confiderably increafed. The Americans had almoft completed an
extenfive work—wooden piers for defending the approaches to the
line of funken frames that croffed the channel of the river. To remove thefe obftructions, fo as to open a communication between

VOL. I. Q q the

the fleet and the army, was an object of the utmost importance, but which could not be accomplished without previously reducing the forts, by which they were defended. Preparations for this purpose were accordingly made immediately after the arrival of the fleet. Some heavy cannon were landed from the ships, and batteries were begun on Province Island, which was formed by the conflux of the rivers Schuylkill and Delaware, and was opposite to the fort on Mud Island; but, owing to the swampiness of the ground, the works advanced slowly, and the approaches were made with difficulty. Major Vatap, of the tenth regiment, who commanded a detachment of the British on Province Island, to cover the working parties, abandoned most shamefully his artillery, upon the Americans having landed a small body of men on the island. From the gallantry, however, of a subaltern officer, the artillery was retaken, and the enemy compelled to retire. Major Vatap was obliged to quit the service, and sell out below the regulated price.

As soon as the enemy perceived the designs of the English, they dispatched two frigates and a schooner, with some row-gallies, to demolish the batteries and cannonade the town. For some time the vessels kept up a heavy fire upon the town, but, on the falling of the tide in the Delaware, one of the frigates ran a-ground, and was taken; the rest of the fleet were under the necessity of retreating as fast as possible.

General Washington, who was at this time encamped at Skippack Creek, on the eastern side of the Schuylkill, about seventeen miles from German Town, being reinforced by fifteen hundred troops from Peek's Kill, and one thousand Virginians, on receiving intelligence of the large detachments that were sent to take possession of Philadelphia, to cover the convoys and destroy the works on the

Delaware,

Action at
German
Town;

Delaware, formed the defign of furprifing the camp at German Town. At fix in the evening of the third of October, the enemy quitted their encampment at Skippack Creek, and under cover of a thick fog, made an attack on the troops pofted at the head of the village, at dawn of day, on the fourth. There, after a vigorous re-fiftance, they were driven into the village, and general Wafhington advancing with his army, divided into five columns, endeavoured to enter the north end of the village, in order to feparate the Britifh force, and thereby to enfure fuccefs to the different attacks on the Britifh flanks. The fortieth regiment, which lay at the head of the village, had been under the neceffity of retreating before the enemy; neverthelefs lieutenant-colonel Mufgrave, who commanded this regiment, by his addrefs and activity had contrived to keep five companies of the regiment together. In order to impede the pro-grefs of the enemy he threw them into a large ftone houfe in the village, that lay in the front of the enemy. This gallant conduct arrefted the Americans in their career, and in the event prevented the feparation of the right and left wings of the Britifh troops; by which means time was afforded to the reft of the Britifh line to get under arms. General Wafhington immediately ordered a brigade to furround the houfe. Colonel Mufgrave, however, and his brave men, refufed to furrender, and from the windows pouring a heavy fire upon the enemy, did confiderable execution. Four pieces of cannon were then brought againft him, the fire of which he conti-nued to brave till he received affiftance from major-general Grey, who, with the third brigade, and brigadier-general Agnew with the fourth brigade, attacked the enemy with great fpirit. The engage-ment for fome time was very warm. At length, part of the right wing attacking the enemy on the oppofite fide of the village, they

gave

gave ground, and retired with great precipitation. They attempted to rally upon some rising grounds, and made a shew of renewing the action ; but it was only a feint to secure a retreat. This they effected, with all their artillery, under cover of the fog, which rendered it difficult for the British troops to discover their movements. This fog, which had at first been so advantageous to the Americans, was alleged to have greatly contributed to the disappointment of the scheme, inasmuch as it prevented the different bodies of the American army from discovering each other's operations.

On the part of the English six hundred were killed and wounded. Among the former were brigadier-general Agnew, and colonel Bird, officers of distinguished reputation. The loss on the side of the Americans was supposed to amount to between two and three hundred killed, six hundred wounded, and above four hundred made prisoners. General Nash and a great number of officers were among the slain. The neglect of the commander in chief in the action at German Town was extreme. He was acquainted with the intentions of general Washington on the evening before the attack, and therefore could have provided against it. Had he adopted such a mode of conduct, the American army would certainly have been destroyed. It was the general opinion of the officers of both armies, that, had the Americans advanced immediately, instead of attaching the fortieth regiment, the total defeat of the British must have ensued. But the delay occasioned by the several attempts to reduce Chew's House afforded time for the British line to get under arms; and that circumstance was justly considered as the salvation of the royal army. Notwithstanding the importance of the capture of Philadelphia, it was seen that the army

I   could

could not maintain itself during the winter, unless Mud Island
should be reduced. In order to effect the reduction of this, the
royal army removed from German Town to Philadelphia. The
enemy after the action at German Town had returned to their old
camp at Skippack Creek.

In consequence of measures concerted between the commander
in chief and lord Howe, a joint attack was resolved to be made on
Mud Island and Red Bank.

Colonel Stirling, after destroying the American works at Billing's
Port, saw the necessity of forming a post at Red Bank, not yet occupied by the enemy, it being of no great consequence while they
retained possession of the other post just mentioned. But when they
had lost that station, it became of the utmost importance, being the only
key to the fort on Mud Island; the only spot from which it could
be relieved or supplied. And, had this post been taken and occupied
by British troops, the fort and water-guard would have been placed
in the midst of a triangle, and constantly exposed to the cannon
from posts on each of its sides; from Red Bank on the east, the
Province Island on the west side of the Delaware, and from the
men of war on the south in the river below. Possessed of these,
colonel Stirling desired permission to take possession of Red Bank,
but it was not granted him. The rebels, taking advantage of this
blunder, immediately fortified it: And, under its cannon, they
constantly covered their water-guard, which sallied out from this
advantageous post when they wished, either to supply or relieve the
fort, or to annoy the ships of war. The subsistence of the British
troops in Philadelphia depended so much on the surrender of this
fort, that Washington exerted every nerve to preserve it. He
offered one hundred pounds extraordinary bounty to every soldier
who should serve in defending it during the siege. These men were

relieved

CHAP.
XV.

1777.

at Red Bank.

relieved every fix hours from Red Bank, and therefore the defence was extremely obftinate.

On the nineteenth of October the Britifh army was withdrawn from German Town, and encamped in the immediate vicinity of Philadelphia, as a more convenient fituation, from which detachments might be made, and occafional reinforcements fent to reduce the forts upon the river : And foon after this movement an attempt was made to carry the redoubt and intrenchment at Red Bank by affault. The execution of this enterprife was intrufted to colonel Donop, a brave and high-fpirited German officer, who, with three battalions of Heffian grenadiers, the regiment of Mirbach, and the infantry chaffeurs, paffed the Delaware, from Philadelphia, on the twenty-firft of October, and, on the following day in the afternoon, reached the place of his deftination. A difpofition for the attack was inftantly made, and the brave Donop, with undaunted firmnefs, led on his troops to the affault, through a tremendous fire, not only from the works at Red Bank, but from the provincial gallies and floating batteries upon the river; and whilft deftruction every inftant thinned their ranks, the German battalions advanced, unmoved, to the charge, and forced an extenfive outwork, from which the enemy were driven, and obliged to flee for fhelter within the redoubt. By this time the intrepid Donop had fallen, his thigh having been fractured by a mufket fhot, and the fecond in command was alfo wounded. The redoubt was found to be more than eight feet high, with a parapet boarded and frized, and could not be forced without fcaling-ladders. Why the affailants were not furnifhed with this neceffary implement has not been explained ; but for want of it, in the moment of victory, and with the object of the enterprife within their grafp, they were obliged precipitately to retire through fuch a fire as that under which they had advanced,

leaving

leaving their brave commander behind them, who died of his wound
fome few days after, whilft a prifoner in the hands of the Americans.

But this was not the only misfortune that happened at this time.
It was intended that a part of the fleet, by moving up the river as
far as it could go, fhould make a diverfion in favour of the attack
by land. For this purpofe the Augufta, Roebuck, Liverpool, Pearl,
and Merlin floop, were ordered to pafs through the opening in the
lower chevaux de frize, and be in readinefs. And as foon as Donop's
attack commenced thefe fhips flipped their cables and moved flowly
up the river with the flood tide ; but the natural courfe of the channel having been altered by the artificial obftructions thrown acrofs it,
and fand-banks being collected where there were none before, two of
thefe fhips, the Augufta and the Merlin, unfortunately got a-ground
a little below the fecond line of chevaux de frize. At the next tide
of flood every exertion was made to get them off, but in vain, the
flow of the tide having been prevented from rifing to its ufual
height by a ftrong northerly wind. It was not until the following
morning that the fituation of thefe fhips was perceived by the enemy, when they began to fire upon them from their works, gallies,
and floating batteries, and fent down feveral fire-fhips with the expectation of deftroying them. The fire-fhips were however towed
off without doing any injury, by the activity and dexterity of the
feamen ; but, unfortunately, the Augufta, by fome accident, caught
fire, and the flames, fpreading fo rapidly that they could not be got
under, it was with the utmoft difficulty that the greateft part of the
crew were faved. Only a few, and amongft thefe the fecond-lieute-
nant, chaplain, and gunner, perifhed in the flames. It now became neceffary to remove with all hafte the frigates which lay near
the Augufta, that they might not fuffer by her explofion ; and as

the

the Merlin could not be got off, orders were given to abandon and
deftroy her.   Such were the unfortuante confequences of the attack
on Red Bank fort.

In the mean time the preparations for reducing the fort on Mud
Ifland were going forward on the weftern fhore of the Delaware;
but, from the difficulty of conftructing works in marfhy grounds,
and the length of time required for tranfporting through fwamps
fuch heavy ftores as were indifpenfably neceffary, the batteries were
not opened before the tenth of November.   Immediately below
Mud Ifland, and ranging nearly in a line with this, were two others,
called Province and Hog Iflands.   Between thefe and the weftern
fhore was a narrow channel of fufficient depth to admit fhips of a
moderate draught of water.   For fome days, that part of the fleet
which was deftined to co-operate in the attack, was prevented by
contrary winds from moving up the river; but on the fifteenth of
November, the wind proving favourable, and every thing being in
readinefs, the Vigilant armed fhip, followed by a hulk, both of them
mounted with heavy cannon, paffed through between Province and
Hog Ifland, and got into the channel behind, fo as to bring their
guns to bear upon that part of the fort which was leaft provided
with defences.   At the fame time two of the large fhips, the Ifis and
the Somerfet, with the Roebuck, and feveral frigates, failed up the
main channel of the river, and lay as near the front of the fort as
the fecond line of the chevaux de frize would permit.   The fhips
being thus difpofed, a heavy cannonade commenced as well from
them as from the batteries on fhore, which difmounted feveral of
the guns in the fort, and otherwife fo damaged its defences, that the
garrifon, fearful of an affault, quitted it the enfuing night, and were
carried off by their fhipping.   Two days after the redoubt at Red
Bank was alfo abandoned upon the approach of lord Cornwallis with
a detach-

Mud Ifland
and Red
Bank taken.

a detachment from camp fent to reduce it; and the provincial water force, being now no longer protected by the works on fhore, quitted its ftation, and retired up the river. Some few of the fmaller gallies, by keeping clofe on the Jerfey fhore, paffed Philadelphia in the night, and efcaped. The reft were abandoned and burnt. And thus a communication by the Delaware was at laft opened between the navy and army.

General Wafhington, after receiving a reinforcement of four thoufand men from the northern army, left his ftrong fituation at Skippack Creek, drew nearer to the Britifh lines, and encamped at White Marfh, an advantageous ftation, about fourteen miles from Philadelphia. A valley and a rivulet were in his front; and to the fouth and eaft an abbatis of trees, their top branches pointed and lying outwards.

Sir William Howe hoped that, in confequence of this reinforcement, Wafhington might be tempted to rifque an engagement in the view of regaining poffeffion of the capital of Penfylvania. With this expectation he marched with the army from Philadelphia on the fourth of December at night, and on the following morning took poft on Chefnut Hill, in front of the right wing of the provincial encampment. Here the Britifh army remained for two days, offering battle to the provincials, but the latter continued within their lines, except a corps of about one thoufand men, which being fent out to fkirmifh with the light-infantry, under lieutenant-colonel Abercrombie, who were pofted in front, was quickly repulfed with lofs.

On the fixth at night the army was again put in motion, and the following morning took poft on Edge Hill, an eminence one mile in front of the enemy's left, which was occupied by a ftrong corps of northern provincials, and from whence they were driven by the van-guard of the army under lord Cornwallis. The fame

VOL. I.   R r   morning,

Margin notes:
CHAP. XV.
1777.
American fleet burnt.
Removal of the royal army to White Marfh, where general Wafhington was encamped.

morning, another out-poſt of the enemy was forced by a column
of the army under major-general Grey, and ſo nearly ſurrounded by
a rapid movement of the light-infantry of the guards to turn their
left, that the provincials, in making their eſcape, were driven acroſs
the fire of the centre and left of the general's diviſion, and ſuſtained
a conſiderable loſs in killed and wounded.

During all this time general Waſhington remained quiet within
his lines; and ſir William Howe, ſeeing no proſpect of being able
to provoke him to an engagement, and, after having viewed the
right, left, and centre, of his encampment, judging it unadviſable
to attack him in his preſent ſtrong poſition, returned on the eighth
with the army to Philadelphia: The enemy ſtill keeping ſo cloſe
within their lines, that the rear-guard of the army under lord Cornwallis, which did not leave its ground till four in the afternoon, was
ſuffered to retire unmoleſted. It was generally expected that the
commander in chief would have made ſome farther attempts on general Waſhington. It is true he made ſome movements on the
enemy's front, right, and left, but none on their rear, where they
were vulnerable without difficulty. By the ſame movement he
would have cut off Waſhington from his baggage and proviſions,
which lay five miles diſtant. The American general dreaded this,
and was prepared for flight. Our troops, notwithſtanding, retired,
to the ſurpriſe of all who were acquainted with the ground on
which general Waſhington was encamped, and the variety of excellent roads that led round to his rear. It was even well known that
Waſhington's army was under the greateſt apprehenſion, and con-
ſtantly expecting the neceſſity of attempting a hazardous movement
to eſcape.

Not long after the retreat of the Britiſh troops from White
Marſh, general Waſhington quitted his camp at that place in the
night,

night, croffed the Schuylkill, and took poft at Valley Forge, about twenty-fix miles diftant from Philadelphia.

Had the American army retired to Lancafter, York, and Carlifle, the neareft towns where they could have been accommodated with winter-quarters, a large and fertile diftrict of country would have been left open for the Britifh troops to forage in at pleafure, the inhabitants of which being left without protection might have been tempted to accept of thofe pardons which were fo liberally offered, and to fubmit themfelves again, and become reconciled to the authority of the mother-country.

The American general, moved by thefe confiderations, determined to remain during the winter in the pofition which he then occupied at Valley Forge, recommending it to his troops to build huts in the woods for fheltering themfelves from the inclemency of the weather. And it is perhaps one of the moft ftriking traits in general Wafhington's character, that he poffeffed the faculty of gaining fuch an afcendancy over his raw and undifciplined followers, moft of whom were deftitute of proper winter clothing, and otherwife unprovided with neceffaries, as to be able to prevail upon fo many of them to remain with him, during the winter, in fo diftrefsful a fituation. With immenfe labour he raifed wooden huts, covered with ftraw and earth; which formed very uncomfortable quarters. On the eaft and fouth an intrenchment was made; the ditch fix feet wide and three in depth—the mound not four feet high, very narrow, and fuch as might eafily have been beat down by cannon. Two redoubts were alfo begun, but never completed. The Schuylkill was on his left, with a bridge acrofs. His rear was moftly covered by an impaffable precipice formed by Valley Creek, having only a narrow paffage near the Schuylkill. On the right his camp was acceffible with fome difficulty, but the approach on his front was on ground nearly on a level with his camp. It is indeed

deed

deed difficult to give an adequate defcription of his mifery in this
fituation. His army was deftitute of almoft every neceffary of
clothing, nay, almoft naked; and very often on fhort allowance of
provifions; an extreme mortality raged in his hofpitals, nor had he
any of the moft proper medicines to relieve the fick. There were
perpetual defertions of parties from him of ten to fifty at a time.
In three months he had not four thoufand men, and thefe by no
means to be termed effective. Not lefs than five hundred horfes
perifhed from want and the feverity of the feafon. He had often
not three days provifion in his camp, and at times not enough for
one day. In this infirm and dangerous ftate he continued from December to May, during all which time every perfon expected that
the commander in chief would have ftormed or befieged his camp,
the fituation of which equally invited either attempt. To have
pofted two thoufand men on a commanding ground near the bridge,
on the north fide of the Schuylkill, would have rendered his efcape
on the left impoffible; two thoufand men placed on a like ground
oppofite the narrow pafs, would have as effectually prevented a retreat by his rear; and five or fix thoufand men, ftationed on the
front and right of his camp, would have deprived him of flight on
thofe fides. The pofitions were fuch, that, if any of the corps
were attacked, they could have been inftantly fupported. Under
fuch propitious circumftances what mortal could doubt of fuccefs?
But our army, neglecting all thefe opportunities, was fuffered to
continue at Philadelphia, where the whole winter was fpent in diffipation. A want of difcipline and proper fubordination pervaded the
whole army; and if difeafe and ficknefs thinned the American army
encamped at Valley Forge, indolence and luxury perhaps did no lefs
injury to the Britifh troops at Philadelphia. During the winter a
very unfortunate inattention was fhown to the feelings of the inhabitants of Philadelphia, whofe fatisfaction fhould have been vigi-
lantly

lantly confulted, both from gratitude and from intereft. They experienced many of the horrors of civil war. The foldiers infulted and plundered them ; and their houfes were occupied as barracks, without any compenfation being made to them. Some of the firft families were compelled to receive into their habitations individual officers, who were even indecent enough to introduce their miftreffes into the manfions of their hofpitable entertainers. This foured the minds of the inhabitants, many of whom were Quakers.

But the refidence of the army at Philadelphia occafioned diftreffes which will probably be confidered, by the generality of mankind, as of a more grievous nature. It was with difficulty that fewel could be got on any terms. Provifions were moft exorbitantly high. Gaming of every fpecies was permitted, and even fanctioned. This vice not only debauched the mind, but, by fedentary confinement, and the want of feafonable repofe, enervated the body. A foreign officer held the bank at the game of pharo, by which he made a very confiderable fortune ; and but too many refpectable families in Britain have to lament its baneful effects. Officers who might have rendered honourable fervice to their country, were compelled, by what was termed a bad run of luck, to difpofe of their commiffions, and return pennylefs to their friends in Europe. The father who thought he had made a provifion for his fon by purchafing a commiffion for him in the army, ultimately found that he had put his fon to fchool to learn the fcience of gambling, not the art of war. Diffipation had fpread through the army, and indolence, and want of fubordination, its natural concomitants : For if the officer be not vigilant, the foldier will never be alert.

Sir William Howe, from the manners and religious opinions of the Philadelphians, fhould have been particularly cautious: For this public diffolutenefs of the troops could not but be regarded by fuch

people

people as a contempt of them, as well as an offence againſt piety; and it influenced all the repreſentations which they made to their countrymen reſpecting the Britiſh. They inferred from it alſo, that the commander could not be ſufficiently intent on the plans of either conciliation or ſubjugation; ſo that the opinions of the Philadelphians, whether erroneous or not, materially promoted the cauſe of congreſs. During the whole of this long winter of riot and diſſipation, general Waſhington was ſuffered to continue, with the remains of his army, not exceeding five thouſand effective men at moſt, undiſturbed at the Valley Forge: Conſiderable arrears of pay due to them; almoſt in a ſtate of nature, for want of clothing; the Europeans in the American ſervice diſguſted, and deſerting in great numbers, and indeed in companies, to the Britiſh army; and the natives tired of the war. Yet, under all theſe favourable circumſtances for the Britiſh intereſt, no one ſtep was taken to diſlodge Waſhington, whoſe cannon were frozen up, and could not be moved. If ſir William Howe had marched out in the night, he might have brought Waſhington to action; or if he had retreated, he muſt have left his ſick, cannon, ammunition, and heavy baggage behind. A nocturnal attack on the Americans would have had this further good effect: It would have depreſſed the ſpirit of revolt, confirmed the wavering, and attached them to the Britiſh intereſt. It would have opened a paſſage for ſupplies to the city, which was in great want of proviſions for the inhabitants. It would have ſhaken off that lethargy in which the Britiſh ſoldiers had been immerged during the winter. It would have convinced the well-affected that the Britiſh leader was in earneſt. If Waſhington had retreated, we could have followed. With one of the beſt appointed, in every reſpect, and fineſt armies (conſiſting of at leaſt fourteen thouſand effective men) ever aſſembled in any country, a number of officers of approved ſervice, wiſhing only to be led to action, this dilatory commander, ſir William Howe, dragged

I

out

out the winter, without doing any one thing to obtain the end for which he was commiffioned. Proclamation was iffued after proclamation, calling upon the people of America to repair to the Britifh ftandard, promifing them remiffion of their political fins, and an affurance of protection in both perfon and property; but thefe promifes were confined merely to paper. The beft perfonal fecurity to the inhabitants was an attack by the army, and the beft fecurity of property was peace; and this to be purchafed by fuccefsful war. For, had fir William Howe led on his troops to action, victory was in his power, and conqueft in his train. During fir William Howe's ftay at Philadelphia a number of difaffected citizens were fuffered to remain in the garrifon; thefe people were ever upon the watch, and communicated to Wafhington every intelligence he could wifh for. Sir William Howe ought not to have fuffered the avowedly hoftile to remain in the city. A commander in chief fhould form his plans with fecrefy. Whenever any foraging parties were fent from the garrifon, the enemy were always apprized of it. This will account why our fupplies were always fo fcanty, and our rear always haraffed. That war is neceffary, in fome cafes, is certain; but it is the duty of every commander to leffen the horrors of war, and to abridge their period. Severity in the early part of the war would have been mercy in the end. Thoufands of lives would have been faved on both fides; the enormous load of the national debt would not have fwelled to its prefent amount; America might have been taught the neceffity of peace; and Britain, the juftice and policy of granting honourable terms. But, unfortunately for this country, the inftant the war fhould be at an end, the multiplication of pounds, fhillings, and pence, would ceafe to be carried on by individual characters, who wifhed to make a fund, or aggregate fum, to retire upon. In confirmation of the diftrefs in the American army above related we fhall here infert a letter from the committee of congrefs.

A LET-

A LETTER from the Committee of Congrefs to the Prefident;
found among the Papers of HENRY LAURENS, Efq.

" SIR,   ·   *Camp at Valley Forge, Feb.* 12, 1778.

" WE had flattered ourfelves, that, before this time, the pleafure of
congrefs would be made known to us, refpecting the quarter-mafter's
department. We fear our letter upon this fubject has mifcarried, or
the confideration of it yielded to other bufinefs. You will therefore
pardon us, fir, when we again folicit your attention to it, as an
object of the laft importance; on which not only the future fuccefs
of your arms, but the prefent exiftence of your army, immediately
depend. The influence of this office is fo diffufive through every
part of your military fyftem, that neither the wifdom of arrangement, the fpirit of enterprife, or favourable opportunity, will
be of any avail, if this great wheel in the machine ftops, or moves
heavily. We find ourfelves embarraffed in entering on this fubject,
left a bare recital of facts fhould carry an imputation (which we do
not intend) on thofe gentlemen who have lately conducted it. We
are fenfible, great and juft allowances are to be made for the pecu-
liarity of their fituation, and we are perhaps not fully acquainted
with all their difficulties. It is our duty, fir, to inform you it is
not our intention to cenfure; and be affured, nothing but a fenfe of
the obligation we are under, to poftpone all other confiderations to
the public fafety, could induce us to perform the unpleafing tafk.—
We find, fir, the property of the continent difperfed over the whole
country; not an encampment, route of the army, or confiderable
road, but abounds with waggons, left to the mercy of the weather,
and the will of the inhabitants; large quantities of intrenching tools
have, in like manner, been left in various hands, under no other fecurity that we can learn, than the honefty of thofe who have them
in poffeffion. Not lefs than three thoufand fpades and fhovels, and
                                                        the

the like number of tomahawks, have been lately difcovered and collected in the vicinity of the camp, by an order from one of the general officers. In the fame way, a quantity of tents and tent cloth, after having lain a whole fummer in a farmer's barn, and unknown to the officer of the department, was lately difcovered, and brought to camp by a fpecial order from the general. From thefe inftances, we prefume there may be many other ftores yet unknown and uncollected, which require immediate care and attention.

" When, in compliance with the expectations of congrefs, and the wifhes of the country, the army was thrown into huts, inftead of retiring to more diftant and convenient quarters, the troops juftly expected every comfort which the furrounding country could afford. Among thefe, a providential care in the article of ftraw, would probably have faved the lives of many of your brave foldiers who have now paid the great debt of nature. Unprovided with this, or materials to raife them from the cold and wet earth, ficknefs and mortality have fpread through their quarters in an aftonifhing degree. Notwithftanding the diligence of the phyficians and furgeons, of whom we hear no complaint, the fick and dead lift has increafed one-third in the laft week's returns, which was one-third greater than the week preceding; and, from the prefent inclement weather, will probably increafe in a much greater proportion.—Nothing, fir, can equal their fufferings, except the patience and fortitude with which the faithful part of the army endure them. Thofe of a different character defert in confiderable numbers.

" We muft alfo obferve, that a number of the troops have now fome time been prepared for inoculation; but the operation muft be delayed, for want of this [ftraw] and other neceffaries within the providence of this department. We need not point out the fatal confequences of this delay in forming a new army, or the prefervation of this. Almoſt every day furniſhes inſtances of the ſmall-pox in the natural way. Hitherto ſuch vigilance and care has been uſed, that the contagion has not ſpread ; but ſurely it is highly incumbent upon us, if poſſible, to annihilate the danger.

" We need not point out the effect this circumſtance will have upon the new-draughted troops, if not carefully guarded ; they are too obvious to need enumeration. In conference with the forage-maſter on this ſubject (which, though in appearance trivial, is really important), he acquainted us, that, though out of his line, he would have procured it, if waggons could have been furniſhed him for that purpoſe.

" The want of horſes and waggons for the ordinary as well as extraordinary occaſions of the army, preſſes upon us, if poſſible, with equal force ; almoſt every ſpecies of camp tranſportation is now performed by men, who, without a murmur, patiently yoke themſelves to little carriages of their own making, or load their wood and proviſions on their backs.—Should the enemy, encouraged by the growing weakneſs of your troops, be led to make a ſucceſsful impreſſion upon your camp, your artillery would now undoubtedly fall into their hands, for want of horſes to remove it.—But theſe are ſmaller and tolerable evils, when compared with the imminent danger of your troops, periſhing with famine, or diſperſing in ſearch of food. The commiſſaries, in addition to their ſupplies of live cattle, which are precarious, have found a quantity of pork in New Jerſey, of which, by a failure of waggons, not one barrel has reached the camp.

" The orders were given for that purpoſe as early as the fourth of January.—In yeſterday's conference with the general he informed us, that ſome brigades had been four days without meat ; and that even the common ſoldiers had been at his quarters to make known

their

their wants.—At prefent, fir, there is not one gentleman of any rank in this department, though the duties of the office require a conftant and unremitted attention. In whatever view, therefore, the object prefents itfelf, we truft you will difcern, that the moft effential interefts are connected with it. The feafon of preparation for next campaign is paffing fwiftly away. Be affured, fir, that its operations will be ineffectual, either for offence or protection, if an arrangement is not immediately made, and the moft vigorous exertions ufed to procure the neceffary fupplies.—Permit us to fay, that a moment's time fhould not be loft in placing a man of approved abilities and extenfive capacity at the head of the department, who will reftore it to fome degree of regularity and order; whofe provident care will immediately relieve the prefent wants of the army, and extend itfelf to thofe which muft be fatisfied, before we can expect vigour, enterprife, or fuccefs.—When your committee reflect upon the increafed difficulties of procuring waggons, horfes, tents, and the numerous train of articles dependent on this office, without which your army cannot even move; they feel the greateft anxiety, left the utmoft fkill, diligence, and addrefs, will prove ineffectual to fatisfy the growing demand. All other confiderations vanifh before this object; and we moft earneftly wifh congrefs may be impreffed in a proper degree with its neceffity and importance.

" A report has reached us, that colonel Lutterlogh is a candidate for the office of quarter-mafter-general; we have therefore been led to make fome inquiry into his character and conduct. We fhould be far from doing injuftice to his abilities and experience in a fubordinate line; but, exclufive of the danger of entrufting fo confidential an office to a ftranger, whofe attachment to this country muft be light and tranfient, and whofe intereft may be fo eafily diftinguifhed from ours, we cannot find that he poffeffes talents or activity equal to this important office.—We find, in the courfe of the campaign, neceffary tools and ftores have often been wanting; important and

feafonable

seasonable movements of the army delayed; in some instances, wholly frustrated; and favourable opportunities lost, through the deficiencies of this department.—The rapid marches of our army, and unforeseen disasters which attended it during the summer season, partly claim some allowances ; but that disorder and confusion prevail through the department, which requires some able hand to reform and reduce it, is a certain and melancholy truth.

" Unacquainted with the resolution of congress with respect to general Schuyler, we have hesitated what further to propose. Time is so extremely precarious, that we are unwilling to lose a single unneeessary moment ; and have therefore been induced to extend our views to the disapprobation of this gentleman, and make some provision for that event. A character has presented itself, which, in a great degree, meets our approbation, judgment, and wishes. We have opened the subject to him, and it is now under his consideration. When we are at liberty, we shall introduce him to your notice; but delicacy forbids our doing it, until he has made up his mind on the subject, and given his consent to the nomination.—Another gentleman of extensive connexions, great activity, and comprehensive genius, but intirely in civil life, has also been proposed. As he is at a distance, we have not been able to consult him; and are restrained, by similar motives of delicacy, from making his character and name a subject of discussion without his consent.

" By the time we are favoured with the determination respecting general Schuyler, and he should not be approved, we hope to be able to announce both these gentlemen for your consideration.

" We are, with the greatest regard and respect,
" S I R,
" Your most obedient, and very humble servants,
" (THE COMMITTEE.)
* To the President of Congress.   (Signed) FRA. DANA."

IE

IT muſt be confeſſed that, on the whole, the Britiſh arms under ſir William Howe were attended with ſuccefs ; but this ſuccefs was never duly followed up and improved. That commander had ſe-veral opportunities of defeating the American army, and thereby of putting an end to the war. At Long Iſland, in the Jerſeys, at Brandywine, at White Marſh, and at Valley Forge, fortune had placed the enemy within his graſp, but he declined to ſeize the offered advantage. None of his military exploits poſſeſſed either plan, object, or deciſion. And the only fruit derived from the ſeveral victories of ſir William Howe, during the campaign of 1777, amounted to no more than the acquiſition of good win-ter-quarters for the Britiſh army at Philadelphia.

CHAP. XVI.

*Canadian Operations—General Burgoyne invested with the Command
of the Northern Army—General Carleton, offended with this Appointment, resigns his Government—Opinions on the Employment
of the Savages—Number of Troops under General Burgoyne—
Expedition under Colonel St. Leger—Burgoyne's Manifesto—Ticonderoga and Mount Independence invested—The Forts abandoned by the Americans—American Galleys destroyed near Skenesborough—Americans abandon their Works—Their Rear overtaken
—General St. Clair arrives at Fort Edward—Americans repulsed by Colonel Hill—Americans abandon Fort Anne—Difficulties encountered in the March of the Royal Army to Fort Edward—Americans retire to Saratoga.*

CHAP.
XVI.

1777.
Canadian
operations.

General Bur-
goyne invest-
ed with the
command of
the northern
army.

IT will be necessary now to turn our attention from the south
to the north; from the plains of Pensylvania to those of Canada:
where, instead of victories mixed with loss, we meet with nothing
but disappointment, disaster, and defeat.

The administration of Great Britain resolved to carry on the war
upon the side of Canada and the Lakes with activity and energy.
The command of this expedition was entrusted to general Burgoyne.
Sir Guy Carleton was certainly, and with much reason, offended
with this appointment, which, indeed, could not be justified on any
grounds of reason or of prudence. General Burgoyne, without
doubt, possessed bravery, and some military knowledge; but it must
be allowed that general Carleton was better qualified for the im-

portant

portant expedition, which, under his direction, would probably have been attended with fuccefs. From his long refidence in Canada, he knew more accurately than general Burgoyne, the fituation of the country, the manners of the inhabitants, and the extent of its refources ; and he united greater authority with more military experience. He would have been more aware of the difficulties to be encountered, and better prepared for furmounting them. But general Burgoyne was a member of parliament, and it was one of thofe miferable expedients which the minifter fubftituted for grandeur of defign, to beftow fome of the moft important employments, both military and naval, on men who were in the habits of oppofing the meafures of adminiftration. By this pitiful policy he was enabled to fecure himfelf againft parliamentary attack, and to carry his meafures more eafily in the houfe of commons.

That general Carleton was offended with the appointment of general Burgoyne is fufficiently evident, from his immediate refignation of his government. Much was expected from this expedition, and, to do the minifter juftice, nothing was wanting on his part to render fuccefs probable. A large body of veteran troops was fent from England, well provided with every neceffary, and great quantities of warlike ftores were alfo tranfmitted in order to fupply thofe inhabitants who were expected to declare in favour of the Britifh caufe.

General Carleton, offended at this appointment, refigns his government.

In addition to the ftrength already poffeffed by the Englifh in Canada, feveral nations of favages who inhabit the back fettlements of that province, and the borders of the Weftern Lakes, refolved to take up arms againft the Americans. The acceptance of their affiftance has occafioned much difcuffion, and a variety of opinions. General Burgoyne was certainly induced to adopt this meafure from a knowledge of their warlike character, and from a well-grounded fuppofition that, if he refufed their offers, they would inftantly join

Opinions on the employment of the favages.

the

the Americans.   But he refolved to bring them into action as little
as poffible.   In the preceding year he did not make much ufe of
them, and he determined to purfue, as far as he could with prudence, the fame line of conduct in the prefent year.   He knew that
their object in all wars was murder, defolation, and deftruction; and
though he certainly wifhed to conquer the revolted Americans, yet
he did not wifh to exterminate them.   His conduct however, in
this refpect, did not receive general approbation; for it was contended
that partial feverity was general mercy, and that, to put a fpeedy
end to the rebellion, the moft vigorous and refolute meafures
fhould be adopted.   Among the opponents of general Burgoyne on
this fubject was the minifter himfelf; who, accordingly, tranfmitted
orders to general Carleton to ufe all his influence in fecuring the
affiftance of the Indian nations.   This he did fo effectually, that he
became fearful at length of obtaining a larger number than was neceffary.

The army under general Burgoyne confifted of Britifh and German troops, amounting to feven thoufand one hundred and feventy-
three men, exclufive of the corps of artillery.   Of thefe the foreign
troops amounted to near one half.   This body of troops accorded
very nearly with the plan fubmitted to the minifter by general
Burgoyne.   He had required eight thoufand regulars, rank and file,
exclufive of the artillery, a corps of watermen, two thoufand Canadians, including hatchet-men, with a thoufand favages.

General Burgoyne was furnifhed with picked and experienced
officers.   The moft eminent of thefe were major-general Philips,
brigadier-generals Frazer, Powel, and Hamilton; the Brunfwick
major-general Reidefel, and brigadier-general Specht.   This large
body of veteran troops was to be kept together as much as poffible.
In order to produce this effect, the inhabitants of Canada were commanded to furnifh men fufficient to occupy the woods on the

S   frontiers,

frontiers, to prevent defertion, to procure intelligence, and to in- tercept all communication between the enemy and the malcontents in the province. They were alfo required to provide men for the completion of the fortifications at Sorel, St. John's, Chamblée, and Ifle aux Noix, for the carriage of provifions, artillery, and ftores, and for making roads. In addition to this, they were to furnifh an adequate quantity of horfes and carts.

Colonel St. Leger, with a body of light troops and Indians, *Expedition under colonel St. Leger.* amounting to between feven and eight hundred men, having been previoufly detached by the way of Lake Ontario, and the Mohawk river, in order to make a diverfion in favour of the army, general Burgoyne fet out from St. John's on the fixteenth of June 1777.

The naval force, under the command of commodore Lutwych, preceded the army, and opened the way for its advances, detachments of Indians having been previoufly made from the river Bouquet, as well to act upon the enemy's convoys and communications on the fide of Otter Creek, as to cover the reconnoitre of South Bay, through which country it was probable that the enemy would pafs, if Ticonderoga fhould fall into the hands of the Britifh. The fleet proceeded without any oppofition, and, under its protection, the troops were landed about the middle of June, and encamped at a fmall diftance from Crown Point on the north fide. The advanced parties of the enemy retired on the approach of our army.

At this place general Burgoyne thought proper to give the Indians a war-feaft, and to make a fpeech to them. The purport of it was, to induce them to refrain from cruelty, and to mitigate their natural ferocity.

Before the royal army advanced to Ticonderoga general Burgoyne *Burgoyne's manifefto.* iffued a proclamation or manifefto, in which, with a moft ill-judged policy, he threatened to punifh, with the utmoft feverity, thofe who

VOL. I.   T t   refufed

refused to attach themselves to the British cause. At the same time he magnified the ferocity of the savages, animadverting with peculiar emphasis of diction on the eagerness which they discovered to butcher those who continued hostile to the mother-country, whose interests they had espoused. Having remained at Crown Point a few days, in order to rest themselves, and to establish magazines, the whole army proceeded with caution to Ticonderoga, which place it was resolved to invest.

Ticonderoga invested,

· Ticonderoga is situated on the western shore, a few miles to the northward of that narrow inlet which unites Lake George to Lake Champlain. Crown Point lies more northward than Ticonderoga, and is situated on an angle of land washed on two sides by water flowing over rocks. A deep morass covered the third side, except in a small part, where formerly the French had erected lines, which still continued, and which the Americans had now strengthened by additional works.

and Mount Independence.

Opposite to Ticonderoga, on the eastern shore, the Americans had with great industry fortified a high hill called Mount Independence. On the top of it, which is flat, a star fort had been erected, containing extensive barracks well supplied with artillery. The mountain stretched in a sloping direction into the water, strongly entrenched to its base, and well supplied with heavy artillery. Midway up the mountain, another battery was erected to cover the lower works. With infinite labour the Americans had united Ticonderoga and Mount Independence by a strong bridge of communications over the inlet. Twenty-two sunken piers supported the bridge at equal distances. Between the piers floats were placed, fastened together with chains and rivets, and bound to the sunken piers. On the Lake Champlain side of the bridge, a boom, composed of very large timber, was erected, fastened together by rivetted bolts and double chains, made of iron an inch and a half

square.

fquare. This bridge effectually prevented any attack by water from
the northern fide. But Ticonderoga, notwithftanding its apparent ftrength, had one difadvantage to contend with. To the fouthward of the bridge of communications was a hill, called Sugar Hill, which overlooked and commanded both the works at Ticonderoga, and on Mount Independence. This place the Americans were unable to fortify, on account of the want of men; general St. Clair, who commanded at Ticonderoga, not having above three thoufand men.

The royal army, when they left Crown Point, advanced with the greateft circumfpection and prudence on both fides of the Lake, the fleet keeping in the centre till the army had enclofed the enemy on the land fide, and the fleet had arrived juft out. of cannon-fhot of their works. On the approach of the right wing on the fecond of July, the enemy inftantly relinquifhed and fet fire to their works on the fide of Lake George. Major-general Philips therefore immediately fecured the poffeffion of an important place called Mount Hope, which commanded the enemy's line, and cut off all communication with Lake George.

The royal army having arrived at Ticonderoga, proceeded with great expedition and alacrity in conftructing works neceffary for the inveftment of that place. By the fifth of July thefe works were completed, and a road made to the top of Sugar Hill for the conftruction of a battery there. The enemy, difcovering thefe vigorous operations, thought proper to hold a council of war, in which it was refolved to evacuate Ticonderoga and Mount Independence immediately. In confequence of this determination, their baggage, provifions, and ftores, were embarked in two hundred batteaux, and difpatched up the fouth river to Skenefborough. The army took the Caftle Town road, in order to reach Skenefborough by land. The American general conceived that his retreat would be made

The forts abandoned by the Americans.

without

without any difficulty, on account of the obſtacles which the Engliſh muſt neceſſarily overcome before they could purſue him. The dawn of the day, on the ſixth of July, diſcovered this unexpected retreat. Commodore Lutwych immediately began to prepare for a purſuit by removing an immenſe work of framed timber ſunk in the water, and by cutting away the boom that obſtructed the paſſage, and which had coſt, in the completion of it, near twelve months labour. As ſoon as theſe obſtructions were removed (which taſk was effected by nine o'clock in the morning), captain Carter of the artillery, who commanded a brigade of gun-boats, gave chaſe, and purſued that diviſion of the enemy which was making its retreat by water. So great was the ſpeed with which he executed the truſt repoſed in him, that he overtook them near the Falls of Skeneſborough, engaged and captured ſome of their largeſt gallies, obliging them to ſet the others on fire, together with a conſiderable number of their batteaux.

The grand diviſion of the army under general Burgoyne, in gunboats, the Royal George, and Inflexible frigates, approaching the Falls, were ſaluted by a diſcharge of cannon from the works at Skeenſborough. On this account the general thought proper to return and land his army at South Bay, where part of the batteaux of the enemy had taken refuge. Theſe would certainly have been deſtroyed if the day had not been too far advanced. Immediately on the landing of the Engliſh the enemy evacuated their ſtockade fort, and other works, to which, as well as to the mills and ſtorehouſes, they ſet fire previous to their departure.

During theſe operations by water, brigadier-general Frazer, at the head of the advanced corps of grenadiers and light infantry, preſſed hard upon the rear of that diviſion of the enemy which had taken the route of Hubberton, and which he overtook at five o'clock on the morning of the ſixth of July. This diviſion conſiſted of near one thouſand

five

five hundred of the beſt markſmen and choſen troops, under the command of colonel Francis. They were poſted on ſtrong ground, and received the attack of the Britiſh from behind breaſtworks compoſed of logs and old trees. General Frazer's detachment was not equal in point of number to the enemy; neverthelefs he commenced the engagement, becauſe he expected a reinforcement of troops under the German general Reidefel. The Americans maintained their poſt with great reſolution and bravery. The reinforcement did not arrive ſo ſoon as was expected, and victory for a long time was doubtful. The arrival however of general Reidefel decided the fate of the day. Hearing the firing of guns he puſhed forwards with a ſmall number of men, and joined general Frazer with a full band of muſic playing. The enemy conceiving from this circumſtance that the whole of the German troops had advanced into the field, immediately retreated with great precipitation.

The Americans loſt in this action their brave commander, ſeveral other officers, and above two hundred men killed. The ſame number were taken priſoners; and it was ſuppoſed that not leſs than ſix hundred wounded died in the woods.

The loſs on the part of the Britiſh did not exceed twenty officers, none, except major Grant, of any rank; and about one hundred and twenty men killed and wounded. During this engagement general St. Clair was at Caſtle Town, about ſix miles diſtant from the field of battle. Immediately on receiving intelligence of this defeat, he bent his courſe to the woods on his left, fearful of being intercepted at Fort Anne, but yet uncertain whether he ſhould proceed to the upper part of the Connecticut, or to Fort Edward. In the mean time a party of the enemy having taken the road by Wood Creek, in order to proceed beyond Fort Anne, after their retreat from Skeneſborough, were purſued by colonel Hill and the

ninth

ninth regiment, and overtaken near Fort Anne. A warm engagement immediately commenced, the enemy having infinitely the advantage in point of number. But colonel Hill had posted himself in such a judicious manner, that all the attacks of the enemy in front were ineffectual. A disposition was then made to surround him, which the British commander, with admirable dexterity, avoided, by changing his situation in the heat of the action. The engagement still continued, with various success, for three hours, when the Americans were repulsed with great slaughter, and forced to retreat, after setting fire to Fort Anne, to Fort Edward. The artillery lost, by the evacuation of the northern posts, and taken or destroyed in the armed vessels at Skenesborough, was prodigious, amounting to no less than one hundred and twenty-eight pieces, serviceable and unserviceable. The loss of flower, biscuit, pork, and beef, was also very considerable. At Fort Edward, where general Schuyler was joined by general St. Clair on the twelfth, after a fatiguing march, the whole strength of the Americans did not exceed four thousand four hundred men, including militia. It may not be improper to relate here one of those stratagems in which the genius of the Americans, during the whole course of the war, was remarkably fertile. Schuyler took out of a canteen with a false bottom, a letter from a person in the interest of the provincials to general Sullivan, and prepared an answer to it, drawn up in such a strain as to perplex and distract Burgoyne, and leave him in doubt what course to follow. This letter, which fell, as was intended, into the English general's hands, had the desired effect; for he was completely duped and puzzled by it for several days, and at a loss whether to advance or retreat.

General Burgoyne, after remaining some time at Skenesborough, left that place, with an intention of taking the road that leads to Hudson's River, and thence to Albany, in order to open a communication

cation with Lake George, on which he had embarked the heavy artillery and baggage. In this undertaking, the difficulties which the royal army had to encounter were infinite. Swamps and moraffes were to be paffed. Bridges were to be conftructed, not only over creeks, but over ravines and gullies. The roads were to be cleared of the foreft trees, which had been felled and difpofed in fuch a manner as to interfect each other. Notwithftanding, however, all thefe obftacles, in a fultry feafon of the year, and in a clofe country, which the numerous infects render almoft intolerable to Europeans, the royal army endured this amazing fatigue with great cheerfulnefs, and oppofed themfelves to difficulty and danger with untired perfeverance and unabated fortitude. This general has, with much reafon, been blamed for adopting this difficult and tardy mode of conduct; by returning to Ticonderoga, and embarking again on Lake George, he might have eafily proceeded to Fort George, whence there was a waggon-road to the place of his deftination, Fort Edward. The reafon he gave for not purfuing this line of conduct was, that a retrograde motion would have checked the vigour and animation of the troops. Whether the mode he chofe to adopt was likely to increafe them it is not very difficult to determine. As foon as the Britifh troops had fecured the poffeffion of Skenefborough, that active officer major-general Philips returned to Lake George, to tranfport the artillery, provifions, and baggage, over the lake, to Fort George, and thence by land to Fort Edward, on Hudfon's River, together with a large number of boats and batteaux for the ufe of the army in the intended defcent to Albany. General Schuyler, who at this time commanded the northern American army, had pofted himfelf, immediately after the affair of Hubberton, as already obferved, at Fort Edward. On the advance of the royal army he retreated down Hudfon's River to Saratoga, where he iffued a proclamation calculated to counteract the effect intended to be pro-

S   duced

C H A P.   duced by the manifesto published by general Burgoyne.   The royal
   XVI.   army, on account of the numberless difficulties they had to encoun-
   1777.   ter, advanced but flowly; and it was not till the thirtieth of July
           that they arrived on Hudson's River.   Here their progress was
           checked for fome time, becaufe it was neceffary, before they could.
           proceed, that the provifions, ftores, and other neceffaries, which had
           been brought to Fort George from Ticonderoga, by general Philips,
           fhould be embarked.   The army of courfe was immediately em-
           ployed in the profecution of this fervice.

CHAP. XVII.

Difficulties experienced at Fort Edward—Colonel St. Leger's Ex-
pedition—Detachment to Bennington—Baum and Breyman defeated
—Fort Stanwix invested—Attempt to relieve it by General Harke-
mer—St. Leger obliged to raise the Siege of Fort Stanwix—Ge-
neral Gates takes the Command of the American Army in the North
—Action at Still Water—Distressed Situation of General Burgoyne
—Desertion of the Indians—Retreat to Saratoga—Royal Army
nearly surrounded—Convention with General Gates.

THE delays which had been occasioned by the route which
general Burgoyne thought proper to take, had afforded time for
the Americans to recover their fortitude and to recruit their strength.
Where the Mohawk falls into Hudson's River, about eight miles
from Albany, is an island in the shape of an half-moon, call Still
Water. On this place general Schuyler, who had assembled about
two thousand seven hundred men at Saratoga, on receiving a reinforcement of men and artillery, under the command of general
Arnold, posted his army, in order to check the progress of colonel
St. Leger, who early in June had been detached from Lashene,
six miles from Montreal, by the way of Lake Ontario and the
Mohawk River, in order, as already observed, to make a diversion
in favour of the main army. He had under his command a confiderable number of savages, who, in spite of general Burgoyne's
address to them, could not be restrained from the commission of fe-

U u   veral

C H A P.
XVII.

1797.
Difficulties
experienced
at Fort Ed-
ward.
Colonel St.
Leger's ex-
pedition.

veral acts of ferocity. General Burgoyne still remained in the neighbourhood of Fort Edward, where, on account of the difficulty of bringing the stores from Fort George to Hudson's River, the army began to experience great hardships. At this juncture he received intelligence that colonel St. Leger had advanced up the St. Lawrence, and had commenced his operations against Stanwix, a fort situated on a rising ground at the upper end of the Mohawk River, about three hundred yards from its source, and about half a mile from the source of Wood Creek, which runs into Lake Onida, and through the Onandigo into Lake Ontario. General Burgoyne saw the necessity of co-operating with colonel St. Leger, and of immediately making a rapid movement forward. But this intention could not be carried into execution under the present circumstances. Ox-teams, carriages, and other necessaries, were indispenfably necessary; to procure which, the commander in chief resolved to detach a body of troops to Bennington, a place situated between the forks of the Hosick River, and about twenty-four miles to the eastward of Hudson's River. The northern army received supplies of cattle, provisions, and stores, from the New England provinces by way of the Connecticut, Manchester, and Arlington; which supplies were deposited at Bennington. On this expedition the German colonel Baum was dispatched with about six hundred men, mostly Germans, including a detachment of Reidesel's dragoons. This number was in every respect too small. A loyalist who was well acquainted with the road, and had undertaken to accompany colonel Baum, stated to general Burgoyne that the expedition required a force of not less than three thousand men; for the roads were very bad, through a thick woody country, and the tardiness of the German method of marching would, he knew, enable the enemy to prepare for their reception. The general, however, paid no attention to the repre-

Detachment
to Benning-
ton.

fentation

fentation of this gentleman, whom he piqued on the point of honour.
The idea of fending German troops on this fervice was oppofed by
fome of the officers of the army; but particularly by general Frazer,
who, it is faid, not only remonftrated with general Burgoyne, but reduced his remonftrance into writing. The Germans were heavy and
tardy in marching, and, as ufual, were loaded with accoutrements that
prevented thofe exertions which fuch an expedition required. In the
whole army a corps could not have poffibly been found fo unfit for
a fervice that required rapidity of motion as Reidefel's dragoons.
Their very hats and fwords weighed very nearly as much as the whole
equipment of one of our foldiers. The worft Britifh regiment in the
fervice would with eafe have marched two miles for their one. Colonel Baum was a brave officer, but he was totally unacquainted
with the country, with the people, and with the language, infomuch,
it was reported, that he hardly knew, when he underftood that they
were rifing in arms, whether to confider them as friends or foes.

Colonel Baum, accompanied by the loyalift as his guide, began his
march. On the firft day Baum furprifed a large body of the enemy
who had affembled for the purpofe of oppofing the progrefs of his
detachment. This body of men, however, were, from a too
refined principle of generofity, on the fucceeding day liberated
by colonel Skeene, the infpector-general, who joined the detachment and fuperfeded the loyalift. This mode of conduct it
was fuppofed would detach them from the American caufe. Unfortunately however it produced an effect diametrically oppofite;
for this very body of the enemy were afterwards the moft formidable
opponents of the Englifh at Bennington.

On the fecond day's march of colonel Baum's detachment, they
captured fome cattle, and routed a fmall part of the enemy near a
village called Cambridge. Here the colonel received intelligence

U u 2 that

that the enemy were affembling from New Hampfhire, and the borders of Connecticut, for the defence of Bennington. Neverthelefs he advanced as far as Walloon Creek, about feven miles from Bennington, where the intelligence he had received at Cambridge was confirmed, and no doubt remained of a formidable oppofition. In confequence of this information he thought proper to halt, and to poft his detachment in as advantageous a manner as poffible. This laft meafure he was induced to adopt from the reprefentations of a number of loyalifts, under the command of a colonel Phifter, who joined him, and acquainted him that the enemy were ftrongly intrenched at Bennington, and that, as foon as they had received a reinforcement of men, it was intended to attack him. Colonel Baum having tranfmitted thefe particulars to general Burgoyne, a detachment of five hundred Germans, under the command of lieutenant-colonel Breyman, was fent to his affiftance. The roads were bad; nor was the mode in which the Germans marched calculated to promote expedition. They halted ten times in an hour to drefs their ranks, which, through the embarraffments attending their march, were liable to be broken at every turn.

The American general, Starke, with a body of one thoufand men from New Hampfhire and Maffachufet, was at this period on his route to join general Schuyler. Having received intelligence, however, of the approach of colonel Baum, he altered his courfe, and haftened towards Bennington, where, joining the continental troops under colonel Warner, he fet out on the fixteenth of Auguft, and, by ten o'clock in the morning, furrounded colonel Baum at St. Coieck's Mill, on Walloon Creek. The German officer, a ftranger to the country, and to the language of the inhabitants, was at firft perfuaded by the loyalifts who had joined him that they were friends. General
                                                                    Starke,

Starke, however, commencing a furious attack upon him on all sides, soon convinced him of their error. Neverthelefs he refolved to make a vigorous defence. For upwards of an hour he endured a terrible difcharge of mufquetry, and during that period drove the enemy feveral times from the high ground on which they were ftationed. But their number increafing every moment, and colonel Baum having loft his artillery, the German troops were under the neceffity of retreating into the woods, leaving their commander mortally wounded on the field of battle. The favages who had accompanied colonel Baum behaved in a fhameful manner, retreating at the commencement of the engagement. Flufhed with this victory, the enemy advanced againft the detachment under colonel Breyman, who, ignorant of the defeat of Baum, was advancing to his relief; but the tardinefs of their method of marching, added to the obftacles which the roads prefented, had retarded their progrefs in fuch a manner, that twenty-four hours were fpent in marching fixteen miles. The confequence was, that Breyman came up juft in time to join the fugitives of Baum's detachment. The Americans began a vigorous attack on Breyman, who was obliged to retreat, after having made a very gallant refiftance, and having expended all his ammunition. The lofs of men in thefe two engagements amounted to about fix hundred.

This was the firft check which the northern army received, and indeed it muft be chiefly attributed to the commander in chief. The troops he difpatched on the expedition to Bennington were too few in number, and, being foreigners, improper for it. The general ought to have rectified his miftake, when colonel Baum fent for a reinforcement. Had he fent Frazer's brigade, according to that general's requeft, the fatal confequences that enfued might in all probability have been prevented. Immediately after the

defeat

Baum and
Breyman
defeated.

defeat of colonel Baum, and the retreat of colonel Breyman, the royal army which had advanced to Saratoga, drew back.

1777.
Fort Stanwix
invested.

In the mean time colonel St. Leger had commenced his attack upon Fort Stanwix, a small square log fort with four bastions and a stockaded covered-way, without any other outworks. It was defended by colonels Gansevert and Willet, and seven hundred men. The commencement of the siege was attended with very favourable circumstances. On the fifth of August colonel St. Leger received intelligence that one thousand provincials, under the command of

Attempt to
relieve it by
general Har-
kemer.

general Harkemer, were advancing to the relief of the fort. Sir John Johnson therefore, with a party of regulars, and a number of savages, was dispatched into the woods, where he placed his men in ambush. The enemy advanced incautiously, and fell into the trap that was laid for them. A sudden and unexpected fire was poured upon them from behind trees and bushes, and the savages rushing from their concealment, made a dreadful slaughter with their spears and tomahawks. The enemy, though surprised and somewhat dismayed, did not retreat precipitately, but recovered a rising ground, which enabled them, by a kind of running fight, to preserve about one third of their detachment. The number of killed and wounded on the part of the enemy amounted to near four hundred. The besieged being informed of the approach of general Harkemer, made a sally under colonel Willet, which was attended with some success. Having received, however, intelligence of the defeat of the provincials, he and another officer undertook a very perilous expedition. They penetrated at the dead of night through the camp of the besiegers, and traversed a space of fifty miles, through deserts, woods, and morasses, in order to bring relief to the fort. The enemy perceiving that the artillery of the besiegers was too light, and insufficient to make any impression on the defences of the fort, treated

3

every

every propofal for a furrender with derifion and contempt. On the twenty-fecond of Auguft a man belonging to the fort purpofely conveyed himfelf into the Britifh camp, and declared that he had efcaped from the enemy at the hazard of his life, in order to inform the Britifh commander that general Arnold, with two thoufand men and ten pieces of cannon, was advancing rapidly to raife the fiege. He alfo acquainted him that general Burgoyne had been defeated, and his army cut to pieces. Colonel St. Leger was not intimidated by this information; nor did he give much credit to it; but it produced an immediate effect on the favages. The Britifh commander called a council of their chiefs, and endeavoured, by the influence of fir John Johnfon, and the other fuperintendants, co-lonels Claus and Butler, to induce them not to withdraw their affiftance. Every effort however was ineffectual; a large party of the favages departed while the council was fitting; and the reft threatened to follow their example, unlefs the Britifh commander would immediately make a retreat. To this mortifying propofition he was under the neceffity of acceding. The tents were left ftand-ing, and the artillery and ftores fell into the poffeffion of the gar-rifon. One of the chief caufes of the failure of fuccefs in this expedition was the inadequacy of the force under colonel St. Leger, and the infufficiency and fmallnefs of the artillery, which were in-capable of making any breach on the enemy's works. The fupe-riority of the favages in number over the Britifh troops, was another caufe. Their fubfequent defertion, and the approach of Arnold, rendered a retreat a meafure of neceffity, though it certainly might have been conducted in a more regular manner.

With refpect to the intimation of general Arnold's approach to the relief of Fort Stanwix, it was in part true. He was advancing up the Mohawk River with two thoufand men; but, in order to arrive more fpeedily at the place of his deftination, he had left the

main

C H A P.
XVII.

1777.
General
Gates takes
the command
of the Ame-
rican army in
the north.
main body, and moved rapidly forward with a body of about nine hundred men. He arrived at the fort two days after the fiege had been raifed. His affiftance being now unneceffary, he returned with his army to reinforce general Gates, who had a fhort time before taken the command of the American army in the north.

General Burgoyne having by unremitting induftry collected about thirty days provifions, and a bridge of boats being conftructed in lieu of the bridge of rafts which had been carried away by inceffant rains, the whole army croffed Hudfon's River on the thirteenth and fourteenth of September, and encamped on the heights and plains of Saratoga, with a vaft train of artillery. The movements of the army were of courfe regulated by the advances of the artillery, which were not only retarded by the deftruction of the bridges, but by the rains, which had rendered the roads almoft impaffable. On the nineteenth of September the army advanced in front of the enemy at Still Water in the following order: The right wing was commanded by general Burgoyne, and covered by general Frazer and colonel Breyman, with the grenadiers and light-infantry, who were pofted along fome high grounds on the right. The front and flanks were covered by Indians, Provincials, and Canadians. The left wing and artillery were commanded by majors-general Philips and Reidefel, who proceeded along the great road. The nature of the country preventing the enemy from beholding the different movements of the Britifh army, they detached a body of five thoufand men to attempt turning the right wing, and attacking general Burgoyne in his rear. Being checked in their defign by general Frazer, they made a rapid movement, which the peculiar fituation of the country prevented from being difcovered, and advanced to

attack the Britifh line on the right. The engagement began at three o'clock in the afternoon of the nineteenth of September, and continued till after fun-fet. The enemy were led to the battle by

general

general Arnold, who diftinguiſhed himſelf in an extraordinary manner. Unfortunately, the engagament was only partial on the part of the Englifh. The chief burden of the battle of courſe lay on the regiments which were poſted in the plain. Theſe were the twentieth, the twenty-firſt, and the fixty-fecond. They behaved with great gallantry and firmneſs, receiving and returning the heavy fire of the enemy with equal coolneſs and intrepidity, for the ſpace of four hours. Several other regiments alſo diftinguiſhed themſelves. The twenty-fourth regiment, with the grenadiers and light-infantry, were for ſome time engaged with great ſpirit and bravery. The German troops were not much in the battle, on account of their ſituation, which it was not judged adviſable to relinquiſh. As ſoon as the battle commenced, major-general Philips contrived to convey through a thick part of the wood ſome artillery, which was of eſſential ſervice.

The enemy, during the whole of the engagement, were ſupplied with freſh men by general Gates, who was poſted at a ſtar redoubt. As day-light cloſed they thought proper to retire, and leave the Britifh maſters of the field of battle.

The loſs on each ſide was nearly equal; ſix hundred being killed and wounded on the part of the Britiſh, and the ſame number on the ſide of the Americans. It muſt be confeſſed that the engagement would have been more deciſive on the part of the Engliſh, if general Burgoyne had not burdened himſelf with ſuch a train of artillery as not only rendered his marching tardy, but made it neceſſary for him to extend his lines more than the nature of his ſituation rendered prudent. No ſolid advantages reſulted to the Britiſh troops from this encounter. The conduct of the enemy had fully convinced every one that they were able to ſuſtain an attack in open plains with the intrepidity, the ſpirit, and the coolneſs of veterans. For four hours they maintained a conteſt hand to hand;

VOL. I. X x and

and when they retired, it was not becaufe they were conquered, but becaufe the approach of night made a retreat to their camp abfo-lutely neceffary.

The Britifh army lay all night on their arms in the field of battle, and the next day works were erected within cannon-fhot of the enemy, the right being fortified by ftrong redoubts. It is faid that, had the lines of the enemy been attacked on the morning after the battle, they would have retreated, their baggage being loaded, and every thing prepared for flight, if the Britifh general had thought proper to have adopted fuch a meafure. It muft be confeffed, how-ever, that fuch an affertion is not fupported by circumftances or pro-babilities; for the manner in which the enemy were pofted was pe-culiary ftrong. On the right, any approach or attack was impracti-cable; and on the left not to be made without great hazard. The intrepidity of captain Jones, of the Britifh artillery, who fell in this action, was particularly diftinguifhed. Few actions have been more remarkable than this, for both vigour of attack and obftinacy of refiftance.

Diftreffed fituation of general Bur-goyne.

Every poffible method was now taken to inform fir William Howe and general Clinton of the fituation of general Burgoyne, and argu-ments ufed that might induce them to make a diverfion in his favour. Under the conviction that they would adopt fuch a mode of conduct, he had croffed Hudfon's River, and given up all com-munication with the Lakes. He had expected that a diverfion would have been made before this period. Such a diverfion was indeed made about this time, and that without orders, by fir Henry Clinton, againft Forts Clinton and Montgomery in the lower parts of Hudfon's River.

After the battle of Still Water the favages, as already obferved, had difcovered a difinclination to continue with general Burgoyne. They had been difappointed in their hopes of plunder, and the

3　　　　　　　　　　　　　　　　　　　**check**

check which the Englifh had received at Bennington and Fort Stanwix had chilled that ardour and enthufiafm which they had at firft manifefted. The feafon for hunting was now arrived; and never do they on any pretence forego it. On this account they withdrew their affiftance, and deferted general Burgoyne, deaf to every confideration of honour, and unmoved by any reprefentations made to them of the diftrefs in which their feceffion would involve him. The royal army was by this defertion extremely weakened; but the Britifh general did not think it advifable to retreat from the enemy.

Both armies lay in fight of each other for fome time, each fortifying their camp in the ftrongeft manner poffible. This delay was extremely beneficial to the Americans, inafmuch as it enabled them to increafe their number of men, and to obtain a powerful reinforcement of ftores and provifions from the fouthern provinces. But the American generals were not folely employed in fortifying their camp, or in increafing their refources. They knew the embarraffment of general Burgoyne's fituation, and the dilemma to which he was reduced. The only probable means of faving himfelf from deftruction lay in a retreat. An expedition was therefore planned by generals Gates and Arnold, to prevent the adoption of this laft fad meafure, by cutting off all communication with the Lakes, and, by recovering the poffeffion of Ticonderoga and Mount Independence.

This expedition was entrufted to the command of colonel Brown, who with great fecrefy and diligence gained the rear of the royal army undifcovered. He arrived on the eighteenth of September at the north end of Lake George, where one fmall floop and the boats employed in tranfporting provifions to the army were furprifed and taken, with a number of Canadians and a few feamen. Three com-

Defertion of the Indians.

Retreat to Saratoga.

panies

panies of the fifty-third regiment were at the fame time made pri-. foners. Immediately after they had fecured the poffeffion of the. armed veffels, they began to attack Ticonderoga with two pieces of cannon, which they had obtained from the captured floop.

Brigadier-general Powel, who commanded the garrifon, defended it for four days againft the attempts of the enemy, who, at the ex-. piration of that period, were induced to retire, from an apprehenfion of being intercepted in their retreat by a detachment of troops from Canada. In their way back the enemy made another attempt upon Diamond Ifland, fituated in the fouthern part of the lake, which was as unfuccefsful as that made againft Ticonderoga.

General Burgoyne's difficulties began now to increafe daily. The enemy had augmented their ftrength iu fuch a manner as to render him diffident of the poffibility of making good his retreat. His army was reduced to little more than five thoufand men, who were limited to half the ufual allowance of provifions. The ftock of forage was entirely exhaufted, and the horfes were perifhing in, great numbers for the want of it. In addition to thefe circumftances, no intelligence had yet been received of the approach of general Clinton, or of the diverfion which was to be made. Environed thus by difficulty and danger, general Burgoyne refolved to try the dif-pofition of the enemy, to examine the poffibility of advancing, and of diflodging them from their pofts on the left, which would en-able him to adopt the melancholy refource of retreating to the lakes. Purfuant to this determination he detached a body of fifteen hun-dred men, which he headed himfelf, being attended by generals Philips, Reidefel, and Frazer. The camp was defended on the high grounds by generals Hamilton and Specht; and the redoubts and parts adjacent to the river, by brigadier Gell. This detachment had, fcarce formed, within lefs than half a mile of the enemy's intrench-

ments,

·ments, when a furious attack was made on the left, where the grenadiers were pofted. Major Ackland, who commanded the grenadiers, conducted himfelf with great coolnefs and intrepidity. His
·poft was extremely difficult and dangerous, and it was not poffible
to detach any affiftance to him from the German corps, becaufe the
fuperiority in number of the enemy enabled them at the fame time to
extend their line of attack againft them. The right had not yet been
·employed, but it being obferved that the enemy were making a movement round their flank to prevent their retreat, the light-infantry
and the twenty-fourth regiment inftantly formed, in order to
fruftrate the enemy's intentions.

The left wing in the mean time, overpowered by numbers, was
obliged to retreat, and would inevitably have been cut to pieces, but
for the intervention of the light-infantry and twenty-fourth regiment. The whole detachment was now under the neceffity of retiring, with the lofs of fix pieces of artillery. Scarce had the Britifh troops entered the lines when they were again impetuoufly attacked by the enemy, who, notwithftanding a moft heavy fire,
began a furious affault upon their intrenchments. They were led
by the gallant general Arnold, who attacked lord Balcarras's light-
infantry with great eagernefs. The refiftance was firm, and the
engagement for a long while doubtful. A wound which Arnold received at length gave the victory to the Englifh, and the Americans
were repulfed from this quarter. In another, however, they were
more fuccefsful. The intrenchments defended by the German
troops under colonel Breyman were carried fword in hand. The
colonel was killed, and his troops retreated, with the lofs of all
their baggage, artillery, &c. Night clofed the dreadful fcene. The
Englifh loft, this day, general Frazer, colonel Breyman, and feveral other officers of note, befides a confiderable number of
wounded. The Americans took upwards of two hundred officers
and

privates prifoners; befides nine pieces of brafs artillery, and the encampment of a German brigade, with all their equipage. But
what was of the greateft confequence, they obtained from the fpoils
of the field a large fupply of ammunition, under a fcarcity of which
they had long laboured.

General Burgoyne was now moft critically fituated. He could
not continue in his prefent pofition without a certainty of deftruction. He therefore refolved to make a total and immediate change
of pofition. With great fecrefy and filence the whole army removed, with all their baggage and artillery, to the heights above the
hofpital during the night. This movement reduced the enemy to
the neceffity of making a new difpofition. On the fucceeding day,
the eighth of October, feveral attempts were made to induce the
enemy to hazard a battle. They were however ineffectual, and the
whole day was occupied in continued fkirmifhes.

The enemy had refufed to hazard a battle becaufe they were
preparing to carry meafures into execution which would have
immediately completed the ruin of the Britifh army. Thefe were
to turn general Burgoyne's right, which, if effected, would have
inclofed him on all fides. The Britifh general, however, difcovered
thefe intentions before they were carried into execution. An inftant
retreat therefore to Saratoga was now the only alternative left. At
nine o'clock on the evening of the eighth of October the army was
ordered to relinquifh their pofition on the heights above the hofpital.
The retreat to Saratoga was effected without lofs, and without any
obftruction on the part of the enemy; but it was impoffible, encumbered as the army was with baggage and artillery, to carry off the
fick and wounded from the hofpital. General Gates, however,
behaved with his wonted humanity, and the unfortunate tenants of
the hofpital were treated with all imaginable tendernefs. General
Burgoyne having ordered the roads and the bridges to be broken in
                                                        their

their march forward, the movement of the army in their retreat was neceffarily tardy. The fords of Fifh Kill Creek, which are fome-what to the northward of Saratoga, were not paffed till ten o'clock on the fucceeding morning. The enemy, watching every motion with the moft anxious attention, had already arrived at this place before them; but on the approach of the Britifh troops, they retired over the river Hudfon, to a larger force, which had been detached there to obftruct the paffage of the royal troops.

An attempt was now made to retreat to Fort George. A detach-ment of artificers under a ftrong efcort was accordingly difpatched before the army, in order to repair the bridges and open the road to Fort Edward. The appearance of the enemy, however, prevented the artificers from effecting their purpofe, and they were under the neceffity of making a precipitate retreat on account of the defertion of their efcort. The enemy ftretching along the farther fhore of the river Hudfon, annoyed the batteaux of the royal army in fuch a manner that they were forced to land the provifions and convey them to the camp up a fteep hill, the enemy pouring, during the whole time, a moft tremendous fire on the men employed in this fervice.

Surrounded in this manner by deftruction and difmay, general Burgoyne refolved to attempt a retreat by night to Fort Edward, each foldier carrying his provifion on his back. The artillery was to be left behind, on account of the impoffibility, under the prefent circum-ftance, of conveying it away. But even this fad alternative was ren-dered impracticable. While the army were preparing to march, in-telligence was received that the enemy had already poffeffed them-felves of the road to Fort Edward, and that they were well provided with artillery. In the courfe of the difaftrous events here enume-rated, large quantities of baggage, provifions, boats, and other ar-ticles, fell into the hands of the Americans; both regular troops, called continentals, and militia. The American militia were fo eager

after

C H A P.
XVII.

1777.

after plunder, that they would often rob the provincial regulars of what booty they had fecured, and fell it on their own account. Irregularities of this kind were carried to fuch a height, that the American commander, in general orders iffued on the twelfth of October, declared " that he faw fo many fcandalous and mean tranfactions committed " by perfons who fought more after plunder than the honour of " doing their duty, that it was his unalterable refolution to have the " firft perfon who fhould thereafter be detected in pillaging the bag- " gage and ftores taken from the enemy tried and punifhed with the " utmoft feverity."

The fituation of general Burgoyne had now attainted the climax of difficulty and danger. Inceffant toil had enervated the whole army. Out of eight thoufand men, of which the army confifted after the capture of Ticonderoga, not more than three thoufand five hundred fighting men remained, one half of which only were Britifh. Provifions were almoft exhaufted, and no hope remained of procuring a frefh fupply. Added to this, an enemy four times greater in point of number, and increafing every day, almoft encircled them. An engagement was ftudioufly avoided by the Americans, on account of their knowledge of the defperate fituation of the Britifh troops; and the enemy were pofted in fo advantageous a manner that they could not be attacked.

Every hope of relief being now at an end, on the thirteenth of October 1777, general Burgoyne ordered an exact ftatement to be made of the ftock of provifions, which was found not to exceed feven or eight days fubfiftence for the troops.

The general inftantly called a council of war, at which not only field officers but every captain was ordered to affift.

Convention with general Gates.

After fome confultation on the emergency of affairs, it was unanimoufly refolved to enter into a convention with general Gates. The following were the fteps preliminary to it:

No.

No. I.

October 13, 1777.

Lieutenant-general Burgoyne is desirous of sending a field-officer with a message to major-general Gates, upon a matter of high moment to both armies. He requests to be informed at what hour general Gates will receive him to-morrow morning.

Major-general Gates.

Answer.

Major-general Gates will receive a field-officer from lieutenant-general Burgoyne at the advanced post of the army of the United States at ten o'clock to-morrow morning, from whence he will be conducted to head-quarters.

Camp at Saratoga, nine o'clock P. M. thirteenth October.

Lieutenant-general Burgoyne.

No. II.

Major Kingston delivered the following message to major-general Gates, October 14, 1777.

After having fought you twice, lieutenant-general Burgoyne has waited some days in his present position, determined to try a third conflict against any force you could bring against him. He is apprised of the superiority of your numbers, and the disposition of your troops to impede his supplies, and render his retreat a scene of carnage on both sides. In this situation he is impelled by humanity, and thinks himself justified by established principles and precedents of state and war, to spare the lives of brave men upon honourable terms. Should major-general Gates be inclined to treat upon that idea, general Burgoyne would propose a cessation of arms during the time necessary to communicate the preliminary terms, by which, in any extremity, he and his army mean to abide.

No. III.

Major-general Gates's Propofals, together with Lieutenant-general
Burgoyne's Anfwers.

1. General Burgoyne's army being exceedingly reduced by repeated defeats, by defertion, ficknefs, &c. their provifions exhaufted,
their military horfes, tents, and baggage taken or deftroyed, their
retreat cut off, and their camp invefted, they can only be allowed
to furrender prifoners of war.

Anf. Lieutenant-general Burgoyne's army, however reduced, will
never admit that their retreat is cut off while they have arms in
their hands.

2. The officers and foldiers may keep the baggage belonging to
them. The generals of the United States never permit individuals
to be pillaged.

3. The troops under his excellency general Burgoyne will be
conducted by the moft convenient route to New England, marching by eafy marches, and fufficiently provided for by the way.

Anf. This article is anfwered by general Burgoyne's firft propofal,
which is here annexed.

4. The officers will be admitted on parole; may wear their fide
arms, and will be treated with the liberality cuftomary in Europe,
fo long as they, by proper behaviour, continue to deferve it; but
thofe who are apprehended having broke their parole, as fome Britifh officers have done, muft expect to be clofe confined.

Anf. There being no officer in this army under, or capable of
being under the defcription of breaking parole, this article needs
no anfwer.

5. All public ftores, artillery, arms, ammunition, carriages, horfes,
&c. muft be delivered to commiffaries appointed to receive them.

                                                    Anf.

Anf. All public ftores may be delivered, arms excepted.

6. Thefe terms being agreed to, and figned, the troops under his excellency general Burgoyne's command may be drawn up in their encampments, where they will be ordered to ground their arms, and may thereupon be marched to the river fide to be paffed over in their way towards Bennington.

Anf. This article inadmiffible in any extremity. Sooner than this army will confent to ground their arms in their encampment, they will rufh on the enemy, determined to take no quarter.

7. A ceffation of arms to continue till fun-fet, to receive general Burgoyne's anfwer.

(Signed) HORATIO GATES.

Camp at Saratoga, October 14, 1777.

No. IV.

Lieutenant-general Burgoyne's Propofals, together with Major-general Gates's Anfwers.

The annexed anfwers being given to major-general Gates's propofals, it remains for lieutenant-general Burgoyne, and the army under his command, to ftate the following preliminary articles on their part:

1. The troops to march out of their camp with the honours of war, and the artillery of the intrenchments, which will be left as hereafter may be regulated,

1. The troops to march out of their camp with the honours of war, and the artillery of the intrenchments to the verge of the river where the Old Ford ftood, where their arms and artillery muft be left.

2. A free paffage to be granted to this army to Great Britain, upon condition of not ferving again in North America during the

Y y 2   prefent

prefent conteft, and a proper port to be affigned for the entry of tranfports to receive the troops wherever general Howe fhall fo order.

2. Agreed to, for the port of Bofton.

3. Should any cartel take place, by which this army, or any part of it, may be exchanged, the foregoing article to be void, as far as fuch exchange fhall be made.

3. Agreed.

4. All officers to retain their carriages, bat-horfes, and other cattle; and no baggage to be molefted or fearched, the lieutenant-general giving his honour that there are no public ftores fecreted therein. Major-general Gates will of courfe take the neceffary meafures for the fecurity of this article.

4. Agreed.

5. Upon the march, the officers are not to be feparated from their men; and in quarters the officers fhall be lodged according to rank, and are not to be hindered from affembling their men for roll-calling and other neceffary purpofes of regularity.

5. Agreed to, as far as circumftances will admit.

6. There are various corps in this army compofed of failors, batteau-men, artificers, drivers, independent companies, and followers of the army; and it is expected that thofe perfons, of whatever country, fhall be included in the fulleft fenfe and utmoft extent of the above articles, and comprehended in every refpect as Britifh fubjects.

6. Agreed to in the fulleft extent.

7. All Canadians and perfons belonging to the eftablifhment in Canada to be permitted to return there.

7. Agreed.

8. Paffports

8. Passports to be immediately granted for three officers, not exceeding the rank of captain, who shall be appointed by general Burgoyne to carry dispatches to sir W. Howe, sir G. Carleton, and to Great Britain by the way of New York, and the public faith to be engaged that these dispatches are not to be opened.

8. Agreed.

9. The foregoing articles are to be considered only as preliminary for framing a treaty, in the course of which others may arise to be considered by both parties; for which purpose it is proposed that two officers of each army shall meet and report their deliberations to their respective generals.

9. This capitulation to be finished by two o'clock this day, and the troops to march from their encampment at five, and be in readiness to move towards Boston to-morrow morning.

10. Lieutenant-general Burgoyne will send his deputy adjutant-general to receive major-general Gates's answer to-morrow morning at ten o'clock.

10. Complied with.

(Signed) HORATIO GATES.

Saratoga, October 15, 1777.

On the following day the subsequent articles of convention between lieutenant-general Burgoyne and major-general Gates were settled.

1. The troops under lieutenant-general Burgoyne to march out of their camp with the honours of war, and the artillery of the intrenchments to the verge of the river where the Old Ford stood, where the arms and artillery are to be left; the arms to be piled by word of command from their own officers.

2. A

2. A free paſſage to be granted the army under lieutenant-general Burgoyne to Great Britain, on condition of not ſerving again in North America during the preſent conteſt; and the port of Boſton is aſſigned for the entry of tranſports to receive the troops whenever general Howe ſhall ſo order.

3. Should any cartel take place by which the army under general Burgoyne, or any part of it, may be exchanged, the foregoing article to be void, as far as ſuch exchange ſhall be made.

4. The army under lieutenant-general Burgoyne to march to Maſſachuſet's Bay by the eaſieſt, moſt expeditious, and convenient route; and to be quartered in, near, or as convenient as poſſible to Boſton, that the march of the troops may not be delayed when tranſports arrive to receive them.

5. The troops to be ſupplied, on their march and during their being in quarters, with proviſions, by major-general Gates's orders, at the ſame rate of rations as the troops of his own army; and, if poſſible, the officers' horſes and cattle to be ſupplied with forage at the uſual rates.

6. All officers to retain their carriages, bat-horſes, and other cattle; and no baggage to be moleſted or ſearched, lieutenant-general Burgoyne giving his honour that there are no public ſtores ſecreted therein. Major-general Gates will of courſe take the neceſſary meaſures for a due performance of this article. Should any carriages be wanted during the march, for the tranſportation of officers baggage, they are, if poſſible, to be ſupplied by the country at the uſual rates.

7. Upon the march, and during the time the army ſhall remain in quarters in the Maſſachuſets Bay, the officers are not to be ſeparated from their men, as far as circumſtances will admit. The officers are to be quartered according to their rank, and are not to

6   be

be hindered from affembling their men for roll-callings, and other neceffary purpofes of regularity.

8. All corps whatever of general Burgoyne's army, whether compofed of failors, batteau-men, artificers, drivers, independent companies and followers of the army, of whatever country, fhall be included in the fulleft fenfe and utmoft extent of the above articles, and comprehended in every refpect as Britifh fubjects.

9. All Canadians and perfons belonging to the Canadian eftablifhment, confifting of failors, batteau-men, &c. are to be permitted to return there; they are to be conducted immediately by the fhorteft route, to the firft Britifh port on Lake George, are to be fupplied with provifions in the fame manner as the other troops, and are to be bound by the fame condition of not ferving during the prefent conteft in North America.

10. Paffports to be immediately granted for three officers, not exceeding the rank of captains, who fhall be appointed by lieutenant-general Burgoyne to carry difpaches to fir William Howe, fir Guy Carleton, and to Great Britain by the way of New York; and major-general Gates engages the public faith that thefe difpatches are not to be opened. Thefe officers are to fet out immediately, after receiving their difpatches, and are to travel the fhorteft route, and in the moft expeditious manner.

11. During the ftay of the troops in the Maffachufets Bay, the officers are to be admitted on parole, and are to be permitted to wear their fide-arms.

12. Should the army under lieutenant-general Burgoyne find it neceffary to fend for their clothing, and other baggage from Canada, they are to be permitted to do it in the moft expeditious manner, and the neceffary paffports granted for that purpofe.

13. Thefe

13. Thefe articles are to be mutually figned and exchanged to-morrow morning at nine o'clock; and the troops under lieutenant-general Burgoyne are to march out of their intrenchments at three o'clock in the afternoon.

HORATIO GATES, Major-general.

Camp at Saratoga, Oct. 16, 1777.

To prevent any doubts that might arife from lieutenant-general Burgoyne's name not being mentioned in the above treaty, major-general Gates hereby declares that he is underftood to be compre-hended in it as fully as if his name had been fpecifically men-tioned.

HORATIO GATES.

General Gates's conduct in this melancholy event was peculiarly generous and humane. It is faid that when the Britifh troops piled their arms he would not fuffer his own men to be witnefs to the fad fpectacle.

The number of men who furrendered, amounted, including Ca-nadians and Provincials, to near fix thoufand. The fick and wounded in the hofpitals amounted to fix hundred; and it was com-puted that the lofs in killed, taken, and deferted, fubfequent to the capture of Ticonderoga, was near three thoufand men. The artil-lery taken, confifted of thirty-five pieces of different dimenfions.

Such was the melancholy event of a campaign from which the moft important benefits were predicted. The tardinefs of movement, however, occafioned by the large and fuperfluous train of artillery which general Burgoyne carried with him, certainly contributed not a little to produce thofe difafters and diftrefles which at length over-whelmed him. But tracing the failure of his expedition further back, it will be found to have been occafioned alfo by other caufes, which,

though

though when considered singly, may be deemed only remote, yet, condensed into one general prospect, they will be found to have immediately produced that fatal consummation which has already been recorded.

During the winter of 1776 no steps whatever were taken in Canada to provide horses, carts, or forage, for the expedition that was to take place in the ensuing year: It was not till the tenth of June 1777 that any contract was made for those articles. This tardiness of conduct delayed the movement of the army for three weeks, and rendered every subsequent operation equally flow; for the carriages for the transport service being constructed in haste, and of fresh unseasoned wood, were insufficient for the purposes for which they were designed, and were almost all destroyed on the road to Fort Edward. This circumstance detained the army so long at Fort Edward, that it ultimately occasioned the unfortunate, ill-conducted expedition to Bennington. The defeat of colonels Baum, Breyman, and St. Leger, enervated the British cause in an extraordinary degree. There were several of the inhabitants who were not attached to either party by principle, and who had resolved to join themselves to that which should be successful. Those men, after the disasters at Bennington and Fort Stanwix, added a sudden and powerful increase of strength to the Americans.

General Burgoyne, it was generally thought, after his disappointment, and the defeat at Bennington, ought not by any means to have crossed the Hudson. Any attempt to proceed to Albany was then improper. The distance from Fort Edward was sixty-four miles; the road was difficult and dangerous, being commanded by high and strong grounds, where an active enemy, well acquainted with the country, had many advantages, even with an inferior force. General Burgoyne should have posted himself, it was said, on the heights of Fort Edward; which would have secured a communication

munication with Canada, and enabled him to advance or to retreat according to contingent circumftances. He was cenfured alfo for remaining fo long at Skenefborough, and confuming eighteen days in making roads through moraffes and fwamps. Had he returned to Ticonderoga, and croffed Lake St. George, he would have reached Fort Edward at leaft ten or twelve days fooner. He fhould have detached general Frazer from Skenefborough to Fort George; by which means a quantity of provifions and ftores, deftined by the Americans for Ticonderoga, would have been fecured, as well as a fupply of carts, waggons, and draft bullocks. This conduct would have enabled him to have penetrated to Albany before the enemy were fufficiently powerful to oppofe him. Another caufe of the failure of the expedition was the want of a fyftem of co-operation between general Burgoyne and general Carleton, and the neglect of fir William Howe to take any fteps to facilitate the operations of the northern army. When general Burgoyne found himfelf under the neceffity of relinquifhing the communication with Canada, he wrote to general Carleton, requefting, in the moft preffing terms, that he would fend a regiment to garrifon Ticonderoga, that he might take the regiment then on duty there with him, and thereby endeavour ftill to preferve a communication with Canada. This favour, however, was pofitively refufed. General Burgoyne was alfo difappointed in not receiving an increafe of ftrength by the junction of a body of loyalifts on his advancing beyond Ticonderoga. Offended with general Carleton for refufing to inveft Ticonderoga in the preceding year, they refolved to remain inactive, and to afford no affiftance to the Britifh army. But indeed the grand caufe was the appointment of general Burgoyne in preference to general Carleton. Of the former, it muft be allowed that he poffeffed courage, a tolerable degree of military knowledge, with much addrefs. The latter had many of thefe

qualities,

6

qualities, with the addition of a knowledge of the country, its
refources, and its local ftrength and weaknefs. He was likewife well acquainted with the temper and difpofition of the inhabitants.

The unfortunate Burgoyne, reduced from the lofty language of
his proclamation to the ftyle of defence and recrimination, endeavoured to lay the blame of his mifcarriages upon fir William
Howe, for not having fent a force for co-operation up the North
River to Albany; on lord George Germaine, the Britifh fecretary of ftate, for having tied up his hands by orders
pofitive and unqualified, in inftances where latitude fhould be
given to a general to act according to circumftances; and on
the flownefs with which the Germans had marched to Bennington, the centre and fource of his misfortunes. But it was
urged, in anfwer to all the general's excufes, that the force put
into his hands for the intended march through Canada, was nearly, if
not fully, equal to what he himfelf had demanded : That he ought
not, on any doubtful profpect of a co-operating army from New
York, to have given up his communication with the Lakes; and
that his conduct, in fending fo fmall a detachment to Bennington, and this confifting of foreigners, and of all foreigners the
floweft in their motions, was an abfurdity bordering on infatuation.

It was alfo contended, on the iffue of Burgoyne's unfortunate
expedition, that he had carried along with him a quantity of artillery totally incompatible with that celerity of movement on which
his fuccefs entirely depended. If a juncture afterwards arofe which
feemed to demand this formidable apparatus, it was the very movement of that apparatus that created the neceffity of employing it.
The army was confined in its operations to the motions of the
artillery; and the enormous delays, occafioned in a great degree by

Z z 2

the

the flownefs of its progrefs, gave time to the provincials to recover from their panic, and again to collect that army which had
been completely difperfed. Whereas, had he advanced rapidly,
without incumbrance or delay, he would neither have found men
to oppofe nor works to interrupt his progrefs through the country.
But not only had general Burgoyne embarraffed himfelf with every
incumbrance that could retard the progrefs of an army; he had
adopted a route calculated to add to every delay, and to augment
every difficulty. Inftead of the direct and common road to Hudfon's River, by the way of Lake George, he had thought proper,
at the expence of much time and labour, to cut a road through an
extent of country the moft difficult and impracticable. If general
Gates himfelf, it was faid, had directed his operations, he could
not have planned meafures more conducive to the completion of his
own views. The flight from Ticonderoga had made fuch an impreffion on the fpirits of the Americans, that it was impoffible immediately to collect an army, or to infpire them with that confidence
which is neceffary to enfure fuccefs; but in time that impreffion
would wear off, unlefs it fhould be continued or renewed by the
rapid movements of the king's troops. When, inftead of fuch
movements, they faw thofe troops wafting days, weeks, and months,
without making the fmalleft progrefs, it is no wonder that they recovered their fpirits, and affembled in much greater force than ever.
In the whole of general Burgoyne's vindication, it was obferved,
his method was to ftate a neceffity for every one of his meafures
taken fingly, and not as links of one chain or fyftem of action,
taking care to pafs over one material circumftance, that *that neceffity*
invariably originated, on his own part, from fome previous omiffion
or blunder. The deportment of this commander, after the furrender of his army, was as pitiful as his conduct before that melancholy event was weak and unfortunate. He refufed, having been

fe-

fet at liberty on his parole, to join his captive army, threw himfelf,

like other unfuccefsful commanders, into the hands of oppofition, railed at his majefty's minifters, introduced himfelf on every occafion in the debates in parliament, demanding a public trial, complaining, even while a prifoner to the enemy, that he was denied accefs to the king, and that his merit and fufferings were equally unnoticed.

C H A P.   XVIII.

Expedition up the North River under Sir Henry Clinton—Reduction
of the Forts Montgomery and Clinton.—Burning of Æsopus.

C H A P.
XVIII.

1777.
Expedition
up the North
River under
fir Henry
Clinton.

A BODY of recruits arrived from Europe at New York about the clofe of September 1777. This reinforcement enabled fir Henry Clinton to undertake an expedition which he could not before have attempted, without leaving the defences of New York too feebly guarded. It may here be obferved, that the fituation of New York, commanded in a variety of points, which were thence of neceffity to be occupied by the Britifh, had a very unfavourable influence on the conduct of the war; for the protection of that great depofitary of our ftores required fo confiderable a number of men as moft materially cramped exertion in the field. The object of fir Henry Clinton's expedition was to take poffeffion of the forts which forbad the paffage of our veffels up to Albany; and the ulterior view in the meafure was not fo much to create a diverfion in favour of general Burgoyne (the neceffity of which was not fufpected), as to open a communication which might have been important when that commander fhould have fixed himfelf at Albany. The enterprife was entirely fpontaneous on the part of fir Henry Clinton, and was conducted with more energy than moft of the military operations that took place in America. A force amounting nearly to three thoufand men was embarked on board craft of different kinds, convoyed by fome fhips of war under the command of commodore Hotham. This armament proceeded up the Hudfon

to

to Verplank's Point, on the eaſt ſhore of that river (forty miles from
New York), which ſtation of the enemy lord Rawdon had ſome time
before been diſpatched to reconnoitre in a frigate. The landing-
places being defended only by ſlight breaſtworks with two twelve-
pounders, and the corps ſtationed there being fearful· that their
retreat might be cut off at the neck of the peninſula, the de-
barkation was made with little or no reſiſtance, and the firſt troops
who landed, purſuing rapidly the flying enemy, obliged them to
abandon one of the twelve-pounders. Sir Henry Clinton paſſed
the night upon this peninſula. This feint had the effect which it
was hoped it might produce; for it inſpired general Putnam, who
commanded in that diſtrict, with the opinion that ſir Henry Clinton
meant to puſh through the eaſtern highlands, in order to co-operate
with Burgoyne. Putnam, under this perſuaſion, haſtened with two
thouſand men, principally drawn from the forts, to occupy the
paſſes on the eaſtern ſhore. On the ſixth of October at day-break,
two thouſand one hundred men, without any artillery, were tranſ-
ported to Stoney Point, on the weſtern bank of the river; the
remainder of the troops being left to ſecure Verplanks. The only
road from Stoney Point to the forts (at leaſt the only one without a
prodigious circuit) was a path acroſs the Donderberg, a very ſteep
mountain, which with its precipices overhangs the North River.
As the path would not admit above three men to march abreaſt, and
by its windings would have expoſed the troops, during their paſſage,
to be deſtroyed at the pleaſure of any force ſtationed at the top of the
hill, the moſt trifling guard would have been ſufficient to have
rendered the attempt of the Britiſh abortive. The very difficulties
however of the attempt ſecured the paſſage to ſir Henry Clinton;
this having induced the Americans to ſuppoſe that it was ſuperfluous
to watch it; and a ſmall advanced guard, ſent forward to explore if
the

C H A P. the pafs was undefended, having made a fignal that the coaft was
  XVIII. clear, the main body of the Britifh afcended the hill with all poffible
  1777. expedition.   Having refted a while, they traverfed the fummit, and
descended on the oppofite fide, at the bottom of which they ftumbled upon a detachment fent too tardily for the defence of the pafs. The difperfion of this fmall corps deftroyed the hope that the forts might be furprifed; but the enterprife was not thence profecuted with lefs refolution.   The diftance from Stoney Point to the fort is twelve miles; but the nature of the country rendered the march fo flow and fatiguing, that it wanted but about an hour of funfet when the Britifh arrived within a mile of their deftination.   They feparated into two columns: The one, confifting of nine hundred men, under lieutenant-colonel Campbell of the fifty-fecond regiment, was def-

Reduction of tined for the attack of Fort Montgomery; whilft the remainder,
the Forts under the immediate command of fir Henry Clinton, were to ftorm
Montgomery the ftronger poft of Fort Clinton.   The two forts were only divided
and Clinton. by a creek called Poplop's Kill, which empties itfelf into the Hudfon's River, communicating by a wooden bridge of confiderable length acrofs that ftream.   The affault was made upon both forts at the fame inftant.   The point affailed at Fort Montgomery, was not very ftrong, either from fituation or works, nor did the enemy make a very obftinate refiftance; fo that the fort was carried by our troops with little lofs, excepting that the death of fo valuable an officer as lieutenant-colonel Campbell muft be confidered as material in the balance againft the fuccefs.   Almoft all the garrifon, confifting of eight hundred men, made their efcape.

Againft Fort Clinton the enterprife was more ferious; the fort was built upon a rocky elevation, the only approach to which, for the Britifh troops, was over a fpecies of pafs of about four hundred yards fquare, between a lake and a precipice which overhung
                                                          the

the Hudfon's River. This fpot was covered with felled trees, fo
that the approach of the affailants could not be conducted with rapidity or with much regularity, and ten pieces of artillery bore upon
that narrow pafs, whilft the Britifh had not a fingle cannon to cover
their affault. Their only chance confifted in preffing forward with
as much velocity as the ground would admit; and the troops were
ftrictly ordered upon no account to fire. The flank companies of
the feventh and twenty-fixth regiments, with a company of Anfpach
grenadiers, led the attack upon one point, whilft the fixty-third
regiment endeavoured to penetrate at another.

In no inftance during the American war was more invincible refolution exhibited than in this attack. The Britifh and foreign
troops preffed forward filently, under a dreadful fire, and arriving
at the foot of the work, actually pufhed one another up into the
embrafures. The garrifon, confifting of four hundred men, for a
little while longer contefted the rampart. Some of our men were
killed in the very embrafures, and feveral were wounded with bayonets in the ftruggle; fo that it muft be admitted the Americans
defended themfelves courageoufly. At length the rampart was
cleared. The Americans retiring to the other fide of the efplanade,
difcharged a laft volley, and threw down their arms. Notwithftanding this provocation, there was not a fingle man of the
enemy put to death, except fuch as fell in the actual ftruggle upon
the rampart. This fact we mention, not only as difplaying a moft
generous moderation on the part of the victors, contrary to what
ufually happens in fuch affaults, but as refuting an impudent affertion advanced in fome of the French accounts, that the whole garrifon
had been put to death by their conquerors. We are happy in refcuing
from the fhade which the magnitude of general Burgoyne's misfortune
at the time threw over it, an enterprife equally worthy of atten-

VOL. I. 3 A tion

tion for its boldnefs and the degree of injury that it did to the enemy.

The lofs on the part of the affailants was not fo fevere as might have been expected, for it amounted to only one hundred and forty killed and wounded. About three hundred of the Americans were killed, wounded, and taken prifoners.

The fmall lofs of the Britifh is only to be accounted for by the dufk, and by the American artillery being ferved with more attention to quicknefs in firing than accuracy in pointing. Captain Stewart, who commanded the grenadiers, and major Sill, who led the fixty-third regiment, were killed upon the fpot, both pierced with many wounds. Count Graboufky, a Polifh nobleman, who had croffed the Atlantic on purpofe to make a campaign as a volunteer with the Britifh, like-wife fell on this occafion. But his death was attended with a little circumftance which ought to be mentioned in honour to his me-mory. He had advanced to the ftorm in company with lord Raw-don amongft the grenadiers, but was feparated from him amongft the felled trees, which forced every man to find a path for himfelf. Arriving at the foot of the work he fell, after having received three balls : When giving his fword to a grenadier, he conjured him, with his expiring voice, to deliver it to lord Rawdon, and to affure his lordfhip that he died in a manner becoming one who had fhared the dangers of fuch gallant troops.

It is not amifs here to correct an error which has crept into former accounts, from an expreffion ufed by fir Henry Clinton, with a view of doing juftice to the zeal of the fquadron under commodore Hotham. In the Annual Regifter it is men-tioned as one of the circumftances which fhook the courage of the Americans, and flackened their refiftance, that the Britifh gal-lies advanced fo near as to ftrike the walls of the fort with their oars,

oars. The fort being on a precipice at leaft one hundred and twenty feet above the level of the river, this reprefentation muft appear abfurd. Sir Henry Clinton, in his letter on the fubject, mentions the appearance of the gallies, which was not effected without infinite exertion, to a diftance whence they thought they might, by their fire, in fome degree diftract the attention of the garrifon; and fir Henry Clinton, doing juftice to this purpofed diverfion, meant to exprefs that feveral of the balls had actually reached the fort.

High praife is due to commodore, now admiral, Hotham, for his arrangements and efforts upon this expedition; and the officers ferving under him nobly imitated his example.

Night came on immediately after the Britifh had completed their conqueft; but its obfcurity was not of long continuance. Two frigates, two gallies, and an armed floop belonging to the enemy, lay at anchor in the river under the guns of the forts. Thefe veffels were fecured from our fquadron by a defence which ftrongly marked the indefatigable induftry of the Americans. A boom, confifting of vaft rafts of timber connected by cables, ftretched acrofs the Hudfon's River (in that part fix hundred yards wide) from the projecting point on which Fort Montgomery ftands to a mountain, called St. Anthony's Nofe, that rifes immediately from the other margin of the ftream. This boom was ftrengthened by a chain, which alone was fuppofed to have coft the Americans about fifty thoufand pounds. The chain weighed above fifty tons, and the links were about two inches and a half fquare. Behind this bulwark the American veffels bid defiance to any attempt by water; but it was clear that as foon as daylight returned they muft be deftroyed by the cannon of the forts, unlefs they furrendered themfelves to the victors. To avoid this fate they filently flipped their cables, and fetting all their fails attempted to get up the river. The wind

3 A 2   happened

happened to be fo adverfe, that it was foon found impracticable to complete their efcape; upon which the crews quitted the veffels in their boats, previoufly fetting fire to the frigates and gallies. The flames fuddenly broke forth; and, as every fail was fet, the veffels foon became magnificent pyramids of fire. The reflection on the fteep face of the oppofite mountain, and the long train of ruddy light that fhone upon the water for a prodigious diftance, had a wonderful effect; whilft the ear was awfully filled with the continued echoes from the rocky fhores, as the flames gradually reached the cannon. The whole was fublimely terminated by the explofions, which again left all to darknefs.

No fooner was the reduction of the Forts Montgomery and Clinton known, than Fort Conftitution, on a rock fome miles higher up the river, was demolifhed without the orders of the governor, and without a removal of the artillery and ftores*.

Not far from the forts, thus reduced or demolifhed, lay a new fettlement called the Continental Village, which contained barracks for fifteen hundred men. Thefe, befides feveral ftore-houfes and

---

* Return of Cannon, Stores, Ammunition, &c. taken and deftroyed upon the Expedition up the North River, October 6, 1777.

Cannon.—Thirty-two pounders 6; eighteen pounders 3; twelve pounders 7; nine pounders 3; fix pounders 41; four pounders 3; three pounders 2; two pounders 2. Total 67.

Two frigates built for 30 and 36 guns were burnt by the Americans on the forts being taken. The guns aboard them, and two gallies which were likewife burnt, amounted to above 30. One floop with 10 guns fell into our hands. The whole lofs therefore is above 100 pieces.

Powder.—54 cafks; 11 ¼ barrels; 12,236 lb. exclufive of what was aboard the veffels.

Cartridges fitted.—1852 cannon; 57,396 mufquet.

Cannon fhot.—9530 round; 886 double headed; 2483 grape and cafe; 36 cwt. 1 qr. 15lb. langridge.

For mufquets.—1279 wt. of ball; 116 wt. of buck-fhot; 5400 flints.

Every article belonging to the laboratory in the greateft perfection. Other ftores, fuch as port-fires, match, harnefs, fpare gun carriages, tools, inftruments, &c. &c. in great plenty.

I   loaded

loaded waggons, of the articles contained in which no account could be taken, were deftroyed by a detachment under major-general Tryon.

A fervice was now completed, which, it was imagined, might open effential communication with general Burgoyne; of whofe diftrefs the moft remote fufpicion was not then entertained.

Whilft the fleet was on its paffage from New York to the forts, an officer from general Burgoyne, who had made his way through the country in difguife, reached fir Henry Clinton; but the object of his miffion was only to folicit the facilitation of general Burgoyne's progrefs by fome fuch expedition as that in which the officer found fir Henry Clinton engaged.

The day after the capture of the forts another officer from the northern army reached fir Henry Clinton, and his reprefentation alfo amounted only to this point, That if general Burgoyne did not hear of co-operation by the tenth of October, he fhould, on that day, be conftrained, by the terror of wanting provifions, to return to Fort Edward. The ignorance of the difficulties which at that time furrounded general Burgoyne's army is the lefs to be lamented, as it does not appear that it would have been practicable for fir Henry Clinton to have taken any fteps which could at all have fuc-coured that army.

A flying fquadron under fir James Wallace was now fent up the river, deftroying a number of veffels as they failed along. Under cover of this naval force, general Vaughan, on the thirteenth of October, with a detachment from the little army under fir Henry Clinton, landed at Æfopus Creek, where he found two batteries; one of two, another of three guns; and an armed galley at the mouth of the Creek. The Americans made little refiftance; but, abandoning the batteries and row-galley, took to flight.

October.

From

From this place the general continued his march about five miles farther to the town of Æfopus; which, having been fired at by fome people as he entered it, he reduced to afhes with a vaft collection of ftores and provifions. A few of the townfmen, and fome of the country people, affembled; but, after making fome fhew of oppofition, drew back.

Sir James Wallace at the fame time deftroyed the fhipping and fmall craft that had taken fhelter in the creek which leads up to the town. Our troops, having performed thefe fervices, re-embarked for New-York.

C H A P. XIX.

Expedition under the Command of Lieutenant-colonel Mawhood—
Action at Quintin's Bridge—At Hancock's Bridge—Ingenious Stra-
tagem of an Americau Loyalist—Colonel Abercrombie's Expedition
against the Americans under Lacey near Crooked Billet—Colonel
Maitland's Expedition up the Delaware,—Attempt on La Fayette.
—1778.

WHILE the Britifh army lay in winter-quarters at Philadelphia, the efforts made for their own conveniency, and for annoying the enemy, were as follow :—

In the beginning of March, lieutenant-colonel Mawhood, with a detachment from the main army, confifting of the twenty-feventh and forty-fixth regiments, and New Jerfey volunteers, made a defcent on the coaft of Jerfey, near Salem, for the purpofe of procuring forage, of which the army ftood in great need, and of opening a communication with the loyalifts of that part of the country, groaning under the tyranny of Livingfton the governor. Colonel Mawhood carried with him fpare arms to put into the hands of fuch as chofe to repair to his ftandard. This detachment embarked on board tranfports on the twelfth of March, fell down the Delaware, and landed fafely at the place of their deftination.

Colonel Mawhood, being reinforced on the feventeenth by the queen's rangers, confifting of about two hundred and feventy infantry, rank and file, and thirty cavalry, gave directions for the forage to take place on the eighteenth, accompanied by the ftricteft charge againft plunder.

C H A P.
XIX.
1778.

Expedition under colonel Mawhood.

The

The town of Salem, near to which, as has juft been obferved, our detachment landed, lies upon a creek of that name, falling into the Delaware nearly oppofite to Reedy Ifland.   The Alewas Creek runs almoft parallel to that of Salem, and falls into the Delaware to the fouth of it.   Over the Alewas Creek three bridges were extended: Hancock's Bridge the lower; Quintin's that in the centre; and Thompfon's the fartheft up.   Between thefe Creeks, then, on the Delaware, forming a peninfula, at its greateft feven, and at its leaft four miles in width, the foraging was to commence.   The provincial militia was pofted at Hancock's and Quintin's Bridge, which they had defended by breaftworks.   Colonel Mawhood made detachments to mafk thefe bridges, and foraged in their rear.

Action at
Quintin's
Bridge.

The officer who commanded the detachment at Quintin's having fent information that the enemy were affembled in great numbers at the bridge, and would probably pafs over it whenever he fhould quit it, in which cafe his party would be in great danger, colonel Mawhood marched with the queen's rangers to his affiftance, and by a fuccefsful feint and ambufcade, firft drew a divifion of the enemy over the bridge, and then vigoroufly attacked them.   Not a few of them were taken prifoners, but the greater part were drowned in the Alewas Creek.   Among the prifoners was their commanding officer, who proved to be a Frenchman.   The rangers had one huffar mortally wounded.   Here we fhall give place to an anecdote, authenticated by the authority of colonel Simcoe, who commanded the rangers, that affords a fpecimen of that bafe and ungenerous fpirit with which many individuals in the American armies fhewed themfelues in the courfe of the war to be actuated.   The huffar was wounded by a man whom, in the eagernefs of the purfuit, he had paffed, and given quarters to him without difarming him.   The villain was killed by another huffar.

The

The Americans, who had for a moment quitted the bridge, but who, when they perceived that colonel Mawhood did not think it to his purpose to pass it, returned, still occupied the posts at Quintin's and Hancock's Bridge, their numbers gradually increasing. Colonel Mawhood determined to attack them at Hancock's Bridge, where, from all reports, they were assembled to the number of four hundred men. This enterprise was entrusted to major Simcoe, who embarked with the rangers on board flat-bottomed boats on the twentieth at night. He was to be landed at an inlet seven miles below Alewas Creek, when the boats were to be immediately returned; and by a private road he was to reach Hancock's Bridge, opposite to which major Mitchell was to co-operate with him, at the head of the twenty-seventh regiment. Major Simcoe, though the enemy were nearly double his numbers, and his retreat was cut off by the absolute orders to send back the boats, considered that every thing depended on surprise, and reposed just confidence in the silence, attention, and spirit of the corps under his command. By an oversight in the naval department, when the boats arrived off Alewas Creek, the tide set so strong against them, that, in the opinion of the officer of the navy, they could not reach the place of their destination till mid-day. Major Simcoe determined, however, not to return, but to land at the mouth of the Alewas Creek on the marshes. They soon found out a landing-place, and, after a march of two miles through marshes up to the knees in mud and water, at length arrived at a wood upon dry land, where the major formed his men for the attack. There was no public road that led to Hancock's Bridge but that of which the rangers were now in possession; but a bank or dyke, on which there was a footway, led from Hancock's to Quintin's Bridge. This dyke captain Saunders, with a party, was sent to ambuscade, and to take up a small bridge that was upon it, as the enemy would probably flee that way, and if not pursued too closely, would thus be the more easily defeated.

There was at Hancock's Bridge a large brick dwelling-house, called Hancock's House, around which were many stone houses, and some few cottages. Captain Dunlop was detached to the rear of Hancock's House, in which it was presumed the American officers were quartered, and directed to force, occupy, and barricade it, as it commanded the passage of the bridge. Different detachments were allotted to the small houses in the rear of Hancock's, supposed to be the enemy's quarters. Having mastered these, they were ordered to assemble at Hancock's, which the light-infantry who were in reserve reached by the road, and forced the front door at the same time that captain Dunlop, by a more difficult way, entered the back door. As it was very dark, these companies were on the point of falling on one another. The surprise was complete, which it would have been, even if the whole of the enemy's force had been present; but, fortunately for them, they had quitted it the evening before, leaving a detachment of twenty or thirty men, all of whom were killed.

The roads that led to the country were immediately ambuscaded, and lieutenant Whitlock was detached to surprise a patrole of seven men who had been sent down the Creek, which he completely effected. On their refusal to surrender he was obliged to fire on them, when only one made his escape. It was the firing on this small party that communicated to the twenty-seventh regiment the success of the enterprise: Two days after, the queen's rangers patrolled Thomson's Bridge. The enemy, who had been posted there, were alarmed at the approach of a cow the night before, fired at it, and then fled. They also abandoned Quintin's Bridge, and retired to a creek, sixteen miles from Alewas Creek.

5

Major

Major Simcoe continued to drive the fmall parties of the enemy before him, wherever he went for the protection of the foragers: And even the main force of the enemy, in thofe parts, affembled at Cohanfey, might have been eafily furprifed ; but colonel Mawhood judged, that, having completed his forage with perfect fuccefs, his bufinefs was to return to head-quarters, which he did accordingly. The troops reimbarked on board the boats, and returned, without any accident, to Philadelphia.

Though patroles were made now as regularly as ever, as fpring approached the enemy's cavalry came nearer to our lines, and owed their efcape more than once to the fleetnefs of their horfes. Some of thefe that fell into the hands of our parties were decorated with eggs, women's fhoes, and other articles, of which they had plundered the country-people coming to and returning from market ; and thus accoutred, were paraded through the ftreets to prifon. A number of loyalifts in arms under the command of Mr. Thomas, their captain, with Hoveden's and James's troops of provincials, made excurfions into the country, and carried off from the Americans, provifions, clothing, and other articles of ufe to the Britifh army and their adherents. On fuch excurfions they were ufually fupported, and their return to their friends fecured, by the queen's rangers.

A ftratagem for procuring provifions for our army at Philadelphia, equally pleafant and fuccefsful, was played off by one of the loyalifts againft the Americans. General Wafhington drew his fupplies of fat cattle from New England. A drove of this kind was met about thirty miles from Philadelphia, between the Delaware and Schuylkill, by a friend of government, who paffed himfelf upon the drivers for one of general Wafhington's commiffaries, billeted them at a neighbouring farm, and then immediately galloped to Philadelphia, from whence a party of dragoons were fent for the cattle, and the whole drove was fafely conducted to Philadelphia.

Ingenious ftratagem of an American loyalift.

About

C H A P.
XIX.

1778.
Colonel
Abercrom-
bie's expedi-
tion againft
the Ameri-
cans under
general La-
cy near
Crooked
Billet.

About the beginning of May, a great part of an American brigade, not lefs than one thoufand men, commanded by brigadier Lacy, general of the Penfylvania militia, took poft at a place called the Crooked Billet, about feventeen miles from Philadelphia, on one of the great roads of communication between that town and the country. From this ftation the Americans, in fmall parties, overawed and impeded the country-people in their approaches with provifions to the Philadelphia market. By the way of Crooked Billet lay the main road between Philadelphia and New York; and, at lefs than half a mile from it, on the Philadelphia fide, there was another road which led, by the way of Horfham Meeting, to general Wafhington's camp. Major Simcoe, who had been the firft that gave intelligence to the commander in chief of the fituation, ftrength, and probable views of brigadier-general Lacy, propofed that he fhould march with the rangers, and, by a circuit, get to the road in the rear of the Crooked Billet; and that a detachment fhould march, and ambufcade themfelves in a wood (for according to his intelligence there was one adapted to the purpofe) on the road which led to Wafhington's camp, by the Horfham meeting-houfe. This party was to remain in ambufcade till they fhould hear the firing of the queen's rangers. It was prefumed that, if the furprife fhould not be complete, the ambufcade would enfure fuccefs, by fupporting the rangers if they fhould be checked, and by intercepting the enemy if they fhould attempt to retreat, as they probably would, and that towards their main army. This plan being adopted, lieutenant-colonel Abercrombie, on the night preceding the fourth of May, was detached to the place of ambufcade, with about four hundred light-infantry, a large party of light dragoons, and horfes to mount part of his infantry for the greater expedition.

Major Simcoe's march was difficult, as he judged it neceffary to make many circuits; in order to avoid places where the enemy had

3   pofts

posts or patroles. He was well guided; and fortunately had information about twilight that prevented him from committing a
difaftrous error. The armed refugees under their leader captain
Thomas, had been fent by Mr. Galloway to efcort fome of his furniture into Philadelphia. Hearing by fome means or other of the
prefent expedition; they were encouraged to feize the opportunity
which it afforded of effecting their object with the greater certainty
and fafety. They marched up the roads which the rangers had fo
carefully avoided, but without meeting with any interruption or
alarm. They fortunately paffed a houfe at which major Simcoe
called; otherwife he would certainly, when he overtook them, have
miftaken them for the enemy. This little adventure of the refugees, with the narrow efcape they made from a fatal onfet by their
own friends, ferves, among many other inftances with which the
hiftory of war is replete, to fhew the neceffity of different military operations going on at the fame time, being concerted and
carried on under the direction of one mind. The refugees were
directed to keep themfelves undifcovered, and the rangers marched
on as faft as poffible. Although daylight appeared, major Simcoe
was under no apprehenfions of difcovery, nor yet of colonel Abercrombie's having met with any accident, as the parties were within
hearing of each other's fire, and none was heard. He was therefore, as he had now quitted the road, in order to make his laft circuit to reach the Billet, informing his officers of his plan of attack,
when all of a fudden a flight firing was heard.

Colonel Abercrombie, although affifted by horfes, could not arrive at his poft at the appointed time, before day-break. But, being
anxious to fupport major Simcoe, he detached to the place of ambufcade his cavalry and mounted light-infantry. The officer who
commanded this detached party patrolled as far as Lacy's out-poft,
and being fired at by the centinels did not retire. Lacy, rightly
judging

judging that he was fupported by a force adequate to fuch confidence, collecting his ftrength, began to retreat up the country. At this crifis, the rangers arrived nearly in his rear, upon his right flank. They ftopped, and turned fome fmaller parties who were making their efcape from the light-infantry, and who were killed; but the main body retreated in a mafs without order, and in great precipitation; nor could our infantry, by their utmoft efforts, overtake them. The huffars of the rangers were unfortunately left at Philadelphia, their horfes having been fatigued by a long courfe of duty, and a fevere patrole the day before. Thirty dragoons, who were with the rangers, were fent to intercept the baggage-waggons, and ftaid to guard them. As the enemy were paffing through a wood, major Simcoe, galloping up to the edge of it, fummoned them to furrender: They were in great confternation, but continued to prefs forward. The major then gave the word of command, " make ready," " prefent,". " fire," hoping that the in_ tervening fence and thickets between him and them might lead them to fuppofe that he was accompanied by a body of men, and that they might halt; in which cafe a few moments would have been de_ cifive. At the word " fire," they crouched down, but ftill moved on, and foon got out of all reach *.

                                                                    Our

* In the Hiftory of Great Britain, from the Time of Cromwell to the Acceffion of George I., by Mr. Alexander Cunningham, the tutor and the companion of John duke of Argyle, in his campaigns in the Netherlands, which is generally admitted to contain a more particular, clear, and intelligible account of the conduct, ftratagems, and incidents, of war, than any hif- tory in the Englifh language, we read the following paffage relating to the celebrated earl of Peterborough, commander of the Britifh troops in Spain in the war of the fucceffion :

    " The earl of Peterborough had alarmed all the country, far and near, with dreadful ru-
" mours and meffages of his approach ; and, carefully concealing the fmall number of his troops,
" caufed reports to be fpread that the confederates had a large army. It is faid he had not above
" twelve hundred men, who were reduced to great weaknefs, when he thus, by ftratagem, put
" to flight feven thoufand of the enemy [under the condé de las Torres, who had laid fiege to
" the town of San Mattheo, which had fubmitted to king Charles].

                                                                    " After

Our troops returned to Philadelphia. The commander in chief ordered the baggage to be fold for their benefit, which produced a dollar a man. This excurfion, though it failed of that fuccefs which was expected, had the full effect of intimidating the militia, who never afterwards appeared but in fmall parties like robbers. The fuccefs of the expedition would have been more fignal, had not our

"After this he thought it worth his while to attempt the town of Nules, which the inha..,
"bitants held out for king Philip; but as he neither had foldiers, nor any thing in readinefs
"neceffary for war, he himfelf rode full fpeed up to the gate of the town, and calling for one of
"the magiftrates or priefts, demanded the town to be furrendered to him. He told them that
"if they would yield immediately, they might expect good terms; but that if they refufed, he
"would inftantly give orders to his army to plunder the town, allowing them only fix minutes·
"time to confult, and return their anfwer; at the fame time calling out aloud for his cannon
"(although he had none) to be planted againft the walls. As great revolutions are brought abo.it
"by fmall accidents, the word was no fooner faid, than the town was delivered·up: And other
"places alfo he went and took with the fame celerity, all which he added to the dominions of
"king Charles. By this manner of making war, the earl of Peterborough, in a fhort fpace of
"time, performed fuch wonderful exploits in Spain, that the Spaniards even began to give credit
"to all the fabulous ftories of the valour and atchievements of Don Quixote; and the Englifh alfo
"thought his praifes an obfcuration of the duke of Marlborough's glory. He farther pretended
"to be furnifhed with horfes as it were fprung out of the earth, and drew brigadier Mahoni into
"a conference, in which he dexteroufly operated on his mind, and managed his paffions as it
"fuited his own purpofe. Then he took Molviedro, and feized Valencia, and, by his ru-
"mours and fpies, caufed the Spaniards to make war upon one another, and defeated the duke
"d'Arcas. And, laftly, he fupported the priefts by his liberality, and fuch of the country peo-
"ple as would take up arms for king Charles."

"In a word, the earl of Peterborough, in the hiftory of his conduct, is ftyled the father of
"ftratagems, and Fortune is faid always to have attended his undertakings."

Had the chief command of our army in America been placed in the hands of fuch a man as the earl of Peterborough, whofe vigilance, invention, and celerity of action on a fcene not alto-gether diffimilar to the divided ftate of the American colonifts, form a direct contraft to the flownefs, and circuitous movements of fir William Howe, it is extremely probable that the iffue of the American war would have been reverfed. Neither military genius, nor alert-nefs of conduct, nor promptitude of action, were wanting in the Britifh army; nor is major Simcoe the only inftance in which thefe qualities were difplayed in a very confpicuous man-ner; though not in that ftation in which they could produce the greateft and moft decifive confequences.

troops.

C H A P.
XIX.

1778.

Expedition
up the Dela-
ware under
major Mait-
land.

Attempt on
La Fayette.

troops been too much fatigued by the very great length of the march, which favoured the enemy in their flight, and had our cavalry pushed on when they first discovered the American centinels.

A joint attempt was made, on the seventh of May by sea and land to destroy the gallies and other vessels that had escaped up the Delaware after the reduction of Mud Island, and the shipping that the enemy had in the river between Philadelphia and Trenton. This enterprise was effectually accomplished by the skill and activity of captain Henry of the navy, and major Maitland of the marines. A considerable quantity of stores and provisions was also destroyed; and a number of the enemy, who made no great opposition, were killed. Not fewer than forty-four American vessels were burnt, some of them of considerable value.

About the nineteenth of May 1778, General Washington detached the marquis de la Fayette to take post with nearly three thousand men upon Barren Hill, a position seven miles advanced from the camp of Valley Forge; but upon the opposite or eastern side of the river.

The object of this step is not very clear. The position was still too distant from Philadelphia to give any interruption of consequence to such supplies as were carried into that city by the neighbouring country. Possibly, as the intended evacuation of Philadelphia was now well known, general Washington might have thought that it would keep up the spirits of his party if he seemed to press upon the British in their retreat; for he must have been aware that his then force could not allow him to expect that he should make any real advantage of such an attempt: And the distance of Barren Hill from Philadelphia appeared to secure the detachment from any hazard. This supposed security proved illusive. On the night of May the twentieth, five thousand of the choicest troops in the British army set out from Philadelphia, marching by the road which keeps close

to

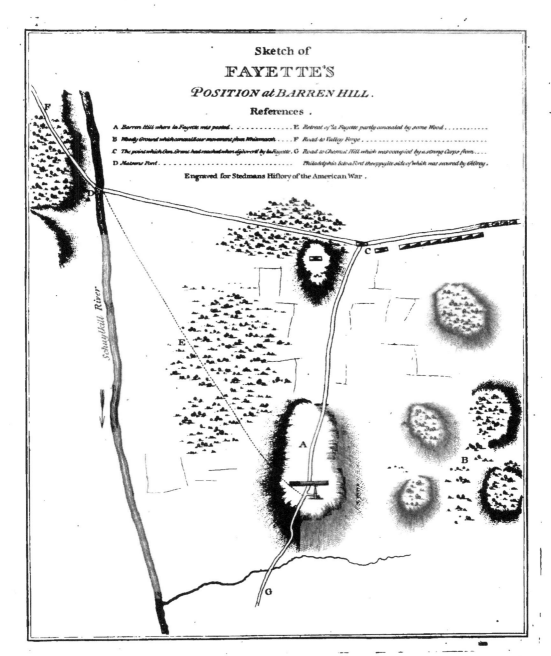

Sketch of
FAYETTE'S
POSITION at BARREN HILL.

References .

A *Barren Hill where la Fayette was posted* . . . . E. *Retreat of la Fayette partly concealed by some Wood* . . . .

B *Woody Ground which conceald our movement from Whitemarsh* . . . . F *Road to Valley Forge* . . . .

C. *The point which Gen. Grant had reached when discoverd by la Fayette.* G *Road to Chesnut Hill which was occupied by a strong Corps from* . . . . .

D *Matsons Ford* . . . . *Philadelphia &to a Ford the opposite side of which was secured by Gl. Grey* .

Engraved for Stedmans History of the American War .

Schuylkill River

to the Delaware, and which, therefore, diverges from the direction of Barren Hill. After the detachment had proceeded fome miles, it turned to the left, and paffing White Marfh foon after day-break, it reached at length its deftined point, without having fallen in with any patrole or out-poft of the enemy. This point was directly in the rear of La Fayette's pofition, confequently was between him and the camp of general Wafhington. The road here forked ; one branch led to the camp of La Fayette, at the diftance of a fhort mile ; the other went to Matfon's Ford acrofs the Schuylkill, at about the fame diftance. In the courfe of the night a ftrong detachment, under the command of general Grey, had marched from Philadelphia along the weftern branch of the Schuylkill, and ftationed themfelves at a ford two or three miles in front of La Fayette's right flank, whilft the remainder of the Britifh army advanced to Chefnut Hill.

The retreat of La Fayette was thus cut off from every paffage but Matfon's Ford ; and as the line from La Fayette's pofition formed the bafe of an obtufe-angled triangle with the two roads above men-tioned, it was obvious that his diftance from it was much greater than that of the Britifh. When general Grant arrived at the point above defcribed, the confufed galloping of fome of the enemy's horfemen, who advanced to reconnoitre, intimated that the approach of the Britifh was then firft perceived. At the fame time the column was difcovered by glaffes from the camp of general Wafhington, who, by the firing of cannon, attempted to give his detachment notice of the danger. Confiderable time feems to have been loft in making a difpofition for the intended attack, during which delay a corps of cavalry, that had formed the advanced guard on the march, took poffeffion of a hill between the two roads. From this elevation the corps of La Fayette was difcovered retreating towards Matfon's Ford through the low woody grounds which border the river. The diforder and precipitation, apparent in the rear of that column, fufficiently indicated the terror with which they were attempting their escape. Information of this circumftance is faid to have been given to general Grant, and his fuperior proximity to Matfon's Ford is reported to have been urged to him, and even pointed out in the ftrongeft manner; but under the perfuafion that this was only a part of La Fayette's troops, detached for fome unaccountable reafon, the general perfifted in his refolution of advancing to Barren Hill, notwithftanding the ftrong remonftrances of Sir William Erfkine againft that meafure. This poft was unluckily concealed from view by intervening trees, otherwife the defertion of it by the enemy would have been perceived. The Britifh having advanced to the church, and found the camp abandoned, undertook the purfuit of the enemy by the very track which La Fayette had taken. In the mean time that officer had reached the Ford; but his troops, being overcome with apprehenfion, had hurried acrofs the river, leaving behind them the fix field-pieces which they had brought from camp to the bank of the river. La Fayette having formed his battalions on the other fide, and perceiving that the Britifh did not approach by the road in which he apprehended them, fent a corps acrofs for his cannon, ordering fome fmall parties to be advanced into the woods to retard the progrefs of the Britifh advanced guard, fhould it approach whilft the artillery was in the river. The cannon were dragged over, but before the parties of obfervation could retire, the Britifh cavalry fell upon them, and killed or took about forty. The Britifh generals advancing to the Ford, perceived that La Fayette was fo advantageoufly pofted on the other fide of the river, with his artillery on the high and broken grounds which arofe from the water's edge, that nothing further could be attempted againft him. Thus unfortunately failed the object of the expedition. It is faid general Wafhington thought the cafe fo hopelefs, that he broke his bridge from Valley Forge acrofs the Schuylkill, left the fuccefs fhould

6   the

be purfued againſt himſelf.   It is obvious that he could not attempt
to ſuccour La Fayette; becauſe, as he had but four thouſand men
remaining in his camp, the Britiſh detachment was of itſelf equal
to give him battle, could he poſſibly have joined La Fayette; and
that was a ſtake which every intereſt forbade.   But as the body of
the Britiſh army was at Cheſnut Hill, at hand to give general Grant
immediate ſupport, general Waſhington could not have interfered
without every probability of incurring ruin.

As the time approached when the army was to move from Philadelphia, American patroles were paſſed over the Delaware from the
Jerſeys.   One of theſe, after a long chaſe, was taken by the huſſars
belonging to the queen's rangers.   The quarter-maſter-general,
ſir William Erſkine, being in great want of horſes, commiſſaries
were ſent to procure them, eſcorted by the rangers under major
Simcoe.   The major entered on this office with much regret, as
the horſes were to be taken from people whom he had hitherto uniformly protected.

3 C 2

C H A P. XX.

*Sir William Howe refigns the Command of the Army—Feftival called. Mifchianza, in honour of Sir William Howe—He is fucceeded in the Command of the Army by Sir Henry Clinton—Returns to England —Complains of Defamation, and folicits and obtaius a Parliament- ary Inquiry into his Conduct.—*1778.

THESE, then, with occafional parties fent out to cover the loyalifts, were the only movements made by the Britifh commander in chief while he lay in his winter-quarters, from October 1777 to June 1778, at Philadelphia.

It would feem, however, that fir William Howe imagined that all that could be done for the royal caufe had been now performed: For to a deputy fent to the commander in chief from the magiftrates, on a rumour of the intended evacuation of Philadelphia, requefting his advice how to act, he faid that the beft thing they could do would be to go over and make their peace with general Wafhington. And as he himfelf was on the eve of quitting the army, he told them to go to fir Henry Clinton, his deftined fucceffor, for a flag of truce in order to go out to Wafhington for that purpofe. The deputy accordingly went to fir Henry Clinton, who faid that he could not grant a flag on fuch an occafion; that the game was not up; that the war was not over, but would ftill be

vigor-

vigoroufly carried on; and that they ought not by any means to entertain a thought of going over to the enemy.

CHAP.
XX.
1778.
Sir William
Howe refigns
the command
of the army.

Sir William Howe had formed the refolution of refigning his
office fo early as the month of October. In a letter of his of the
twenty-eighth of that month, he wrote to the fecretary of ftate for
the American department, lord George Germaine, as follows:——
" From the little attention, my lord, given to my recommenda-
" tions fince the commencement of my command, I am led to hope
" that I may be relieved from this very painful fervice, wherein I
" have not the good fortune to enjoy the neceffary confidence and
" fupport of my fuperiors, but which I conclude will be extended
" to fir Henry Clinton, my prefumptive fucceffor. By the return
" of the packet I humbly requeft I may have his majefty's per-
" miffion to refign." That permiffion he received on the fourteenth
of April 1778; but in the fame letter which conveyed leave to refign, he was ordered by his majefty, while he fhould continue in
command, to lay hold of every opportunity of putting an end to
the war, by a due exertion of the force under his orders.

The commander in chief's letter, in which he alleges, as the
ground of his refignation, the want of neceffary confidence and fupport on the part of adminiftration, was matter of equal aftonifhment
and indignation to the parties againft whom that charge was made;
while it inevitably led the unprejudiced and impartial fpectator to
contraft the languor and reluctance too vifibly apparent in the whole
conduct of fir William Howe with that alacrity and zeal with
which the miniftry, and particularly the minifter for American affairs, provided and furnifhed the means of carrying on the war,
and that difpofition which they manifefted to invite and reward the
efforts of the general by all poffible encouragement. When meafures

C H A P. fures for reducing the revolted colonies were refolved on, and fir
   XX.   William Howe was appointed to the command of the army, fuch
  1778. was the difpofition of government to gratify him in whatever he
fhould defire, that the fecretary for the American department declared, " the meafures of force fhould be the wifhes of the ge-
" neral." The general, who was then in America, and had the
ftate of the war under his eye, was the beft judge of what force
would be competent to its fuppreffion. On his judgment, therefore,
government relied; but inftead of ftinting, they furpaffed his wifhes.
In his letter to lord Germaine *, after long and mature deliberation,
he only requires nineteen thoufand men; which, he fays, will be
" adequate to an active offenfive campaign on the fide of New
" York and Rhode Ifland." Inftead of nineteen thoufand men, he
was furnifhed with thirty-one thoufand four hundred and feventy-
fix. And, although he expected to meet a force of thirty thoufand
men, the whole American army did not amount to eighteen thoufand. With the force now fent, amounting to eleven thoufand
men more than he required, the general appeared to be more than
fatisfied, and declared his utter aftonifhment at the uncommon exertions of government. He acknowledged, in his letter to government †, that the fucceffes of the army under his command had intimidated the leaders of rebellion, and nearly induced a general fubmiffion;—an admiffion which was ftrictly juft; for farther oppofition
was univerfally defpaired of by all America, except a few defperate
men in general Wafhington's army; and that army was reduced to
a number not exceeding four thoufand men. And yet, at that pe-

* Of the 26th of November 1775.
† Of the 30th of November 1776, and the 20th of January 1777.

                                                        riod,

riod, we find him making a demand, first of fifteen thousand, and then of twenty thousand rank and file. The general, it is true, did not make this extravagant demand without affigning reafons for it; but thefe reafons were ill-founded. In his letter of the twelfth of February 1778 he informed the fecretary of ftate that " the rebels had profpects of bringing into the field more than " fifty thoufand men. They are moft fanguine in their expecta- " tions," fays he, " and confcious that their whole ftake depends upon " the fuccefs of the next campaign, ufe every compulfory means to " thofe who do not enter voluntarily into their fervice." We know however, that, inftead of fifty thoufand men, they were not able to bring into the field, when the general met their force at Hillfborough, more than eight thoufand men; and even at the Brandywine, not more than fixteen thoufand, militia included, after he had, contrarily to all policy, given them two months, by every poffible exertion, to recruit their feeble army. It thus appears, that if the reinforcement required on this occafion fell fhort of that which was demanded by the general, the expected reinforcement of the Americans, which was the reafon affigned for that requifition, failed in a much greater proportion. More than one half of the force required was fent, and not more than one fifth of that of the Americans was raifed. The account of the armed force in 1777 ftood thus: Britifh, forty thoufand eight hundred and feventy-four, veteran troops. American regular army at Hillfborough, eight thoufand; at Brandywine, eleven thoufand; and, in the fpring, at Valley Forge, not four thoufand undifciplined troops. With what juftice, then, it was faid, could the general complain of his want of force? and how extravagant his attempt to throw the blame of his own mifconduct on that adminiftration which had, by fuch uncommon
exertions,

exertions, thus gratified him in all his wifhes. The longer contemplation was indulged on this fubject, the more were the minds
of men inflamed with warm emotions.

" While the friends of the colonifts," it was faid, " were bringing
" their plot to maturity in Britain ; while the natural refources of
" this country were cried down, to the great encouragement of our
" foreign enemies, and a national defpondency was generally effect-
" ed ; while the opponents of adminiftration were advifing and con-
" tending in both houfes of parliament for withdrawing the troops
" from America, and, at the fame time, oppofing every meafure
" which was neceffary for the recovery of the revolted colonies,
" the flownefs and procraftination of the general accorded but too
" well with thofe fentiments, and contributed not a little to render
" adminiftration more and more odious to the people, whofe dif-
" guft and indignation rofe in proportion as the minifter de-
" manded more and more fupplies, and as the general neglected
" to improve the great opportunities, that were at different times
" prefented, of putting an end to the war."

The violence of oppofition on the one part, and the extreme
tendernefs of fir William Howe towards the Americans on the
other, feemed to many obfervers to be linked together by a kind
of connection fomewhat fimilar to that between caufe and effect.
He certainly fuffered the enemy, with lefs than four thoufand men,
to re-conquer a province which he had lately reduced, and to
lay a kind of fiege to his army in his winter-quarters. He unfortunately wafted the feafon of military operation, giving them
time to recruit their reduced force. Though the fpirit of revolt was
occafionally depreffed by the valour of our troops, it was uniformly
revived by the mifconduct of the general.

Such

Such were the obfervations that were very generally made on the conduct of fir William Howe, when he not only refigned his office without attaining, in any degree, the end for which he took it upon him, but endeavoured to fhift his want of fuccefs from his own fhoulders upon that of the fecretary of ftate for the American department.

The fame or fimilar obfervations were made, and re-echoed with ftill greater energy over all the Britifh empire, on another unfortunate occafion, which, like the grounds alleged for the refignation of his office, induced and provoked men to compare the importance of his fervices with the merit he affumed, and the gravity with which he fuftained the moft exceffive praife and adulation. It is to the famous Mifchianza that we allude, or feftival given in honour of fir William Howe, by fome of the Britifh officers at Philadelphia, when he was about to give up his command, and to return to England. This entertainment not only far exceeded any thing that had ever been feen in America, but rivalled the magnificent exhibitions of that vain-glorious monarch and conqueror, Louis XIV. of France. All the colours of the army were placed in a gránd avenue three hundred feet in length, lined with the king's troops, between two triumphal arches, for the two brothers, the admiral, lord Howe, and the general, fir William Howe, to march along in pompous proceffion, followed by a numerous train of attendants, with feven filken knights of the blended rofe, and feven more of the burning mountain, and fourteen damfels dreffed in the Turkifh fafhion, to an area of one hundred and fifty yards fquare, lined alfo with the king's troops, for the exhibition of a tilt and tournament, or mock fight of old chivalry, in honour of thofe two heroes. On the top of each triumphal arch, was a figure of Fame, befpangled with ftars, blowing from her trumpet in letters of light, *Tes lauriers font immortels* *.

Feftival called Mifchianza in honour of fir William Howe.

* Thy laurels are immortal.

This

This romantic triumph, after fo many difgraces and difappoint-
ments, did not efcape the fevereft fatire, both in private converfation
and in printed papers; among which a letter addreffed to fir William
Howe in a publication called The American Crifis, by Paine,
the author of the pamphlet ftyled *Common Senfe*, was moft diftinguifhed for fhrewdnefs of remark, vigour of conception, and
energy of expreffion.

We fhall here infert a very excellent letter, which corroborates
many of the facts ftated by us, written in 1777, by M. Du Portail,
minifter at war in France to the conftituent affembly in 1791 and
1792, but at the period of the letter being wrote, a colonel in the
French fervice, and acting as a brigadier-general in the American
army †.

Sir

† (COPIE.)

A Monfeigneur le Comte de St. Germain, Miniftre de la Guerre (pour vous feulement,
Monfeigneur.)

Du Camp de White Marfh, à quartre lieues de Philadelphie,
Monseigneur,   le 12me Novembre 1777.

J'AI eu l'honneur de vous rendre conte des battailles de Brandywine et de German Town,
et de vous en envoyer les plans; ainfi que celui de Philadelphie, avec fes environs, à cinq lieues,
à la ronde; afin que vous puiffiez juger de la fituation du général Howe. J'efpere que tout
cela vous fera parvenu. Jufqu' à préfent le général Howe n'eft pas encore maitre des deux
petits forts, qui font dans la riviere, et qui empêchent fes vaiffeaux de remonter jufqu' à la
ville; ce qui le réduit à ne communiquer avec eux que par le petit chemin que j'ai marqué fur
la carte; chemin que nous pouvons bien lui couper cet hiver, quand nous aurons reçu un
renfort des troupes victorieufes du nord. Nous comptons auffi mettre un corps de deux ou
trois mille hommes de l'autre côté de la Schaylkill. Il y à déja des troupes dans le Jerfeys;
de cette façon le général Howe fera bloqué dans Philadelphie, et en danger de mourir de faim;
à moins qu'il ne fe rembarque; mais pour dire la vérité, nous ne l'efperons pas. Il prendra pro-
bablement les forts, s'il les attaque bien; et il aura alors une communication fure avec fes
vaiffeaux, quoiqu' il en foit, Monfeigneur, vous voyez que pour des gens battus deux fois,
nous

Sir William Howe, foon after receiving the fplendid teftimony of
efteem which has been juft defcribed, fet fail for England, leaving
the

C H A P.
XX.

1778.

nous ne fommes pas en trop mauvaife pofture. Nous devons cela à ce que les Anglois n'ont
que très peu de cavalerie ; de forte qu'ils ne peuvent pourfuivre leur victoire. Nous le devons
encore plus à nos bois, et aux obftacles de toute efpéce d'ont le pays eft défendu. Maintenant d'après l'expérience de cette campagne, il eft naturel, de fe faire cette queftion : Les
Americains réuffiront-ils à fe rendre libres, ou non? En France, où l'on ne peut juger que
par les faits, on jugera pour l' affirmative. Nous, qui avons vu comment les chofes fe font
paffées, ne penferons pas de même. A parler franchement, ce n'eft pas par la bonne conduite des
Americains, que la campagne en général s'eft terminée affez heureufement ; mais par la faute
des Anglois. Ce fut une faute capitale du gouvernement Britannique, de vouloir que le
général Burgoyne traverfat plus de deux cens lieues de pays, et prefque défert, pour fe joindre
aux generaux Howe et Clinton. Ce plan pouvoit paroitre grand dans le cabinet de Londres; mais miférable aux yeux de ceux qui avoient une exacte connoiffance de la nature du pays.
Mon obfervation n'eft pas en conféquence de l' événement ; car vous vous rappelerez peut-être,
Monfeigneur, que j'ai eu l' honneur de vous écrire, il y a deux mois que j' étois bien aife que
les Anglois, ne nous oppofaffent ici que dix mille hommes, & que j'efpérois beaucoup que la
jonction des généraux Burgoyne et Howe n'auroit lieu que quand la campagne ne feroit plus
tenable ; et que même fon armée feroit détruite de la moitié, par la faim, la fatigue, la défertion,
et les pertes qu'ils effuyeroient tous les jours par nos troupes, et nos milices poftées dans les bois.
L'iffue à furpaffé mon attente. Si les Anglois, au lieu de s' amufer avoint dirigé leur attaque
contre le général Wafhington, avec dix-huit ou vingt mille hommes, je ne fais pas trop ce que
nous ferions devenus; parceque fi nous avions doublé le nombre de nos troupes, nous n'aurions
pas doublé nos forces ; mais triplé nos embarras.

Si nous jettons les yeux fur le plan de campagne, en examinant la conduite du général
Howe ; nous verrons qu'il n'a pas même fait, tout ce qu'il étoit en fon pouvoir de faire ;
Comme j'ai eu l'honneur de vous le mander après la bataille de Brandywine. Car s'il eut
profité de fes avantages, il ne feroit plus queftion de l'armée du général Wafhington ; et il
a mis depuis dans toutes fes opérations une lenteur et une timidité, qui m'ont toujours étonné.
Mais il peut fe ravifer, & l' on peut envoyer un autre général de Londres ; alors nous ne pou-
rions peut-être pas fi bien nous tirer d'affaire. Aurefte puifque les événements qui dépendent
de l'habilité des généraux ne peuvent fe prévoir ; ils ne doivent pas entrer dans les conjectures
qu' on peut faire à l' avenir. Faifons feulement attention au nombre de troupes ; et j'oferai
dire que fi les Anglois pouvoient avoir ici trente mille hommes ; ils pourroient réduire le pays.
Une feconde caufe qui pourroit hâter cette réduction, et même l'opérer feule, c'eft le manque
de munition de guerre, et des chofes néceffaires à la vie. A l' égard des chofes néceffaires pour
la continuation de la guerre, il leur manque prefque tout. Il n'ont ni drap, ni linge, ni fel,

3 D 2

the command of the army to fir Henry Clinton, of whofe actions in the courfe of the prefent war we have already made mention; but

ni eau de vie, ni fucre; et ces derniers articles font plus importans qu'on ne le croiroit d'abord. Avant la guerre, les peuples Américains fans vivre dans le luxe, jouiffoient de tout ce qui eft néceffaire pour rendre la vie agréable et heureufe. Ils paffoient une grande partie de leur tems à fumer et à boire du thé, ou des liqueurs fpiritueufes. Telles étoient les habitudes de ces peuples. Il ne feroit donc pas furprenant que le changement d'une vie efféminée, transformée fubitement en celle de geurrier, qui eft dure et penible, leur fit préférer le joug des Anglois, à une liberté achetée aux dépens des douceurs de la vie. Ce que je vous dis ne peut que vous furprendre, Monfeigneur, mais tel eft ce peuple, qui, mou, fans énergie, fans vigueur, fans paffion pour la caufe dans laquelle il s'eft engagé ne fe foutient que parcequ'il fuit l'impulfion qu'on lui a premierement donnée. Il y a cent fois plus d'enthoufiafme pour cette revolution dans quelque caffé de Paris que ce foit qu'il n'y en a dans les Provinces Unies enfemble. Il eft donc néceffaire, pour achever cette revolution, que la France fourniffe à ce peuple tout ce qui lui eft néceffaire; afin qu'il trouve la guerre moins dure à foutenir. Il eft vrai qu'il lui encoutera quelques millions; mais ils feront bien employés en anéantiffant le pouvoir de l'Angleterre qui dépouillée de fes colonies, fans marine, et fans commerce, perdra fa grandeur, et laiffera la France fans rivale. Cependant quelques perfonnes penfent (entr' autres l'Abbé Réynal) qu'il ne feroit pas de l'intérêt de la France donner la liberté aux colonies Angloifes, et qu'elle rifqueroit de perdre les fiennes. Mais pour ceux qui connoiffent ce-pays-ci, il eft evident, qu'il fe paffera bien des années avant qu'ils puiffent être en état de mettre une flotte en mer, pour faire des conquêtes. La jaloufie entre les provinces (dont on voit déja le germe) les aura divifés en tant de différens intérêts, qu'aucune d'elles ne fera à craindre.

On pouroit demander, fi pour opérer plutôt la révolution en Amérique, il ne feroit pas plus prudent que la France fit un traité avec les Etats Unis, et que de concert avec eux, elle fit paffer ici douze ou quinze mille hommes. Ce feroit là le moyen de tout gâter. Le peuple ici, quoiqu' en guerre avec les Anglois (nous le voyons journellement), et malgré tout ce que la France a fait, et à intention de faire pour eux, préféreroit de fe réconcilier avec les Anglois, plutôt que de recevoir des forces de ceux qu'ils ont le plus raifon de craindre: Ou s'ils y confentoient d'abord, bientôt après l'antipathie naturelle entre les deux nations, fe manifefteroit par les plus terribles diffentions. Quiconque habite ce pays-ci doit favoir que la chofe eft impracticable.

Il y a encore un projet à examiner. La France, dans le cas où elle feroit de faire la guerre aux Anglois ouvertement, ne pourroit-elle pas de concert avec le congrés tenter de prendre le Canada? Par l'obfervation precedente, il eft naturel de fuppofer que le congrés ne voudroit pas accéder à une telle propofition. Le voifinage des François les dégouteroit entierement de cette liberté qu'ils croiroient n'être pas capable de garder long-tems; et dépendance pour dépendance,

but concerning whom, for gratifying our readers, it may be proper
farther to remark, that he had in the war with France from 1754 to
1763,

pendance, ils aimeroient mieux dépendre des Anglois. Mais feroit-il avantageux pour nous
d'avoir le Canada? Je fens que pour difcuter ce point, il faudroit avoir une connoiffance exacte des productions du pays ; ce que je n'ai pas. En confiderant la chofe en général, il me paroit que ce qui fe paffe maintenant en Amérique doit dégouter les Eu-
ropéens, d'avoir aucune affaire à démêler avec les colonies de ce continent. Car foit que les
colonies fe rendent à préfent indépendantes ou non il n'y a pas de doute qu'elles ne le foient
dans cent ans ; et avec elles toutes les parties feptentrionales. C'eft fe préparer a une guerre
certaine, que d'avoir des établiffemens ici ; il me paroit donc plus avantageux pour la France,
d'avoir des ifles qu'elle puiffe plus aifément contenir fous fa domination. Parmi ces ifles, je
choifirois celle dont les productions ne font pas naturelles à la France ; et qui cependant lui
font effentiellement néceffaires, comme le fucre, le caffé, &c. Car d'avoir des colonies qui ne
produifent que du blé, quoi de plus inutile à la France? Elle n'a qu'à bien cultiver fon terrain,
défricher celui qui a été laiffé inculte, et elle créera chez elle-même des colonies qui ne lui
conteront rien à defendre. Je crois par toutes ces raifons, que fi la France déclare la guerre
à l'Angleterre, ce n'eft pas le Canada qu'elle doit attaquer ; mais la Jamaïque, et les autres
poffeffions Angloifes de cette nature. Si elle ne déclare pas la guerre, celle doit employer tous
les moyens que la politique lui fuggerera pour empêcher les Anglois d'avoir jamais plus
de vingt cinq mille hommes ici. Nous n'avions durant toute cette campagne, que trente
mille hommes, favoir, l'armée de Mr. Wafhington qui n'a jamais excédé quinze mille hommes,
celle du general Putnam cinq ou fix mille ; et celle de Mr. Gates dix mille. Si l'on trouvoit
qu'il fût néceffaire d'augmenter le tout d'un tiers, je ne crois pas que la chofe fût poffible.

Je fuis peut-être Monfeigneur, entré dans un trop grand détail ; mais vous pardonnerez la
longueur de mes differtations, caufée feulement par l'envie que j'ai eue de fatisfaire vos défirs, et
de rendre mon féjour ici auffi utile qu'il m'eft poffible.

J'ai l'honneur d'être,

MONSEIGNEUR,

Votre très humble et très obéifant Serviteur,

DU PORTAIL.

Le congrés m'a élevé au rang de brigadier-général.

TRANS-

1763, been aid-de-camp to prince Ferdinand of Brunfwick, by whom he was held in the higheft eftimation. Thus he was undoubtedly bred

TRANSLATION.

To the Count de St. Germain, Minifter of War (for you only, Sir).

SIR,

Camp at White Marfh, four Leagues from Philadelphia,
12th November 1777.

I HAD the honour to fend you an accountof the battles of Brandywine and German Town, together with the plans, as well as that of Philadelphia and its environs to the extent of five leagues, that you might be enabled to judge of the fituation of general Howe. I hope they have come to hand. Hitherto general Howe is not mafter of two fmall forts in the river, which prevent his veffels from coming up to the city, and his communication with them, except by means of a by-way I have marked on the map, and from which we fhall cut him off in the winter, when we have received a reinforcement of victorious troops from the north. We purpofe, likewife, to poft a body of two or three thoufand men on the other fide of the Schuyl-kill. There are already troops in the Jerfeys, fo that general Howe will be blocked up in Philadelphia, and in danger of dying with hunger, unlefs he reimbarks. But, to fpeak the truth, we do not expect quite that. He probably will take the forts, if he attacks them pro-perly, and will then have a communication with his fhipping. Be that as it may, you fee, Sir, for people who have been twice beaten we are not in fo very bad plight; for this we are in-debted to the fmall number of Englifh cavalry, which prevented the enemy from following up their victory, and ftill more to the woods and other obftacles by which the country is defended. Now, after the experience of this campaign, it is natural to put this queftion, Will the Ame-ricans fucceed in obtaining their liberty, or no? In France, where you can only form your judgment from the facts, you will anfwer in the affirmative; we, on the fpot, who have feen how things have gone, think differently. To fpeak plain, it has not been owing to the good conduct of the Americans that the campaign, upon the whole, has terminated rather fortunately, but to the fault of the Englifh. It was an egregious error in the Britifh government, to direct general Burgoyne to traverfe about two hundred leagues, of a wretched and almoft defert country, to join the generals Howe and Clinton. The plan might appear grand in the cabinet of London, but miferable in the opinion of thofe who had paid attention to the nature of the country. The obfervation is not in confequence of the event; for you will probably, Sir, call to recollection that, two months ago, I had the honour to write you word, I was well pleafed the Englifh oppofed us here with only ten thoufand men; and that I was in great hopes that general Burgoyne would not effect a junction with general Howe, till it would be no longer

4   poffible

bred in one of the firſt military ſchools in Europe. With ſuch perſonal merit, the advantage of being of the family of Newcaſtle, and
alſo

poſſible to keep the field, and even then with his army half deſtroyed by famine, fatigue, and deſertion, and the daily loſs he would neceſſarily ſuſtain from our troops, and the militia poſted in the woods. The event exceeded my expectations. Had the Engliſh, inſtead of making ſo many diverſions, directed their attack againſt general Waſhington with eighteen or twenty thouſand men, I do not very well know what would have become of us; becauſe, in doubling the number of our troops, we ſhould not have added double ſtrength to our army, and our embarraſſments would have been increaſed threefold.

In looking over the plans of the campaign, if we examine the conduct of general Howe, we ſhall find he has not even done that which he had it in his power to do, as I had the honour to write you word after the battle of Brandywine; for, had he followed up the advantages which that gave him, there had been an end of general Waſhington's army; and, ſince that, all his operations have been carried on ſo ſlowly, and with ſo much timidity, they have become the object of my aſtoniſhment: But, perhaps, he may recollect himſelf; perhaps another general may be ſent from London, and then poſſibly we may not extricate ourſelves ſo well. However, ſince the events which depend on the ſkill of generals cannot be foreſeen, they ſhould make no part of the conjectures we may form for the future; let us pay attention ſolely to the number of troops, and I would hazard my opinion, *that, if the Engliſh could have here thirty thouſand men, they ought to reduce the country.* A ſecond cauſe, which might haſten that reduction, and even operate alone, is the want of warlike ſtores and the neceſſaries of life. With reſpect to the requiſites for carrying on war, the Americans want almoſt every thing; and as to other matters, linen, ſalt, brandy, ſugar, &c. are wanting; and theſe laſt articles are of more importance than one is at firſt aware. Before the war, the American people, though they did not live in luxury, enjoyed in abundance every requiſite to make life comfortable and happy; they paſſed great part of their time either in ſmoking, drinking tea or ſpirituous liquors. Such was the diſpoſition of theſe people. Sore againſt the grain then, as it muſt be of a ſudden, the tranſ-form into ſoldiers, reduced to lead a life of hardſhips and frugality, it would not be ſur-priſing that they ſhould prefer the yoke of the Engliſh to a liberty purchaſed at the expence of the comforts of life.

You will be aſtoniſhed, Sir, at this language; but ſuch are theſe people, that they move without ſpring or energy, without vigour, and without paſſion for a cauſe in which they are engaged, and which they follow only as the impulſe of the hand that firſt put them in motion directs. There is an hundred times more enthuſiaſm for this revolution in any one coffee-houſe at Paris, than in all the Thirteen Provinces united. It is neceſſary then that France, to ac-compliſh this revolution, ſhould furniſh theſe people with every requiſite to leſſen the hardſhips of war. True, it will coſt ſome millions; but they will be well laid out in annihilating the

power

C H A P.
XX.

1778.

also the next in command to fir William Howe, fir Henry Clinton was naturally appointed, on the refignation of fir William, to the chief command of the Britifh army.

Sir

power of England, which, when bereft of her colonies, without a navy and without commerce, will lofe her confequence in the world, and leave France without a rival.

Neverthelefs, there are fome, and amongft them the Abbé Raynal in his publication, who think France would not find her account in liberating the Englifh colonies, that fhe would run a rifk of lofing her own; but, to any one acquainted with this country, it is evident that ages muft pafs before fhe would be in a condition to fend out a fleet to make conquefts. The jealoufies between the Provinces (the feeds of which are already fown) will have divided them into fo many different interefts and ftates, that no one of them will be to be feared.

It may be afked, whether, to bring about the revolution in America, it would not be advifable for France to make a treaty with the United States, and, in concert with them, crofs over twelve or fifteen thoufand men? That would be the way to mar all. The people here, though at war with the Englifh (we fee it every day), and, in fpite of all that France has done and means to do for them, would prefer a reconciliation with the Englifh rather than receive in force the men in the world they moft fear; or, if they fhould confent at firft, it would not be long ere the natural antipathy between the two nations would break out into the moft terrible diffenfions *. Whoever inhabits this country muft know the thing to be abfolutely impracticable.

There is yet another projeét to examine. In the event of France being obliged to carry on the war openly againft the Englifh, might not fhe, in concert with congrefs, attempt Canada? From the preceding obfervation, it is natural to fuppofe congrefs would not accede to fuch an arrangement. The French neighbourhood alone would give them a difguft to that liberty which they would apprehend themfelves not long able to preferve, and dependance for dependance, they had rather be dependant on the Englifh.

But, would it be very advantageous for us to have Canada? I am fenfible, to difcufs this point, a moft minute and accurate knowledge of the produce of the country is neceffary, which I have not; yet, to confider the thing in general, it appears to me, that what is now going on in America ought to difguft every European power from having any concern with colonies on this continent. For, whether the Englifh colonies become independent or not at prefent, a century hence, no doubt, they will; and, with them, all the northern parts of this continent. It is laying the foundation of certain war to have eftablifhments here. It appears to me, then,

* In confirmation of what M. du Portail has here advanced, we recollect having heard, whilft we were in America during the war, and from good authority, " that, upon fome difagreement with the French, the Americans difliking the manner in which they conducted themfelves, the people were clamorous for putting arms into the hands of general Burgoyne's foldiers, and making a caufe common with them to drive the French out of the country."

more

Sir William Howe, upon his arrival in England, found that his conduct was generally condemned, and threw him- felf for protection and exculpation into the arms of a party, the oppofition to government in parliament, who received him with gladnefs, and boldly vindicated his conduct both in and out of the fenate. Anonymous charges againft the general were carried into parliament, that thereby the way might be prepared for a parliamentary inquiry into his conduct. He complained, in the houfe of commons, that many fevere cen- fures had been thrown out againft him, and that minifters had been filent. He alleged, among other charges againft adminiftration, that he had not the cordial confidence and fupport of miniftry; that

more advantageous for France to have iflands, which fhe can eafily defend from this contagion of independence; and, amongft the iflands, I fhould chufe that whofe productions were not natural to France, and which, neverthelefs, are become effentially neceffary; fuch as fugar, coffee, &c. &c.; for to have colonies producing only corn, what could be of lefs ufe to France? She has nothing to do but well till her own lands, to put under the plough thofe which have hitherto lain uncultivated, and fhe will create at home colonies which will coft her nothing to defend.

For all thefe reafons, I think, fhould France declare war againft England; it is not to Ca- nada, but Jamaica and other Englifh poffeffions of that fort, fhe fhould direct her attacks. If fhe does not declare war, fhe fhould employ the beft means which policy may fuggeft to prevent the Englifh from ever having more than twenty-five thoufand men here. We had no more than thirty thoufand in the whole of this campaign, to wit, the army of Mr. Wafhington never exceeded fifteen thoufand, that of general Putnam five or fix thoufand, and that of Mr. Gates ten thoufand. Should it be found neceffary to increafe the whole a third, I do not know that it could be done. I have perhaps, Sir, in my letter exceeded what you required; but pardon the length of the differtations I have gone into, from a defire to fatisfy your wifhes, and render my ftay here as ufeful as in my power to make it.

With the moft profound refpect,

I am, S I R,

Your moft humble and moft obedient fervant,

DU PORTAIL.

Congrefs has promoted me to the rank of brigadier-general.

his orders from government had not been clear, but ambiguous, and such as might be easily explained away in case, of any adverse accident arising from their execution; and that they had concealed from parliament the true state of our affairs in America, promising success when they knew there was no reason to expect it. Lord George Germaine had said, that he had learned from his intelligence the difficulties the Americans were under in raising troops; that he hoped that he (sir William) should be able to get a sufficient force in Pensylvania for the defence of that province; and that he still hoped that this campaign would be the last, "so that, in spite of my " positive assurances," said the general, " from the spot, the minister's " delusive hopes and conjectures were to influence him in opposition " to my certain knowledge." In the animation of debate, the allegations of the general were placed in a stronger point of view. Ministers were charged with having " treacherously and traitorously deceived " this country; inasmuch as they had declared to the house of " commons, that they had reason to expect a successful campaign, " when they had it in their pockets, under the general's own hand, " that nothing was to be expected."

With regard to the first of these charges, respecting confidence and support, the vast exertions of the minister for the American department were recapitulated, and the letters of sir William Howe acknowledging them. With regard to the second, it was proved, by the correspondence between the general and the secretary for American affairs, that every plan proposed by the former was sure to meet with the approbation of the latter; and that stronger proof of confidence in a general could not be given by those who employed him, than that he should be left unconstrained by particular instructions, uncontrolled by superior power, at entire liberty to follow his own plans, and prosecute a war according to his own ideas; nor was it ever before made a matter of serious complaint against a minister, that he

did

did not furnifh military plans in detail to a commander in chief, efpe- cially when repeated proofs were given of a fincere difpofition to co-operate with the military commander, and furnifh the means of executing whatever plan he might judge to be the moft expedient for the public fervice. The fecretary of ftate for the American department, in a letter of the twenty-fecond of October 1776, exprefsly fays, " His majefty does not intend that the general, in his " plans of operation, fhould be confined to any particular province : " His choice of fituation muft in that refpect be governed by his " own judgment." How many times, it was farther urged on this fubject, did fir William Howe alter his plan for the campaign of 1777 in the courfe of a few months ? Between the months of November and April no lefs than four plans, effentially different from each other, were propofed, and yet, by the general's own account, each of them, in its turn, was approved of. The minifter for American affairs, in a letter to the general of the third of March 1777, fays, " I am now commanded to acquaint you that the king entirely " approves of your deviation from the plan which you formerly " fuggefted." And again, May the eighteenth, "As you muft, from " your fituation and military fkill, be a competent judge of the pro- " priety of every plan, his majefty does not hefitate to approve the " alterations which you propofe." The nature of the American fervice, indeed, required that the general fhould be at liberty to vary his plan of operations according to the varying circumftances of the war : And accordingly, as appears from the whole of the official correfpondence on the fubject of the American war, the fulleft confidence was placed in fir William Howe from the time of his appointment to the chief command to that of his afking leave to return to Britain. Not only was he fupported by the whole weight of government, but was indulged in all his wifhes for himfelf and his friends. On this head, therefore, they who faw more matter

3 E 2   of

of accufation in the inactivity and blunders of fir William Howe, than in the conduct of lord George Germaine, which feemed, on the whole, to be well defigned, and towards the general full of confidence and generofity, enjoyed a complete triumph. It was with greater plaufibility that fir William and his friends infifted on the third charge, juft mentioned, againft the minifter; that his hopes and conjectures, refpecting the ftate of America and the iffue of the war, were more fanguine and favourable than the general's corre-fpondence warranted him to entertain. Yet, even here, it was fhewn from their correfpondence, that the minifter's intelligence was not materially different from that of the general, nor his hopes of fuc-cefs on the whole much lefs lively.

Still, however, the friends of fir William Howe, the members of parliament in oppofition to adminiftration, with his concurrence, in-fifted on a public inquiry into the conduct of the American war, that our national difgraces and misfortunes might be traced to their real fource. Lord Howe, in a fpeech in the houfe of commons, April the twenty-ninth, 1779, demanded an inquiry into his own and his brother's conduct, for the following reafons: They had been arraign-ed in pamphlets and in newfpapers, written by perfons in high cre-dit and confidence with minifters, by feveral members of that houfe,

and folicits and obtains a parliamenta-ry inquiry in-to his con-duct.

in that houfe, in the face of the nation; by fome of great credit and refpect in their public characters, known to be countenanced by ad-miniftration; and that one of them in particular, governor John-ftone, had made the moft direct and fpecific charges. Their charac-ters, therefore, fo publicly attacked, and in fuch a place, were to be vindicated in the great councils of the ftate, and no-where elfe.

In vain did the minifters of the crown, who had employed him, declare, that they had no accufations againft either the general or admiral. They, with their friends, infifted on a public examination, which was obtained, and in which they, for fome time, took the lead.

But,

But, at length it plainly appeared that, under pretence of vindicating the general, their real defign was to condemn the conduct of adminiftration. The parliamentary inquiry that had been inftituted, the miniftry and their adherents confidered as a factious intrigue.

It was, perhaps, imagined that his majefty, alarmed at the dangers that began, by this time, to threaten Great Britain, not only in America, but in other quarters, would change his confidential fervants, and commit the conduct of government to thofe very hands that hitherto had been employed in various attempts to baffle its defigns, and fruftrate all the meafures that had been taken for carrying them into execution. But the king, amidft multiplying diftreffes, with proper firmnefs withftood their machinations, determined to continue his countenance to thofe who wifhed not to fruftrate nor procraftinate the war *, but to bring it, as foon as poffible, to a fafe and honourable conclufion. The oppofition, therefore, difappointed in their expectations from the higheft quarter in the ftate, ferioufly intended, what they loudly threatened, to impeach the fervants of the crown, and by that means to drive them from their places by a kind of violence.

Adminiftration, eafily penetrating this defign, refolved no longer to permit their opponents to run in the race of examination alone, but to vindicate the meafures they had taken. Many gentlemen of undoubted reputation, perfectly acquainted with the conduct of the war, and the ftate of America, were fummoned to give evidence refpecting thofe fubjects. Of this the movers of the inquiry were apprized, and they foon began to lofe courage. Only two witneffes were examined, on what may be called, in the language of judicial trials, the fide of adminiftration: Major-general Robertfon, who had ferved twenty-

* It is believed that the king on fome occafions went fo far as to fuggeft his ideas of the proper plan for carrying on the war, which were very judicious, and which, had they been adopted by the general, might probably have been productive of good effects.

four

four years in America as quarter-mafter-general, brigadier and major-general; and Mr. Galloway, a gentleman of Penfylvania, of fortune and confequence, as well as good abilities, who was bred to the law, and had been a member of congrefs, but who had come over to the royal army in December 1776. But fuch was the circumftantiality, credibility, and weight of their evidence, that the movers or managers fhrunk from the inquiry; as, the more it was carried on, the more parliament, as well as the nation at large, feemed to be convinced that the conduct of adminiftration, in refpect to the American war, was on the whole juftified. The friends of the general and admiral, therefore, moved to diffolve the committee which they had been fo ftudious to obtain; and it was diffolved accordingly.

But although fir William Howe, as well as his friends, was difappointed in his hopes of fomething even more than exculpation, from an indulgent houfe of commons, he neither wanted a fufficient number of partifans to keep him in countenance amidft all that cenfure that was poured on his conduct, nor political friends of fufficient confequence to compenfate for that cenfure by an honourable and lucrative ftation which he now holds under government: Nor is this the only inftance in the hiftory of Britain at this period, of great inequality in the public retribution of rewards and punifh-ments. When we reflect on the different and even oppofite reception given to fuccefsful genius actuated by the pureft patriotifm on the one hand, and to monotonous mediocrity, not only unfuccefs-ful, if fuccefs is to be meafured by effects conducive to the public good, but even of ambiguous intentions; what are we to think of the fpirit which influences and directs the public councils?

In the decline of free governments we ever obferve the influence of faction to predominate over ideas of patriotifm, juftice, and duty, on which alone liberty is founded, and a propenfity in the citizens to range themfelves under the banners of a Marius or a Sylla, a Pompey

Pompey or a Cæsar. Hence the servants of the state are apt to become less and less sensible to honour, and the voice of fame, the
great incentives to glorious actions, well knowing that their conduct,
however meritorious, may still be condemned, or however exceptionable, still be palliated, and even applauded, to advance the
views of faction and ambition; while the great body of the people,
distracted and confounded by the oppofite opinions and declarations
of their superiors, who are supposed to have the best means of information, know not where to place their hopes, their confidence,
or their fears.

It is the province of the historian to correct these errors, and to
animate the patriot, the sage, and the hero, under temporary neglect or detraction, by carrying an appeal in their behalf to a tribu-
nal more candid than their misguided cotemporaries, and that, raised
on a theatre more extended than their native country.

END OF VOLUME FIRST.